Robert Thang's work on the land-theology of the [...] jor theme in Old Testament theology, with impo[...] tions, by means of a focused study on a single [...] the deep connection between land and the prop[...] of angles, dealing with major concepts and topics in the book, such as Zion, northern and southern kingdoms, and other places of worship. The topic of land is also shown to relate to a range of other theological topics, such as creation, salvation, justice and eschatology. Finally, the study enables further reflection on various Old Testament theologies of land-possession, and the relationship between the land of Israel and land in the context of Yahweh's relation to other peoples. The book makes a unique and well-documented contribution to an abiding topic, in biblical as well as Old Testament theology.

J. G. McConville
Professor of Old Testament Theology,
University of Gloucestershire

At a time when biblical scholarship is at last beginning to pay more sustained attention to ecological issues and other questions relating to the land or earth, it is pleasing to see the publication of this detailed study of the land in Amos 7-9. Robert Thang offers a thoughtful and important exploration of Amos's theology of the land in relation to a number of significant theological themes, including creation, salvation, Sabbath, justice and eschatology. The book makes a welcome contribution to the contemporary debate surrounding these and similar issues.

Karl Möller
Senior Lecturer in Theology and Religious Studies,
University of Cumbria

The Theology of the Land in Amos 7-9

Robert Khua Hnin Thang

Langham
MONOGRAPHS

© 2014 by Robert Khua Hnin Thang

Published 2014 by Langham Monographs
an imprint of Langham Creative Projects

Langham Partnership
PO Box 296, Carlisle, Cumbria CA3 9WZ, UK
www.langham.org

ISBNs:
978-1-78368-966-8 Print
978-1-78368-965-1 Mobi
978-1-78368-964-4 ePub

Robert Khua Hnin Thang has asserted his right under the Copyright, Designs and Patents Act, 1988 to be identified as the Author of this work.

All rights reserved. No part of this publication may be reproduced, stored in a retrieval system or transmitted, in any form or by any means, electronic, mechanical, photocopying, recording or otherwise, without the prior written permission of the publisher or the Copyright Licensing Agency.

All Scripture quotations, unless otherwise indicated, are from the Holy Bible, New International Version®, NIV®. Copyright © 1973, 1978, 1984, 2011 by Biblica, Inc.™ Used by permission of Zondervan. All rights reserved worldwide. www.zondervan.com The "NIV" and "New International Version" are trademarks registered in the United States Patent and Trademark Office by Biblica, Inc.™

British Library Cataloguing in Publication Data
Thang, Robert Khua Hnin, author.
 The theology of the land in Amos 7-9.
 1. Bible. Amos--Criticism, Textual. 2. Land use in the
 Bible.
 I. Title
 224.8'066-dc23
 ISBN-13: 9781783689668

Cover & Book Design: projectluz.com

Langham Partnership actively supports theological dialogue and a scholar's right to publish but does not necessarily endorse the views and opinions set forth, and works referenced within this publication or guarantee its technical and grammatical correctness. Langham Partnership does not accept any responsibility or liability to persons or property as a consequence of the reading, use or interpretation of its published content.

Contents

Abstract ix
Acknowledgments xi
Abbreviations xiii

Chapter 1 1
The Aspects of the Theology of the Land in Amos
   1.1 Introduction 1
   1.2 The 'Land': אֶרֶץ and אֲדָמָה in Amos 1
      1.2.1 The Term ארץ in Amos 2
      1.2.2 The Term אדמה in Amos 8
   1.3 The Semantic Range of the Land (אדמה/ארץ) in Amos 10
      1.3.1 Land as Territory 10
      1.3.2 Land as Fruitful 11
      1.3.3 Land as Cosmic 12
   1.4 The Theology of the Land (אדמה/ארץ) in Amos 12
      1.4.1 Land as Promised 13
      1.4.2 Land as Gift 16
      1.4.3 Land as Inheritance 21
      1.4.4 Land as a Place of Justice 21
   1.5 Conclusion 22

Chapter 2 23
Theological Themes Linked to the Land in Amos
   2.1 Introduction 23
   2.2 Zion 24
      2.2.1 Zion and the Theme of Worship and Justice 24
      2.2.2 Zion and the Relationship between North and South 29
      2.2.3 Zion and Its Relationship with Natural World 30
   2.3 Covenant-Election 33
      2.3.1 Election: Its Responsibility of Justice 33
      2.3.2 Election: Its Connection with Land 37
   2.4 Israel 39
   2.5 Creation 41
   2.6 Justice 46
      2.6.1 Justice in Social Context 46
      2.6.2 Justice in Cultic Context 48

        2.6.3 Justice in Creation Context 50
    2.7 Conclusion 51

Chapter 3 53
    The Land in Amos 7
        3.1 The Land in Amos 7:1-9 53
            3.1.1 Introduction 53
            3.1.2 The Visions and Response of YHWH 54
            3.1.3 The Use of Jacob/Isaac/Israel in Amos 7-9 60
            3.1.4 Land in the Context of the First Three Visions 72
            3.1.5 Conclusion 81
        3.2 The Land in Amos 7:10-17 82
            3.2.1 Introduction 82
            3.2.2 The Insertion between the Third and Fourth Visions 82
            3.2.3 The House of Israel and the Concept of Land 87
            3.2.4 The Meaning of Land 89
            3.2.5 Conclusion 103

Chapter 4 105
    The Land in Amos 8
        4.1 The Land in Amos 8:1-3 105
            4.1.1 Introduction 105
            4.1.2 The Summer Fruit 105
            4.1.3 I Will Never Again Pass Them By 108
            4.1.4 The Temple and Land 109
            4.1.5 Conclusion 113
        4.2 The Land in Amos 8:4-6 114
            4.2.1 Introduction 114
            4.2.2 Sabbath in the Ancient Near East 115
            4.2.3 Sabbath in the Pentateuch 116
            4.2.4 Amos' Theology of Sabbath 124
            4.2.5 Conclusion 134
        4.3 The Land in Amos 8:7-14 135
            4.3.1 Introduction 135
            4.3.2 Earthquake 136
            4.3.3 Eclipse 140
            4.3.4 Famine 143
            4.3.5 Conclusion 146

Chapter 5 149
The Land in Amos 9
    5.1 The Land in Amos 9:1-6 149
        5.1.1 Introduction 149
        5.1.2 Temple (Altar): A Symbol of YHWH's Universal Rule 149
        5.1.3 The Certainty of YHWH's Judgment 157
        5.1.4 YHWH's Presence and His Power over the Creation 159
        5.1.5 YHWH's Power in Heaven and Earth 164
        5.1.6 Conclusion 171
    5.2 The Land in Amos 9:7-10 172
        5.2.1 Introduction 172
        5.2.2 Election in Relation to Land in 3:2 172
        5.2.3 Election in Relation to Land in 9:7 173
        5.2.4 The Relation of 3:2 with 9:7: A Rhetorical Purpose 174
        5.2.5 Election: YHWH's Ultimate Purpose for the
             Whole World 177
        5.2.6 Conclusion 179
    5.3 The Land in Amos 9:11-15 180
        5.3.1 Introduction 180
        5.3.2 Authenticity 180
        5.3.3 Intertextual Relationship between Amos 9:11-15 and
             Other Parts of the Book 187
        5.3.4 Eschatology: Various Aspects of Amos' Land-Theology ... 194
        5.3.5 Conclusion 210
Conclusion 213
Bibliography 221

Abstract

This thesis aims to give an account of Amos' specific contribution to the Old Testament's theology of land. It seeks to explore the theme of land as a key aspect of the background to Amos' prophecy, and also of the book's overall theology of the relationship between YHWH, Israel, and the world. In Amos, the language about land is extensive, including terms and ideas such as Zion, Carmel, YHWH's bringing of Israel into the land, references to various sanctuaries and places, harvest and famine, other geographical indications, the relationship between the northern kingdom and Judah, and references to the land of other nations.

The topic of land, however, has often been studied incidentally to other themes, but less often as a theological topic in its own right. This thesis shows how deeply embedded the topic of land is in Amos, and argues this by showing its relation to other theological themes, including Zion, the covenant-election tradition, Israel, creation, salvation, Sabbath, justice, and eschatology. That is, the study of land in Amos has wider dimensions. The study is therefore set in a wide context in the Old Testament, and raises questions about the relation of Amos to other important theological traditions about land.

The study is essentially theological analysis. The argument will follow an essentially synchronic reading. It will also employ textual, literary and historical criticism, and the thesis analyzes carefully the text of Amos 7-9 for its literary coherence and inner relationships. It attempts to demonstrate what theological assumptions are made about the land in each section in Amos 7-9, and the relationship of Amos' land-theology to other Old Testament theological traditions. While the findings are set in the context of the book as a whole, the study focuses on this one section of the book, chapters 7-9, in order to explore the topic in close detail.

Acknowledgments

I wish to thank Langham Partnership International for the financial support that covered my tuition fees and living expenses during my study in the UK since October 2007; especially Dr. John Stott the founder of the partnership, Dr. Howard Peskett the former Director of Langham Scholars, and Dr. Ian J. Shaw the present Associate Director of Langham Scholars, and the scholarship committee. It is no exaggeration to say that without a Langham scholarship this research would not have been possible.

I am most grateful to my first supervisor, Professor Gordon McConville, for his careful reading and correcting of my many drafts, and his patience and guidance in encouraging my work all along. He also taught me the importance of asking better questions of the terms אֶרֶץ and אֲדָמָה for 'land' and he constantly provokes my thinking to be critical. To him I owe an enormous debt. A word of appreciation is also extended to my second supervisor, Dr. Karl Möller (University of Cumbria), for his valuable advice and comments. My thanks are also extended to friends who shared the office with me during my study: Jason LeCureux, Luke Devine, Michael Johnstone, Andrew Lee, and Carl Sweatman.

I extend my warm appreciation beyond words to my wife, Kyu Kyu Win, for encouraging and supporting me through prayer and words; and taking care of our daughters, Hannah Cer Dim Par and Abishag Saw Dim Tial, during my study. I highly cherish the love, endurance, and support of my family. Mention must be made of my church, Chaungkhuah Baptist Church, Kalay, Myanmar, for their ardent prayer support. Above all else I thank almighty God for leading me to the completion of my study. To God be the Glory!

יְהוָה שְׁמוֹ
YHWH is His Name (Amos 9:6)

Abbreviations

AB	Anchor Bible
ABD	*The Anchor Bible Dictionary*
AJT	*Asia Journal of Theology*
AOTC	Apollos Old Testament Commentary
ASV	American Standard Version
AUSS	*Andrews University Seminary Studies*
BASOR	*Bulletin of the American Schools of Oriental Research*
BEATAJ	Beiträge zur Erforschung des Alten Testaments und des Antiken Judentums
BHS	Biblia Hebraica Stuttgartensia
Bib	*Biblica*
BO	Berit Olam
BRS	The Biblical Resource Series
BS	*Bibliotheca Sacra*
BSC	Bible Student's Commentary
BSem	The Biblical Seminar
BulBR	*Bulletin for Biblical Research*
BZAW	Beihefte zur Zeitschrift für die alttestamentliche Wissenschaft
CBC	The Cambridge Bible Commentary
CBQ	*Catholic Biblical Quarterly*
CCen	*Christian Century*
CC	Continental Commentary
DBR	*Dictionary of Bible and Religion*
DDD	*Dictionary of Deities and Demons in the Bible*
DG	*The Drew Gateway*
DL	*DavarLogos*

EC	Epworth Commentaries
ed.	Editor, edited by
EDB	*Eerdmans Dictionary of the Bible*
EDT	*Evangelical Dictionary of Theology*
EJL	Early Judaism and Its Literature
EJT	*European Journal of Theology*
ESV	English Standard Version
et al.	And others
ExA	*Ex Auditu*
ExpTim	*Expository Times*
FAT	Forschungen zum Alten Testament
HAR	*Hebrew Annual Review*
Hor	*Horizons*
HSMS	Harvard Semitic Monograph Series
HTR	*Harvard Theological Review*
HUCA	*Hebrew Union College Annual*
IBCTP	Interpretation, A Bible Commentary for Teaching and Preaching
ICC	The International Critical Commentary
IDB	*Interpreter's Dictionary of the Bible*
IDBSup	*Interpreter's Dictionary of the Bible: Supplementary Volume*
Int	*Interpretation*
IRT	Issues in Religion and Theology
JBL	*Journal of Biblical Literature*
JETS	*Journal of the Evangelical Theological Society*
JITC	*Journal of the Interdenominational Theological Center*
JPSTC	The Jewish Publication Society Torah Commentary
JR	*Journal of Religion*
JRT	*The Journal of Religious Thought*
JSOT	*Journal for the Study of the Old Testament*
JSOTSS	Journal for the Study of the Old Testament Supplement Series
JST	*Journal of Semitic Studies*
JTSA	*Journal of Theology for Southern Africa*
Jud	*Judaism*

KJV	King James Version
LBI	Library of Biblical Interpretation
LXE	LXX English Translation
LXX	Septuagint
MT	Masoretic Text
MTL	Marshall's Theological Library
NAB	The New American Bible
NAC	The New American Commentary
NAS	New American Standard Bible (1977)
NAU	New American Standard Bible (1995)
NCBC	The New Century Bible Commentary
NDBT	*New Dictionary of Biblical Theology*
NIBC	New International Biblical Commentary
NICOT	New International Commentary on the Old Testament
NID	*New International Dictionary*
NIDB	*New Interpreter's Dictionary of the Bible*
NIDOTTE	*New International Dictionary of Old Testament Theology and Exegesis*
NIV	New International Version
NJB	The New Jerusalem Bible
NKJ	New King James Version
NRS	New Revised Standard Version
NSBT	New Studies in Biblical Theology
OBT	Overtures to Biblical Theology
OTG	Old Testament Guides
OTL	Old Testament Library
OTS	Old Testament Series
PSB	*Princeton Seminary Bulletin*
RB	*Revue Biblique*
RE	*Review and Expositor*
rev.	Revision, revised by
RQ	*Restoration Quarterly*
RSV	Revised Standard Version
SBL	Studies in Biblical Literature

SBLDS	Society of Biblical Literature Dissertation Series
SHBC	Smyth and Helwys Bible Commentary
SJT	*Scottish Journal of Theology*
SS	Symposium Series (Society of Biblical Literature)
TB	*Tyndale Bulletin*
TBC	Torch Bible Commentaries
TBS	Teach the Bible Series
TDOT	*Theological Dictionary of the Old Testament*
TE	*The Theological Educator*
ThT	*Theology Today*
TOTC	Tyndale Old Testament Commentaries
trans.	Translation, translated by
TTS	Theologische Texte und Studien
VetEcc	*Verbum et Ecclesia*
VT	*Vetus Testamentum*
VTSup	*Vetus Testamentum Supplements*
WBC	Word Biblical Commentary
WW	*Word & World*
YLT	Young's Literal Translation
ZAW	*Zeitschrift für die alttestamentliche Wissenschaft*

CHAPTER 1

The Aspects of the Theology of the Land in Amos

1.1 Introduction

This section aims to survey the language and concepts of 'land' in Amos. We begin by considering the occurrences of the terms אֶרֶץ and אֲדָמָה for 'land', and the range of their meaning. It will be suggested that both terms אֶרֶץ and אֲדָמָה may refer to the land as 'earth', 'land', 'ground', or sometimes 'soil'. We will go on to consider traditions concerning land in the Old Testament, and ask if they occur in Amos. In doing so we will try to highlight some of the significant theological ideas about land in Amos.

1.2 The 'Land': אֶרֶץ and אֲדָמָה in Amos

Generally, although אֶרֶץ rather than אֲדָמָה may have cosmological, geographical, and political overtones, both terms have certain physical and theological meanings.[1] As Wright suggests, the theological meaning of אֶרֶץ has two dominant senses: 'the earth and the land of Israel'.[2] The term ארץ may be used to refer to the whole earth or cosmos, or the land as territory

---

1. Michael A. Grisanti, 'אֲדָמָה,' in *NIDOTTE*, ed. Willem A. VanGemeren et al., vol. 1 (Carlisle: Paternoster Press, 1996), 273.
2. Christopher J. H. Wright, 'אֶרֶץ,' in *NIDOTTE*, ed. Willem A. VanGemeren et al., vol. 1 (Carlisle: Paternoster Press, 1996), 518.

with political boundaries, while אדמה tends to mean with ground, 'soil', the agricultural soil, the dwelling place of humankind.[3] This understanding of 'land' vocabulary ארץ and אדמה is used in Amos as well. According to Linville, the term אדמה in Amos stresses the actual 'life-giving soil' while ארץ is used in reference to the political state of the king (Amos 7:10).[4] And for Hans W. Wolff, what is meant by 'land' (אדמה) is used elsewhere in Amos to refer to the native 'soil' of Israel (5:2; 7:11b, 17b; 9:8).[5]

However, both terms ארץ and אדמה in Amos undoubtedly designate the full semantic range of the 'land' in terms of land as territory, land as fruitful (e.g. ארץ in 7:2; אדמה in 9:15), and land as cosmic or the whole earth (3:2; 4:13, 5:8, 9; 8:9; 9:5, 6, 8). As will be shown, both terms are used with several significant theological traditions of land: land as promised (9:15; 7:2, 5, 8, 11), land as gift (2:10; 3:1; 9:7, 9:15), land as inheritance (2:10; 7:4), and land as the place where justice is expected (8:4). These two terms function almost as synonyms and are used interchangeably in Amos. As Snyman suggests, Amos 7:10-17 could be set as an example: for Amaziah, the land (ארץ) cannot bear Amos' word (7:10) because Israel will go into exile away from their land (אדמה) (7:11). Amos was told to go back to his land (ארץ) (7:12). Amos responded to Amaziah that his land (אדמה) will be divided and he will die in an unclean land (אדמה), and Israel will go into exile away from their land (אדמה) (7:17).[6]

1.2.1 The Term ארץ in Amos

Out of thirty-three occurrences of 'land' vocabulary – both אֶרֶץ and אֲדָמָה – אֶרֶץ appears twenty-three times in twenty-one verses (2:7, 10 [twice]; 3:1, 5, 9, 11, 14; 4:13; 5:7, 8; 7:2, 10, 12; 8:4, 8, 9, 11; 9:5, 6 [twice], 7, 9). In three cases it refers to the land (ארץ) of Egypt (2:10; 3:1; 9:7). The

---

3. Horst Dietrich Preuss, *Old Testament Theology*, vol. 1 (Edinburgh: T & T Clark, 1995), 118.
4. Jame R. Linville, *Amos and the Cosmic Imagination* (Hampshire: Ashgate, 2008), 148.
5. Hans Walter Wolff, *A Commentary on the Books of the Prophets Joel and Amos*, trans. by Waldemar Janzen, S. Dean McBride, Jr., and Charles A. Muenchow, ed. by S. Dean McBride, Jr. (Philadelphia: Fortress Press, 1969), 315. Also see Grisanti, 'אֲדָמָה,' 271.
6. S. D. Fanie Snyman, 'The Land as a *Leitmotiv* in the Book of Amos,' *VetEcc* 26, no. 02 (2005), 529.

ארץ could mean 'land', 'earth', and 'ground'. Sometimes it is hard to decide which meaning is most suitable.

1.2.1.1 The Term ארץ as 'Land'

It is more likely that in the following references, in all cases the term ארץ as 'land' denotes territory. Most translations[7] translate the term ארץ as 'land' in Amos 2:10; 3:1, 9, 11; 7:2, 10, 12; 8:4, 8, 11; 9:7. The reference to ארץ in these passages shows that ארץ is related to the territory of a particular nation or people. In Amos 2:10, the term ארץ occurs two times referring to the land of Egypt and Amorites. Most scholars translate the term ארץ which appears in 2:10 as 'land',[8] a reference to granting of land to Israel.[9]

As in 2:10, the term ארץ in 3:1 is used to refer to the land of Egypt, from which YHWH brought the people of Israel out. Again, in Amos 3:9, ארץ refers to the land of Egypt. With the term ארץ as 'land', Snyman argues that Amos 3:9 also indicates the giving of land to the people of Israel. Egypt is mentioned to remind Israel of the exodus event, and Ashdod, in the same verse, functions as a reminder of the conquest of the land (Josh 13:3; 15:47). Egypt and Ashdod serve as witnesses to oppression in Samaria. An enemy will overturn the land of Israel and destroy their fortresses (3:11). In this sense, the people of Israel are in danger of losing the land given by YHWH during the period of the conquest of the land.[10] Snyman concludes that, 'the possible loss of the land thus stands over against the initial granting of the land alluded to by the mentioning of Ashdod.'[11] In Amos 3:11, Amos shows that the enemies of Israel will

---

7. ASV, ESV, KJV, NAB, NAS, NIV, RSV.
8. See, for example, Wolff, *Prophets*, 134; James Luther Mays, *Amos: A Commentary*, OTL, (London: SCM Press, 1969), 50-51; Andersen and Freedman, *Amos: A New Translation with Introduction and Commentary*, 324; Douglas K. Stuart, *Hosea-Jonah*, WBC, (Waco, Texas: Word Books. 1987), 306; Shalom M. Paul, *A Commentary on the Book of Amos*, edited by Frank Moore Cross, (Minneapolis: Fortress Press, 1991), 44; Jörg Jeremias, *Book of Amos*, OTL, (Louisville, Kentucky: Westminster John Knox Press, 1995), 32; Snyman, '*Leitmotiv*', 529.
9. S. D. Fanie Snyman, 'Eretz and Adama in Amos,' in *Stimulation from Leiden: Collected Communications to the XVIIIth Congress of the International Organization for the Study of the Old Testament, Leiden 2004*, edited by Hermann Michael Niemann and Matthias Augustin, 137-146. BEATAJ 54, (Frankfurt am Main: Peter Lang, 2006), 137.
10. Snyman, 'Eretz and Adama', 138.
11. Ibid., 138-139.

overtake the land (ארץ) and destroy its fortresses. The context is clearly the destruction of the land of Israel.[12]

Similarly, the ארץ in 7:2 indicates 'land'[13] as the territory which is threatened by locusts, a disaster sent by YHWH. The fertile land is also in view here. Therefore, term ארץ, 'land' may designate both territory and fruitful land at the same time. However, as we have noted above, in the confrontation between Amos and Amaziah at Bethel, the term ארץ refers to the land of Israel.[14] In Amos 7:10, Amaziah accused Amos of conspiracy against the king and thus the 'land' (ארץ) could not bear the prophet's words. And in 7:12, he tells Amos to turn back to the 'land' (ארץ) of Judah where he came from.[15]

The word ארץ is used to mean 'land' in Amos 8:4, 8, 11. In Amos 8:4, it refers to the 'land' of Israel as the place where the poor lived.[16] As Snyman argues, in fact, the ארץ 'land' is a place where justice is to be carried out.[17] Amos condemns the landed wealthy class who oppress the landless farmers in the land of Israel (8:4-6). Some translate the term ארץ in Amos 8:8 as the 'whole earth'[18] while others translate it as 'land.'[19] The ארץ itself will turn against the people in a dreadful earthquake and eclipse as a result of their acts of injustice against the needy and poor of the land.[20] There will

---

12. See Wolff, *Prophets*, 190; Mays, *Amos*, 63; Andersen and Freedman, *Amos*, 401; Stuart, *Hosea-Jonah*, 327; Paul, *Amos*, 115; Jeremias, *Book of Amos*, 55.

13. For this, see Snyman, 'Eretz and Adama', 142; Wolff, *Prophets*, 292; Mays, *Amos*, 127; Andersen and Freedman, *Amos*, 739; Paul, *Amos*, 226; Jeremias, *Book of Amos*, 123.

14. See Wolff, *Prophets*, 306; Mays, *Amos*, 134; Andersen and Freedman, *Amos*, 762; Stuart, *Hosea-Jonah*, 374; Jeremias, *Book of Amos*, 135.

15. For this view, see Wolff, *Prophets*, 306; Mays, *Amos*, 134; Andersen and Freedman, *Amos*, 762; Paul, *Amos*, 238; Jeremias, *Book of Amos*, 135.

16. See Wolff, *Prophets*, 321; Mays, *Amos*, 142; Andersen and Freedman, *Amos*, 799; Stuart, *Hosea-Jonah*, 381; Paul, *Amos*, 256; Jeremias, *Book of Amos*, 143; Jeffrey Niehaus, 'Amos', in *The Minor Prophets: An Exegetical and Expository Commentary*, edited by Thomas Edward McComiskey, Vol. 1. (Grand Rapids, Michigan: Baker Book House, 1992), 470.

17. Snyman, 'Eretz and Adama', 143.

18. Those who prefer to translate ארץ as 'earth,' see Andersen and Freedman, *Amos*, 800, 810; Stuart, *Hosea-Jonah*, 381; Paul, *Amos*, 256.

19. The ארץ as 'land,' see Wolff, *Prophets*, 322; Mays, *Amos*, 142; Jeremias, *Book of Amos*, 143; Niehaus, 'Amos,' 473; Snyman, '*Leitmotiv*,' 536.

20. Snyman, 'Eretz and Adama', 143.

be a famine throughout the 'land' (ארץ).[21] Regarding the term ארץ in 8:4, 8, 11, Niehaus argues that as Amos' prophesies are addressed particularly to the people of Israel it seems convenient to translate ארץ as referring to 'land', the land of Israel, for the judgment is not for the whole earth.[22] However, rather than referring to the territory or whole earth, 'land' here might simply be land as the physical entity, that which shakes in an earthquake, or dries up in a famine. In his rhetorical technique, Amos could also be using it here to extend his thought from 'land' to 'whole earth'. Amos 8 illustrates the overlapping meanings of the word.

1.2.1.2 The term ארץ as 'Earth'

Most translations translate the term ארץ as 'earth' in Amos 4:13; 8:9; 9:6.[23] Here the term ארץ in the first doxology in 4:13 refers to the 'earth' because it deals with the creation of YHWH which includes the whole universe.[24] In 4:13, the words יצר, ברא, and עשה are used, all terms which are used in creation traditions in the Old Testament (Gen 2:7-8, 19; Isa 43:1, 7; 45:7).[25] The term ארץ appears in the second doxology (5:8). The second doxology (5:8-9) also has the theme of creation. Most versions[26] translate ארץ as 'earth' while NIV and NJB translate it as 'land'. The verb עשה occurs again in 5:8 which reflects creation and the content of the passage clearly has creation theme in nature.[27] The context refers to the handiwork of YHWH's creation. In this sense, it is more logical to translate it as 'earth'[28] which includes all the created order of creation. Like Amos 4:13 and 5:8, the term ארץ in 8:9 refers to the 'earth' which will be turned into

---

21. See Wolff, *Prophets*, 322; Mays, *Amos*, 147; Stuart, *Hosea-Jonah*, 381; Paul, *Amos*, 256; Jeremias, *Book of Amos*, 144; Snyman, 'Eretz and Adama', 143. However, Andersen and Freedman, *Amos*, 822, translate as 'earth.'
22. Niehaus, 'Amos,' 473.
23. ASV, ESV, KJV, LXE, NAB, NAS, NAU, NIV, NKJ, NRS, RSV.
24. See Wolff, *Prophets*, 211; Mays, *Amos*, 77; Andersen and Freedman, *Amos*, 453; Stuart, *Hosea-Jonah*, 335; Paul, *Amos*, 138; Jeremias, *Book of Amos*, 67.
25. Snyman, 'Eretz and Adama', 145.
26. ASV, ESV, KJV, LXE, NAB, NAU, NKJ, NRS, RSV, YLT.
27. Snyman, 'Eretz and Adama', 145.
28. See Wolff, *Prophets*, 229; Mays, *Amos*, 95; Andersen and Freedman, *Amos*, 486; Stuart, *Hosea-Jonah*, 342; Paul, *Amos*, 157; Jeremias, *Book of Amos*, 82.

darkness by the power of YHWH.²⁹ Amos 4:13, 5:8, and 8:9 all use ארץ in the same way, not referring to the conquest of the land by YHWH, but rather reflecting creation theology.³⁰

Linked with 2:10 and 3:1, the text in 9:7 alludes to the act of YHWH, who brought Israel and other nations from exile implying that Israel's exodus and occupation of land was not unique.³¹ Following 9:5-6, 9:7 shows YHWH's bringing of all peoples and thus it indicates YHWH's lordship over all creation. The term ארץ (9:5-6) has a universal sense, embracing all the peoples who live in all corners of the world. YHWH is sovereign over the entire cosmos (9:1-6).³² In this third doxology, ארץ appears three times. Some versions translate ארץ in 9:5 as 'earth',³³ while others take it as 'land'.³⁴ The context is similar to 5:8 which denotes the creation of YHWH. In this case, the term ארץ is better taken to refer to the 'earth'.³⁵ In 9:6, the term ארץ refers twice to the 'earth'.³⁶ YHWH is celebrated and praised as the God of creation of the earth, that is, the whole universe.³⁷

1.2.1.3 The Term ארץ as 'Ground'

Most translations³⁸ are in agreement in translating the term ארץ as 'ground' in Amos 3:14. James Luther Mays translates it as 'earth',³⁹ but in this case

---

29. Wolff, *Prophets*, 322; Mays, *Amos*, 146; Andersen and Freedman, *Amos*, 819, 821; Stuart, *Hosea-Jonah*, 381; Paul, *Amos*, 262; Jeremias, *Book of Amos*, 144.
30. Snyman, 'Eretz and Adama', 145.
31. See Wolff, *Prophets*, 344; Mays, *Amos*, 156; Andersen and Freedman, *Amos*, 867; Stuart, *Hosea-Jonah*, 389; Paul, *Amos*, 282; Jeremias, *Book of Amos*, 160.
32. See Joyce Rilett Wood, *Amos in Song and Book Culture* (JSOTSS 337; London: Sheffield Academic Press, 2002), 86; Regina Smith, 'A New Perspective on Amos 9:7a: "To Me, O Israel, You are just like the Kushites,"' *JITC* 22, no. 01 (Fall 1994): 47.
33. ESV, NAB, NIV, NJB, NKJ, NRS, RSV.
34. ASV, KJV, LXE, NAS, NAU, YLT.
35. See Wolff, *Prophets*, 336; Mays, *Amos*, 151; Andersen and Freedman, *Amos*, 844; Stuart, *Hosea-Jonah*, 398; Paul, *Amos*, 273; Jeremias, *Book of Amos*, 154.
36. ASV, ESV, KJV, LXE, NAB, NAS, NAU, NIV, NJB, NKJ, NRS, RSV, YLT.
37. Wolff, *Prophets*, 336; Mays, *Amos*, 151; Andersen and Freedman, *Amos*, 844; Stuart, *Hosea-Jonah*, 389; Paul, *Amos*, 273; Jeremias, *Book of Amos*, 154.
38. ASV, ESV, KJV, LXE, NAB, NAS, NIV, NJB, NKJ, NRS, RSV. Cf. for example, Wolff, *Prophets*, 199; Mays, *Amos*, 151; Andersen and Freedman, *Amos*, 453; Stuart, *Hosea-Jonah*, 327; Paul, *Amos*, 123; Jeremias, *Book of Amos:*, 56.
39. Mays, *Amos*, 68.

'earth' simply means 'ground'. The passage refers to YHWH's destruction of the altar at Bethel so that the horns of the altars will fall on the ground. In this sense, the 'ground' simply means the surface of the land, and an area of land used for a particular purpose. Theologically, the term 'ground' is not important because it merely indicates that which people walk on or something falls on.

Amos 2:7; 3:5; 5:7; 9:9 are differently translated as 'earth' or 'ground'. Most versions[40] translate ארץ in 2:7 as 'earth' while NIV translates it as 'ground'. Some scholars also translate it as 'earth'[41] while others prefer 'ground'.[42] The text points to the oppression of the poor, in which the wealthy class tramples them into the dust of the 'ground'. In 3:5, English versions also show different translations of the term ארץ as 'earth'[43] and 'ground'.[44] Commentators vary in a similar way.[45] The context shows Amos' knowledge about nature of the land of Israel, which includes the wildlife, that is, trees and forest with wild animals. Again, the term ארץ in 5:7 is also taken as both 'earth'[46] and 'ground'.[47] Some commentators consider that it is suitable to translate it as 'earth', since justice and righteousness are the main concern for the whole universe and the earth is the location of the deeds of humans and YHWH.[48] Others, however, take it as 'ground'.[49]

Finally, in Amos 9:9, as in 3:5, the English versions show that the term ארץ may mean either 'earth'[50] or 'ground'.[51] Some commentators take it

---

40. ASV, ESV, KJV, LXE, NAB, NAS, NAU, NKJ, NRS, RSV.
41. Wolff, *Prophets*, 133; Mays, *Amos*, 42; Andersen and Freedman, *Amos*, 306; Jeremias, *Book of Amos*, 32.
42. For example, Paul, *Amos*, 44.
43. ASV, ESV, KJV, LXE, NAB, NKJ, RSV.
44. NAB, NAS, NIV, NJB.
45. For those who prefer ארץ in 3:5 as 'earth,' see Mays, *Amos*, 59; Jeremias, *Book of Amos*, 47. Those who translate ארץ in 3:5 as 'ground,' are, for example, Wolff, *Prophets*, 140; Andersen and Freedman, *Amos*, 383; Stuart, *Hosea-Jonah*, 323; Paul, *Amos*, 104.
46. ASV, ESV, KJV, LXE, NAS, NAU, NKJV, RSV.
47. NAB, NIV, NJB, NRS.
48. For instance, see Mays, *Amos*, 91; Andersen and Freedman, *Amos*, 482; Stuart, *Hosea-Jonah*, 306.
49. See Stuart, *Hosea-Jonah*, 229; Jeremias, *Book of Amos*, 82.
50. ASV, ESV, KJV, LXE, RSV.
51. NAB, NAS, NAU, NIV, NJB, NKJ, NRS.

as 'earth',[52] others as 'ground'.[53] This verse suggests the act of YHWH's judgment upon the people of Israel among other nations. In this context, the shaking of Israel among all other nations is compared to the shaking of grain in a sieve in which no pebble shall fall upon the ground. Thus, the term ארץ can be taken as either 'earth' or 'ground' in 2:7; 3:5; 5:7; 9:9. Here 'ground' is a suitable translation yet the context is the whole 'earth'. The different translations of these texts show that the English word 'earth' has a semantic range which covers some of the meanings of the Hebrew ארץ. It is often hard to judge between the meanings. Context must decide, and 5:7 and 9:9 are good examples of this.

1.2.2 The Term אדמה in Amos

Amos' use of 'land' vocabulary אֲדָמָה occurs ten times in seven verses in Amos (3:2, 5; 5:2; 7:11, 17 [three times]; 9:8, 15 [twice]). Like ארץ, אדמה also refers to 'land', 'earth', 'ground', and sometimes 'soil' in the sense of fruitful land. Therefore, the function of the two terms ארץ and אדמה for 'land' as synonyms can be clearly seen throughout the book.

1.2.2.1 The Term אדמה as 'Land'

The term אדמה in Amos 5:2; 7:11, 17 [three times]; 9:15 [twice] is generally translated 'land'. In 5:2, the context is a lament for Israel, depicted as a virgin who has died on her 'land'.[54] This could mean the land of Israel.[55] Others, however, prefer to use 'soil',[56] with attention to the fruitful dwelling-place of Israel. 'Soil' and land as territory could overlap in this case. A further possibility is that אדמה here refers to a person's property. This is the

---

52. For example, Wolff, *Prophets*, 344; Mays, *Amos*, 160.
53. See Andersen and Freedman, *Amos*, 870; Stuart, *Hosea-Jonah*, 389; Paul, *Amos*, 282; Jeremias, *Book of Amos*, 161.
54. ASV, ESV, KJV, LXE, NAB, NAS, NAU, NIV, NKJ. NRS, RSV, YLT. However, NJB translates it as 'soil,' focusing on the very dwelling place of Israel which could also mean 'land.'
55. Wilfried Warning, 'Terminological Patterns and Amos 9:11-15,' *DL* 5, no. 02 (2006): 131; Mays, *Amos*, 84; Andersen and Freedman, *Amos*, 472; Stuart, *Hosea-Jonah*, 341; Jeremias, *Book of Amos*, 81; Snyman, '*Leitmotiv*,' 537.
56. See Wolff, *Prophets*, 227; Paul, *Amos*, 157.

piece of land that belongs in a special way to the 'virgin' who stands for Israel in this image.[57]

In the encounter between Amos and Amaziah in 7:11-17, the term אדמה figures prominently, and can be translated 'land' in each case.[58] Amos predicted that King Jeroboam would go into exile from his own land.[59] But different aspects of land appear here. The term אדמה appears three times in 7:17. The second of these three occurrences refers to a foreign land. The other two could both refer to the land of Israel.[60] However, as in 5:2, the first occurrence in 7:17 could designate the property that belonged to Amaziah in particular. This is another case where it is hard to decide between meanings of the word. This is because there is a close connection between the thought that Amaziah will lose his property and that Israel will lose its land.

Finally, in the closing verse of the book (9:15), Amos focuses on the reassurance of YHWH's restoration of the land of Israel (אדמה). Here again the term is best translated 'land'. But it is hard to separate the idea of land as territory from the idea of land as fruitful. Once again, the senses of 'land' overlap and merge into each other.

1.2.2.2 The Term אדמה as 'Earth'

Amos 3:2 shows the theme of Israel's election from all the peoples of the world. It is clear that the term אדמה refers here to the whole 'earth',[61] all the nations of the world. The phrase 'All the families of the earth' in 3:2

---

57. See Wolff, *Prophets*, 315.
58. ASV, ESV, KJV, LXE, NAB, NAS, NAU, NIV, NJB, NKJ, NRS, RSV, YLT.
59. See Wolff, *Prophets*, 307; Mays, *Amos*, 134; Andersen and Freedman, *Amos*, 634, 762; Stuart, *Hosea-Jonah*, 374; Paul, *Amos*, 238; Jeremias, *Book of Amos*, 135; Warning, 'Patterns', 130-131.
60. See Warning, 'Patterns', 130-131; Wolff, *Prophets*, 307, 315-316; Mays, *Amos*, 134; Andersen and Freedman, *Amos*, 635, 763; Stuart, *Hosea-Jonah*, 374; Paul, *Amos*, 238; Jeremias, *Book of Amos*, 135; Snyman, 'Eretz and Adama', 144. For English translations, see ASV, ESV, KJV, LXE, NAB, NIV, NJB, NKJ. NRS, RSV, YLT. In the reference to the foreign nation, NAS, NAU, and NJB prefer to use unclean or polluted 'soil' whereas NIV uses foreign 'country.'
61. See Wolff, *Prophets*, 174; Mays, *Amos*, 54; Andersen and Freedman, *Amos*, 378; Stuart, *Hosea-Jonah*, 321; Paul, *Amos*, 100; Jeremias, *Book of Amos*, 47; Warning, 'Patterns', 131. Also see the English Translations, ASV, ESV, KJV, LXE, NAB, NAS, NAU, NIV, NJB, NKJ, NRS, RSV.

has connections with the blessings of YHWH upon all the peoples of the earth (Gen 12:3; 28:14).[62] Again, in Amos 9:8, אדמה indicates the whole 'earth'. The term is variously translated 'earth'[63] and 'ground'.[64] It is more relevant to translate as 'earth'[65] since in this context, the nation is depicted in relation to the whole earth.

1.2.2.3 The Term אדמה as 'Ground'

In Amos 3:5, both ארץ and אדמה occur in the same sense denoting 'ground'. Some scholars and English versions translate אדמה as 'earth'[66] while others take it as 'ground'.[67] Here, in any case, 'earth' means 'ground'.

1.3 The Semantic Range of the Land (אדמה/ארץ) in Amos

1.3.1 Land as Territory

The survey of the terms ארץ and אדמה shows that both terms can carry the meanings of 'earth', 'fruitful land', 'territory', and 'ground'. In addition, אדמה may be able to refer to an individual's property.[68] And the meanings sometimes overlap or relate closely to each other. In Amos 7:10-17, Amos is reported as saying that Israel would go into exile away from *their* land (אדמה) (7:11). Amaziah orders Amos to go back to *his* land (ארץ) (7:12), and Amos responds '*your* land (אדמה) will be divided and you will die in an unclean land (אדמה) and Israel will go into exile away from *their* land (אדמה)' (7:17). Here, 'territory' overlaps with individual 'property'. Amos

---

62. Paul, *Amos*, 101; Snyman, 'Eretz and Adama', 138.
63. ASV, KJV, LXE, NAB, NAS, NAU, NIV, NJB, NKJ, NRS.
64. ESV, RSV, YLT.
65. See Wolff, *Prophets*, 344; Mays, *Amos*, 156; Andersen and Freedman, *Amos*, 867; Stuart, *Hosea-Jonah*, 389; Paul, *Amos*, 282; Jeremias, *Book of Amos*, 160; Warning, 'Patterns', 131.
66. See Warning 'Patterns', 131; and English versions such as KJV, NAU, NIV.
67. For this translation, see Wolff, *Prophets*, 180, 315-316; Mays, *Amos*, 59; Andersen and Freedman, *Amos*, 383; Stuart, *Hosea-Jonah*, 323; Paul, *Amos*, 104; Jeremias, *Book of Amos*, 47. For English translation, see ESV, NJB, NRS.
68. See Waldemar Janzen, 'Land,' in *ABD (K-N)*, ed. David Noel Freedman et al. (London: Doubleday, 1992), 144.

also uses the term גְּבוּל for the territories of the Amorites (1:13), and of Calneh, Hamath, and the Philistines (6:2).

As Keita asserts, Amos 2.10 implies that the land belongs to Israel. This is confirmed by 7:11 (אדמתו). However, she points out that the phrase ארץ ישראל does not occur in Amos, and argues that for the concept of 'land of Israel' the term used is always אדמה (5:2; 7:11, 17; 9:15 – contrast only once in Hosea, Hos 2:20).[69] This leads her to the conclusion that in Amos the territorial-political aspect of the land is less prominent than the agrarian aspect ('Das lässt darauf schliessen, dass bei Amos der territorial-politische Aspekt des Landes insgesamt hinter dem agrarischen Aspekt zurücktritt').[70] My view is different from Keita's assessment here because I have shown that both ארץ and אדמה can be used in the territorial sense as well as the agrarian.

1.3.2 Land as Fruitful

In Amos 5:2, Israel appears in the metaphor of a young woman (בְּתוּלָה) who has fallen dead on her 'land'. The 'land' (אדמה) here is 'fruitful land' (cf. 5:11, 17).[71] Keita finds the land referred to as אדמה ten times in Amos as against only twice in Hosea, and she therefore thinks that the theme of fruitful land is much stronger in Amos than in Hosea. The young woman and the vineyards share the idea of wasted or pointless fertility ('sinnlosen Fruchtbarkeit').[72] Amos 5:7 echoes 5:2 as the young woman falls dead to the earth (אדמה), so righteousness (*sedaqa*) is thrown down to the earth (ארץ). Righteousness is thus portrayed as 'dying' like the virgin; and the fruitful land suffers from unrealized potential.[73]

In the vision of locusts in Amos 7:2, YHWH sends the natural disaster of locusts upon the land of Israel. The 'land' (ארץ) is threatened by locusts and the land itself endangers the life of both human and animals,

---

69. Katrin Keita, *Gottes Land: Exegetische Studien zur Land-Thematik im Hoseabuch in kanonischer Perspektive*, TTS 13, (Hildeshheim: Georg Oms Verlag, 2007), 273.
70. Ibid.
71. Ibid., 258.
72. Ibid., fn. 7.
73. Ibid., 259.

for it yields no grass for animals or crops for humans.[74] As Shalom M. Paul points out, the phrase עשׂב הארץ 'vegetation of the land' indicates plant growth which is necessary for both humans and animals.[75] The context of 7:2 shows that the land is also in view as a fruitful land because the land produces vegetation and crops before its destruction by locusts.

The term אדמה (9:15) often means the 'soil',[76] that is, the fruitful land (9:13-15),[77] and therefore the term often suggests an agricultural image.[78] The land (אדמה) may be fruitful (7:1; 8:2) or unfruitful (1:2; 4:7, 9; 5:11), but finally becomes bountiful (9:13-14). In some of these texts it is hard to distinguish between the land as fruitful and as territorial.

1.3.3 Land as Cosmic

The semantic range of both ארץ and אדמה includes the cosmic aspect, where either of the terms can stand for the whole earth, or even universe (אדמה – 3:2; 9:8; ארץ – 4:13, 5:8, 8:9; 9:5, 6). The doxologies (4:13, 5:8, 9; 9:5, 6) together reflect the handiwork of YHWH's creation of the whole cosmos. The natural disasters of earthquake and eclipse in 8:8-9 also show land as cosmic because of the disruption even of Egypt and the Nile.

1.4 The Theology of the Land (אדמה/ארץ) in Amos

We have shown the range of possible meanings of ארץ and אדמה. Now, we come to identify topics for further considerations and raise a new question about the theological traditions concerning land that underlie the message of Amos. Köckert carefully distinguishes a number of possibilities of understanding land in Amos' time, identifying several separate traditions. He sets them out as follows: land promised to the patriarchs, land given

---

74. Snyman, 'Eretz and Adama', 142.
75. Paul, *Amos*, 228.
76. Preuss, *Old Testament Theology*, 1: 118.
77. Ellen Davis, *Scripture, Culture, and Agriculture: An Agrarian Reading of the Bible*, (Cambridge: Cambridge University Press, 2009), 129.
78. Duane A. Garrett, *Amos: A Handbook on the Hebrew Text* (Waco, Texas: Baylor University Press, 2008), 290.

by YHWH (Amos 9:15; Hos 2:17; Deut 6:10ff.; 7:12ff.; 8:7ff.; 11:10 ff; 26:5-10), land taken by YHWH in war (Amos 2:9; Judg 11:23-24; Deut 33:26-29), and land as YHWH's property (1 Kgs 20:23; 2 Kgs 17:26; 1 Sam 26:19; Amos 7:17; Hos 9:3; Ezek 4:13).[79] According to Köckert, up until the eighth century, the relationship between God, Israel and the land was 'natural.' However, the eighth-century prophets, Amos and Hosea, began to loosen this 'natural' bond.[80] Köckert's critical assumption is that in Hosea and Amos the promise tradition and the theology of gift are silent.[81] This assumes that Amos and Hosea do not know the Deuteronomic land-theology. With Köckert's view in mind, we turn now to consider theological traditions underlying Amos.

1.4.1 Land as Promised

According to Köckert, land as promised to the patriarchs is not the same as mere occupation of land, or conquest of it.[82] He further argues that Amos and Hosea would have referred to this promise tradition if they had known about it, as it would have suited their purpose very well. However as they are silent about it, they cannot have known it. The promise of land arises from theologizing in the context of the threatened *loss* of the land at the time of the exile. Amos and Hosea did not yet know this theology.[83] The same conclusion must follow for the tradition of YHWH's oath to the patriarchs, since this is a particular form of the promise-theology.[84]

Köckert may be right here since there is no exact word for 'promise' in 2:9. However, arguably the idea of this land promised is already inherent in Amos in relation to the exodus traditions. As Snyman suggests, the land is promised and given (2:9-10; 3:1-2, 9) to Israel.[85] It is true that these texts do

---

79. Mattias Köckert, 'Gottesvolk und Land: Jahwe, Israel und das Land bei den Propheten Amos und Hosea,' in *Gottesvolk: Beiträge zu einem Thema biblischer Theologie. Festschrift S Wagner*, edited by Arndt Meinhold and Rüdiger Lux, (Berlin: Evangelische Verlagsanstalt, 1991) 43-73.
80. Ibid., 43.
81. Ibid., 45.
82. Ibid., 44.
83. Ibid., 45.
84. Ibid., 45-46.
85. Snyman, '*Leitmotiv*,' 527-542.

not directly and explicitly mention promise and gift. However, a different judgment could be made in Amos in association with other traditions. In his book, *A History of Pentateuchal Traditions*, Martin Noth recognized that the Pentateuch has different traditions which set out a new model for the composition of the Pentateuch. He identified some key Pentateuchal traditions namely, promise to the patriarchs (e.g. Deut 26:5-9), exodus from Egypt (e.g. Exod 20:2; Lev 25:38; Num 23:22; 24:8; Deut 5:6; 6:21; 26:8), revelation at Sinai (e.g. Exod 19-20; Num 3:1; Deut 33:2) or Horeb (Deut 5), guidance in the wilderness (e.g. Deut 29:4-5), and guidance into the arable land or taking possession of the arable land (e.g. Lev 25:38; Deut 4:38; 6:23; 26:9).[86] Noth then convincingly demonstrated that in essence, both themes of 'the exodus from Egypt' and 'the taking possession of the arable land' are closely related and the Pentateuchal tradition rests between these two themes.[87] Noth gives a way of thinking that suggests keeping an open mind about what Amos knew. In this sense, Amos is likely to be drawing on other biblical traditions outside Amos in the Old Testament. It looks as if Amos knows the Pentateuchal traditions of a conquest (2:9) and exodus (2:10; 3:1; 9:7), wilderness (2:10; 5:25), and gift of land (9:15).

Although there is no clear evidence of promise in Amos there is a clear connection with the Jacob and Bethel traditions which also serve as hints. In Amos, the land, ארץ (7:2) or אדמה (9:8), seems to be closely associated with Jacob, the patriarch (7:2, 5), and 'Jacob' could call to mind the promise or oath (3:13; 8:7). These references might imply the memory of the oath to the patriarchs and thus hint at the land as promised to patriarchs, though admittedly this cannot be proved. Land is also connected with the Bethel tradition (3:14; 4:4; 5:5-6; 7:10, 13), since Bethel is associated with the promise to give the land to Israel (Gen 28:13).

The references to Bethel and other sanctuaries in Amos may hint at a theology of promise. Amos mentions the sanctuaries of Bethel (3:14; 4:4; 5:5, 6; 7:10, 13), Gilgal (4:4; 5:5), Samaria (3:9, 12; 4:1; 6:1; 8:14), Dan (8:14), and Beersheba (5:5; 8:14). Bethel, Gilgal, and Beersheba

---

86. Martin Noth, *A History of Pentateuchal Traditions*, trans. with an Intro. Bernhard W. Anderson (Englewood Cliffs: Prentice-Hall, 1972), 46-62.
87. Ibid., 47.

were worship places from ancient times connected with the patriarchs.[88] The high places of Isaac may indicate the sanctuaries at Bethel, Gilgal, Beersheba, and Dan (Amos 3:12; 4:4; 5:5-6; 6:1, 6; 8:14),[89] embracing the whole historic land of Israel.[90]

Amaziah's confrontation with Amos at Bethel suggests the concept of land as promised to the patriarchs. Amaziah claims לֹא־תוּכַל הָאָרֶץ לְהָכִיל אֶת־כָּל־דְּבָרָיו 'the land cannot bear all his words' (7:10). Amos then responds to Amaziah by quoting his divine commission and authority (7:14-15) to prophesy to Israel at Bethel,[91] who are among the covenant people, 'my people of Israel'. Bethel is a 'house of God' associated with Jacob (Gen 28:19) and the patriarchal promises (Gen 12:8; 13:3; 28:10-22). In the dream of Jacob, YHWH promised him the land: 'I will give you and your descendants the land on which you are lying' (Gen 28:13; NIV). In the patriarchal tradition, Bethel is thus related to the promise of the land.

Bethel is a place promised to Jacob for possession, and it is a sanctuary where the people of Israel celebrated (Gen 28:10-22; 1 Kgs 12:28 29)[92] and offered sacrifices and feasts, along with Gilgal (Amos 4:4-5; 5:5-6). It is reasonable to suggest, as argued by Klaus Koch, that the cultic place at Bethel is connected with the gift of the land by YHWH to Israel and it was

---

88. See Billy K. Smith and Frank S. Page, *Amos, Obadiah, Jonah*, NAC, (Broadman and Holman Publishers, 1995), 99; Gene M. Tucker, 'Amos the Prophet and Amos the Book: Historical Framework,' in *Israel's Prophets and Israel's Past: Essays on the Relationship of Prophetic Texts and Israelite History in Honor of John H. Hayes*, ed. Brad E. Kelle and Megan Bishop Moore (London: T & T Clark, 2006), 93.

89. See Erling Hammershaimb, *The Book of Amos: A Commentary*, trans by John Sturdy, (Oxford: Basil Blackwell, 1970), 112; R. Dennis Cole, 'The Visions of Amos 7-9,' *TE* no. 52 (Fall 1995): 61; J. Alberto Soggin, *The Prophet Amos: A Translation and Commentary*, trans. John Bowden (London: SCM Press, 1987), 117; Elizabeth Achtemeier, *Minor Prophets I* (NIBC; OTS 17; Peabody, Massachusetts: Hendrickson Publishers, 1996), 221.

90. J. Gordon McConville, '"How Can Jacob Stand? He is So Small!" (Amos 7:2): The Prophetic Word and the Re-Imagining of Israel,' in *Israel's Prophets and Israel's Past: Essays on the Relationship of Prophetic Texts and Israelite History in Honor of John H. Hayes*, edited by Brad E. Kelle and Megan Bishop Moore, (London: T & T Clark, 2006), 147-148, refers to Samaria, Dan, and Beersheba (Amos 8:13-14) and the pairing of Dan and Beersheba (1 Sam 3:20; 2 Sam 3:10; 17:11; 24:2) and Beersheba in connection with the patriarch to imply the whole land.

91. A. G. Auld, *Amos* (Sheffield: Sheffield Academic Press, 1995), 25.

92. Klaus Koch, *The Prophets: The Assyrian Period*, Vol 1 (London: SCM Press, 1982) 1: 37.

celebrated in remembrance of the promise of YHWH to the patriarchs in the ancient days.[93] Not only is Bethel regarded as the place which YHWH promised to the patriarchs as their possession but also as בֵּית מַמְלָכָה, the temple of the kingdom. It is possible that the house of Jeroboam fitted itself into this view of history by adopting Bethel. In this way, the monarchy took for itself the possession of the land promised by YHWH.[94] This land as promised is threatened, however.

Amos laments for Israel, depicted as a young woman who has died and is deserted in her own land (אדמה) (5:2). He also announces the loss of the land (אדמה) in exile (7:11, 17). The land threatened with exile is mentioned elsewhere (3:11; 4:2-3; 5:2, 5, 26-27; 6:7; 9:1, 4, 8-9). As Aaron Park argues, exile is one remarkable theological theme in Amos. It is also a prominent theme in the Oracles against the Nations, including Damascus, Gaza, Tyre, and Ammon (1:3-5, 6-8, 9-12, 13-15). The threat of exile becomes more specific as the book progresses (5:5; 5:27; 6:7; 7:17); however, in the disputed last section of the book, exile ends with restoration (9:14).[95] YHWH promises to restore this land by raising again the fallen booth of David (9:11). Finally, YHWH undertakes to restore the land (אדמה) once promised to fathers: 'And I will plant them upon their land (אדמה), and they shall never again be uprooted from their land (אדמה)' (9:15).

1.4.2 Land as Gift

For Köckert, land as YHWH's property means an exclusive connection between the god and the land. He thinks that the idea of land as YHWH's property contradicts the idea of the gift of land. In this theology, the god's power is limited to the land (e.g. 1 Kgs 20:23; 2 Kgs 17:26).[96] For him, Amos 2:9 indicates an exclusive connection between God, the people, and the land, and is not necessarily about the gift of land. And this is used by Amos only to bring up the 'impossible possibility' of Israel's present deeds. Israel sees its own future in the fate of the Amorites – who were completely

---

93. Ibid., 1: 55.
94. Ibid., 1: 37.
95. Aaron W. Park, *The Book of Amos as Composed and Read in Antiquity* (SBL 37; New York: Peter Lang, 2001), 117.
96. Köckert, 'Gottesvolk und Land', 49.

destroyed from the land.[97] According to Köckert, this theology does not yet see the relationship between land and people as a problem; it is simply a story of a people and its victorious god. Amos knows this kind of land-theology (2:9), land taken by YHWH in war, which belongs to the common Ancient Near East war-ideology.[98] Keita agrees with Köckert's assessment that land as gift and land as conquest are to be differentiated, and that in Amos only the land as conquest appears. She also agrees with him that the conquest motif has the purpose of warning Israel that they too could be driven out. She differs from him in his view that the whole people is judged equally – she thinks a distinction is made between offenders and victims in Israel (3:9-15; 4; 5:11-17).[99]

There are several prophetic examples which show the exclusive claims of YHWH on Israel's worship (Hos 9:3, 15; Jer 2:7-8; 16:18), and the threat of foreign nations to YHWH's land (Hos 8.1; Jer 12:7ff.; 50.11; Ezek 36:5, 20; 38:16; Isa 14:2, 25; Joel 1:6; 4:2, 6; Zech 9:8; Ps 10:16). Strikingly, in none of these cases does the idea of *gift* of the land occur. In fact the idea of 'gift' would contradict the idea of YHWH as owner.[100] The idea that the land where Israel lived was YHWH's land is one of the fundamental tenets of their faith. The land ultimately belongs to YHWH (Deut 32:43; Lev 25:23; Josh 22:19; Isa 14:2, 25).[101] The prophets and Psalms often mention this concept of YHWH's ownership of land.[102] It can be argued, however, that the traditions of YHWH's ownership of land and land as divine gift are closely associated.[103] According to a certain way of thinking in the Old Testament, YHWH owns the whole earth (e.g. Exod 19:5; Ps 24:1) by right of creation (Gen 1-2; cf. Amos 4:13; 5:8-9; 9:5-6). In this sense, YHWH's ownership of the land is close to the concept that YHWH has the right to give the land to his people (Gen 12:1-3; 13:14-16; 15:18-21;

---

97. Ibid., 52.
98. Ibid., 48.
99. Keita, *Gottes Land*, 277.
100. Köckert, 'Gottesvolk und Land', 50.
101. For YHWH as the owner of the land, see Waldow, 'Israel and Her Land: Some Theological Considerations,' 493-496.
102. Christopher J. H. Wright, *The Mission of God: Unlocking the Bible's Grand Narrative* (Nottingham: Inter-Varsity Press, 2006), 292.
103. Ibid.

21:8; 26:3-4, 24; 28:3-4, 13-15; 35:9-12).[104] Therefore, certain texts can be taken to imply that land is a *gift*.

Köckert is right that there is no mention of *gift* except in 9:15 which, along with many scholars, he assigns not to Amos but to the exilic period.[105] Deuteronomy 26:5-10 contains an ancient ritual of thanksgiving for harvest, which focuses on land as fruitful. This aspect of land-theology often appears in Deuteronomy (6:10ff.; 7:12ff.; 8:7ff., 11ff.; 11:10ff. etc).[106] According to Köckert, Amos 9:15 which similarly speaks of a paradisal land, comes from the exile at the earliest.[107] Köckert concludes that there is no clear evidence for the theology of land-as-gift before Deuteronomy.[108] This suggests that Amos does not know the Deuteronomic land-theology.

However, the terms ארץ and אדמה are closely associated with עלה, and ירש in texts about Israel's possession of the land (Amos 2:10; 3:1; 9:7, 12). In Deuteronomy, ירש (possess) and נתן (give) are closely associated. YHWH swears (שבע) to the forefathers to give (נתן) them the land (e.g. Deut 7:13; 11:9; 28:11; 31:7) and Israel possesses (ירש) it (Deut 30:18; 31:13; 32:47).[109] Gerhard von Rad considers that the idea of land in Deuteronomy has to do with a possession which YHWH gave to Israel (Deut 12:1; 17:14; 18:9; 19:1; 21:1; 26:1), that they may have long life in it (Deut 4:25, 26; 6:18; 8:1; 11:8, 9, 18-21; 16:20).[110] Von Rad argues that, 'Deuteronomy is dominated from beginning to end by the idea of the land which is to be taken in possession.'[111] Therefore, the terms נתן and ירש are Deuteronomic language for YHWH's giving of the land (ארץ,

---

104. J. Gary Millar, 'Land,' in *NDBT*, eds. T. Desmond Alexander et al. (Leicester: InterVarsity Press, 2000), 623.
105. Köckert, 'Gottesvolk und Land', 47.
106. Ibid., 46.
107. Ibid.
108. Ibid., 47.
109. Josef G. Plöger, 'אֲדָמָה,' in *TDOT*, ed. G. Johannes Botterweck and Helmer Ringgren, trans. John T. Willis, vol. 1 (Grand Rapids, Michigan: William B. Eerdmans Publishing Company, 1974), 96-97.
110. Gerhard Von Rad, 'The Promised Land and Yahweh's Land in the Hexateuch,' in *The Problem of the Hexateuch and Other Essays*, trans. E. W. Trueman Dicken; intro. Norman W. Porteous (London: Oliver &Boyd, 1966), 91.
111. Von Rad, 'The Promised Land,' 90.

אדמה).[112] The Book of Amos concludes the theology of the land with the idea of *gift* in the phrase אֲשֶׁר נָתַתִּי לָהֶם 'which I have given to them' (9:15). This phrase clearly recalls the covenantal vocabulary of 'the land that I have given them' (e.g. Deut 1:8; 6:3; 7:13; 11:9; 26:9; 30:5).[113] As noted above, 9:15 is often considered secondary. Many scholars defend it as authentic, however. And in any case, it draws out an implication of the texts which I have reviewed.

Keita, though she agrees with Köckert that the theology of gift is not explicit in Amos, understands that Israel had to take possession of the land. It once belonged to others. YHWH created the conditions in which they could take it. As YHWH could violently remove the previous inhabitants, so he can also remove Israel (2:13-16; cf. 8:2; 9:1-4).[114] As Amos 2:10 declares that the land belongs to Israel, this is strengthened and verified by 'his land' (אדמתו) in 7:11.[115] Zimmerli understands the motif of annihilation of the previous inhabitants as a 'land-gift.' He argues that the land was first given to Israel by their God in their early history when he destroyed the Amorites (Amos 2:9) and thus the people of Israel acknowledge that they are not indigenous to their land.[116] Snyman too argues that 2:10 is a reference to the giving of land to Israel, the land as promised is given to Israel (2:9-10; 3:1-2, 9).[117] That is, land as gift and land as conquest are not totally different. So, even though נתן (give) appears only in the disputed 9:15, it is reasonable to find the concept of the gift of the land in Amos.

---

112. See J. Gordon McConville, *Law and Theology in Deuteronomy* (JSOTSS 33; Sheffield: JSOT Press, 1984), 11-13; Patrick D. Miller, Jr., 'The Gift of God: The Deuteronomic Theology of the Land,' *Int* 23, no. 04 (October 1969): 451-465; Eryl W. Davies, 'Land: Its Rights and Privileges,' in *The World of Ancient Israel: Sociological, Anthropological, and Political Perspectives*, ed. Ronald E. Clements (Cambridge: Cambridge University Press, 1989), 350-351.
113. Niehaus, 'Amos,' 494.
114. Keita, *Gottes Land*, 272-273.
115. Ibid.
116. Walter Zimmerli, 'The "Land" in the Pre-Exilic and Early Post-Exilic Prophets,' in *Understanding the Word: Essays in Honor of Bernhard W. Anderson*, ed. by James T. Butler, Edgar W. Conrad, and Ben C. Ollenburger, JSOTSS 37, (Sheffield: JSOT Press, 1985), 247.
117. Snyman, 'Eretz and Adama', 137.

At the same time, it is to be admitted that there is no exact word for 'promise' and 'gift' in the references to exodus and wilderness traditions (Amos 2:9-10; 3:1). However, what is clear is that YHWH gave the land to fulfil what was promised to the patriarchs by the events of exodus and conquest. As already mentioned, it seems as if Amos knows the conquest, exodus, and wilderness traditions. The land had been given to Israel through the exodus redemptive history. Therefore, the land was 'the goal of the exodus *redemption* tradition'.[118] Both exodus and wilderness wandering gradually led to the conquest of the land by YHWH's act. In this way, both the exodus and wilderness wandering find their ultimate goal in YHWH's extending his favour to his people in the possession of the land of the Amorite; hence, the *gift* of land.[119] The exodus from Egypt and wilderness wandering for forty years would be meaningless apart from the gift of the land.[120]

'Wilderness' appears only in reference to the past in Amos (as in Hos 9:10; 13:4-6), but not in reference to the future (as in Hos 2:17; 12:10). In Amos 2:10, references to Exodus, wilderness and occupation of land occur in the same order as in the Pentateuch. There is also reference to the forty-year duration of the wilderness period in 2:10 and 5:25. This period is understood differently from the Pentateuch, because here it is seen as a time when YHWH *cared for* Israel. Amos thus shares the reception of the wilderness tradition with Hosea, since in both books it is associated with YHWH's care for Israel, their intimate relationship.[121] Amos 5:25 contains two points: the relationship between YHWH and Israel was intact; and Israel's sacrificial worship is regarded negatively. The wilderness is seen as a time of close relationship between God and Israel *without* sacrifice. Therefore, *that* time (wilderness) is contrasted with *this* time (land).[122] Land and people, then, are always closely related in Amos. YHWH's bringing back of his people into their own אדמה and planting them there (9:15) is a

---

118. Wright, *Mission,* 292.
119. Paul, *Amos,* 91; Niehaus, 'Amos,' 369.
120. Snyman, '*Leitmotiv*,' 530.
121. Keita, *Gottes Land,* 261.
122. Ibid., 262-263.

fulfilment and confirmation of YHWH's land promise as a 'New Exodus'.[123] Therefore, Amos' theology of land is consistent in terms of the 'exodus' event by which YHWH brought them from Egypt and gave them land (2:10; 3:1; 9:7) and Amos reaffirms their possession of it again (9:14-15).

1.4.3 Land as Inheritance

Amos uses the term ירש in 2:10 to designate the possession of the land of the Amorites. In Deuteronomy, the people of Israel possess (ירש) the land (Deut 30:18; 31:13; 32:47),[124] and ירש is used in parallel with נַחֲלָה, 'inheritance' (Deut 26:1). The term נחלה does not occur in Amos. However, Amos uses the term חֵלֶק to denote the concept of inheritance (7:4) in relation to Jacob (7:5). Andersen and Freedman argue that the term חֵלֶק usually refers to the 'patrimonial land',[125] the inheritance received from YHWH. A number of scholars suggest that the term חֵלֶק may refer to the land of Israel as an inherited 'portion' (cf. Mic 2:4).[126] The land of Israel as חֵלֶק depends on the idea of YHWH's giving it as an inheritance. The LXX adds κυρίου, and thus it reads the 'Lord's portion'[127] or the 'Lord's field'.[128]

1.4.4 Land as a Place of Justice

The land is also a place where it is expected that justice will be practiced (8:4-6; cf. 2:6-8; 3:10; 4:1; 5:7, 11-12; 24).[129] The demand of YHWH who brought Israel into its land is that Israel should practice justice and righteousness in it (5:24).[130] However, 'land' becomes an occasion to pervert

---

123. Plöger, 'אֲדָמָה,' 98.
124. Ibid., 96-97.
125. Andersen and Freedman, *Amos*, 747.
126. See Mays, *Amos*, 131; James R Linville, *Amos and the Cosmic Imagination*, (Hampshire: Ashgate, 2008), 137; Smith and Page, *Amos, Obadiah, Jonah*, 131.
127. See Wolff, *Prophets*, 293. Further, it seems that the term חֵלֶק also alludes to Israel as the 'Lord's portion' since Jacob, YHWH's people, is referred to as the Lord's portion in Deuteronomy 32:9. See Mays, *Amos*, 131; Richard James Coggins, *Joel and Amos* (NCBC: Sheffield: Sheffield Academic Press, 2000), 139.
128. See Gary V. Smith, *Amos*, 221; Stuart, *Hosea-Jonah*, 370-371.
129. Snyman, '*Leitmotiv*,' 536.
130. Zimmerli, 'Land', 248.

justice (Deut 24:17-18; see Amos 5:10-12).[131] Koch argues that 'Amos had in mind a particular constitutional ideal: that the equal rights of participation in the actual soil of the Promised Land belonged to Israel, with all its members, as the people of YHWH.'[132] The people of Israel have to enjoy benefits of the land under YHWH's ownership and protection.[133] However, in practice the poor have no privilege to share the bounty of the land. The conditions of ordinary people show that they need their share in the land to be protected.

1.5 Conclusion

From the above investigation of the terms ארץ and אדמה for 'land' the following conclusions can now be drawn. First, both the terms ארץ and אדמה function as synonyms referring to 'earth', 'land', and 'ground'. Second, the language and concepts of 'land' – אֶרֶץ and אֲדָמָה – with attention to the theology of the land run through to the climax of the book, with its reaffirmation of the gift of the land. The theology of the land, therefore, is closely connected with one of the most influential and important themes in the book of Amos, that of justice. However, this does not deny the existence of other important theological themes in Amos.

Third, the survey of the terms ארץ and אדמה for 'land' indicates both semantic and theological meanings. Semantically, there are a variety of meanings which the terms carry, namely, land as territory, land as fruitful, and land as cosmic. In addition, these terms ארץ and אדמה denote various aspects of the theology of the land in Amos, namely, land as promised, land as a gift of YHWH (both territory and fruitful land), land as inheritance, and land as a place to practice justice. These theological ways of speaking concerning land in the book of Amos will be further explored in detail later.

---

131. Brueggemann, *The Land: Place as Gift, Promise, and Challenge in Biblical Faith.* 2nd ed. OBT. (Minneapolis: Fortress Press, 2002), 62.
132. Koch, *Prophets*, 1: 49-50.
133. Wright, *Mission*, 293.

CHAPTER 2

Theological Themes Linked to the Land in Amos

2.1 Introduction

Within Amos' understanding of land, various theological themes, including Zion, covenant, Israel, creation, and justice are linked to the theology of land. That is, the study of land in Amos has wider dimensions. Zion (Amos 1:2), which implies the claim to be the place of worship in Israel, connects both with the theme of worship and with the question of the relationship between the northern and southern kingdoms. The covenant-election tradition implies that Amos anticipates the covenant with Israel as a whole. It also shows the connection between the election of Israel and the theme of oppression and justice. The relationship between the two kingdoms, and the question about who Amos' message is really for, raises the question about what the 'land' really refers to. In this connection, the book's terminology for the people of 'Israel' is closely relevant to its understanding of the concept of land. It is also suggested that in a number of places the language of land has broader connotations of the whole creation. Finally, one of the leading theological themes is its prophetic criticism of injustice in Israel. The aim of this chapter is to show the relationship between the concept of land and the concepts of Zion, the covenant-election tradition, Israel, creation, and justice in Amos.

2.2 Zion

In Amos 1:2, Zion has a specific purpose in relation to the land. Many scholars view this text as the motto of the entire book.[1] The roar of YHWH from Zion (1:2a) shows its effect especially upon the land and thus the land is at risk in 1:2b: 'the pastures of the shepherds shall dry up, and the top of Carmel withers.'[2] In this connection, the critical question must be asked: How does Zion and the whole theme of worship relate to the land? How does it function in the relationship between the northern and southern kingdoms? Why is Zion important to Amos and how does it relate to the natural world and to justice?

2.2.1 Zion and the Theme of Worship and Justice

Zion is originally the name of the fortress of the Jebusites located near the southeastern hill of Jerusalem. It was named 'the city of David' after David captured it. Later 'the city of David' was used as the name for the hill, including the Jerusalem Temple, and finally it referred to Jerusalem proper.[3] Jerusalem was assumed to be the place of the worship of YHWH in which Melchizedek, king of Salem, priest of God Most High, blessed Abram, saying, 'blessed be Abram by God Most High, Creator of heaven and earth' (Gen 14:18-20). And Jerusalem alone was the legal sanctuary of the covenant, the only place of worship (Deut 12; 1 Kgs 9:3; 2 Chr 13:9-11; Pss 2, 76, 110).[4] Zion is the chief of the mountains, and Jerusalem was the only proper place to worship.[5] Zion, the temple mount, is YHWH's dwelling

---

1. For instance, William Rainey Harper, *A Critical and Exegetical Commentary on Amos and Hosea* (ICC; Edinburgh: T & T Clark, 1905), 9; Hammershaimb, *Book of Amos,* 19, 21; Wolff, *Prophets,* 119; Mays, *Amos,* 21; Stuart, *Hosea-Jonah,* 300; Jeremias, *Book of Amos,* 13-14; Sweeney, *The Twelve Prophets,* 1: 194, 198-199; Gerhard F. Hasel, *Understanding of Amos: Basic Issues in Current Interpretations* (Grand Rapids, Michigan: Baker Book House, 1991), 19; Paul, *Amos,* 36; Stephen J. Bramer, 'Analysis,' *BS* 156, no. 622 (April-June 1999): 172.
2. Snyman, 'Eretz and Adama', 140.
3. Hammershaimb, *Book of Amos,* 20.
4. Stuart, *Hosea-Jonah,* 337-338, 346.
5. Andersen and Freedman, *Amos,* 46, 223-228, 566.

place (Pss 9:11; 76:2; 132:13),[6] the place of Temple and the royal city (Amos 9:6; cf. Ps 78:68, 69),[7] and the seat of his government from which his decrees come.[8] The placement of the Ark on Zion indicates YHWH's dwelling in Jerusalem (Ps 132).[9] From these perspectives, it is clear that Zion can be used interchangeably with Jerusalem.[10]

The traditions of the bringing of the Ark of Covenant to Jerusalem by David (2 Sam 6-7; cf. Ps 132) and the building and dedicating of the temple in Jerusalem by Solomon (1 Kgs 8) may well have influenced Amos' understanding of Zion as God's dwelling place.[11] And therefore, Amos may be speaking YHWH's words coming from the Temple of Zion.[12] Niehaus argues in relation to Amos that, 'Zion was the place where Yahweh chose to put his name so that it would be available for his people' (as in 1 Kgs 9:1-9).[13] Zion is superior to other sanctuaries, the heavenly king is enthroned there, and he exercises his authority from there (cf. Ps 14:7; 53:6; Joel 3:16).[14] Zion is the place where the covenant people hear the word of YHWH.[15]

Since Zion is the site of the Temple (1 Kgs 8; Ps 78:68, 69), it is the place of worship accompanied by offerings such as tithes and the firstfruits of the ground which are related to the land. In the Old Testament and specifically in Amos, worship is always connected with the land in this way. However, in Amos YHWH does not accept the people's worship. Amos' social criticisms are primarily directed against their false worship

---

6. See Ben C. Ollenburger, *Zion, the City of the Great King: A Theological Symbol of the Jerusalem Cult* (JSOTSS 41; Sheffield: JSOT Press, 1987), 23; Mays, *Amos*, 21; Mox E. Polley, *Amos and the Davidic Empire: A Socio-Historical Approach*, (Oxford: Oxford University Press, 1989), 44; Gary Smith, *Amos: A Commentary*, 21; Niehaus, 'Amos,' 338.

7. John H. Hayes, *Amos, the Eighth Century Prophet: His Times and His Preaching*, (Nashville: Abingdon Press, 1988), 63-64; Andersen and Freedman, *Amos*, 721, 854.

8. Jon Douglas Levenson, *Sinai and Zion: An Entry into the Jewish Bible* (Minneapolis: Winston Press, 1985), 187.

9. Ollenburger, *Zion*, 24.

10. See Niehaus, 'Amos,' 338; Hammershaimb, *The Book of Amos*, 20.

11. See Gary Smith, *Amos: A Commentary*, 21, 26; Polley, *Davidic Empire*, 44.

12. See Hammershaimb, *The Book of Amos*, 19; Richard S. Cripps, *A Critical and Exegetical Commentary on the Book of Amos* (London: SPCK, 1929), 115.

13. Niehaus, 'Amos,' 338.

14. Soggin, *The Prophet*, 28.

15. Smith and Page, *Amos, Obadiah, Jonah*, 38-39.

and sacrifices without justice (4:4-5; 5:21-24). David Allan Hubbard argues that Zion functions as a rebuke upon Israel's false worship at Bethel, Gilgal (4:4; 5:5), Beersheba (5:5; 8:14), Samaria and Dan (8:14).[16]

Amos seems to use דרש 'seek' to illustrate the concept of worship in Israel. Hubbard suggests that דרש is asking YHWH for help and abiding in loyalty to him.[17] It denotes seeking YHWH for a particular response[18] and inquiring about the will of YHWH through prophets who are his spokesmen.[19] Amos 5:14-15 gives an explanation about what kind of 'seeking' (דרש) is approved. It is none other than to do or seek good, hate evil, and maintain justice in the gate.[20] Amos may well have thought there was no revelation of YHWH at Bethel, Gilgal or Beersheba.[21] According to Polley, Amos' intention was to call the northern kingdom to seek YHWH in Jerusalem. And Amos 1:2 functions as an introduction to his polemic against northern shrines (Amos 5:4-6).[22] It is clear that for Polley, Amos supported the worship of God in Jerusalem and wanted the north to return to Jerusalem. Marvin Sweeney, in line with Polley, argues that, though the sanctuaries in the north would have been places for offerings and worship, Amos calls the northerners to return to the Jerusalem Temple (cf. Amos 9:11-15).[23]

However, for Amos, the traditional worship at Bethel, Gilgal (4:4-5), and other sanctuaries rather proved their unwillingness to return to YHWH with their full heart.[24] The refrain וְלֹא־שַׁבְתֶּם עָדַי 'yet you did

---

16. David Allan Hubbard, *Joel and Amos: An Introduction and Commentary*, TOTC, (Leicester: Inter-Varsity Press, 1989), 126.
17. Ibid., 166.
18. David Denninger, 'דרש', m in *NIDOTTE*, ed. Willem A. VanGemeren et al., vol. 1 (Carlisle: Paternoster Press, 1996), 995.
19. See Paul, *Amos*, 162; Leonard J. Coppes, 'דָּרַשׁ,' in *Theological Wordbook of the Old Testament*, ed. R. Laird Harris, vol. 1 (Chicago: Moody Press, 1981), 198.
20. S. Wagner, 'דָּרַשׁ', in *TDOT*, eds. G. Johannes Botterweck and Helmer Ringgren, trans. John T. Wills, Geoffrey W. Bromiley, and David E. Green, vol. 3 (Grand Rapids, Michigan: William B. Eerdmans Publishing Company, 1978), 298.
21. Hubbard, *Joel and Amos*, 126.
22. Polley, *Davidic Empire*, 154. Also see Aaron Schart, 'The First Section of the Book of the Twelve Prophets: Hosea-Joel-Amos,' *Int* 61, no. 02 (April 2007): 145.
23. Sweeney, *The Twelve Prophets*, 1: 234.
24. Gary Smith, *Amos: A Commentary*, 133.

not return to me' exposes the meaningless sacrifices offered at Bethel and Gilgal.[25] Amos 4:4-13 was a covenant renewal ceremony which took place at Bethel and Gilgal, because these were places where covenant renewal took place.[26] However, instead of going there for covenant renewal, Amos rhetorically and ironically depicts the people's worship at Bethel and Gilgal as 'transgression' (4:4), because they failed to return to YHWH.[27]

Wolff argues that there is no evidence in the Old Testament that worshippers would call upon YHWH in a sanctuary, but they rather seek (דרש) YHWH through a prophet.[28] Similarly, Paul argues that people must not 'seek' (דרש) the sanctuaries, but YHWH, and return to him.[29] Amos also explains that to 'seek' (דרש) YHWH is to 'seek' (דרש) good and not evil (cf. 5:4-6; 14-15). Andersen and Freedman are right to argue that, 'the key is in finding not the right place to go, but the right thing to do and the right way to do it. The true search for God, like the search for the true God, begins in the heart; and in the practice of justice and righteousness.'[30] Amos as a prophet of social justice condemned total depravity in the courts and the common places and he called persuasively to Israel to establish justice and do righteousness (5:15, 24).[31] However, people neglected the covenant, which is characterized by justice (מִשְׁפָּט) and righteousness (צְדָקָה).[32]

Zion in Amos arguably relates to this theme of justice. Amos, from Tekoa (1:1), referred to Zion/Jerusalem in his pronouncement on the northern kingdom. For Polley, Amos' call for justice and righteousness may have been connected with the judicial reforms of Jehoshaphat. According to the Chronicler, Jehoshaphat's reforms included appointing the judges in the

---

25. Ibid.
26. Walter Brueggemann, 'Covenant Worship,' *VT* 15, no. 01 (January 1965): 9, 11-13; cf. John Bright, *A History of Israel*, 4th ed. (Louisville: The Westminster John Knox Press, 2000), 169-170; Martin Noth, *The History of Israel* (London: SCM Press, 1990), 94-95.
27. George Snyder, 'The Law and Covenant in Amos,' *RQ* 25, no. 03 (1982): 163-164.
28. Wolff, *Prophets*, 238.
29. Paul, *Amos*, 165.
30. Andersen and Freedman, *Amos,* 482.
31. Polley, *Davidic Empire*, 126.
32. Elizabeth R. Achtemeier, 'Righteousness in the OT,' in *IDB (R-Z)*, ed. George Arthur Buttrick (Nashville: Abingdon Press, 1962), 80-85; Achtemeier, *Minor Prophets I*, 170-171.

cities of Judah including Tekoa (2 Chr 19:5-7, cf. 11:5-12), and the establishment of a court in Jerusalem (2 Chr 19:8-11).[33] The King as YHWH's representative is responsible for establishing justice and righteousness at the court (Ps 72:1-2; 2 Sam 8:15), defending the poor and the needy. For the Chronicler, Jehoshaphat, a righteous King of Judah,[34] established this royal court system centred on Jerusalem.[35] Amos' own city, Tekoa, was part of this royal court system (2 Chr 11:5-12; 19:5). If Jehoshaphat's reform has a historical basis,[36] it sheds some light on Amos' call for social justice in Israel.[37]

Mays argues that in Amos' eyes, 'the court in the gates seems to have been the most crucial institution in Israel's life. It was the place where righteousness should bear its fruit and justice be established (6:12; 5:15).'[38] Amos was appealing 'to standards of justice the northerners would recognize as valid.'[39] Amos views YHWH as the God of nature (1:1, 2), the God of the entire world, and of righteousness, and justice. YHWH demands these qualities both from Israel particularly and from other nations.[40] Stuart argues: 'the mention of Zion/Jerusalem as the origin of Yahweh's word and destructive action is a tacit condemnation of the false, degenerate northern cult that Amos was called by God to condemn.'[41] The roar of YHWH comes from Zion (1:2), condemning Israel's injustice.

---

33. Polley, *Davidic Empire*, 126-128.

34. See Steven L. McKenzie, *1-2 Chronicles* (AOTC; Nashville: Abingdon Press, 2004), 286-294; Polley, *Davidic Empire*, 137.

35. Polley, *Davidic Empire*, 137.

36. For further and detail discussion on the Jehoshaphat's judicial reform, see some examples, H. G. M. Williamson, *1 and 2 Chronicles* (NCBC; Grand Rapids, Michigan: William B. Eerdmans Publication Company, 1982), 287-291; William Johnstone, *1 & 2 Chronicles-2 Chronicles 10-36: Guilt and Atonement*, vol. 2 (JSOTSS 254; Sheffield: Sheffield Academic Press, 1997), 93-94; J. A. Thompson, *1, 2 Chronicles*, vol. 9 (NAC; Nashville, Tennessee: Broadman & Holman Publishers, 1994), 288-290; Steven S. Tuell, *First and Second Chronicles* (IBCTP; Louisville, Kentucky: John Knox Press, 2001), 175-184.

37. See Polley, *Davidic Empire*, 131-138.

38. Mays, *Amos*, 11.

39. Robert B. Coote, *Amos Among the Prophets: Composition and Theology* (Philadelphia: Fortress Press, 1981), 52.

40. Cripps, *Exegetical Commentary*, 22-24.

41. Stuart, *Hosea-Jonah*, 302.

The connection between Zion and justice is also seen in the other parts of the Old Testament. In a number of Psalms, the kingship of YHWH is exercised on Zion (Pss 24; 47; 48:1-2; 76).[42] Zion, the seat of YHWH (Ps 76:2), relates to justice (Ps 9:7-12; cf. 72:2). The Zion tradition in the Old Testament thus seems to have a close connection with YHWH's kingship – a kingship grounded on justice (Ps 9:7-12), in which YHWH exercises his judgment on the whole world. In my view, it is reasonable to suppose that there is such a connection between Zion and justice also in Amos.

Justice is related to the court (6:12) and righteousness is a norm used for a relationship between YHWH and people in the form of covenant and cult. Amos' critique of Israel's worship is primarily linked with justice and righteousness.[43] In addition to the rebellious government that supported the sanctuaries, the rejection of sacrifice in these sanctuaries is due to lack of justice and righteousness (5:15, 24).[44] The people's many offerings at Bethel and other places show a concern to celebrate the good things of the land – yet they fail to understand the most important thing about occupying the land – that they must do justice in it. In my view, this connection between worship and justice in Amos may be related to his understanding of Zion.

2.2.2 Zion and the Relationship between North and South

The question of the relationship between the northern and southern kingdoms is also a question about the extent and definition of 'land' in Amos. Amos pronounces the destruction of Israel (9:1-10), the death of Jeroboam (7:10-17), and the restoration of the fallen house of David (9:11-15).[45] These factors led Sweeney to argue that Amos called for 'the reunification of the entire nation Israel around YHWH's Jerusalem and the Davidic monarchy.'[46] According to Polley, Amos condemned the nations including Israel for rebelling against Davidic rule together with the temple and priest-

---

42. Ollenburger, *Zion*, 44-46.
43. See Mays, *Amos*, 91-93; Philip J. King, *Amos, Hosea, Micah: An Archaeological Commentary* (Philadelphia: Westminster Press, 1988), 88-89.
44. Polley, *Davidic Empire*, 101.
45. Sweeney, *The Twelve Prophets*, 1: 200.
46. Sweeney, *The Twelve Prophets*, 1: 200; also in *Form and Intertextuality in Prophetic and Apocalyptic Literature* (FAT 45; Tübingen: Mohr Siebeck, 2005), 182.

hood at Zion.[47] Therefore, for Polley, true worship will be established only through reunion with the south, and rejecting the northern cult and monarchy. Amos expected the restoration of the two kingdoms under Davidic rule (9:9-12).[48]

That is, the restoration of 'the fallen booth of David' (9:11) will bring the reunion of the two kingdoms under the Davidic dynasty again (see Isa 9:1-7; 11:10-14; Hos 1:11; 3:5).[49] David had first united the whole people of Israel (Hos 3:5; Isa 9:7).[50] However, Zion suggests the nature of people and land. Ronald E. Clements argued that, 'the very name "Zion" became a part of the special vocabulary concerning the elect status of God's people' (cf. Isa 40:9; 51:3).[51] Amos, as prophet of eschatological doom and hope, is looking forward to a successful future of the people and land.[52] I shall argue, however, that Amos is not merely paying attention to the relationship between the northern and southern kingdoms; he is more interested in the reality of keeping the covenant with YHWH, which is based on justice and righteousness. This is what will enable the ancient land promises to be fulfilled.

2.2.3 Zion and Its Relationship with Natural World

Further, the action of YHWH from Zion is connected with the natural world: the mourning or drying up of the pastures and the top of Carmel. Marlow argues that the natural world functions as part of a cosmic dialogue

---

47. In the Ancient Near East, priesthood and monarchy usually go hand in hand, they support each other. For example in Amos' confrontation with Amaziah at Bethel (7:10-17), Amaziah understood that Amos' attack upon the priesthood at Bethel was the same as attacking the monarchy. When Amos announced the destruction of Bethel and Gilgal (5:5), it referred to the end of the northern kingdom (7:11). Polley, *Davidic Empire*, 94-107.

48. Ibid., 138.

49. See Chisholm, *Handbook on the Prophets: Isaiah, Jeremiah, Lamentations, Ezekiel, Daniel, Minor Prophets*, 402; H. Richardson, '*SKT* (Amos 9:11): "Booth" or "Succoth"?,' 381; Polley, *Davidic Empire*, 138; Sweeney, *The Twelve Prophets*, 1: 200; G. Davies, 'Amos—the Prophet of Reunion,' 196-199; Stuart, *Hosea-Jonah*, 398.

50. Stuart, *Hosea-Jonah*, 398.

51. Ronald E. Clements, *Old Testament Theology: A Fresh Approach* (MTL; London: Marshall, Morgan and Scott, 1978), 92.

52. Gerhard F. Hasel, 'The Alleged "No" of Amos's Eschatology,' *AUSS* 29, no. 01 (Spring 1991): 18.

between *Creator* and *creation*. YHWH's voice has a powerful effect on the natural world.[53] This natural world undergoes 'a significant and visible change' as a reaction to YHWH's voice. It affects the non-human creation, which is symbolized by the 'drying up' or 'mourning' (אבל) of the pastures of the shepherds and the top of Carmel (1:2; 9:3).[54] The non-human creation in 1:2 is shifted to the human in Amos 9:5. This implies that 'the relationship between YHWH and natural world is more subtle than first appears.'[55] Human beings who are the inhabitants of the earth mourn (אבל) (9:5) and Carmel, the non-human creation (1:2), gives no hiding place for people those who tried to escape from YHWH (9:3). That is, Carmel works against the people.[56]

YHWH's action of uttering his voice קוֹל portrays his relationship with the land: 'the pastures of the shepherds shall dry up, and the top of Carmel shall wither' (1:2). As Stuart points out, in addition to the meaning of 'voice', or 'sound', the word קוֹל has a distinctive meaning in the Old Testament. The plural form קוֹלוֹת is frequently translated as 'thunder' (e.g. Exod 9:23; 19:16). It seems that Amos uses this קוֹל יִתֵּן to connote 'thundering'.[57] Since usually 'thunder' accompanies rain,[58] there is a clear picture of agricultural fertility.[59] However, in the context of Amos, YHWH's thunder brings the opposite effect. That is, instead of giving productive rain it brings devastating drought, and hence disaster on the land.[60] YHWH's voice is compared to a lion's roar. As a lion's roar indicates devastation and death, YHWH's voice is a symbol of his wrath which brings destruction in the land (cf. Jer 2:15).[61] The land became a place of disaster (1:2). Even Carmel, a garden or fertile land with plenty of water (Isa 35:2;

---

53. Hilary Marlow, *Biblical Prophets and Contemporary Environmental Ethics*, (Oxford: Oxford University Press, 2009), 132-133.
54. Ibid., 134-135.
55. Ibid., 135.
56. Marlow, *Ethics*, 135.
57. Stuart, *Hosea-Jonah*, 301.
58. See Hammershaimb, *Book of Amos*, 20; Stuart, *Hosea-Jonah*, 301; Smith and Page, *Amos, Obadiah, Jonah*, 39.
59. Stuart, *Hosea-Jonah*, 301.
60. Smith and Page, *Amos, Obadiah, Jonah*, 39-40; Stuart, *Hosea-Jonah*, 301.
61. Hammershaimb, *Book of Amos*, 20.

Jer 50:19; Nah 1:4) is depicted as suffering a disastrous drought, recalling the covenant drought curses (Lev 26:19; Deut 28:22-24).[62] Amos, then, declares that YHWH's קוֹל from Zion brings about natural disasters affecting agriculture, and the devastation of the land.

YHWH's voice thunders (1:2) and rain is withheld (4:7-8). Drought occurs as one of YHWH's judgments (4:7; 7:4; Isa 5:6; 19:17). There are drought and blight (4:6-11), and the wailing of the farmers and the wailing in the vineyards (5:16-17).[63] The natural disasters of 4:6-11 may possibly be the background of 1:2.[64] In 1:2, YHWH's thunder from Zion causes the withering of the 'pastures of the shepherds' and the fertile Carmel ridge,[65] implying the complete desolation of the fruitful places[66] and of the whole land.[67] YHWH's bringing of natural disaster from Zion (1:2) immediately follows the reference to the earthquake in 1:1. Joel 3:16 draws from Amos 1:2 and includes the effect of the trembling of the 'heaven and earth'.[68] This shows YHWH's power to bring judgment from Zion over all creation.[69] According to James Nogalski, Joel (3:16 [Heb 4:16]) adapts Amos 1:2, and broadens it by portraying the trembling of the 'heavens and earth', and points forward to YHWH's judgment of the nations in Amos 1-2.[70] Accordingly, immediately following the reference to the earthquake in 1:1, Amos announces YHWH's judgment from Zion (1:2), and he brings it to bear on the nations in 1:3-2:16. That is, the action of YHWH from Zion is connected with the natural world and the whole creation.

---

62. Stuart, *Hosea-Jonah*, 301.
63. Gary Smith, *Amos: A Commentary*, 27.
64. Andersen and Freedman, *Amos*, 228.
65. See Mays, *Amos*, 22; Gary Smith, *Amos: A Commentary*, 27; Paul, *Amos*, 39.
66. Paul, *Amos*, 40.
67. Hammershaimb, *Book of Amos*, 20.
68. Sweeney, *Apocalyptic Literature*, 203.
69. Ibid., 205.
70. James D. Nogalski, 'Intertextuality and the Twelve,' in *Forming Prophetic Literature: Essays on Isaiah and the Twelve in Honor of John D. W. Watts*, ed. James W. Watts and Paul R. House (JSOTSS 235; Sheffield: Sheffield Academic Press, 1996), 107-108.

2.3 Covenant-Election

Amos 3:2 addresses the special status of Israel as the 'chosen people' among the nations of the world. The covenant-election tradition is stressed in 3:2, with the connection between the election of Israel and the theme of oppression and justice. Amos 3:9-11 could be seen as a sequel to 3:2. Election requires responsibility and it essentially relates to justice and land.

2.3.1 Election: Its Responsibility of Justice

The most prominent statement of the theology of election is found in Deuteronomy 7:6-8: 'YHWH has "chosen" בָּחַר Israel' out of all the people of the earth[71] and this concept of election is rooted in the exodus event (cf. Pss 106:5-48; 135:4-21).[72] Amos 3:2 applies that concept of election to Israel.[73] In relation to the exodus event (3:1), Amos rather uses the common verb [74]יָדַע which suggests an intimate relationship between persons (Gen 4:1; 1 Kgs 1:4),[75] but here signifies election, that is, an intimate covenantal relationship between YHWH and his people.[76] In this way, the

---

71. See Clements, *Old Testament Theology*, 87-89; Preuss, *Old Testament Theology*, 1: 28, 33.

72. Preuss, *Old Testament Theology*, 1: 28.

73. John Goldingay, *Old Testament Theology: Israel's Faith*, vol. 2 (Downers Grove, Illinois: InterVarsity Press, 2006), 193.

74. The term יָדַע has variety of meaning such as 'know, observe, realize, understand, notice, recognize, perceive, care for, be acquainted with, have insight into, have sex with, and choose.' See Terence E. Fretheim, 'יָדַע,' in *NIDOTTE*, ed. Willem A. VanGemeren, vol. 2 (Carlisle: Paternoster Press, 1997), 409; Stuart, *Hosea-Jonah*, 322; Johannes Lindblom, *Prophecy in Ancient Israel* (Oxford: Blackwell, 1962), 326; Paul R. Gilchrist, 'יָדַע', in *Theological Wordbook of the Old Testament*, ed. R. Laird Harris, vol. 1 (Chicago: Moody Press, 1981), 366.

75. See Edmond Jacob, *Theology of the Old Testament*, trans. Arthur W. Heathcote and Philip J. Allcock (London: Hodder and Stoughton, 1958), 202; Andersen and Freedman, *Amos*, 381-382; Seock-Tae Sohn, *The Divine Election of Israel* (Grand Rapids, Michigan: William B. Eerdmans Publishing Company, 1991), 10; Daniel J. Simundson, 'Reading Amos: Is It an Advantage to Be God's Special People?,' *WW* 28, no. 02 (Spring 2008): 134.

76. See, Martin Buber, *The Prophetic Faith* (New York: Harper & Row Publishers, 1960), 99, 115; Wolff, *Prophets*, 176; Gary Smith, *Amos: A Commentary*, 105; Hayes, *Amos*, 123; Paul, *Amos*, 101; Harry Mowvley, *The Books of Amos and Hosea* (EC; London: Epworth Press, 1991), 37-38; Andersen and Freedman, *Amos*, 381; Mays, *Amos*, 56; Stuart, *Hosea-Jonah*, 322; Jeremias, *Book of Amos: A Commentary*, 50; Simundson, 'Reading Amos', 134; Yehoshua Gitay, 'A Study of Amos's Art of Speech: A Rhetorical Analysis of Amos

Deuteronomic technical term בָּחַר is similar to the term יָדַע (know=choose/elect) in Amos 3:2.[77] The term יָדַע in Amos 3:2 (also see Gen 18:19, Deut 9:24; 2 Sam 7:20; Jer 1:5; Hos 13:5) is used with YHWH as subject to mean knowing and choosing somebody for his own.[78]

The unique status of Israel is also characterized by the term רַק 'you only.'[79] 'All the families of the earth' כֹּל מִשְׁפְּחוֹת הָאֲדָמָה (3:2) is an expression (cf. Gen 12:3; 28:14) referring to the multiple nationalities in the world from whom only Israel is YHWH's unique 'covenant people',[80] or 'covenant partner'.[81] Therefore, the election presupposes the great variety of possibilities among all the families of the earth.[82] The traditions of the exodus from Egypt (3:1) and the election of Israel (3:2) correlate to the covenant,[83] that is, the Mosaic covenant.[84] Amos 3:2 and 9:7 presuppose the tradition of election and exodus. The exodus from Egypt[85] is an essential element in the election of the nation[86] which serves as the foundations for their status and existence[87] and is the decisive event for historic Israel.[88]

3:1-15,' *CBQ* 42, no. 03 (July 1980): 302; Snyder, 'Law and Covenant,' 163; Herbert B. Huffmon, 'The Treaty Background of Hebrew YĀDA',' *BASOR* 181(Fall 1966): 34-35; Marjorie O'Rourke Boyle, 'The Covenant Lawsuit of the Prophet Amos: 3:1-4:13,' *VT* 21, no. 03 (July 1971): 344; Preuss, *Old Testament Theology*, 1: 28-30.

77. Mays, *Amos*, 56.

78. Ernest W. Nicholson, *God and His People: Covenant and Theology in the Old Testament* (Oxford: Clarendon Press, 1986), 80.

79. See Wolff, *Prophets*, 176; Jeremias, *Book of Amos: A Commentary*, 50; Gary Smith, *Amos: A Commentary*, 105; Mays, *Amos*, 56.

80. Stuart, *Hosea-Jonah*, 322.

81. Mays, *Amos*, 57.

82. Walther Zimmerli, *Old Testament Theology in Outline*, trans. David E. Green (Edinburgh: T & T Clark, 1978), 44.

83. See Boyle, 'Covenant Lawsuit', 344; Huffmon, 'The Treaty Background of Hebrew YĀDA',' 33-34; Gary Smith, *Amos: A Commentary*, 98.

84. Snyder, 'Law and Covenant,' 163.

85. The significance of the events of the exodus is mentioned elsewhere (e.g. Hos 11:1; 13:4; Micah 6:3-4; Jer 2:6-7, 16:14; Exod 20:2; Num 24:8; Deut 5:6; Josh 24:5-6). For a further discussion on the dealing of YHWH with Israel in Egypt and the exodus event, see Alec Motyer, *Old Testament Covenant Theology: Four Lectures* (Leicester: Theological Students Fellowship, 1973), 10-17.

86. Preuss, *Old Testament Theology*, 1: 27, 35-36. Also see Horst Dietrich Preuss, *Old Testament Theology*, vol. 2 (Edinburgh: T & T Clark, 1992), 67.

87. Gary Smith, *Amos: A Commentary*, 105-106.

88. Sweeney, *The Twelve Prophets*, 1: 219-220.

It is important that Amos here applies the election concept to Israel. He may or may not be the first to do so, because that depends on how certain texts in the Pentateuch are dated. Amos apparently knows some of the traditions which appeared in the Pentateuch notably in 2:9-10; 3:1-2. He may or may not know the Deuteronomic election tradition. However, he shares with it the belief that election brings the responsibility to act in accordance with YHWH's standards.

Since Amos explicitly sees YHWH as sovereign Lord over all the people of the earth (1:3-2:16; 9:7) by right of creation (4:13; 5:8-9; 9:5-6), he reminds Israel of their unique status (3:2).[89] By choosing Israel, YHWH has given a special responsibility which is made clear by the word יָדַע.[90] Therefore, 'election' is both 'from' and 'to' (Amos 3:2; cf. Deut 7:6; 10:14-15; 14:2), which means 'Israel's election is for service'.[91] The context of Amos 3:2 shows Israel's wrong theological concept of election. They thought that they would be protected in all circumstances and also YHWH would never bring the covenant to an end.[92] Amos insists that it is not unconditional.[93] In Amos' theology, the traditional concept of Israel's unique status is not for the sake of indulgence,[94] but for responsibility[95] and a basis for judgment.[96] The idea is simple: 'the greater opportunities, the more

---

89. Walter C. Kaiser, *Toward an Old Testament Theology* (Grand Rapids, Michigan: Zondervan Publishing House, 1978), 193-194.
90. Edmond Jacob, *Theology of the Old Testament*, 207.
91. Preuss, *Old Testament Theology*, 2: 285.
92. Hammershaimb, *Book of Amos*, 57.
93. Paul, *Amos*, 102.
94. See Paul Joyce, 'Amos,' in *Prophets and Poets: A Companion to the Prophetic Books of the Old Testament*, ed. Grace Emmerson (Oxford: The Bible Reading Fellowship, 1994), 222-223; Mays, *Amos*, 129; William J. Dumbrell, *Covenant and Creation: An Old Testament Covenantal Theology* (Exeter: The Paternoster Press, 1984), 168.
95. See H. Keith Beebe, *The Old Testament: An Introduction to Its Literary, Historical, and Religious Traditions* (Belmont, California: Dickenson Publishing Company, 1970), 228; Wolff, *Prophets*, 176-177; Mays, *Amos*, 57; Smith and Page, *Amos, Obadiah, Jonah*, 161; Joyce, 'Amos,' 222-223; Wright, *Mission*, 96.
96. See Wolff, *Prophets*, 177; Hayes, *Amos*, 123, 218; Mays, *Amos*, 58; Andersen and Freedman, *Amos*, 93, 381-382; Paul, *Amos*, 102; Smith and Page, *Amos, Obadiah, Jonah*, 71; Jeremias, *Book of Amos: A Commentary*, 51; Gerhard von Rad, *The Message of the Prophets* (London: SCM Press, 1968), 104; Gary Smith, *Amos: A Commentary*, 106; Stuart, *Hosea-Jonah*, 321-322; Buber, *Faith*, 99; Snyder, 'Law and Covenant,' 163;

responsibility,'[97] 'the more special and unusual the relationship the more severe the judgment.'[98]

Amos then introduces the punishment of YHWH by using the word 'therefore'.[99] Punishment is not merely because of the status of YHWH's covenant people; rather, it is because of their iniquity: אֵת כָּל־עֲוֺנֹתֵיכֶם 'for all your iniquities'.[100] This traditional covenantal language פֹּקֵד עָוֺן 'punishing iniquities' (Exod 34:6-7; Num 14:18)[101] is a failure to meet the standard of covenant people, that is, breaking of the covenant (cf. Deut 27:15-26; 28:15-68).

Israel's historical opportunity is to be accompanied by obedience to the covenant demands, specifically in terms of social justice. Amos sees that failure to comply with this demand of justice puts Israel on the same level as other nations (9:7).[102] The covenantal relationship entails the concept of justice and righteousness (5:24)[103] and thus practicing them is the legal demand of YHWH who brought Israel out of the land of Egypt into its land (2:9-10; 3:1).[104] The essential factor concerning the covenant-election tradition is Israel's possession of the land, which functions as part of their mission in relation to all peoples.[105]

Huffmon, 'The Treaty Background of Hebrew YĀDA',' 31, 34-35; Boyle, 'Covenant Lawsuit', 344; Sweeney, *The Twelve Prophets*, 1:220; Wood, *Song*, 55.

97. Cripps, *Exegetical Commentary*, 152.

98. Andersen and Freedman, *Amos*, 873.

99. See, for instance, Mays, *Amos*, 56; Smith and Page, *Amos, Obadiah, Jonah*, 71; Mowvley, *Amos and Hosea*, 38; Jeremias, *Book of Amos: A Commentary*, 51; Simundson, 'Reading Amos', 135; Georges Farr, 'The Language of Amos, Popular or Cultic?,' *VT* 16 (1966): 320.

100. Stuart, *Hosea-Jonah*, 321-322.

101. Farr, 'The Language' 320-321.

102. Wright, *Living as the People of God: The Relevance of Old Testament Ethics*, (Leicester: Inter-Varsity Press, 1983), 36.

103. See Brevard S. Childs, *Old Testament Theology in A Canonical Context* (London: SCM Press, 1985), 95, 233; Lawrence Boadt, *Reading the Old Testament: An Introduction* (New York: Paulist Press, 1984), 316; Dumbrell, *Covenant and Creation*, 168; Mays, *Amos*, 56-57; Gary Smith, *Amos: A Commentary*, 104.

104. Zimmerli, 'Land', 248.

105. Christopher J. H. Wright, 'Theology and Ethics of the Land,' in *A Christian Approach to the Environment*, Sam Berry et al. (n.p.: The John Ray Initiative, 2005), 37-38.

As already noted, Amos 3:9-11 could be seen as a sequel to 3:2. Rhetorically, Amos summons Egypt and Ashdod to Samaria to witness Israel's violent life of injustices and oppression. They are instructed to become aware of the dominant practice of oppression and injustices.[106] The invitation of foreigners is intended to see in Samaria, 'a city full of *tumult* instead of order, *oppression* instead of justice.'[107] Although order and justice should be celebrated, disorder and oppression dominated in the city.[108] Violence has destroyed the morality of the people of Israel that they do not know what is right. They have practised injustices against their fellow people (3:9-10).[109] Rather than doing good things they pile up injustices by their violent acts.[110] The people of Israel turn aside from covenant righteousness; they do not know what is right and just and their leaders treasure up unjust gain in their fortresses (3:10).[111] Because they have sinned, YHWH brings punishment in the form of an enemy who will surround the land (3:11). In this sense, Israel's injustices have significant effects on their land.

2.3.2 Election: Its Connection with Land

In this covenant-election tradition (3:2), Wolff suggested the possibility that יָדַע may be a reference to YHWH's giving of the land to Israel in the way that is expressed by the contrast between 2:9 and their behaviour in 2:6-8.[112] Deuteronomy 9:24 uses מִיּוֹם דַּעְתִּי אֶתְכֶם (ie., [since] I [first] knew you) which is precisely used in Amos 3:2 in the expression אֶתְכֶם יָדַעְתִּי (you have I known). In both cases, YHWH is subject of the verb. In Deuteronomy, this verb is preceded by an allusion to the command to possess the land that YHWH gave them (Deut 9:23). In this sense, the root

---

106. See Hammershaimb, *Book of Amos*, 60; Niehaus, 'Amos,' 383; Gary Smith, *Amos: A Commentary*, 118-119; Auld, *Amos*, 61.
107. Mays, *Amos*, 64.
108. Smith and Page, *Amos, Obadiah, Jonah*, 78.
109. Gary Smith, *Amos: A Commentary*, 119-120.
110. Hammershaimb, *Book of Amos*, 61.
111. Niehaus, 'Amos,' 384.
112. Wolff, *Prophets*, 176-177.

ידע is connected with the possession of the land.[113] Further, the context of Deuteronomy 9:23-24 shows that despite the fact that YHWH granted Israel the land they disobeyed and rebelled against him. Amos makes the same connection. YHWH knew them, gave them the land and yet they did not live in accordance with YHWH's command. It seems, therefore, that Amos 3:2 rather assumes the idea of the giving of the land.[114]

Amos assumes that his hearers understand themselves as YHWH's chosen people because of their connection with the exodus tradition, and their settlement in a new land (2:9-10).[115] YHWH also entered into an intimate relationship with Israel (3:2), with the intention that the covenant people would maintain the gift of land. However, at the same time they become liable to be punished for their iniquities. This moral logic relates to the concept of land.[116]

YHWH gave the land to fulfil what was promised to the patriarchs. As a consequence of YHWH fulfilling his promise of giving the land, Israel knew that they are the covenant people of YHWH.[117] Entry into the land is not 'entry into a safe space but into a context of covenant.'[118] The covenant-election theme in Amos 3:2 also reflects the patriarchal tradition in Genesis 18:18-19.[119] Israel's election is related to the land since the promise of the land was a fundamental part of the promise to the patriarch (Gen 12:1-3). Therefore, the land became an essential theme of divine promise for the elected people. As Clements put it, the land acquired a very special significance as a visible expression of Israel's elect status.[120] It is likely that the patriarchal connection with the giving of the land (Gen12:1-3; 18:18-19) is implied in Amos (3:1-2).

---

113. Snyman, 'Eretz and Adama', 138.
114. Ibid.
115. Herbert B. Huffmon, 'The Social Role of Amos's Message,' in *The Quest for the Kingdom of God: Studies in Honor of G. E. Mendenhall*, eds. H. H. Huffmon, F. A. Spina, and A. R. W. Green (Winona Lake, Indiana: Eisenbrauns, 1983), 110, 114.
116. Zimmerli, 'Land', 247.
117. Christopher J. H. Wright, *Old Testament Ethics for the People of God* (Leicester: Inter-Varsity Press, 2004), 88.
118. Brueggemann, *The Land*, 52-53.
119. Mays, *Amos*, 57.
120. Clements, *Old Testament Theology*, 92.

The intimate relationship between YHWH and Israel leads to the formulation of a specific theology of Israel and its land. It suggests that Israel and its land have a special status in comparison with other peoples and their land. Amos 3:2 and 9:7 appear to give quite different views of the election of Israel. Both texts relate to the election of Israel and their occupation of land. Amos 9:7 however, rather than emphasizing the distinctness of Israel from other nations, puts Israel's exodus and occupation of land on the same footing with the histories of other nations. The relationship between these texts will be dealt with in detail at a later point.

2.4 Israel

As already mentioned, Amos 3:1-2 affirms the concept of Israel's election and their covenantal relationship with YHWH, as evidenced by the traditions of the patriarchal promise, the exodus from Egypt, and settlement in land.[121] Israel's unique status characterized by רַק אֶתְכֶם יָדַעְתִּי 'you only have I known'[122] among all the families of the earth (כֹּל מִשְׁפְּחוֹת הָאֲדָמָה) (3:2) shows that only Israel is YHWH's special 'covenant people.'[123] Concerning Israel, the question of covenant raises a further issue: which covenant and with whom? That is, is this a covenant with Israel as a whole, north and south? As in the case of Zion, it raises the question of the extent of the land Amos has in mind. The meaning of 'Israel' is an important factor in the book, as will be shown in more detail later.

The term 'Israel' יִשְׂרָאֵל can bear a number of meanings in the Old Testament. It occurs thirty times in Amos, and its meaning is contested in several texts.[124] It occurs alone and in several combinations. 'Israel' יִשְׂרָאֵל occurs alone ten times (1:1b; 2:6; 3:14; 4:12 [twice]; 7:9, 11, 16, 17; 9:7b), 'my people Israel' עַמִּי יִשְׂרָאֵל four times (7:8, 15; 8:2; 9:14), 'virgin Israel'

---

121. Boyle, 'Covenant Lawsuit,' 344; Huffmon, The Treaty Background of Hebrew YĀDAʻ,' 33-34; Gary Smith, *Amos: A Commentary*, 98.
122. See Wolff, *Prophets*, 176; Jeremias, *Book of Amos: A Commentary*, 50; Gary Smith, *Amos: A Commentary*, 105; Mays, *Amos*, 56.
123. Stuart, *Hosea-Jonah*, 322.
124. Wolff, *Prophets*, 164.

בְּתוּלַת יִשְׂרָאֵל once (5:2), 'sons of Israel' בְּנֵי יִשְׂרָאֵל five times (2:11; 3:1, 12; 4:5; 9:7a), 'house of Israel' בֵּית יִשְׂרָאֵל eight times (5:1, 3, 4, 25; 6:1, 14; 7:10b; 9:9), and 'king of Israel' מֶלֶךְ יִשְׂרָאֵל twice (1:1b; 7:10a).[125] The related terms to 'Israel' such as 'Jacob' יַעֲקֹב (3:13; 6:8; 7:2, 5; 8:7; 9:8), 'Isaac' יִצְחָק (7:9, 16), and 'Joseph' יוֹסֵף (5: 6, 15; 6:6) also occur throughout the book.

The important issue here is whether Amos addresses his message only to the northern kingdom or the people as a whole. Amos' words are said at the outset to be 'concerning Israel' (1:1). How does Amos define this? I will argue that Amos speaks this as 'my people Israel' עַמִּי יִשְׂרָאֵל (7:15), referring to the whole people. Therefore, where it means historic Israel, it is closely related to the ancient covenantal promise of the whole land. As J. G. McConville argues, the interpretation of 'Israel' and 'land' are closely connected.[126] As will be shown later, the central ambiguity of the terms 'Jacob', 'Israel', and 'Isaac' in Amos can best be understood to refer to historic Israel and the whole land. For Amos, Jacob and Isaac would have been associated with the patriarchal narratives and thus Amos appears to understand that his prophecy is to *all* Israel (7:15). In my view, he uses the complex terminology – Jacob, Isaac, Israel, my people Israel, house of Israel, sons of Israel – to refer to both kingdoms as historic Israel. The historic land, therefore, remains in view – as both gift and challenge – even though it may be divided, or parts of it lost.

Further, Amos, as a seer חֹזֶה, is called and commissioned by YHWH, the God of Israel and the God of the universe to prophesy (נבא) (7:15) to that same covenant people, 'my people Israel'. Amos is taken from following the flock which confirms divine appointment to prophesy to all Israel, the entire covenant people and thus the entire land of Israel. The concept of חֹזֶה in relation to the covenant people will be discussed further later.

---

125. Ibid.
126. McConville, 'Jacob', 147-148, 150.

2.5 Creation

YHWH is the creator of the whole world, and lord of the history of Israel and the nations. YHWH's relationship with the patriarchs (Gen 12-50), with Israel as a whole (Exod 1-24), and his election of Israel are set within a concept of humankind as a whole.[127] There is a question, however, about when a belief in YHWH as creator was assimilated into the faith of Israel. What evidence is there for such a belief in Amos?

Von Rad established the direction for the assessment of the theology of creation. He said 'Yahwistic faith of the Old Testament is based on the notion of election, and therefore primarily concerned with redemption.'[128] Von Rad argued that a belief in YHWH's creation of the world is found only in later texts, including Deutero-Isaiah, the Priestly document and a few Psalms which are connected with his redemptive activity.[129] Israel experienced YHWH through her history, and this experience shaped a religion of salvation.[130] Like von Rad, Zimmerli has shown that the primary orientation of creation is seen in the deliverance of Israel out of Egypt. He asserted that it was out of this experience that Israel started to think clearly of God as the creator.[131] Again, von Rad stated: 'creation is regarded as a work of Yahweh in history, a work within time.'[132]

However, as H. H. Schmid suggested, 'creation' should be restored to a leading place in Old Testament theology.[133] Bernhard W. Anderson also

---

127. Preuss, *Old Testament Theology*, 1: 226-227.
128. Gerhard Von Rad, 'The Theological Problem of the Old Testament Doctrine of Creation,' in *The Problem of the Hexateuch and Other Essays,* trans. E. W. Trueman Dicken; intro. Norman W. Porteous (London: Oliver & Boyd, 1966), 131.
129. Gerhard Von Rad, *Old Testament Theology*, trans. D. M. G. Stalker, vol. 1 (London: SCM Press, 1962), 136-139; Von Rad, 'Theological Problem', 131-143; Von Rad, *From Genesis to Chronicles: Explorations in Old Testament Theology*, ed. K. C. Hanson (Minneapolis: Fortress Press, 2005), 177-186.
130. Von Rad, *Old Testament Theology*, 1: 137-139.
131. Zimmerli, *Old Testament Theology in Outline*, trans. By David E Green, (Edinburgh: T&T Clark, 1978), 32-33.
132. Von Rad, *Old Testament Theology*, 1: 139.
133. H. H. Schmid, 'Creation, Righteousness, and Salvation: "Creation Theology" as the Broad Horizon of Biblical Theology,' in *Creation in the Old Testament*, ed. Bernhard W. Anderson (IRT 6; London: SPCK, 1984), 102-103. Also see Henning Graf Reventlow, 'Creation as a Topic in Biblical Theology,' in *Creation in Jewish and Christian Tradition*, ed.

considered that creation is an appropriate theme of Old Testament theology.[134] Schmid asserted that historical events are associated with creation. In this sense, history is defined as an implementation of creation and the portrayal of the creation order. The ancestral history (Gen 12-50) also witnesses to the creation order.[135] The exodus event, the basis of Israel's faith, is regarded as a sort of fulfilment of YHWH's promise to the patriarchs. In Deuteronomy, this exodus event is closely connected with keeping YHWH's commandments, and receiving his blessing. This blessing is none other than 'the harmonious (*Heil*) world order given in creation'.[136] Taking this together, Schmid argued that this idea of world order is the overall horizon of Old Testament faith and theology.[137] Schmid concluded that Israel exercised creation faith and understood the experience of YHWH's salvation in historical events within this perspective of creation.[138]

Rolf P. Knierim followed Schmid on this, and affirmed that 'creation' played a crucial role in Old Testament belief while most works of Old Testament theology paid some attention to the sustenance of the world and the concept of creation they did not develop it fully.[139] While von Rad suggested that time is related to history, and creation is assumed as YHWH's work within history, Knierim asserts that time relates to the 'cosmic space of the ordered world'.[140] Cosmological statements in the Old Testament describe YHWH's relationship to Israel and to the world. Further, creation is considered as the beginning of history in the Pentateuch.[141] That is, Israel's creation theology is not subordinate to its theology of history. Rather, history is subordinated and it is dependent on creation, the cosmos.

Henning Graf Reventlow and Yair Hoffman (JSOTSS 319; London: Sheffield Academic Press, 2002), 153-171.

134. Bernhard W. Anderson, *From Creation to New Creation: Old Testament Perspectives* (Minneapolis: Fortress Press, 1994), 113-131.

135. Schmid, 'Creation', 108.

136. Ibid., 109-110.

137. Ibid., 110-111.

138. Ibid., 111.

139. Rolf P. Knierim, *The Task of Old Testament Theology: Substance, Method, and Cases* (Grand Rapids, Michigan: William B. Eerdmans Publishing Company, 1995), 175-176.

140. Ibid., 180.

141. Ibid.

Terence E. Fretheim also points out that the concept of creation is basic and integral to Israelite faith, and comments that YHWH is the God of the entire cosmos. The scripture starts with creation (Genesis) not with redemption or the experience of YHWH's salvation in historical events (Exodus).[142] Israel's redemptive experience of the exodus event (e.g. Exod 15) rather helps to understand God as creator, an already existent element in Israel's faith. YHWH's work in creation gives the evidence about what God looks like. This is the hypothesis for the interpretation of the exodus event. God-the-Creator is understood to be God-the-Redeemer in this historical event.[143] This suggests that the understanding of God as creator is an important part of Israel's faith from relatively early times.[144] There is thus a close relationship between creation and history. Israel's historical experiences should be understood under the aspect of Israel's theology of creation.

Amos frequently takes up the theme of creation. In exploring the book of Amos as a literary product of the Persian period, Linville demonstrates that it contains mythical conceptions of divine revelation and a pattern of destruction and recreation of the cosmos. The mythic world moves back and forth between heaven and earth. Behind the picture of the natural world is a heavenly, cosmic temple. The mythic motif in the final vision in Amos 9 evokes the macrocosmic temple in heaven.[145] Linville demonstrates that mythic motifs and images are fundamental to the book of Amos, expressing its paradigmatic cosmic theme.[146] Linville has made a considerable contribution to the study of the book of Amos as mythic text, paying attention to some of the key elements in the cosmic imagination displayed in the book of Amos. For instance, Amos 9:1-4 shows YHWH's sovereign power in both the natural world and human history. In Amos, the mythological and cosmological picture of the whole creation functions to indicate the work of YHWH in ordinary time and space.

---

142. Terence E. Fretheim, *God and World in the Old Testament: A Relational Theology of Creation* (Nashville: Abingdon Press, 2005), xiv.
143. Ibid., xv, xvi.
144. Ibid., xvi.
145. Linville, *Cosmic*, 3-8, 33.
146. Linville, *Cosmic*, 3.

Paas studies creation imagery employed in the eighth century prophetic literature, including Amos. He explores how the books of Amos, Hosea, and Isaiah use creation language with respect to the concept of YHWH as creator. Paas gives important insights into mythical language and concepts in Amos and does a lengthy study of creation hymns (4:13; 5:8-9; 9:5-6), including 6:14; 7:1, 4; 9:11.[147] Marlow also identifies creation themes in the biblical prophets of Amos, Hosea, and First Isaiah.[148] She stresses the creation dialogue particularly in the Book of Amos, indicating the interconnection between God and the world, and between human and non-human creation.[149] The non-human creation functions to test human behaviour (Amos 6:12) and evaluate the trials of human life (7:1-3; 8:1-2). It also serves to show the sovereign power of YHWH to human beings (4:13; 5:8-9; 9:5-6).[150]

Unlike von Rad, Paas maintains that creation faith is initiated in Israel's religion long before the exile. He asserts that the belief in YHWH as creator in Israel's concept of deity could have Canaanite origins.[151] Paas argues that originally, Israel was a Canaanite people who worshipped El along with other gods. 'YHWH is likely an Israelite derivative of the Canaanite royal god El. El was known already previously as creator.'[152] It means that creation theology may have been characteristic of Israelite religion from the earliest times. Paas' work supports an understanding that Israel's faith in God as creator was somewhat early.[153]

The theme of creation brackets the book of Amos as a whole, turning from the withering of the land as YHWH's judgment (1:2) to the flourishing of the land as YHWH's new creative act (9:11-15).[154] YHWH's act of universal judgment (1:3-2:3) corresponds to his universal presence, con-

---

147. Paas, *Creation and Judgment: Creation Texts in Some Eighth Century Prophets*, (Leiden: Brill, 2003), 183-326.
148. Marlow, *Ethics*, 115-243.
149. Ibid., 120-157.
150. Ibid., 265.
151. Paas, *Creation and Judgment*, 121.
152. Ibid., 422.
153. Ibid., 176.
154. Fretheim, *God and World*, 168.

trol, and activity (9:1-8). Amos' prophetic words to Israel, therefore, clearly connect creation and judgment throughout the book (4:13; 5:8-9; 9:5-6).[155] Each hymn describes the attributes of YHWH in terms of his creation and control of the cosmos. YHWH is portrayed as the God who communes with both human (4:13) and non-human creation (5:8; 9:6).[156] The hymns intertwine the themes of originating creation and its continuity. Amos 4:1-12 supports YHWH as creator in 4:13. YHWH's actions in texts such as 'I gave, withheld, struck, laid waste, sent' thoroughly relate to the natural order, including famine, drought, blight, locust, and so on.[157] Amos 4:1-11 reminds of Israel's failure to respond to YHWH, and thus it is followed by YHWH's judgment by natural disasters which affect the land. Amos 4:13 is supposed to answer the question 'who is this God?' and confirms the cosmic power of YHWH who is the all-powerful creator and sustainer of the whole cosmos.[158]

Preceded by a lament for the fall of the nation and land (5:1-2) and a call to seek YHWH (5:3-7), the second hymn (5:8-9) is followed by oracles of judgment (5:10-17).[159] The descriptions of Pleiades and Orion, day and night, darkness and light show that they work according to their created order.[160] This hymn (5:8-9) contains the creation of the constellations including Pleiades and Orion which are associated with seasonal changes from winter to summer. This suggests that YHWH maintains the annual rhythms of the earth. This hymn therefore extends the picture of YHWH's cosmic power in 4:13.[161]

Following a picture of YHWH's universal reach in which no one can escape from judgment (9:1-4), the final hymn (9:5-6) portrays YHWH's power, with its destructive capacity, extending over the whole cosmos.[162]

---

155. See Paas, *Creation and Judgment*, 310, 324; Fretherim, *God and World in the Old Testament: A Relational Theology of Creation*, 168-171.
156. Marlow, *Ethics*, 139.
157. Fretheim, *God and World*, 168-169.
158. Marlow, *Ethics*, 140-141.
159. Fretheim, *God and World*, 170.
160. Ibid.
161. Marlow, *Ethics*, 143-144.
162. Ibid., 145.

The same idea is continued in 9:7, where YHWH is the God of all peoples and brings them into their land. The hymn is bracketed by the impossibility of escape from YHWH's eye (9:4, 8). This idea is already introduced in the oracle against the nations (1:3-2:16), in which all nations are put under YHWH's judgment.[163] In each of these creation hymns, YHWH is seen as the powerful creator and sustainer of the whole cosmos.

Gillingham argues that the book of Amos has a 'creation-theology'. That is, YHWH's relationship with the created order pictures God not just as creator but as the God who comes to destroy (4:13; 5:8-9; 9:5-6). YHWH can bring life to the land, but also destruction (4:4-5, 6-12; 5:18-20; 7:1-3, 4-6; 8:9-10).[164] That is, YHWH is powerful over all creation and thus he can also bring judgment to the whole created order specifically the land, witnessing his sovereign authority upon both Israel and other nations. The creation concept, therefore, clearly relates to the theme of land in Amos.

2.6 Justice

2.6.1 Justice in Social Context

Amos condemns the people of Israel for their social injustice in the land (2:6-8; 3:9-11, 13-15; 4:1-3; 5:7, 10-13; 6:1-8, 11-12; 8:4-6).[165] His fundamental ethical message is 'a call for justice and righteousness' (5:7, 24; 6:12).[166] Amos addresses injustices in the land of Israel, such as selling the righteous and the needy for a pair of sandals (2:6), oppression of the poor (2:7), sexual immorality (2:7), excessive fines and collecting tribute (2:8), accumulating wealth (3:10-12, 15; 6:4), enjoying a luxurious life (4:1; 5:11; 6:4-7), corrupt court systems (5:7, 10), injustices in the courts (5:10-

---

163. Fretheim, *God and World*, 170.
164. Gillingham, '"Who Makes the Morning Darkness": God and Creation in the Book of Amos,' 165-184. Also see Paul R. House, 'The Character of God in the Book of the Twelve,' in *Reading and Hearing the Book of the Twelve*, ed. James D. Nogalski and Marvin A. Sweeney (SB 15; Atlanta: Society of Biblical Literature, 2000), 133.
165. See Hasel, *Understanding of Amos*, 102; Auld, *Amos*, 60; Bob Fyall, *Teaching Amos: Unlocking the Prophecy of Amos for the Bible Teacher* (TBS; London: Proclamation Trust Media, 2006), 154.
166. Polley, *Davidic Empire*, 135.

12), turning justice to wormwood (5:7; 6:12), extracting taxes (5:11), bribery (5:12), trampling the needy and poor (8:4), and economic injustices (8:5-6).[167] The profits gained by unjust conduct are kept in private stores (3:10), possibly to be used for drink (4:1) or for sexual pleasure (2:7).[168] The corrupted order of Israel's society breaks 'the šālôm with God and among men'.[169]

Instead of this, Amos demands justice (5:24). As Wright puts it, YHWH is the source of all righteousness and justice, and to know him is to follow the practice of justice. The wicked might find no obstruction in the court (5:10-13), but they have to prepare to meet YHWH (4:12).[170] Amos' social critiques 'correspond in most cases with stipulations of the so-called Covenant Code (Exod 20:23-23:19) and therefore cohere in an ideal society willed by God to be just and righteous.'[171] For example in Amos 2:8, refusal to return the garment taken in pledge to a poor person violates a specific covenant stipulation of Exodus 22:26-27. This covenant regulation is intended to protect the poor.[172]

Polley considers that Amos' favourite topic is his condemnation of the oppression of the poor and needy (2:6-7; 4:1; 5:11-12; 8:4-6),[173] and he condemns the wealthy upper class for this.[174] The poor are synonymously paralleled with the 'oppressed'.[175] The expression 'cows of Bashan' in Amos

---

167. See Hasel, *Understanding of Amos*, 102; Whybray, *The Good Life in the Old Testament*, 267; Victor H. Matthews, *The Social World of the Hebrew Prophets* (Peabody, Massachusetts: Hendrickson Publishers, 2001), 69-70; Gary V. Smith, 'Amos 5:13: The Deadly Silence of the Prosperous,' *JBL* 107, no. 02 (June 1988): 290-291; Blenkinsopp, *A History of Prophecy in Israel: From the Settlement in the Land to the Hellenistic Period*, 96; James Limburg, 'Sevenfold Structures in the Book of Amos,' *JBL* 106, no. 02 (1987): 219; Craig Loscalzo, 'Preaching Themes from Amos,' *RE* 92 (Spring 1995): 195.
168. Whybray, *Good Life*, 267.
169. Hasel, *Understanding of Amos*, 102.
170. Wright, *People of God*, 146.
171. Blenkinsopp, *History of Prophecy*, 96.
172. Ibid.
173. Polley, *Davidic Empire*, 131.
174. Gary Smith, 'Deadly Silence', 290-291.
175. See Terence Kleven, 'The Cows of Bashan: A Single Metaphor at Amos 4:1-3,' *CBQ* 58, no. 02 (April 1996): 216; Whybray, *Good Life*, 266; King, *Amos, Hosea, Micah*, 139; G. H. Wittenberg, 'Amos 6:1-7: "They Dismiss the Day of Disaster but You Bring Near the Rule of Violence,"' *JTSA* 58, no. 01 (March 1987): 62; Polley, *Davidic Empire*, 132.

4:1 is apparently connected with Canaanite cults. The cow symbolizes fertility of the land in the Ancient Near East.[176] Therefore, the wealthy women who are like cows of fertile Bashan abuse the gift of the land. Kleven asserts that the oppression of the poor is one of the most constant aspects of Israel's error.[177] However, YHWH's judgment is that the rich's abuse of the poor for their profit will come to an end (4:2).[178]

Not only did the leaders or upper wealthy class pervert justice, bribe judges, and oppress the poor (2:6-7; 5:10, 12), but they also cheated the poor in the market place (5:11),[179] taking them for their own economic benefit (5:11; 8:5-6).[180] This economic injustice abuses the gift of land because the poor thereby lose their legitimate interest in it. Wright argues that threatening a person's possession of land is to threaten one's membership of the covenant people. In Amos, this kind of loss of land is not merely economic disaster; it rather disastrously hinders one's very relationship with YHWH. 'That is why the wealthy establishment was so appalled at the language of Amos, when he insisted on calling "the righteous" those who were being oppressed and dispossessed' (2:6; 5:12).[181]

2.6.2 Justice in Cultic Context

It is also evident that 'justice' and 'righteousness' appear in a cultic context in relation to land. Amos points to the false celebration of the gifts of the land (5:21-22). YHWH rejects the people's cultic sacrifices because they do not treat the land properly. He condemns religious ceremonies without justice (5:21-24). Adri Wal argues that Amos' concern for justice and righteousness (5:7-6:12) is 'set beside concern for feasts and offerings' (5:21-23).[182] As Michael Walzer suggests, the aim of these ceremonies and

---

176. Hans Barstad, *The Religious Polemics of Amos: Studies in the Preaching of Amos 2:7b-8; 4:1-13; 5:1-27; 6:4-7; 8:14* (VTSup 34; Leiden: E. J. Brill, 1984), 42-43.
177. Kleven, 'Bashan', 216-127.
178. Ibid.
179. Jannie du Preez, '"Let Justice Roll On Like....": Some Explanatory Notes on Amos 5:24,' *JTSA* 109 (March 2001): 95.
180. Carol J. Dempsey, *The Prophets: A Liberation-Critical Reading* (Minneapolis: Fortress Press, 2002), 20.
181. Wright, *People of God*, 56.
182. Adri van der Wal, 'The Structure of Amos,' *JSOT* 26, no. 01 (June 1983): 112.

feasts is a reminder of Israel's commitment to YHWH's law and covenant.[183] Gerhard Hasel thinks that the terms 'justice' and 'righteousness' originated in the covenant-election traditions.[184] These terms are used to portray the characteristics of YHWH and to illustrate the covenant relationship between YHWH and his people Israel.[185]

The covenant relationship is to be restored by seeking YHWH (5:4, 6), seeking good and not evil (5:14).[186] Amos urges: 'Hate evil, love good' (5:15). 'Good' is connected with the tradition of covenant and thus to do good means to obey the covenant laws.[187] Therefore, ceasing to seek YHWH and seeking instead one's own interests will hinder the practice of justice in political, religious, moral or economic spheres.[188] Evil (5:10-13) will continue to characterize the time as long as the poor are trampled, and injustices are practiced.[189]

Amos' concern for justice is to break up the confidence of the traditionally pious: 'Woe to them that are ease in Zion, and to you who feel secure on Mount Samaria' (6:1).[190] Amos knows that justice and righteousness are the core value of Israel's traditions. He identifies the life of the poor in Israel with their experience as slaves in Egypt (2:10; 3:1; 9:7). In this way, he points to justice as the fundamental religious demand.[191] Zimmerli argues that 'the most zealous worship at the holy place in the pure land is no substitute for it.'[192] Amidst a climate of social injustices in the land of Israel, the moral failures in relation to justice are said to be the reason for YHWH's rejection of their religious ceremonies (5:21-23).[193] Their worship, feasts, and offering had become empty ritual and meaningless (4:4-5;

---

183. Michael Walzer, 'Prophecy and Social Criticism,' *DG* 55 (1984): 23.
184. Hasel, *Understanding of Amos*, 103-104.
185. Achtemeier, 'Righteousness in the OT,' 80-85.
186. Donoso S. Escobar, 'Social Justice,' *RE* 92 (Spring 1995): 172.
187. M. Daniel Carroll R, 'Seeking the Virtues Among the Prophets: The Book of Amos as A Test Case,' *ExA* 17 (2001): 86.
188. Escobar, 'Social Justice,' 172.
189. See Escobar, 'Social Justice,' 172; Carroll R., 'Virtues', 86.
190. Walzer, 'Social Criticism,' 23.
191. Ibid., 24.
192. Zimmerli, 'Land', 248.
193. Susan Ackerman, 'Amos 5:18-24,' *Int* 57, no. 02 (April 2003): 192.

5:21-23).[194] With his primary concern for justice Amos challenges the leaders, the people, and their ritual practices.

The people offered sacrifices and feasts at the sanctuaries of Bethel and Gilgal (cf. 4:4-5; 5:5-6, 21-23), believing that Israel could never lose the land which YHWH had once given them as a gift: 'YHWH is with us' (5:14). In the same way, the poor also made pilgrimages to the cultic places at Bethel and Gilgal.[195] It is reasonable to suggest, as Koch argues, that these cultic places at Bethel and Gilgal are connected with the gift of the land by YHWH to Israel and the gift of the land was celebrated in remembrance of the promise of YHWH to the patriarchs in the ancient days.[196] But Amos shows that because of the people's practice of injustice the land will turn against them in a dreadful earthquake and eclipse,[197] and will bring them unavoidable judgment in exile (5:5, 27; 6:7; 7:17).[198]

2.6.3 Justice in Creation Context

Furthermore, 'justice' and 'righteousness' also occur in the creation context. The theme of justice (5:7, 10-15; 5:21-6:14) is 'creational in orientation'. And the references to Pleiades and Orion, darkness and light, day and night (5:8-9) are associated with natural order.[199] The land produces its fruitfulness and peace reigns in society as long as justice and righteousness prevail (Ps 72:1-4; Isa 11, 32).[200] Conversely, the people have polluted the land through their lack of justice and concern for the poor, which brings the disruption of both the social order and the cosmic order and results in the cosmic effects of famine and flood (Amos 5:6-8).[201] Actually the social order and cosmic order are closely connected and thus people's social conduct certainly affects the created order,[202] in both natural and political

---

194. Loscalzo, 'Preaching Themes', 195.
195. Koch, *Prophets*, 1: 52-55.
196. Ibid., 1: 55.
197. Snyman, '*Leitmotiv*,' 536.
198. Park, *Antiquity*, 117-118.
199. Fretheim, *God and*, 170.
200. Marlow, *Ethics*, 104.
201. See Fretheim, *God and World*, 170; Marlow, *Ethics*, 104.
202. Fretheim, *God and World*, 171.

spheres.[203] Justice and righteousness create 'harmony between *society* and *nature*' (Ps 27:1-3; Joel 2:21-23),[204] while turning 'justice' into wormwood (Amos 5:7; 6:12) makes the land unfruitful and devastates the natural world (Hos 10:4).[205] Marlow argues that 'when justice fails the earth is disrupted, the harvest fails, cosmic disturbance occurs, and urban infrastructure disintegrates' (Amos 8:4-10; Isa 24:1-13).[206]

The idea that justice (צְדָקָה) is related to the world order is developed by Schmid, who considered the connection between 'creation' and 'justice' צְדָקָה. For him, צְדָקָה is to be regarded as universal world order and comprehensive salvation in terms of its social ethics. The main focus of צְדָקָה is on a well balanced created order of the world.[207] That is, YHWH's 'justice' is imprinted on the creation. Therefore, Amos' view of justice may come in part from his understanding of creation.

It is interesting that the theme of justice appears in 8:4-6, and the subsequent verses of 7-10 bring in the themes of creation.[208] In short, justice in Amos appears in social, cultic, and creation context, all of which are related to the theme of land. The practice of injustice in social and ritual spheres in Israel affects the land (1:2; 4:7, 9; 5:17; 8:8-10). The land is expected to be a place where justice is practiced. However, it is a place where justice is ignored and the poor and needy who are tenant farmers of the land are trampled. Sabbaths (8:4-6) are the only events that defend the needy and poor from selling and buying. The topic of Sabbath in relation to land and justice will be dealt with in more detail below, in chapters 7-9.

2.7 Conclusion

In the description of land in different ways, Amos uses a range of language with different theological implications, including YHWH's 'ownership'

---

203. Schmid, 'Creation', 105.
204. Koch, *Prophets*, 1: 59.
205. Koch, *Prophets*, 1: 59; also see Marlow, *Ethics*, 268.
206. Marlow, *Ethics*, 268.
207. Schmid, 'Creation', 107-108.
208. Fretheim, *God and World*, 170.

and 'gift,' and Israel's 'inheritance' and 'possession.' He also refers to various features of the land. Amos is a farmer and a shepherd. Therefore, his knowledge of the nature of the land and farming life has significant implications for his understanding of it. This no doubt helped to form his theology of land.

Amos has a distinctive view of Israel's land-tradition. The theology of land in Amos is related to other themes, including Zion, covenant-election, the terminology of 'Israel', creation, justice, and eschatology. The Zion tradition has a connection with YHWH's kingship and Amos may assume this. Zion, as YHWH's dwelling place, also has a close connection with the theme of worship, characterized by the practice of justice in it. Since Zion is part of the covenant people's vocabulary (cf. Isa 40:9; 51:3), it functions in Amos to show his interest in the reality of Israel's keeping the covenant, which will enable the ancient land promises to be fulfilled, rather than merely paying attention to the relationship between the northern and southern kingdoms.

As in the case of Zion, the issue of 'Israel' – with different terms – points to the whole covenant people, that is, 'my people Israel' (7:15), who are brought out of the land of Egypt (3:1). The election of Israel in 3:2 rather assumes the idea of the giving of the land. But it raises the question of the extent of the land and what people Amos has in mind. YHWH's action of election intends that the covenant people would maintain the gift of land by complying with their responsibility of keeping the covenant by doing justice. However, Israel's practice of injustice affects their land. Justice in Amos appears in social, cultic, and creation contexts, all of which are related to the theme of land. In Amos, the creation concept apparently links with the theme of land. YHWH is the creator of the whole world, and is powerful over all creation and thus he can also bring judgment to the whole created order and all nations.

CHAPTER 3

The Land in Amos 7

3.1 The Land in Amos 7:1-9

3.1.1 Introduction

The last three chapters of the book contain the visions of Amos.[1] In the first two visions, a plague of locusts and cosmic fire devours the great deep and the land. The destruction of the cultic places, the people, and the royal house in the third vision envisages the total destruction of the land and a severe judgment on the people of Israel. This study will show how these three visions relate to and affect the land. We will ask whether Amos addresses his message only to northern Israel or to the people as a whole, in view of the confrontation with Amaziah at Bethel (7:12-13). In these three visions, as will be shown, the idea of 'Israel' is pictured in different terms: 'Jacob', 'Isaac', and 'Israel' are used to designate historic Israel, and yet in some contexts, 'Israel' particularly focuses on the north. What does Amos believe about 'Israel'? Does he limit it only to the north or include both kingdoms? What has Amos in mind when he talks about the land? What view of the land is being taken? And on what theological basis is it threatened?

---

1. The visions of Amos in chapters 7-9 have been considered prophetic dramas. See William Doan and Terry Giles, *Prophets, Performance, and Power: Performance Criticism of the Hebrew Bible* (London: T & T Clark, 2005), 139-156; W. David Stacey, *Prophetic Drama in the Old Testament* (London: Epworth, 1990); *idem*, 'The Function of Prophetic Drama,' in *The Place Is Too Small for Us: The Israelite Prophets in Recent Scholarship*, ed., Robert P. Gordon (Winona Lake, Indiana: Eisenbarauns, 1995), 112-132.

3.1.2 The Visions and Response of YHWH

3.1.2.1 The First Two Visions

The visions of locusts and fire demonstrate YHWH's longsuffering regarding his own people and the successful intercessions of the prophet. Amos intercedes and YHWH relents and confirms: this shall not be. YHWH shows Amos locusts, an instrument of YHWH's curse upon the people of Israel (Exod 10:12-20; Deut 28:38, 42; Joel 1:4-12; Amos 4:9).[2] The locusts are symbols of devastation because they can devour the vegetation of the land,[3] and so pose a threat to an agricultural community.[4] In ancient times, people were unable to protect their harvest from the locusts.[5] The vision shows that when Amos sees YHWH forming the locusts the coming devastation is apparent. The timing of the vision is essential to the sequence of events. The term לֶקֶשׁ signifies the agricultural season, the late-planting or the latter growth in late spring (Amos 4:7; cf. Zech 10:1; Prov 16:15).[6] The timing of the plague is significant, therefore, because the locusts were envisaged as having devoured the main latter growth just after it began to shoot in March or April (Deut 11:14).[7]

Several suggestions have been made about the meaning of 'after the king's mowing' (גִּזֵּי). Daniel Simundson considers that the first mowing belongs to the king perhaps in terms of tax or the taking of property (1 Kgs 18:5)[8] and A. G. Auld assumes that it is already being kept in the royal barn.[9] However, for the second mowing, Auld asserts that this latter growth

---

2. See Mays, *Amos*, 128; Paul, *Amos*, 228; Gary Smith, *Amos: A Commentary*, 222; Simundson, *Hosea, Joel, Amos, Obadiah, Jonah, Micah*, 214.
3. Cole, 'Visions,' 58.
4. Simundson, *Hosea, Joel, Amos, Obadiah, Jonah, Micah*, 213.
5. Ibid.
6. See John Andrew Dearman, *Property Rights in the Eighth-Century Prophets: The Conflict and Its Background* (Atlanta, Georgia: Scholars Press, 1988), 31; Hammershaimb, *Book of Amos*, 108.
7. See Wolff, *Prophets*, 297; Gary Smith, *Amos: A Commentary*, 222; Cole, 'Visions', 59; Stuart, *Hosea-Jonah*, 371; Hayes, *Amos*, 202; Paul, *Amos*, 227; Smith and Page, *Amos, Obadiah, Jonah*, 128; Fyall, *Teaching Amos*, 115.
8. Simundson, *Hosea, Joel, Amos, Obadiah, Jonah, Micah*, 214.
9. Auld, *Amos*, 17.

was required for local consumption, that is, for the people of the land,[10] and Stuart sees it as a reserve for the farmers themselves and their cattle while the first growth is apparently earmarked for the king in the time of Jeroboam.[11] Following Auld and Stuart, it is clear that the latter growth is essentially intended for the benefit of the farmer or the poor of the land.

It seems that the king had his share of the land's bounty,[12] possibly before the harvest of the people.[13] The latter growth consists of both grain and non-grain crops such as vegetables. This devastation of the latter growth by the locusts brings a severely harmful result especially for the poor.[14] Therefore, this situation may have heightened Amos' sense of compassion for the helpless farmers and the land itself.

The description of the vision in 7:1 gives the scene, and yet no destruction in the land has yet taken place. The following verse (7:2) envisages the threats of destruction which will be brought about by the locusts. The usual translation of אִם־כִּלָּה לֶאֱכוֹל 'when they had finished eating or devouring'[15] or ' make an end of eating'[16] seems to suggest that the intercession of Amos came after the locusts had already destroyed all the vegetation of the land. If this were the case, it would not fit well with Amos' intercession for mercy and forgiveness with the result that YHWH relented and said, 'this shall not be' (7:3). Therefore, some take the perfect form of כִּלָּה, to refer to what was about to happen: 'when it was about to finish'.[17] Conveying the possible nature of the devastation, Stuart interprets it as Amos' vision of the *potential* future in the land of Israel and thus translates, 'It seemed as if they would completely devour the earth's vegetation' (7:2a).[18] Although

---

10. Ibid., 17.
11. Stuart, *Hosea-Jonah*, 371.
12. Mays, *Amos*, 128.
13. See Linville, *Cosmic*, 135; Mays, *Amos*, 128.
14. Paul, *Amos*, 227.
15. ESV, LXE, NAS, RSV, NKJ, NRS.
16. ASV, KJV.
17. For example, Wolff, *Prophets*, 292; Hammershaimb, *Book of Amos*, 109; Mays, *Amos*, 127. BHS suggests וַיְהִי הָא מְכַלֶּה, to convey the same meaning, but Wolff finds it unnecessary.
18. Stuart, *Hosea-Jonah*, 370-371.

it is difficult, something like this seems to be necessary in order to make sense of the text.

The second vision contains YHWH's call for the judgment by fire (לָרִב בָּאֵשׁ). On the basis of the root רִב, James Limburg argues that the verb means, 'to make accusation or complaint' and the noun, 'accusation or complaint', in Amos 7:4.[19] John H. Hayes also sees it as 'a quarrel or controversy'[20] and Limburg further states that it articulates the real complaint or accusation (Neh 5:7; Judg 6:30-32) or accusing question (Gen 31:36-37; Judg 8:1; Neh 13:11, 17; Job 13:6-28). Thus, the sense in Amos 7:4 is, 'Behold, the Lord God was calling for the making of an accusation . . .'[21] Limburg concludes that since YHWH was calling for the making of an accusation or complaint followed by the sending of fire, the acceptable translation could be 'judgment involving fire', or 'judgment with fire'.[22] Therefore, בָּאֵשׁ 'with fire' suggests that YHWH is about to carry out his judgment upon Israel.[23]

Fire (אֵשׁ), the instrument of YHWH's wrath,[24] devours both the sea and the land, and the outcome of it is nothing less than famine and drought throughout the land. Amos' imagery turns here to the realm of mythology.[25] In Amos 7:4, 'fire' is used as an instrument to devour תְּהוֹם רַבָּה the 'great deep' and even חֵלֶק, the land, or the portion of the land. When YHWH has determined to bring the locusts on the vegetation of the land and the cosmic fire to devour the great deep and the land, Amos pleads with YHWH for forgiveness and mercy and YHWH relents.

---

19. James Limburg, 'Amos 7:4: A Judgment with Fire?,' *CBQ* 35, no. 03 (July 1973): 346-349.
20. Hayes, *Amos*, 203.
21. Limburg, 'Amos 7:4', 347.
22. Limburg, 'Amos 7:4', 347-348, further asserts that 'fire' (אֵשׁ) occurs nine times in Amos, seven times in the oracle against the nations (Amos 1-2). Possibly 'devouring fire' in Amos 1-2 can be seen as a clue to understanding the 'devouring fire' in 7:4.
23. Paul, *Amos*, 231.
24. 'Fire' (אֵשׁ) is used as the instrument of YHWH's wrath of judgment in the Old Testament (Amos 1:4, 7, 10, 12, 14; 2:2, 5; cf. Gen. 19:24-25; Lev. 10:2; Num. 11:1; Deut. 9:3; 2 Kings 1:10, 12; Isa. 66:15-16; Joel 1:19-20; 2:5). Also see Paul, *Amos*, 231.
25. Paul, *Amos*, 231-232; Limburg, 'Amos 7:4', 348-349.

3.1.2.2 This Shall Not Be

It is commonly understood that there is movement and development from the first to the second vision. Linville asserts that the response of Amos seems to reflect the more terrible devastation in the second vision than that of the first. In the first vision, Amos cries, סְלַח־נָא 'forgive, I beseech you!' (7:2) while in the second, he says, חֲדַל־נָא 'cease, I beseech you!' (7:5). Amos can only call out 'cease' in the presence of YHWH calling for great fire.[26] Auld considers that 'forgive' in the first vision (7:2) becomes the more distressed 'cease' of the second vision in 7:5.[27] It does not necessarily mean a change of the mind by Amos about the real need of the people of Israel for forgiveness from YHWH. Rather the punishment by fire is so terrible that he can only cry out to YHWH not to do this; thus, 'cease'.[28] For the use of the words סְלַח 'forgive, and חֲדַל 'cease,' Andersen and Freeman remark that the former is a polite word while the latter is colloquial.[29]

In addition to the development from the first to the second vision, the answer of YHWH also slightly differs: first, YHWH says, 'it shall not be' (7:3), but the second adds גַּם הִיא (this also), so 'this also shall not be' (7:6).[30] The locusts devouring the vegetation of the land and cosmic fire devouring the great deep and the land seem to echo the creation language in Genesis. After the appeal of Amos, YHWH said, לֹא תִהְיֶה 'this shall not be'. However, in Genesis, YHWH said יְהִי 'let there be' (1:3, 6, 9, 14, 15). Here, Genesis uses the verb הָיָה for the creation of the world.

Genesis also mentions the creation of waters and the earth's bringing forth of grass and vegetation (וַתּוֹצֵא הָאָרֶץ דֶּשֶׁא) or vegetation of the field (עֵשֶׂב הַשָּׂדֶה, 1:6, 12; 3:18).[31] The earth is empowered to bring forth vegetation. Brueggemann asserts that הָיָה is creation language in which YHWH commanded, and in this command, 'let be', YHWH gives authorization for creation to become into existence.[32] The term הָיָה, YHWH's creative

---

26. Linville, *Cosmic*, 135-136.
27. Auld, *Amos*, 17.
28. Simundson, *Hosea, Joel, Amos, Obadiah, Jonah, Micah*, 215.
29. Andersen and Freedman, *Amos*, 621.
30. See Linville, *Cosmic*, 136; Andersen and Freedman, *Amos*, 621.
31. See Wolff, *Prophets*, 297; Paul, *Amos*, 228.
32. Walter Brueggemann, *Genesis* (IBCTP; Atlanta: John Knox Press, 1982), 30.

word of command, includes the creation of the vegetation or herbs and trees (Gen 1:11-12). Derek Kidner suggests that the language seems well fitted to the concept of creation and thus the fruitfulness is a *created* capacity.[33] It is the creative word of YHWH that enables the earth to bring forth vegetation.[34] In this way, the context in Amos seems to reflect and echo the creation language in Genesis when the vegetation and fruitfulness of the land is in danger.

3.1.2.3 The Third Vision

In the third vision, YHWH is standing beside a wall with a plumb-line (אֲנָךְ) in hand and says that he is setting a plumb-line in the midst of Israel. Scholars have found a confusing problem in the interpretation of the key term אֲנָךְ,[35] which appears four times in this vision but nowhere else in the entire Hebrew Bible. YHWH held אֲנָךְ the 'plumb-line'[36] in his hand to threaten the people.[37] אֲנָךְ in the sense of 'plumb-line' is based on its meaning as 'lead', which is used as a plummet for measuring walls (2 Kgs 21:13; Lam 2:8; Isa 28:17).[38] Here, the interpretation of the term אֲנָךְ as 'plumb-line' suggests a picture of the destruction of the land and the people of Israel.

The אֲנָךְ allows Amos' audience to see the true state of his people Israel and the land. Amos 7:9 is the consequences of the application of the

---

33. Derek Kidner, *Genesis: An Introduction and Commentary* (TOTC; London: The Tyndale Press, 1968), 48.

34. Claus Westermann, *Genesis 1-11: A Commentary*, trans. John J. Scullion S. J. (London: SPCK, 1984), 126.

35. The term אֲנָךְ could cover both 'tin' and 'lead.' Some take אֲנָךְ to refer to 'tin.' For example, see Paul, *Amos*, 233; Stuart, *Hosea-Jonah*, 373; Linville, *Cosmic*, 138; Gary Smith, *Amos: A Commentary*, 234; Benno Landsberger, 'Tin and Lead: The Adventures of Two Vocables,' *JNES* 24, no. 03 (July 1965): 287. Others take it to refer to 'lead.' For example, see Wolff, *Prophets*, 300; Coggins, *Joel and Amos*, 140; Hammershaimb, *Book of Amos*, 112; Mays, *Amos*, 132.

36. Those who take the term אֲנָךְ to mean 'plumb line' include Hammershaimb, *Book of Amos*, 112; Wolff, *Prophets*, 300; Mays, *Amos*, 132; Gary Smith, *Amos: A Commentary*, 233-234; Smith and Page, *Amos, Obadiah, Jonah*, 132; H. G. M. Williamson, 'The Prophet and the Plumb-Line: A Redaction-Critical Study of Amos 7,' in *The Place is Too Small for Us: The Israelite Prophets in Recent Scholarship*, ed. Robert P. Gordon (New York: Snow Lion Publication, 2002), 453-477.

37. Williamson, 'Plumb-line,' 464-467.

38. See Wolff, *Prophets*, 300; Hammershaimb, *Book of Amos*, 112; Mays, *Amos*, 132.

metaphor of the wall built with a 'plumb-line'. As will be shown, the high places and sanctuaries represent the whole land. YHWH will now bring destruction upon the places of idolatrous worship, 'high places', 'sanctuaries', and the 'house of Jeroboam', with the sword. At this point the time for intercession has passed in contrast with the first two visions.

3.1.2.4 I Will Never Again Pass Them By

As we have seen, the first two visions serve as a paradigm of YHWH's longsuffering and the successful intercessions of the prophet. However, in these first two visions, through the intercession of Amos, the punishment is deferred (7:1-6) but it is not completely removed (cf. 7:7-9; 8:1-3).[39] Therefore, this pattern of YHWH's longsuffering is about to change, as we see in the expression לֹא־אוֹסִיף עוֹד עֲבוֹר לוֹ 'I will never again pass them by',[40] in the third vision (7:8), and also because YHWH does not say: 'it shall not be'. This apparently heralds the bringing of judgment among the people of Israel and the land as a whole.

In other contexts, the term עָבַר 'pass over' is also used to indicate the idea of passing through a land. Moses asked the kings of Edom and the Amorite to permit the people of Israel to pass over their territory (Num 20:17; 21:22) in order to enter the Promised Land, which YHWH gave them for their inheritance. Again, the references to Israel's passing over the Jordan to enter the Promised Land (Deut 9:1; 27:3; 30:18) also designates how the people of Israel have to overcome any hindrance or difficulty, in actualizing the fulfilment of the promise of the covenant of YHWH concerning the land, the gift of YHWH. This same emphasis on the Promised Land given to all the people of Israel also appears in Joshua 1:2. Therefore, the term עָבַר is connected with the concept of the Promised Land. It seems that Amos has this in mind when he uses the term עָבַר in 7:8 and 8:2. However, in the context of Amos, the term becomes a destructive word. YHWH is going to destroy the people of Israel, concluding with the

---

39. Gary Smith, *Amos: A Commentary*, 225-226.
40. The similar expression לֹא־אוֹסִיף עוֹד עֲבוֹר לוֹ 'I will never again pass them by' is found in the fourth vision (Amos 8:2).

solemn words, 'I will never again pass them by' (Amos 7:8; 8:2) due to their failure to repent.

3.1.3 The Use of Jacob/Isaac/Israel in Amos 7-9

The use of the term 'Israel' is debated in the book of Amos as to whether it refers to the northern kingdom or the united kingdom. The name 'Israel' יִשְׂרָאֵל occurs a total of thirty times in Amos.[41] Amos' words are primarily addressed towards Israel, 'concerning Israel' (1:1). Gary Smith asserts that Amos was a herdsman from Tekoa of Judea, and his words are addressed to the northern kingdom of Israel, ruled by Jeroboam II. Not only the references to Samaria (3:9, 12; 4:1; 6:1; 8:14), Bethel (3:14; 4:4; 5:5, 6; 7:13), the house of Israel (5:1, 3, 25; 6:1, 14), Jacob (7:2, 5; 9:8) but also several direct and indirect references affirm that these oracles were given in the north, the kingdom of Israel.[42] The response of Amaziah, the priest at Bethel (7:12-13) to Amos takes up the question of his native land and his ministry. He is from Tekoa of Judah (1:2) and prophesies at Bethel of Israel (7:15). The important issue here is whether he addresses his message only to the northern kingdom or the people as a whole. Our concern now is to ask how this question affects our understanding of first three visions of Amos 7:1-9.

3.1.3.1 Jacob in the First Two Visions

The first two visions describe Amos' response to the visions, his message of intercession for Jacob and the gracious response of YHWH to it. In the first, when the locusts had begun to devour the vegetation of the land, Amos cries for help from YHWH[43] no doubt for the poor and the farmers of the land who lost their harvest. Although the poor, orphan, and widow are unimportant and helpless they received the special attention, concern, and care of YHWH (Exod 22:22; Deut 10:18; 24:17-22; 26:12;

---

41. See Wolff, *Prophets*, 164.
42. Gary Smith, *Amos: A Commentary*, 24.
43. Amos intercedes to YHWH for compassion, mercy and forgiveness because YHWH has confirmed elsewhere that he is a God of mercy who is longsuffering, slow to anger, and forgiving (See Exo. 20:6; 34:6-7; Num. 14:18; Deut. 5:10; 7:9; Ps. 103:8; 145:8; Jonah 4:2). Gary Smith, *Amos: A Commentary*, 223.

Ps 146:9; Isa 1:17; Jer 7:6; Zech 7:10). These will become helpless among the rich in Samaria (6:1-7).[44] The second vision, of fire, also pictures the destruction of the great deep and the land. In both cases, Amos intercedes for forgiveness from YHWH: סְלַח־נָא מִי יָקוּם יַעֲקֹב כִּי קָטֹן הוּא 'Forgive! I beseech you: How can Jacob stand for he is so small?' (7:2, 5).

Forgiveness is often associated with the repentance of the people (1 Kgs 8:30-39, 48-50; 2 Chr 7:14; Isa 55:6-7). The same picture generally holds in Amos. In this sense the sins described in Amos 1-6 are regarded as the reason for the locust plague. However, nothing is said throughout Amos about the repentance of the people of Israel. It is, therefore, impossible to think that Israel had repented or would repent in this context.[45] Smith argues that it seems, therefore, that Amos pleads for YHWH's forgiveness and mercy for their sins without repentance.[46] Exceptionally, it may be that Amos desires YHWH's special intervention upon Jacob 'because he is so small'.

When Amos depicts Jacob as small, he seems to mean that he stands as powerless, poor, pitiful, and helpless before YHWH (see 2:6-8; 4:1; 5:11). What then does Jacob refer to in the first two visions? Stuart claims that when Amos addresses the people of Israel as 'Jacob' here, he aims to characterize the nation in terms of an individual, not as a collective, to make them see how hard it is to survive without their harvest.[47] Wolff considers 'Jacob' as a synonym for 'Israel' and he consistently considers that always in Amos the term 'Israel' refers to the northern kingdom. Therefore, the term 'Israel' in the third vision refers to the north, which is further identified by the different uses of Judah and Israel in 7:12, 15.[48] Regarding Amos' use of the term 'Jacob', Wolff considers that it simply acknowledges the smallness of Jacob in terms of its helplessness and it does not necessarily mean any allusion to the traditions, whether promise or election.[49] Similarly, Paul recognizes that when Amos appeals for the mercy and forgiveness of

---

44. Gary Smith, *Amos: A Commentary*, 223.
45. Ibid.
46. Ibid.
47. Stuart, *Hosea-Jonah*, 371.
48. Wolff, *Prophets*, 301.
49. Ibid., 297-298.

YHWH for Jacob, he does not mean the traditional promise of salvation, and there is no overtone of the election of Israel.[50] Like Wolff, Paul also think that when Amos mentions 'Israel' and 'Jacob' and the intercession for 'Jacob' it rather connotes the northern kingdom.[51] For these writers, 'Jacob' is regarded simply as a synonym for 'Israel', that is, the northern kingdom.

However, contrary to Wolff and Paul, Brueggemann suggests that the smallness of 'Jacob' does indeed connote helplessness and insignificance, and that the term 'Jacob' is used in a theological way to refer to the patriarchal tradition. Jacob as the covenant people is still completely dependent upon YHWH.[52] Unlike Wolff, Mays, and Paul, Andersen and Freedman believe that in 7:2 and 7:5, 'Jacob' signifies the descendants of the patriarch and therefore it refers to the whole people of Israel,[53] which is described as 'the whole family' (כָּל־הַמִּשְׁפָּחָה) which YHWH brought up out of the land of Egypt in 3:1.[54] The use of 'Jacob', according to Richard S. Cripps, designates the nation as a whole as in 7:8, 8:2, 9:8.[55] Further, the use of 'Jacob' in a larger sense is made clear by Jörg Jeremias. He asserts that Amos is obviously avoiding the name 'Israel'. For Amos and his hearers, 'Jacob' never refers to the state, but rather it shows the condition that they are always totally dependent on YHWH. In this sense, the address of Jacob as small, and powerless indicates the impossibility of life apart from the help of YHWH. It is assumed then, that YHWH later addresses the people in a more inclusive manner 'my people Israel' (7:8; 8:2), and finally and more vividly, 'all of them' (9:1).[56]

In addition, with the construct form of בֵּית, the term 'house of Jacob' appears in 3:13; 9:8. Some consider it as a reference to the north.[57] However, traditionally, Jacob designates all the descendants of Israel and from Jacob

---

50. Paul, *Amos*, 229.
51. Ibid.
52. Walter Brueggemann, 'Amos' Intercessory Formula,' *VT* 19, no. 04 (October 1969): 386, 388.
53. Andersen and Freedman, *Amos*, 111, 114-115, 121-122.
54. John Rogerson, *Theory and Practice in Old Testament Ethics*, ed. M. Daniel Carroll R. (London: T & T Clark International, 2004), 125.
55. Cripps, *Exegetical Commentary*, 245.
56. Jeremias, *Book of Amos*, 128.
57. See Gary Smith, *Amos: A Commentary*, 124; Mays, *Amos*, 129, 160.

Israel emerged (Gen 35:10). Andersen and Freedman argue that although it is quite difficult to identify the exact group, the term seems to be a replacement for, or correspond to, the 'house of Israel'. Therefore, it refers to both kingdoms since Jacob is a synonym for all of Israel.[58] Again in 6:8, 8:7, 'pride of Jacob' should be the whole of Israel because the range of the term 'Jacob' is unlikely to convey only the northern kingdom.[59] In this way, unlike the perspectives of Wolff, Paul, Smith, and Mays, Andersen and Freedman maintain that 'Jacob' constantly means historic Israel.

McConville carefully examines at length the use of the term 'Jacob' as it occurs in Amos, specifically how that concept is expressed in the sequence of visions of Amos 7-9.[60] McConville asserts that the duality of Judah and Israel is apparent in Amos by pointing to 'Tekoa', the distinction between the kings of Judah and 'Israel', Uzziah and Jeroboam (1:1), the oracles concerning Judah (2:4-5) and Israel (2:6-16), and Zion and Samaria (6:1). Some texts refer expressly to neither Judah nor Israel, but these suggest the concept of the historic people of Israel who were brought out of the land of Egypt (2:10; 3:1-2; 9:7-8).[61]

In my view, the approach of McConville is convincing in its argument that 'Jacob' connotes the historic Israel. McConville suggests that Amos' choice of 'Jacob' in the first two visions (7:1-3, 4-6) brings into question the true nature of Israel, what Israel really is. The visions along with the narrative and oracles within the sequence of visions (7-9) give the answer to this very question. Amos uses this term 'Jacob' to suggest the nature of 'Israel'.[62] In the first two visions, the question of the true nature of Israel is implicitly identified by the strange phrase מִי יָקוּם יַעֲקֹב, generally translated 'How can Jacob stand?' Literally, מִי means 'who' in Biblical Hebrew. According to Wolff, מִי (who) must be interpreted predicatively since Jacob is the subject of יָקוּם, thus; 'As who [=how] can Jacob stand?'[63] McConville considers that Wolff's use of 'as who' could be best taken as equivalent to

---

58. Andersen and Freedman, *Amos*, 103, 124-125.
59. Ibid., 99, 111, 114-115, 121-122. Also see Cripps, *Exegetical Commentary*, 163.
60. McConville, 'Jacob', 132-151.
61. Ibid., 133.
62. Ibid., 132-133, 150.
63. Wolff, *Prophets*, 292.

'how'. However, McConville further argues that the term מִי 'as who' is not merely identical to 'how' but more significantly it has a rhetorical function in putting the question about the authentic nature of Jacob.[64] Erling Hammershaimb, like Paul, considers the term מִי as 'an accusative of circumstance: "as to whom" = "how".'[65]

McConville suggests that Amos' choice of Jacob seems significantly different from 'Israel' because 'Jacob' avoids the potential ambiguity in the nature of 'Israel' between the historic Israel and the north. And Amos thus highlights the question about the false understanding of the nature of Israel which apparently occurs in his time,[66] especially in the conflict with Amaziah at Bethel.

The true nature of Israel, as argued by McConville, is identified by the conflict with Amaziah at Bethel which gives the clue of the division of the kingdoms: north and south. The attempt of Amaziah to equate Israel with the northern kingdom is deconstructed by Amos and Amos draws attention to the essential calling of historic Israel. Following this narrative (7:10-17), the integral ambiguity of the terms in Amos such as 'Israel', 'people', 'land' is best considered to refer to the historic Israel.[67] In this way, taking 'Jacob' as Amos' choice to designate the historic Israel, McConville concludes that the visions, narrative and oracles in Amos 7-9 show that 'Israel' implies the traditions of election and covenant, that it is fulfilling the responsibility of YHWH's elect people that brings salvation.[68] On the other hand, however, one should not ignore the immediate application, since Amos appears particularly at Bethel.

3.1.3.2 Isaac and Israel in the Third Vision

In the first announcement of punishment, the term יִשְׂחָק 'Isaac' is an ambiguous term. Some think that in 7:9 it is a name for the northern kingdom

---

64. McConville, 'Jacob', 143.
65. Hammershaimb, *Book of Amos*, 109.
66. McConville, 'Jacob', 133, 142.
67. Ibid., 150.
68. Ibid., 150-151.

(cf. 7:16).[69] Again in 7:9, 16, the names Israel and Isaac are interchangeably used. The context in 7:9, 16 might seem to suggest a reference to the northern kingdom only, because the essential concern of Amaziah is to warn Amos that he shall not prophesy against the northern kingdom (cf. v. 13).[70] Andersen and Freedman take it in this sense and maintain that the terms 'Joseph' and 'Isaac' are used to replace the term 'Israel'. These therefore denote the northern kingdom, while 'Israel' with various construct forms stands for historic Israel.[71] Although the term 'Isaac' is rarely used outside Genesis, and Amos is unique in his use of it, Andersen and Freedman argue that the context shows that it designates the northern kingdom (7:9, 16).[72] According to Jeremias, the use of the term 'Isaac' is complicated because apart from Amos 7:9, 16, the Old Testament never uses this term in parallel with Israel, and never as a reference to the northern kingdom. If that is the case, the term 'Isaac' seems to refer to both kingdoms, but ironically.[73]

One might expect the term 'Isaac' to apply to at least Israel, the descendants of Jacob, and possibly the Edomites, the descendants of Esau, Israel's brother people. But here, it is impossible that it be taken to refer to the brother people, the Edomites. Probably, Amos is referring to the whole people of Israel.[74] For Stuart also, the parallel of 'Israel' with 'Isaac' in 7:9, 16 clearly reinforces the view that Amos includes all Israel, both north and south. Although 'Israel' is ambiguous to some extent, 'the house of Isaac' (7:16) had also to embrace Judah.[75] The phrase 'the high places of Isaac' in 7:9 is mirrored in the 'house of Isaac' (בֵּית יִשְׂחָק) in 7:16. Its interpretation belongs to the debate between Amaziah and Amos, to which we shall return. But since 'Isaac' is not used elsewhere to refer to the northern

---

69. See Mays, *Amos*, 133; Smith and Page, *Amos, Obadiah, Jonah*, 133; Wolff, *Prophets*, 301-302.
70. Andersen and Freedman, *Amos*, 120-121.
71. Ibid., 99.
72. Ibid.
73. Jeremias, *Book of Amos*, 141, further claims that although YHWH sent Amos 'to my people Israel' (cf. 7:8; 8:2), Amaziah knows only state terminology: 'Do not vilify the house of Isaac.'
74. Cripps, *Exegetical Commentary*, 226.
75. Stuart, *Hosea-Jonah*, 377; Sweeney, *The Twelve Prophets*, 1: 260.

kingdom only, it is reasonable to assume a broader meaning.[76] Further, 'the high places of Isaac' refer implicitly to the sanctuaries at Bethel, Gilgal, Beersheba, and Dan (Amos 3:14; 4:4; 5:5-6; 6:1; 8:14).[77] Since both Dan and Beersheba are included here, a reference to both kingdoms and the whole people is likely (1 Sam 3:20; 2 Sam 3:10; 17:11; 24:2).

The second announcement of judgment includes the destruction of the sanctuaries of Israel. What does 'Israel' here refer to? The term יִשְׂרָאֵל occurs in 7:9, also in 7:11, 17 without the construct forms בֵּית and בְּנֵי. As previously stated, Wolff considers that in Amos the term 'Israel' always refers to the north, and so 'my people Israel' in the third vision refers to the north, as is reinforced by the distinct terms for Judah and Israel in 7:12, 15.[78] Wolff finds Josianic additions in connection with Bethel, associated with the Deuteronomic traditions about Josiah destroying the sanctuary of Bethel, its altar and high place (2 Kgs 23:15). The destruction of the altar of Bethel in 3:14 is one such later addition to the words of Amos, as is Amos 5:5-6.[79] The plan of YHWH for 'Israel' is indicated in 2:6 and 3:14 and, as Wolff has it, 'the end of this history is announced' in the visions and narrative (7:9, 11b, 17b).[80] In this way, Wolff maintains that 'Israel' refers to the north.

Henry McKeating thinks that 'Israel' can be used to refer to the north and south together, as in 3:1 and 6:1, but mostly it means the northern kingdom since Amos appears as a man with a limited mission and prophecy.[81] In the context of the third vision, McKeating further notes that Amos is sent to one particular place, namely the northern kingdom of Israel.[82] As we have seen, like Wolff, Paul considers that the term 'Jacob' is used to refer to the northern kingdom.[83] In the appeal of Amos to YHWH on behalf

---

76. See Clements, 'Amos and the Politics of Israel,' 58; Wood, *Song*, 76.
77. See Hammershaimb, *Book of Amos*, 112; Cole, 'Visions,' 61; Soggin, *The Prophet*, 117; Achtemeier, *Minor Prophets I*, 221.
78. Wolff, *Prophets*, 301.
79. Ibid., 111.
80. Ibid., 164.
81. Henry McKeating, *The Books of Amos, Hosea, and Micah* (CBC; Cambridge: Cambridge University Press, 1971), 13.
82. McKeating, *Amos, Hosea, and Micah*, 13.
83. Paul, *Amos*, 229.

of Jacob (Israel), he is not appealing to the salvation by which YHWH brought them out of Egypt (3:1).[84] Following Wolff, Paul asserts that the reference to 'Israel' in the expression 'my people Israel' refers to the northern kingdom, since when it applies at the same time to Judah, this is indicated by 'the whole family that I brought out of Egypt' (3:1b). However, Amos 3:1b is an editorial addition, though not the Deuteronomic redaction as Wolff suggested.[85]

In considering 'Israel' in relation to the northern kingdom, Andersen and Freedman observe the different names that appear in Amos.[86] The word 'Israel' can be used in different ways to indicate the patriarchs, the twelve-tribe group, or the nation as a whole, or the northern kingdom in particular according to its context. When the terms 'Israel' stands alone, without the construct forms בֵּית, בְּנֵי, or עַמִּי, it means the northern kingdom.[87] Other terms such as 'Joseph' and 'Isaac' are parallels to 'Israel' and also indicate the northern kingdom.[88] In 7:9, 11, 17, also in 2:6 and 3:14, they argue, 'Israel' refers to the northern kingdom because of the preceding reference to Judah. The reference to Judah makes clear that the term 'Israel' in these verses means the land (kingdom) of Israel, since the immediate target of the prophet's remarks is the northern kingdom which is clearly confirmed by the immediate statement 'the house of Jeroboam'.[89] Andersen and Freedman conclude that where the term 'Israel' means the historic people it is combined with the words בֵּית or בְּנֵי as in 3:1 (בְּנֵי יִשְׂרָאֵל), which has the Exodus theme, as also in 2:10.[90] Again in 7:9, 11, 17, Amos speaks these words in the northern kingdom of Jeroboam. The term 'Israel' in these texts thus implies the northern kingdom, and the context is connected with Jeroboam, king of Israel and Amaziah, high priest at Bethel.[91]

---

84. Ibid., 100.
85. Paul, *Amos*, 236, 100.
86. Andersen and Freedman, *Amos*, 98-139.
87. Ibid., 98.
88. Ibid., 99.
89. Ibid., 101, 104-105, 116, 118, 121.
90. Ibid., 122-123.
91. See Gary Smith, *Amos: A Commentary*, 237; Cripps, *Exegetical Commentary*, 139, 229, 239.

However, in this context, 'Israel' is attached to the sanctuaries. This juxtaposition is suggestive of the land as a whole. McConville argues that the final two chapters try to direct attention to Israel as a whole. In the penultimate chapter, for instance, the criticism of the sanctuaries of Samaria, Dan, and Beersheba (8:13-14), and the pairing of Dan and Beersheba (1 Sam 3:20; 2 Sam 3:10; 17:11; 24:2), and Beersheba in connection with the patriarch, express the full extent of the land and therefore it covers both Israel and Judah.[92] It is commonly understood that the expression 'from Dan to Beersheba' refers to the whole land and the whole people (Judg 20:1; 1 Sam 3:20; 2 Sam 3:10; 17:11; 24:22).[93] In Amos 8:14, the sanctuaries of Dan and Beersheba could imply the inclusion of both kingdoms and of the people as the historic Israel. Again, the term 'Israel' in 7:9, along with the high places of Isaac, is qualified by the sanctuaries namely Bethel (3:14; 4:4; 5:5, 6; 7:10, 13), Gilgal (4:4; 5:5), Samaria (3:9, 12; 4:1; 6:1; 8:14), Dan (8:14), and Beersheba (5:5; 8:14). Therefore, McConville argues for the concept of 'Israel' as historic Israel, and the land as the whole land which is granted by YHWH as inheritance.

3.1.3.3 My People Israel in Amos 7-9

The plumb-line symbolizes YHWH's purpose to destroy Israel (7:8). Those who are to be punished are addressed by YHWH as עַמִּי יִשְׂרָאֵל 'my people Israel' (7:8, 15; 8:2; 9:14). Amos has already confirmed that they are the chosen people among the families of the earth (3:2). However, because of the failure of the covenantal responsibility, the people of Israel are to be punished.

'My people Israel' (עַמִּי יִשְׂרָאֵל) renders the personal relationship between YHWH and Israel in covenantal form (Exod 3:10; 6:4-7; Deut 4:20; 7:6-10), which draws both into an intimate relationship. The punishment is none other than judgment on something which is in the realm of YHWH's belonging. Therefore, YHWH's intended action is covenantally based on the nation's failure to maintain their status as the people of

---

92. McConville, 'Jacob', 147-148.
93. See Simon Cohen, 'Beersheba,' in *IDB (A-D)*, ed by George Arthur Buttrick et al., (Nashville: Abingdon Press, 1962), 375; Mobley, 'Dan,' 311.

YHWH.[94] Further, the context also implies that YHWH is testing their loyalty, faithfulness, and moral character as the covenant people.[95]

What does 'my people Israel' refer to and stand for in the context of Amos? As already mentioned above, for Wolff, the term 'Israel' in the use of 'my people Israel' in the vision of plumb-line, refers to the northern kingdom. If Amos had meant the unified people of Israel, Wolff thinks he would have called them, עַמִּי יִשְׂרָאֵל 'Israel, my people'.[96] Paul, like Wolff, suggests that 'my people Israel' refers to the north who are also a chosen people in covenant (3:2).[97] However, regarding the term 'my people Israel', Andersen and Freedman generally take this to refer to both kingdoms. In 7:8 'my people Israel' should be a historic and larger group, since the word 'Israel' is specified by 'my people'. The term 'Israel' here functions with the possessive form עַמִּי in a way identical to the construct forms of בֵּית, בְּנֵי.[98] Similarly, McConville suggests that the term 'my people Israel' designates historic Israel, brought out by YHWH from slavery in Egypt.[99] Again, in 7:15, 'my people Israel' seems at first to refer to the northern kingdom, with reference to Amos' coming to Bethel. But it is possible that the commission of Amos included not only northern Israel, but that he also had a message for Judah. In the first two visions, Amos might even have previously delivered the message in Judah, and the third vision embraced his visit to Bethel, the north.[100]

Interestingly, Andersen and Freedman further suggest that when Amaziah ordered Amos to go back to Judah and prophesy there, Amos does not contradict what he says. Amos' reply to Amaziah is restricted to neither Judah nor Israel. Amos was told by YHWH to go and prophesy to 'my people Israel' (7:15), both kingdoms.[101] In that case, his message was corresponding to those of his contemporary prophets, Hosea, Micah, and

---

94. Gary Smith, *Amos: A Commentary*, 235.
95. Ibid.
96. Wolff, *Prophets*, 301.
97. Paul, *Amos*, 236.
98. Andersen and Freedman, *Amos*, 115.
99. McConville, 'Jacob', 143.
100. Andersen and Freedman, *Amos*, 118-119.
101. Ibid.

Isaiah, who are also said to have prophesied to both kingdoms. Amos was summoned to speak the word of YHWH to his people Israel: 'certainly to the north, but also to the south.'[102] Again in 8:2 as in 7:8, 'my people Israel' refers to the whole people of Israel. In the visions of the plumb-line and the basket of summer fruit, both kingdoms are covered, but the immediate application is to that particular region of Israel, the northern kingdom, since Amos visits Bethel.[103]

Similarly, Smith also confirms the larger group of Israel in the vision of the plumb-line. Precisely in this vision, the term 'my people Israel' connotes the personal relationship between YHWH and Israel as a whole (Exod 3:10; 6:4-7; Deut 4:20; 7:6-10).[104] For Cripps, this phrase in 7:8, 15; 8:2 seems to prohibit a limitation and encourages a wider group. Amos declares that he has heard the call or commission to prophesy to the people of YHWH, all Israel.[105] Andersen and Freedman further argue that even the reference to 'my people' in 9:10 probably stands for the expression 'my people Israel', the whole group of Israel.[106] Again, in 9:14, 'my people Israel' refers to Israel as a whole and an eschatological context for the future restored Israel, similar to the historic Israel of the exodus from the land of Egypt.[107]

According to Andersen and Freedman, when the term 'Israel' stands alone, it refers to the northern kingdom, but the term 'my people Israel' regularly designates historic Israel. However, it is possible that Amos' use of 'Israel' rather refers to the whole people. If Amos' words are primarily addressed towards *Israel*, 'concerning Israel' (1:1), how does Amos understand this? In my view, Amos' use of 'my people Israel', in 7:15 suggests he has the whole people in mind. This concept, then, is closely related to the ancient covenantal promise of the whole land.

In dealing with the concept, argued by Andersen and Freedman, that when and if Amos speaks sometimes about the northern kingdom and

---

102. Ibid., 120.
103. Ibid., 121.
104. Gary Smith, *Amos: A Commentary*, 235.
105. Cripps, *Exegetical Commentary*, 236-237.
106. Andersen and Freedman, *Amos*, 125.
107. Ibid.

sometimes the historic Israel, McConville rightly asserts that Amos may be using the variety of names to consider the true nature of Israel by asking the question of their rhetorical and theological significance.[108] McConville suggests that the juxtaposition of the first four visions and the narrative of Amos' confrontation with Amaziah at Bethel links rhetorically to traditions about the true nature of Israel.[109]

As previously mentioned, McConville considers that Amos' use of 'Jacob' (7:1-3, 4-6), and the final three chapters, answers the question of the true nature of Israel as a historic people.[110] Andersen and Freedman suggest that 'Jacob' in the two visions designates the descendants of the patriarch and therefore it refers to historic Israel.[111] McConville further argues that Amos deconstructs the wrong understanding of Israel held by Amaziah who tried to equate the historic Israel with the north. 'My people Israel' is now understood differently from 'the house of Israel' which is 'the house of Jeroboam'. Then Amos' plea to YHWH, 'how can Jacob stand?' comes into the main focus. Amos of Tekoa, who came to Bethel, confronts his hearers with the destiny of Israel, both north and south.[112]

The reference to YHWH's roaring in Zion (1:2), arcs forward to the songs of the Jerusalem temple in the fourth vision (8:3). The concept of the temple in Amos 9 offers a vision of restoration which focuses on the whole people and land. In the fifth vision, YHWH appears in judgment in the reference to the 'altar' (9:1), which may have been based on the sanctuary at Bethel. However, the language and ideas in this context can equally apply to Jerusalem, since Bethel is not specified here. Amos 8 as a whole can be considered to relate to all the people of Israel in the whole land. In this way, Amos has directed his hearers toward the concepts of the people as the historic Israel and the land as the whole land.[113]

Again, as in 3:2, Amos' rhetoric moves clearly to the concept of the election of Israel in 9:7-8, indicating the idea of the ancient unified people.

---

108. McConville, 'Jacob', 136-137.
109. Ibid., 137-141.
110. Ibid., 132-133, 142.
111. Andersen and Freedman, *Amos*, 111, 114-115, 121-122.
112. McConville, 'Jacob', 147, 150.
113. Ibid., 148.

The thrust of 9:1-10 is the destruction of the historic Israel.[114] The promise to rebuild the fallen booth of David (9:11) and the connection with Edom (9:12) with its origins in the Jacob story traces back the concept of the election of Israel in one way or another. The symbol of the plentiful restored land (9:13) echoes that of Exodus (3:17; 33:3) and Deuteronomy (6:10-11; 8:7-10; 11:10-12). The term 'my people Israel' (9:14) is none other than the historic Israel and the whole land,[115] and it is the historic Israel that shall never again be uprooted from their land which YHWH gave them for their inheritance (9:15). Andersen and Freedman argue that 'my people Israel' in 9:14 refers to the historic Israel within an eschatological context for the future restoration of the land and people.[116] The prediction of the destruction of 'my people Israel' (7:8) seems to have its connection with the promise to restore 'my people Israel' from exile in 9:14. Following McConville, therefore, the central ambiguity of the terms 'Jacob', 'Israel', and 'Isaac' in Amos could be best understood to refer to historic Israel and the whole land. For Amos, Jacob and Isaac would have been associated with the patriarchal narratives, hence Amos' argument that his prophecy is to all Israel. Amos uses complex terminology for 'Israel' by exploring all types of Israel terminology – Jacob, Isaac, Israel, my people Israel, house of Israel, children of Israel – to refer to both kingdoms and so recall the traditions of a historic Israel.

3.1.4 Land in the Context of the First Three Visions

3.1.4.1 Land as Earth

The vision of fire in 7:4 depicts the destruction of the earth and it is so powerful that it consumes the great deep, [117]תְּהוֹם (Gen 1:2) and then devours the land. Possibly, the devouring by fire pictures the whole earth

---

114. Ibid., 148-149.
115. Ibid., 149.
116. Andersen and Freedman, *Amos*, 125.
117. Genesis 1:2 mentions תְּהוֹם and it appears in Gen 8:2; 49:25; Job 28:14; 38:16, 30; 41:24; Ps 42:8; 104:6; Prov 8:27, 28; Ezek 26:19; 31:4, 15; Jonah 2:6; Hab 3:10. The 'great deep' (תְּהוֹם רַבָּה) is found in Gen 7:11; Isa 51:10; Ps 36:7; 78:15 which lies under the earth as the foundation of springs and rivers. See Paul, *Amos*, 232; Mays, *Amos*, 131.

by referring to both the תְּהוֹם רַבָּה, 'great deep' (sea) and חֵלֶק, the land. Specifically, the 'great deep' (תְּהוֹם רַבָּה), which plays a role in many mythic cosmologies in the ancient Near East,[118] derives from the ancient Hebrew concept of cosmology (Gen 7:11).[119] This phrase refers to the cosmic deep,[120] or the primordial chaos present at the creation (Gen 1:1-2, 6-8), connected with the primeval ocean which is assumed to lie under the earth (Gen 7:11),[121] and to be the source of all springs and rivers (Gen 7:11; Ps 36:6; Isa 51:10). The תְּהוֹם is itself part of YHWH's creation (cf. Ps 104:6; Prov 8:27-28)[122] and typically appears in texts about creation, such as Pss 33:7; 104:6; Job 38:16; Prov 8:24-27.[123]

In the vision of the fire, the reference to the 'great deep' looks as if the fire devours the whole earth, and that this has cosmic significance.[124] According to Simundson, this judgment could apply to the land of Israel because the immediate threat to the people of Israel is in view.[125] Linville, however, claims that the whole world may be addressed here.[126] Taking the 'great deep' in connection with the phenomenal world, it would also be compatible with the drought of Amos 4:7-8.[127]

---

118. For discussion see Paul, *Amos*, 232; Linville, *Cosmic*, 137; Mays, *Amos*, 131; Gerhard von Rad, *Genesis: A Commentary*, 3rd rev. ed. (OTL; London: SCM Press, 1972), 49-50; Westermann, *Genesis 1-11*, 104-106. The deep (תְּהוֹם) in Hebrew could be linguistically similar to the word *Tiamat* in the Babylonian creation myth, but תְּהוֹם in the biblical creation story is probably not derived from it. See Kidner, *Genesis*, 45; Robert Davidson, *Genesis 1-11* (Cambridge: Cambridge University Press, 1973), 15-16; Victor P. Hamilton, *The Book of Genesis: Chapters 1-17* (Grand Rapids, Michigan: William B. Eerdmans Publishing Company, 1990), 110-111.
119. Linville, *Cosmic*, 137.
120. Paul, *Amos*, 231; Mays, *Amos*, 131; Von Rad, *Genesis: A Commentary*, 49.
121. See Gordon J. Wenham, *Genesis 1-15* (WBC; Nashville, Tennessee: Thomas Nelson Publishers, 1987), 16; Fyall, *Teaching Amos*, 116.
122. Wenham, *Genesis 1-15*, 16.
123. See Westermann, *Genesis 1-11*, 105; Alan Richardson, *Genesis 1-11: Introduction and Commentary* (London: SCM Press, 1959), 47-48.
124. See Simundson, *Hosea, Joel, Amos, Obadiah, Jonah, Micah*, 216; James R. Linville, 'Visions and Voices: Amos 7-9,' *Bib* 80, no. 01 (1999): 28; John D. W. Watts, *Vision and Prophecy in Amos*, expanded anniversary ed., (Macon, Georgia: Mercer University Press, 1997), 4.
125. Simundson, *Hosea, Joel, Amos, Obadiah, Jonah, Micah*, 216.
126. Linville, *Cosmic*, 136.
127. Andersen and Freedman, *Amos*, 747.

As in Amos' vision the cosmic fire devours the great deep and the land, so in Deuteronomy 32:22, fire consumes even the foundation of the mountains. The description of the fire devouring the 'great deep' in Amos 7:4 fits closely the imagery in Deuteronomy 32:22 because great deep and land are devoured by fire in both texts.[128] The ability to be fruitful in the first vision is temporarily delayed, but in the second there is an advance, because the fundamental resource of the fruitful deep (תְּהוֹם רַבָּה) is destroyed.[129] Although the word תְּהוֹם can suggest blessing and the fertility of the land (Gen 49:25; Deut 8:7; 33:15; Ezek 31:4; Ps 78:15; Prov 8:28),[130] it now endangers human life and the natural order in Amos. The burning up of the land (Amos 7:4) would also be similar to the drought of Amos 4:7-8, and 'great deep' hereby is connected with the phenomenal world, the earth. By these means one can assume that when Amos mentions the devouring of the 'great deep' he seems to have in mind the whole earth.

3.1.4.2 Land as Territory

Andersen and Freedman observe that a comparison of fire in Amos 7:4 with Deuteronomy 32:22 is helpful to understand the concept of land here. They suggest that the 'great deep' in Amos seems similar to 'lowest sheol' (שְׁאוֹל תַּחְתִּית) in Deuteronomy. It is likely that in that case the 'earth' (Deut 32:22) has a mythological meaning.[131] However, although it is persuasive to equate 'the earth and its increase' (Deut 32:22) with חֵלֶק (Amos 7:4), the former must have the ordinary meaning of 'earth', (i.e. fruitful earth) since the word יְבוּל 'increase' connotes the crops.[132] Amos' use of חֵלֶק is different however.

The term חֵלֶק normally refers to the portion of the land of Israel.[133] The devouring of the חֵלֶק is a threat to Jacob, YHWH's people, or his por-

---

128. Stuart, *Hosea-Jonah*, 372.
129. Auld, *Amos*, 17.
130. Westermann, *Genesis 1-11*, 105.
131. Andersen and Freedman, *Amos*, 748.
132. Ibid.
133. See Mays, *Amos*, 131; Linville, *Cosmic*, 137; Smith and Page, *Amos, Obadiah, Jonah*, 131; Leslie C. Allen, *The Books of Joel, Obadiah, Jonah, and Micah* (NICOT; Grand Rapids, Michigan: William B. Eerdmans Publishing Company, 1976), 290-291. Mignon

tion (Deut 32:9). Land is held as the gift of YHWH.[134] However, Amos believes that the land as gift is also distributed to the nations, including Aramaeans and Philistines (9:7).[135] Further, YHWH shows his concern to other nations and puts them under his control (9:7; chs 1-2), and thus YHWH's חֵלֶק may be said to include all other nations. This is why there is no geographical limit to the disasters mentioned in 4:7-11. Therefore, the disasters could be universal, not only local.[136] While חֵלֶק typically refers to a share or portion of land in Israel (Deut 4:19; 2 Chr 23:18; 28:21; Josh 13:7; 14:4; 15:13; 17:2; 19:9),[137] yet in Amos other nations are also in view, and may give it a broader meaning, in which חֵלֶק makes a parallel with תְּהוֹם.

3.1.4.3 Land as Inheritance

The term חֵלֶק usually refers to the 'patrimonial land',[138] the inheritance received from YHWH. The LXX adds κυρίου, and thus it reads the 'Lord's portion'[139] or 'the Lord's field'.[140] The concept of חֵלֶק in Israelite history means the portion from the father's house or the share or inheritance of the father's estate (Gen 31:14). Gordon Wenham asserts that, here, the expression 'share or inheritance' refers to the share of the land as inheritance for every family in Israel.[141] On the other hand, it can be said that the land, that is a promised land of YHWH, is an inheritance for the people of Israel as a whole.

R. Jacobs, *The Conceptual Coherence of the Book of Micah* (Sheffield: Sheffield Academic Press, 2001), 113; Niehaus, 'Amos,' 454.

134. Andersen and Freedman, *Amos*, 748-749.
135. Ibid., 749.
136. Ibid.
137. See Snyman, 'Eretz and Adama', 142.
138. Andersen and Freedman, *Amos*, 747.
139. See Wolff, *Prophets*, 293.
140. See Gary Smith, *Amos: A Commentary*, 221; Stuart, *Hosea-Jonah*, 370-371.
141. Gordon J. Wenham, *Genesis 16-50* (WBC; Dallas, Texas: Word Books, 1994), 272. The Levites have no share or inheritance among their brothers, but YHWH himself is their inheritance (Num. 18:20; Deut. 10:9; 12:12; 18:1). Yet they were shared by other tribes of Israel so that they had their own fields, cities, and pasture land for their livestock (Num 35:1-8; Josh 14:4; 21:1-42; 1 Chr 6:54-72). See J. G. McConville, *Deuteronomy* (AOTC; Downers Grove, Illinois: Inter-Varsity Press, 2002), 297; Wenham, *Genesis 16-50*, 272; Duane L. Christensen, *Deuteronomy*, 395-396.

It is also possible, as suggested by some scholars, that the term חֵלֶק here refers to the people themselves (Deut 32:9).[142] Deuteronomy 32:9 identifies Jacob, 'his people', as YHWH's portion (חֵלֶק). In other texts, Israel is also called the people of YHWH's inheritance (נַחֲלָה) (Deut 4:19-20; Jer 10:16; 51:19).[143] Eugene Merrill makes clear that the description of the people of Israel as the Lord's portion and his special allotted inheritance (Deut 32:9) is to emphasize the centrality of Israel in the redemptive purpose of YHWH.[144] YHWH elected Israel as his own inheritance and possession. Therefore, they are described as 'my treasured possession' out of all the people (Exod 19:5; cf. Deut 7:6; 14:2, 21).[145]

As YHWH's portion is Jacob, 'his people' (Deut 32:9), Jacob's portion is YHWH as well (Jer 10:16; 51:19).[146] The 'portion of Jacob' (חֵלֶק יַעֲקֹב) indicates that YHWH has a special responsibility for Jacob, the people of Israel.[147] The expression is thus a metaphor for YHWH who reveals himself to a particular people, Israel, and makes a relationship with them.[148] Thus, while the term חֵלֶק refers most naturally to the land of Israel, yet, because the term can also refer to the people themselves, the present text may also suggest the destruction of the people. Since the language belongs to the context of the election of Israel, the point is particularly powerful.

Further, the word חֵלֶק is also echoed in Amos' prophecy about the division of Amaziah's land (תְּחֻלָּק) in the following narrative account in 7:17. Therefore, Amos' depiction of the cosmic fire seems to surpass his later prophecy about the fortunes of Amaziah, the priest of Bethel.[149] The theme

---

142. See Mays, *Amos*, 131; Smith and Page, *Amos, Obadiah, Jonah*, 131; Coggins, Joel and Amos, 139.
143. Moshe Weinfeld, *Deuteronomy 1-11: A New Translation with Introduction and Commentary* (AB; London: Doubleday, 1991), 206.
144. Eugene H. Merrill, *Deuteronomy* (NAC; Nashville, Tennessee: Boradman & Holman Publishers, 1994), 413.
145. Merrill, *Deuteronomy*, 413.
146. William McKane, *A Critical and Exegetical Commentary on Jeremiah: Introduction and Commentary on Jeremiah 1-25*, vol. 1 (Edinburgh: T & T Clark, 1986), 228.
147. See McKane, *Jeremiah*, 228; J. A. Thompson, *The Book of Jeremiah* (Grand Rapids, Michigan: William B. Eerdmans Publishing Company, 1980), 331-332.
148. Terence E. Fretheim, *Jeremiah* (SHBC; Macon: Smith & Helwys, 2002), 171-172.
149. Linville, *Cosmic*, 137.

of land in the narrative section (7:10-17) will be dealt with in more detail later.

3.1.4.4 The Destruction of the Land

The application of the vision of the 'plumb line' is described in 7:9. YHWH is measuring his people, and the result will be the destruction of the high places, sanctuaries, and the downfall of the house of Jeroboam. There are two areas of destruction at a national level: the cultic and royal institutions.[150] YHWH rejects both the religious and political institutions represented by high places and sanctuaries, and the royal house of Jeroboam.[151]

3.1.4.4a The High Places and Sanctuaries

Amos uses the term בָּמוֹת (high places),[152] to refer to the sanctuaries which are located on the top of the hills in the land of Israel.[153] The high places of Isaac could cover places such as Bethel (3:14; 4:4; 5:5, 6; 7:13),[154]

---

150. Stuart, *Hosea-Jonah*, 373; Smith, *Amos: A Commentary*, 235.

151. Gary Smith, *Amos: A Commentary*, 235-236. Also see Robert Coote, 'Bethel,' in *NIDB*, ed. Katherine Doob Sakenfeld et al., vol. 1 (Nashville, Tennessee: Abingdon Press, 2006), 441.

152. The high places (בָּמוֹת) are open-air sanctuaries located on the top of the hills which are decorated with incense altars, small horned altars, wooden post or carved stone pillars, and tree groves. See Hammershaimb, *Book of Amos*, 112; Cole, 'Visions', 61.

153. Soggin, *The Prophet*, 117.

154. For discussion of Bethel, see Robert T. Anderson, 'Bethel,' in *EDB*, ed. David Noel Freedman (Grand Rapids, Michigan: William B. Eerdmans, 2000), 170; Coote, 'Bethel', 438-441; Peter J. M. Southwell, 'Bethel,' in *NIDOTTE*, ed. Willem A. VanGemeren et al., vol. 4 (Carlisle: Paternoster Press, 1996), 440-441.

Gilgal (4:4; 5:5),[155] Samaria (3:9, 12; 4:1; 6:1; 8:14),[156] Dan (8:14),[157] and Beersheba (5:5; 8:14).[158] The reference to the pairing of Dan and Beersheba (Judg 20:1; 1 Sam 3:20; 2 Sam 3:10; 17:11; 24:22) points to the whole land of Israel.[159] I have already argued that the 'high places of Isaac' (7:9) is linked to 'house of Isaac' (7:16), which refers to both kingdoms, the whole people of Israel. Therefore, the phrase 'the high places of Isaac' probably suggests that the full extent of the historical land is in view.

Amos condemns these sanctuaries of Bethel, Gilgal, Samaria, Dan, and Beersheba due to the corrupt nature of the cult which has became empty

---

155. The Israelites encamped at Gilgal and set up stones (Josh 4:20), underwent circumcision there (Josh 5:2-9), and first kept Passover (Josh 5:10). It became the first central sanctuary (Josh 4:19-5:15). Samuel acted as a judge there (1 Sam 7:16; 10:8). Saul was affirmed as king there (1 Sam 11:15). The Prophets Hosea and Amos condemned the worship there (Hos 4:15; 9:15; 12:11; Amos 4:4; 5:5). See Roger Good, 'Gilgal,' in *EDB*, ed. David Noel Freedman (Grand Rapids, Michigan: William B. Eerdmans, 2000), 504-505; J. Muilenburg, 'Gilgal,' in *IDB (E-J)*, ed. George Arthur Buttrick et al. (Nashville: Abingdon Press, 1962), 398-399; Mark F. Rooker, 'Gilgal,' in *NIDOTTE*, ed. Willem A. VanGemeren et al., vol. 4 (Carlisle: Paternoster Press, 1996), 683-685; William H. Brownlee, 'Gilgal,' in *The International Standard Bible Encyclopaedia Volume Two (E-J)*, ed. Geoffrey W. Bromiley et al., rev. ed. (Grand Rapids, Michigan: Williams B. Eerdmans Publishing Company, 1982), 470-472.

156. Samaria, named by Omri, king of Israel (1 Kgs 16:24). From the start, people followed other religions (1 Kgs 16:32) and the eighth century prophets condemned their sin (Isa 7:9; 9:8-9; Mic 1:5; Amos 3:12; 6:1, 6). See Ron E. Tappy, 'Samaria,' in *EDB*, ed. David Noel Freedman (Grand Rapids, Michigan: William B. Eerdmans, 2000), 1155-1159; Gus W. Van Beek, 'Samaria,' in *IDB (R-Z)*, ed. George Arthur Buttrick et al. (Nashville: Abingdon Press, 1962), 182-188; Daniel N. Pienaar, 'Samaria,' in *NIDOTTE*, ed. Willem A. VanGemeren et al., vol. 4 (Carlisle: Paternoster Press, 1996), 1163-1165; Andrianus Van Selms, 'Samaria,' in *The International Standard Bible Encyclopaedia Volume Four (Q-Z)*, ed. Geoffrey W. Bromiley et al., rev. ed. (Grand Rapids, Michigan: Williams B. Eerdmans Publishing Company, 1988), 295-298.

157. When the kingdom was divided, Jeroboam I tried to keep the loyalty of the northern tribes by giving them two golden calves to worship: one was at Dan and another at Bethel (1 Kgs 12:25-30). Amos condemned these shrines (Amos 8:14). See Gus W. Van Beek, 'Dan,' in *IDB (A-D)*, ed. George Arthur Buttrick et al. (Nashville: Abingdon Press, 1962), 758-760; Mobley, 'Dan,' 310-311; Judith M. Hadley, 'Dan,' in *NIDOTTE*, ed. Willem A. VanGemeren et al., vol. 4 (Carlisle: Paternoster Press, 1996), 497-498.

158. Beersheba means 'well of an oath' (Gen 21:14, 30-32) or 'well of seven,' (Gen 26:23-33). Abraham offered up Isaac nearby (Gen 22:1-19). Samuel's sons are appointed as judges there (1 Sam 8:2). Josiah destroyed its high places (2 Kgs 23:8). See Bruce C. Cresson, 'Beersheba,' in *EDB*, ed. David Noel Freedman (Grand Rapids, Michigan: William B. Eerdmans, 2000), 161; Simon Cohen, 'Beersheba,' 375-376; Sharon Pace, 'Beersheba,' in *NIDB*, ed. Katherine Doob Sakenfeld et al., vol. 1 (Nashville, Tennessee: Abingdon Press, 2006), 419.

159. McConville, 'Jacob', 147-148.

ritual.[160] For instance, as Philip Davies asserts, Amos 5:26 and 8:14 probably suggest a hint of idolatrous practices in the sanctuaries at Beersheba, Dan, and Samaria, in which Amos envisages their destruction.[161] Davies further suggests that the statements 'I hate, I despise your religious feasts… Did you bring to me sacrifices and offerings for forty years in the desert, O house of Israel?' (5:21-25) seem to relate to all sacrifices in the whole land of Israel, including sacrifices at Jerusalem.[162] Such a reference is understandable in terms of the larger scope of the whole land of Israel. In the giving of offerings and sacrifices to YHWH, the people of Israel claim 'YHWH is with us' (5:14), and thus consider that they will never lose this land which YHWH had once given them as a gift.[163] However, YHWH rejects their religious institutions and brings about the destruction of the high places and sanctuaries of Israel. As McConville suggests, 'the high places of Isaac' and 'sanctuaries of Israel' together designate both south and north, the whole land.[164] Their many offerings and sacrifices at 'the high places of Isaac' and 'sanctuaries of Israel' show a concern to celebrate the good things and the benefits of the land which YHWH has given them, yet they fail to understand the most important thing about possessing and inhabiting the land in the way of practising *justice* in it.

3.1.4.4b House of Jeroboam

Although the 'high places of Isaac' and 'sanctuaries of Israel' together refer to both northern and southern kingdoms, the triad in 7:9 points to the destruction of the royal house of Jeroboam, the northern kingdom. After the superscription (1:1), Jeroboam is mentioned only here and in the confrontation with Amaziah.[165] The third announcement of judgment includes the royal house of Jeroboam which represents the nation of northern Israel.

---

160. See Philip R. Davies, 'Amos, Man and Book,' in *Israel's Prophets and Israel's Past: Essays on the Relationship of Prophetic Texts and Israelite History in Honor of John H. Hayes*, ed. Brad E. Kelle and Megan Bishop Moore (London: T & T Clark, 2006), 120; Hammershaimb, *Book of Amos*, 113; Coote, 'Bethel,' 441.
161. Philip Davies, 'Amos, Man and Book,' 121.
162. Ibid., 120.
163. Koch, *Prophets*, 1: 52, 55.
164. McConville, 'Jacob', 144.
165. Ibid. Also see Ronald E. Clements, 'Politics,' 58.

The sins of Bethel (Amos 3:14; 4:4-5; 5:5-7, 21-24) could be taken as the grounds for bringing destruction upon Jeroboam.[166]

In the specific description of the house of Jeroboam (7:9) and Amaziah's reference to Jeroboam (7:10), Israel is identified as the northern kingdom. Amaziah's accusation of a conspiracy against the king by Amos is placed בְּקֶרֶב בֵּית יִשְׂרָאֵל 'in the midst of the house of Israel'. In this expression, Amaziah echoes the expression בְּקֶרֶב עַמִּי יִשְׂרָאֵל 'in the midst of my people Israel' in the second vision (7:8).[167] In these categories of the people and house of Israel, there are different formulations. First, the election of Israel identified by 'my people' is endangered. Second, the state of the nation represented by 'the house of Israel' is put in jeopardy.[168]

McConville considers that, as Amaziah represents the cult at Bethel in the north, he believes that all his language must be heard accordingly. When Amaziah says 'the land' (האדמה) in his confrontation with Amos (7:8, 11b), Amos retraces and echoes the language of the Deuteronomic understanding of the land (both האדמה and הארץ) which is the gift of YHWH to his chosen people Israel.[169] But in Amaziah's view, it is the land of the state of Israel, which is distinguished by the reference to the land of Judah (אֶרֶץ יְהוּדָה) in 7:12. According to the language of Amaziah, the northern state seems to be the inheritor to the covenant, and so YHWH's chosen people.[170] In Amaziah's view, Amos 7:9 therefore deals with the fate of Israel, the northern kingdom, illustrating the destruction of the sanctuaries and the high places, and bringing them into exile from their land.[171] However, Amos, against the view of Amaziah, echoes covenantal language of land and people, 'go, prophesy to my people Israel' (7:15).

---

166. Gary Smith, *Amos: A Commentary*, 236.
167. McConville, 'Jacob', 145.
168. Jeremias, *Book of Amos*, 138.
169. McConville, 'Jacob', 145-146. For more discussion of the gift of land see Miller, 'The Gift of God' 451-465; E. Davies, 'Land: Its Rights and Privileges,' 350-351.
170. McConville, 'Jacob', 145-146.
171. David Noel Freedman, 'Confrontations in the Book of Amos,' *PSB* 11, no. 03 (1990): 248.

3.1.5 Conclusion

In the first three visions, devastation is brought on the land by the plague of locusts and cosmic fire, and succeeded by the complete destruction of the high places, sanctuaries, and the royal house of Jeroboam. In the first vision, the timing of the locust plague affected possibly the earlier and certainly the latter growths, which endangers the people and the whole land of Israel. In the second vision, the fire (אֵשׁ) is depicted as devouring both the great deep and the land. The summary of judgment which follows the third vision pictures the destruction of the high places, sanctuaries, and the royal house of Israel. The term אֲנָךְ reveals the true state of the people Israel: the corrupt nature of the high places, the sanctuaries, and the royal house (7:9).

The destruction includes both religious and political institutions. Statements of such a judgment are to be found in the earlier oracles of Amos (3:11, 13-15; 6:8, 11, 14). The consequences are depicted as exile (4:2; 5:5, 27; 6:7; 7:17). Amos believes that the judgment of YHWH is based on the measuring of their sin, especially the corruption of the royal house and sanctuaries specifically at Bethel and other places in the land of Israel, both north and south. The cultic places and their land will become desolate. These places are rather connected with the gift of the land and therefore people are expected to worship YHWH truly in the land (Amos 5:24; cf. Amos 4:4-5; 5:5-6).

The term 'my people Israel' in the setting up of the plumb-line (7:8) may have the same connotation with 'my people Israel' in Amos' commission by YHWH to go and prophesy (7:15). Amos thus uses 'Israel' as historic Israel, although it may refer to the northern kingdom in some contexts because of its immediate specific application. Theologically, it could be understood that 'Israel' in the first three visions, as in Amos as a whole, applies to the historic Israel, and the idea of land in terms of the gift of YHWH, that is, as in the Deuteronomic understanding of the land.

The visions show powerfully that Israel cannot take its possession of the land just for granted. As we have seen, there is a progression in the visions. The first two visions show YHWH's longsuffering and the successful intercessions of the prophet. However, in the succession of the visions, judgment becomes more certain, and the language suggests a picture of the destruction of the land and the people as a whole. The visions illustrate Amos' use of poetic language. The images of locust and fire are closely related to the topic of land. In addition, Amos shows that land and institutions cannot be separated. Amos' threat to the land is inseparable from his critique of sanctuaries and the royal house.

3.2 The Land in Amos 7:10-17

3.2.1 Introduction

This section aims to examine the meaning of land in the narrative account of the conflict of Amaziah with Amos in 7:10-17. Amaziah opposes Amos in his report to Jeroboam, 'the land cannot bear all his words'. The 'land' here is apparently used in reference to the condition of the king, and the people, as well as the place itself. What then is wrong with Amos' message in the perspective of Amaziah? Or rather does Amaziah's charge against Amos itself contradict the word of YHWH by Amos? In bringing his message of judgment, Amos stands himself as a representative on behalf of the ordinary people by pointing to his profession as a shepherd and farmer (7:14). He also confirms that his prophetic role comes directly by divine commission (7:15) to prophesy inclusively to the covenant people, עַמִּי יִשְׂרָאֵל 'my people Israel'. The present survey tries to show how the narrative has been inserted between the third and fourth visions and connected by means of verbal links with both. The study then will show how the land is treated in relation to 'house of Israel', Bethel, the terms חֹזֶה and נָבִיא, and the judgment of exile.

3.2.2 The Insertion between the Third and Fourth Visions

Robert Gordis called attention to the fact that since Amos' main focus is to prophesy against northern Israel, Amos passes reasonably lightly over the sins of Judah and its religious and social transgressions (2:4-5; 6:1).[172] His

---

172. Robert Gordis, 'The Composition and Structure of Amos,' *HTR* 33, no. 04 (October 1940): 249.

encounter with Amaziah (7:10-17) consists of a dispute between the two,[173] in which Amaziah sent a message to Jeroboam, king of Israel, consisting of an indictment against Amos along with a quotation of the words of the prophet himself (7:10-11). To Jeroboam, Amaziah accuses Amos of 'conspiracy', and when he addresses Amos, Amaziah speaks of the authority of the king (7:12-13). Then Amaziah commands Amos to leave the country and not to prophesy at Bethel any more. However, Amos then mentions his profession and confirms that his commission came only from YHWH who sent him to prophesy to the covenant people, identified as 'my people Israel' (7:14-15), and followed with a word of judgment on the land, and of exile for the people (7:16-17).

The narrative of the confrontation with Amaziah (7:10-17)[174] occurs between the third (7:7-9) and the fourth visions (8:1-3). The first four visions follow a certain formula. In the narrative, however, the report shifts from the first person to the third person. Therefore, some suppose that Amos 7:10-17 comes from someone other than Amos,[175] or is the work of an editor,[176] and so treat it separately.[177] However, others maintain it to be from Amos himself, although written in the third person[178] and argue that the narrative itself is connected in many ways to its context.[179] The narrative is also linked thematically with the visions.[180]

---

173. Gene M. Tucker, 'Prophetic Authenticity,' *Int* 27, no. 04 (October 1973): 427-428.

174. This narrative (7:10-17) is assumed as biographical. See Stuart, *Hosea-Jonah*, 374; Polley, *Davidic Empire*, 10-11; Hayes, *Amos*, 239; Wood, *Song*, 72-73; Mays, *Amos*, 123; Andersen and Freedman, *Amos*, 763. Gary Smith, *Amos: A Commentary*, 239.

175. For instance, see Wolff, *Prophets*, 295; Stuart, *Hosea-Jonah*, 369-370; Sweeney, *The Twelve Prophets*, 1: 256.

176. For instance, Hayes, *Amos*, 231; Hubbard, *Joel and Amos*, 211; Andersen and Freedman, *A New Translation with Introduction and Commentary*, 763-765.

177. See, for example, Soggin, *The Prophet*, 125-133; Hayes, *Amos*, 229-240.

178. Among those are, for instance, Hammershaimb, *Book of Amos*, 114; Gary Smith, *Amos: A Commentary*, 228-229; Thomas J. Finley, *Joel, Amos, Obadiah: An Exegetical Commentary* (Chicago: Moody Press, 1990), 290; Stanley N. Rosenbaum, *Amos of Israel: A New Interpretation* (Macon, Georgia: Mercer University Press, 1990), 80-83; Watts, *Vision*, 31-35; Gordis, 'Structure of Amos,' 239-251.

179. Jeremias, *Book of Amos*, 137.

180. See Doan and Giles, *Prophets, Performance, and Power*, 151; Paul R. Noble, 'The Literary Structure of Amos: A Thematic Analysis,' *JBL* 114, no. 02 (Summer 1995): 223; Paul R. Noble, 'Amos and Amaziah in Context: Synchronic and Diachronic Approaches to Amos 7-8,' *CBQ* 60, no. 03 (July 1998): 435; Hayes, *Amos*, 231.

The primary question concerns its present location and the function of the narrative. Several proposals have been made to explain both the location of the narrative and its unity. Presenting Amos as a prophet like Moses, Meindert Dijkstra believes that Amos is pictured as Moses interceding for the people for forgiveness (Amos 7:2, 5 and Exod 34:9; Num 14:19-20).[181] Dijkstra asserts that the prophetic personality of Amos stood in the tradition of Moses who has no relation to a particular group (Levites), or religious professionals (prophecy, priesthood).[182] Dijkstra argues that the insertion of this narrative section in the visionary reports is intentional in order to show Amos in a new type of prophetic role, like that of Moses. Both are prophets not by profession but by virtue of special calling and commission by YHWH.[183] It is this divine commission in 7:15, which is not by virtue of office, that serves as a key to the interpretation of the narrative (7:10-17).[184] This analogy with Moses may be helpful in portraying the land as a gift of YHWH to historic Israel, because of the call of YHWH to Moses to deliver his covenant people from bondage in Egypt and to bring them into the Promised Land (Exod 3:1-22). Amos also refers to this exodus event (2:10; 3:1; 9:7).

Amos 7:10-17 tells of a conflict which is a result of the rejection of the visions.[185] The thematic development of the third vision (7:9) leads into the narrative.[186] It is possible that the narrative and collection of visions could have been created together, and the narrative is inserted after the third vision because of the connection between 7:9 and 7:11 on the basis of the

---

181. Meindert Dijkstra, '"I am neither a prophet nor a prophet's pupil": Amos 7:9-17 as the Presentation of a Prophet like Moses,' in *The Elusive Prophet: The Prophet as a Historical Person, Literary Character and Anonymous Artist*, ed. Johannes C. de Moor (Leiden: Boston, 2001), 123.
182. Dijkstra, 'Presentation of a Prophet', 122.
183. Ibid., 122, 127.
184. Tucker, 'Prophetic Authenticity,' 428, 433.
185. Gary Smith, *Amos: A Commentary*, 8.
186. Noble, 'Literary Structure', 223; *idem*, 'Amos and Amaziah', 435; Hayes, *Amos*, 231.

catchwords 'Jeroboam'[187] and 'sword'.[188] The third vision concludes with YHWH's announcement that he will rise against 'the house of Jeroboam'[189] with the 'sword' (7:9) while the narrative starts with Amaziah who reports that Amos said 'Jeroboam shall die by the sword' (7:10).[190] Verse 9 serves as a transition, with specific interconnections: the expression 'the high places of Isaac' makes a link with 'house of Isaac' (7:16); the 'sanctuaries of Israel' with 'the king's sanctuary' (7:13); and the 'house of Jeroboam' which will be destroyed by 'the sword' with 'Jeroboam shall die by the sword' (7:11a).[191] The effect of these connections is to fill out the significance of 7:9.[192] The insertion of Amos 7:10-17 in to its present position depicts events which occur at the time and so enhance the conflict.[193]

Further, in his analysis of the rhetorical strategy of the book of Amos, Karl Möller argues that the arrangement of Amos is best described in rhetorical terms. Amos aims to persuade his hearers to learn from their failure and respond properly to his message and thus Amos brings up the traditional beliefs of the people. For example, Amos uses the Exodus tradition

---

187. See Mays, *Amos*, 123; Paul, *Amos*, 238; Hammershaimb, *Book of Amos*, 114; Noble, 'Amos and Amaziah', 424; Polley, *Davidic Empire*, 156; Blenkinsopp, *History of Prophecy*, 91.

188. See Freedman, 'Confrontations,' 240-241; Noble, 'Amos and Amaziah', 424; Wood, *Song*, 73; Polley, *Davidic Empire*, 156; Stuart, *Hosea-Jonah*, 370; Paul, *Amos*, 238.

189. The 'house of Jeroboam' refers to Jeroboam II, not Jeroboam I who founded the high places and the northern kingdom. See Hammershaimb, *Book of Amos*, 114; Paul, *Amos*, 237; Gary Smith, *Amos: A Commentary*, 236; Stuart, *Hosea-Jonah*, 370, 375; Blenkinsopp, *History of Prophecy* 90; Soggin, *The Prophet*, 117; Coggins, *Joel and Amos*, 141; Smith and Page, *Amos, Obadiah, Jonah*, 134. For the 'house of Jeroboam' (7:9) in conjunction with 1 Kings 13 implying Jeroboam I, see Philip Davies, 'Amos, Man and Book,' 123-124. However, some scholars have doubted the connection of the 'house of Jeroboam' with 1 Kings 13. See Watts, *Vision*, 66; Åke Viberg, 'Amos 7:14: A Case of Subtle Irony,' *TB* 47, no. 01 (1996): 95-96; Williamson, 'Plumb-Line', 474-475; Peter R. Ackroyd, 'A Judgment Narrative between Kings and Chronicles? An Approach to Amos 7:9-17,' in *Canon and Authority: Essays in Old Testament Religion and Theology*, eds. George W. Coats and Burke O. Long (Philadelphia: Fortress Press, 1977), 71-87.

190. Mays, *Amos*, 123.

191. See Wolff, *Prophets*, 295; Jeremias, *Book of Amos*, 137, 142; Freedman, 'Confrontations,' 244, 248; Jörg Jeremias, 'The Interrelationship between Amos and Hosea,' in *Forming Prophetic Literature: Essays on Isaiah and the Twelve in Honor of John D. W. Watts*, ed. James W. Watts and Paul R. House (JSOTSS 235; Sheffield: Sheffield Academic Press, 1996), 180.

192. Clements, 'Politics,' 54-55.

193. See Rosenbaum, *Amos of Israel*, 81; Clements, 'Politics,' 50, 54, 62-64.

(2:10; 3:2; 9:7) and the Day of YHWH (5:18-20).[194] In the confrontation with Amaziah at Bethel (7:10-17), Möller suggests that the narrative, a debate between Amos and the audience, is strategically placed in the development of the book's argument. Specifically, verse 9 shows that YHWH is right to bring punishment upon Israel and the house of Jeroboam, and therefore לֹא־אוֹסִיף עוֹד עֲבוֹר לוֹ 'I will never again pass them by' (7:8; also 8:2) is YHWH's declaration of punishment.[195]

Amos 7:9 therefore functions rhetorically in the interpretation of the book as a debate between Amos and his audience. In this narrative (7:10-17), Amaziah represents the audience and his refusal to hear Amos thus represents the reaction of the audience.[196] Möller then concludes that 'throughout the book the audience's reactions to the prophet's ministry are mostly (though not always) implied, in 7:10-17 the reaction by one of its (more influential) members is reported in some detail.'[197] Möller's point about Amaziah as representing the audience in this narrative is significant for interpreting Amaziah's understanding of 'Israel' and 'land' in 7:10. The catchword links in 7:9 raise the question about how 'Israel' is to be interpreted. Amos 7:9 prepares rhetorically for the narrative in 7:10-17 specifically what is meant by 'Israel' and the extent of land. The rhetorical progression in 7:10-17 deals with this question of the interpretation of 'Israel' and suggests different interpretations of the 'land' between Amaziah and Amos. Amaziah challenges Amos within his personal perspective of 'Israel' and 'land', that is, the northern kingdom, while Amos understands Israel as the historic Israel, and thus the whole land.

In addition to 7:9, which serves as a transition on the basis of the catchwords, as we have seen, the narrative is linked in other ways with the third vision: 'in the midst of my people Israel' (7:8b) with 'in the midst of the house of Israel' (7:10b), and 'I will never again' (7:8b) with 'you never again' (7:13a). The narrative is also connected with the succeeding fourth vision: 'to my people Israel' (7:15b) finds an echo in 'to my people Israel' (8:2b);

---

194. Karl Möller, '"Hear This Word Against You:" A Fresh Look at the Arrangement and the Rhetorical Strategy of the Book of Amos,' *VT* 50, no. 04 (2000): 510-511.
195. Ibid., 515-516.
196. Ibid., 515-517.
197. Ibid., 517.

and 'never again prophesy' (7:13a) in 'I will never again pass by' (8:2b).[198] Watts has argued that the narrative's location after the third vision suggests that the announcement of the end of Israel in the fourth vision (8:2) came after the conflict of Amaziah with Amos at Bethel.[199] YHWH reaffirms that the promise of punishment on the temple (מִקְדָּשׁ) envisaged in the third vision (7:9) will certainly happen in the destruction of the temple (הֵיכָל) in the fourth vision (8:3), which could be a response to Amaziah's allusion to the temple (בַּיִת) in 7:13.[200]

As stated above, several proposals show the link between the narrative and the preceding and succeeding visions, and that the prophecy of the destruction of sanctuaries and monarchy in 7:9 was correspondingly fulfilled in the following events. The narrative's prophecies of the punishment of the land and the monarchy were the result of the earlier oracle. The prophecy to 'my people Israel' (7:15) also imply to the end of 'my people Israel' (8:2). Therefore, the insertion of the narrative between the third and fourth visions shows that it has strong verbal links and a flow of thematic correlations with both the immediately connected visions.

3.2.3 The House of Israel and the Concept of Land

I have argued that Amos has in his mind the picture of historic Israel and the full extent of the land in his prophecy against Bethel and the northern kingdom. He addresses 'Israel' using all types of terminology – Jacob, Isaac, my people Israel, house of Israel, sons of Israel – to refer to both kingdoms. Again, 'Israel' with the construct form of בֵּית appears in 5:1, 3, 4, 25; 6:1, 14; 7:10; 9:9. Therefore, Amos focuses attention on all of Israel who will go into exile away from their land (7:17; cf. 4:2-3; 5:5, 26-27; 6:7; 9:4), the Promised Land that YHWH has given them (cf. 9:15).

As previously stated, Wolff considered that in Amos 'Israel' always refers to the northern kingdom. So too 'house of Israel' in 5:1, 3, 4, 25; 6:1, 14; 7:10; 9:9 refers to the northern kingdom, with its political (5:1, 3; 6:1) and cultic (5:4, 25; cf. 7:13) institutions, as one among the nations (6:14; 9:9).

---

198. Jeremias, *Book of Amos*, 137.
199. Watts, *Vision*, 66.
200. Stuart, *Hosea-Jonah*, 370.

He thinks too that in the confrontation with Amaziah, the term בֵּית יִשְׂרָאֵל (house of Israel) refers to the northern kingdom because the immediate context is connected with the fate of the 'king of Israel' (7:10; cf. 7:9, 11 and 1:1) and thus the northern kingdom.[201] Jeremias has followed Wolff's understanding of 'house of Israel'. This term is prominent in this sense in chapters 5 and 6 (5:1, 3, 4, 25; 6:1, 14).[202]

The 'house of Israel' can refer to the people as much as to the land. Keita suggests that 'the concept "state" can refer as much to collective as to territorial entities. However, even then, land is always in view. Thus, even the thesis that "the house of Israel" points to the state does not lessen the difficulty of understanding the content of the phrase in relation to the land.'[203] People and land are hard to separate. Andersen and Freedman observe that in 5:1, 3, 25, the term 'house of Israel' is identified with all of Israel of the Exodus. In 5:4-5, it apparently covers the two kingdoms; referring to the people who worship at the shrines of northern and southern Israel.[204] In 6:1, it refers to the double kingdom for it mentions both Zion and Samaria. The 'house of Israel' in 6:14 echoes 6:1, which refers to the double kingdom.[205] Perhaps 6:14 reflects the context which focuses attention on all of Israel with the references to Zion and Samaria and 'people of Israel' (6:1), 'two kingdoms' (6:2), and 'Jacob' (6:8).

Also in 9:9, the expression 'house of Israel' refers to both kingdoms. Perhaps because of the parallels in context, the 'people of Israel' of the exodus (9:7) and 'my people' (9:10), the expression stands for the whole people.[206] In this sense, Andersen and Freedman argue that 'at the conclusion of the book, the language is more and more universal and eschatological and properly, therefore, focuses attention on all of Israel.'[207] Cripps also

---

201. Wolff, *Prophets*, 164.
202. Jeremias, *Book of Amos*, 48.
203. "Zudem verfügt der Begriff „Staat" sowohl über kollektive als auch über territoriale Komponenten, so dass auch These, das „Haus Israel" in Am 7, 10 deute auf den „ Staat", eine Entscheidung in Bezug auf den „ Land"-Gehalt der Wortverbindung nicht erleichtert." Keita, *Gottes Land*, 268.
204. Andersen and Freedman, *Amos*, 106, 108.
205. Ibid., 110, 112-113.
206. Ibid., 125.
207. Ibid.

believed that Amos addresses the people as a whole in 5:1, 3, 4, 25; 6:1, 14; 7:10; 9:9.[208] As noted above, there is no doubt that these references refer to both kingdoms since they are connected with exodus themes (5:1, 3, 25), worship at major sanctuaries with a possibility of the shrines of both kingdoms (5:4-5), and the reference to Zion and Samaria, denoting both kingdoms (6:1), and punishment of Israel among other nations (9:9). Specifically in this narrative, בֵּית יִשְׂרָאֵל 'the house of Israel' (7:10) is the target of Amos' prophecy that is identified as עַמִּי יִשְׂרָאֵל 'my people Israel' (7:15), the covenant people of YHWH. Amos then predicts the future of 'the house of Israel' in connection with the exile (4:2-3; 5:5, 26-27; 6:7; 7:11, 17; 9:4) away from their native land (7:11, 17), the Promised Land, which once YHWH granted them for their own possession (Deut 6:10).

As we saw above, Amos often uses the 'house of Israel' to mean historic Israel as a whole or both kingdoms together. However, in this narrative (7:10), the phrase is used by Amaziah in his report to King Jeroboam to mean Jeroboam's northern kingdom; hence, the land (northern kingdom) cannot bear all his words. It seems then that Amaziah challenges Amos with his own view of 'Israel' and the 'land', and conversely, Amos challenges Amaziah's.

3.2.4 *The Meaning of Land*

3.2.4.1 Bethel and the Concept of Land

How then does Amaziah's confrontation with Amos function in terms of the meaning of land? Amaziah's accusation at Bethel directly links with this concern. Amaziah defiantly declares that לֹא־תוּכַל הָאָרֶץ לְהָכִיל אֶת־כָּל־דְּבָרָיו 'the land cannot bear all his words' (7:10). Amaziah, as priest of Bethel (7:10), has a significant role in relation to the nation's religion, and thus for the security of both the nation itself and the land of Israel.[209] In other words, he was responsible for sustaining peace and stability in social and religious matters and his fidelity to the royal house is explained in this way.[210]

---

208. Cripps, *Exegetical Commentary*, 178, 203, 229.
209. See Noble, 'Amos and Amaziah', 428; Gary Smith, *Amos: A Commentary*, 236.
210. Achtemeier, *Minor Prophets I*, 222.

This also explains his words to Amos: 'And Amaziah said to Amos, "Seer, go, flee away to the land of Judah, and eat bread there and prophesy there. But never again prophesy at Bethel, for it is the king's sanctuary and it is the temple of the kingdom"' (7:12-13).

In speaking this, however, Amaziah contradicts the call of Amos to prophesy to the entire covenant people. YHWH's command that Amos should go (לֵךְ) and prophesy (7:15) reflects the order of Amaziah that Amos should go and flee (לֵךְ בְּרַח־לְךָ) and prophesy in Judah (7:12). YHWH reverses Amaziah's order by commanding that Amos should prophesy in the land of the northern kingdom not in Judah.[211] Amaziah believes that he has a right to order Amos in YHWH's name, but in fact his orientation leads him to neglect the demands of covenant and finally to oppose the word of YHWH.[212] As we have seen, Amaziah's order to 'never again' (לֹא־תוֹסִיף עוֹד) prophesy at Bethel (7:13) is echoed by the statement of YHWH, 'I will never again', (לֹא־אוֹסִיף עוֹד) pass by them (8:2).[213] Seeing the text as leading on to the next chapter, Linville asserts that the punishment of the lack of the word of YHWH (8:11-13) ironically shows the ignorance of Amaziah about the word of YHWH through the prophet. It is people like Amaziah who will go hungry and thirsty when the word of YHWH is withdrawn from all the land.[214] Therefore, the rejection of the word of YHWH in 7:10-17 leads to a thirst for the word of YHWH in 8:11-14.[215]

Amaziah's refusal of the words of Amos suggests that he might have thought that Amos' word was his personal message and not the word of YHWH.[216] When Amaziah quotes Amos' word: 'for thus Amos has said', he assumes that Amos is speaking on his own account, because when a prophet speaks the word of God he regularly begins with the messenger formula: 'for thus the Lord says'. However, Amos responds that he speaks

---

211. Linville, *Cosmic*, 145; also see Smith and Page, *Amos, Obadiah, Jonah*, 140.
212. Stuart, *Hosea-Jonah*, 377.
213. Linville, *Cosmic*, 144.
214. Ibid., 146.
215. Gary Smith, *Amos: A Commentary*, 249.
216. Paul, *Amos*, 240.

not for himself but for God.[217] Similarly, Möller considers that the trouble that Amos is facing in confrontation with Amaziah is due to Amaziah's refusal to take the word of Amos as a divine message.[218] For Sweeney, Amos' message is expressed as a prophetic judgment speech referred to as 'the word of YHWH' (7:16), and the messenger formula, לָכֵן כֹּה־אָמַר יְהוָה, 'therefore, thus said YHWH' (7:17) further identifies the message as this.[219] Möller also notes that 'for thus Amos has said' (כִּי־כֹה אָמַר עָמוֹס) in 7:11 reflects 'and YHWH said to me' (וַיֹּאמֶר יְהוָה אֵלַי) in 7:8,[220] the messenger formula.

Further, the commission of Amos is to prophesy to YHWH's covenant people, 'my people Israel' (7:15), who are neither the people of Jeroboam nor Amaziah nor Amos, rather they are the people of YHWH. Therefore, Amaziah is wrong in his attempt to stop Amos from preaching the word of YHWH to them.[221] However, Amaziah shows his disbelief about the message of divine judgment, which Amos addressed to all Israel. His attitude may also suggest that the people of Israel are not ready to accept his message either.[222]

In addition, the formula 'says YHWH' or 'says Lord YHWH' (אֲדֹנָי יְהוִה), in 1:5, 8, 15; 2:1; 5:17, 27; 7:3, 6, refers to his prophetic role assigned by YHWH as the messenger to the people (1:1; 2:11-12; 3:7-8; 7:14-15).[223] If Amaziah assumes that any prophet should begin with the messenger formula or prophetic speech: 'for thus the Lord says', this is covered by Amos when he introduces his words with: 'And YHWH said to me' (וַיֹּאמֶר יְהוָה אֵלַי) in 7:8, and confirmed in the prophetic judgment speech: 'hear the word of YHWH' (שְׁמַע דְּבַר־יְהוָה) in 7:16, then in the messenger formula: 'therefore, thus said YHWH' (לָכֵן כֹּה־אָמַר יְהוָה) in 7:17. Finally Amos concludes the book with the messenger formula: 'says YHWH your

---

217. See Daniel J. Simundson, *Hosea, Joel, Amos, Obadiah, Jonah, Micah* (AOTC; Nashville: Abingdon Press, 2005), 218; Achtemeier, *Minor Prophets I*, 222.
218. Karl Möller, *A Prophet in Debate: The Rhetoric of Persuasion in the Book of Amos* (JSOTSS 372; London: Sheffield Academic Press, 2003), 135.
219. Sweeney, *The Twelve Prophets*, 1: 260.
220. Möller, *Debate*, 135.
221. Smith and Page, *Amos, Obadiah, Jonah*, 141.
222. Möller, *Debate*, 135-136.
223. Hubbard, *Joel and Amos*, 245.

God' (אָמַר יְהוָה אֱלֹהֶיךָ, 9:15). Amos also insists in his vision-reports that his message comes from YHWH.

Having made the claim for YHWH's word, Amos then prophesies against Bethel. Bethel has an important symbolic significance in Israel, and so plays an important part in the argument between Amaziah and Amos. Amaziah's summary of Amos' message includes the destruction of Jeroboam: 'Jeroboam shall die by the sword' (7:11) which reflects the threat to 'rise against the house of Jeroboam with the sword' in 7:9. Amaziah believes that the threat to the king and the danger to the people is not really a punishment of YHWH, but rather it is due to the rebellious act of Amos.[224] The prophecy against the house of Jeroboam (7:9) is echoed in the following few verses (7:10-11).

Amaziah now sends a report to king Jeroboam about the message of Amos[225] as having 'conspired against you'. Why does Amaziah regard Amos' activity as 'conspiracy'? Again, this accusation seems to relate to Bethel, the royal house and royal sanctuary, in connection with the concept of land. Accordingly, it is possible that the accusation of 'conspiracy' implies that his prophecy was understood in terms of giving internal opposition to the royal house of Jeroboam.[226] Amaziah's choice of the term 'conspiracy' could warn Jeroboam that he could hardly ignore the activity of Amos, since kings in ancient Israel controlled religious matters, and Bethel was a royal sanctuary, or temple of the kingdom (בֵּית מַמְלָכָה).[227]

The context here suggests that monarchy and state religion were essentially related,[228] the royal power was absolutized[229] and the national sanctuary was directly under the control of the monarchy.[230] In this context,

---

224. Linville, *Cosmic*, 142.
225. Edgar W. Conrad, *Reading the Latter Prophets: Towards a New Canonical Criticism* (JSOTSS 376; London: T & T Clark International, 2003), 84-85.
226. See Hayes, *Amos*, 232; Andersen and Freedman, *Amos*, 781.
227. Stuart, *Hosea-Jonah*, 375-376, further notes that the tradition of monarchical control of religion was quite apparent especially in the north (1 Kings 12:26-33; 16:26, 30-33; 18:4, 19).
228. See Hammershaimb, *Book of Amos*, 114; Polley, *Davidic Empire*, 17; Achtemeier, *Minor Prophets I*, 222.
229. Achtemeier, *Minor Prophets I*, 222.
230. Hayes, *Amos*, 235.

Bethel is no longer the 'house of God', (7:13),[231] but rather it is politicized and thus it represents the king's sanctuary (מִקְדַּשׁ־מֶלֶךְ) and the temple of the kingdom (בֵּית מַמְלָכָה) (cf. the sanctuaries of 7:9),[232] the national or state temple.[233] This lies behind Amaziah's accusation of conspiracy.[234] Robert Coote suggests that bringing the offering and sacrifices at Bethel is similar to the secular provision of the royal house (1 Kgs 4-5). The royal elite in Israel had authority over the religious elites at Bethel (7:10, 13).[235] As Amaziah reported, threatening YHWH's shrine was a threat to the king's shrine.[236] When Amos predicts the people's captivity away from their native land, he rejects the basis of religion and state. Therefore, Amaziah may be right when he says that Amos is blasphemous and rebellious against the religion and the monarchy.[237]

From Amaziah's perspective, his defence of the cult and monarchy could be logically based on the ancient tradition of Israel that the king as divine (Ps 45) was the chief executive, controlling the religious, social, and political life of the nation. As Solomon had built the temple in Jerusalem, so Jeroboam would have authority over all matters of state and religion (1 Kgs 12:26-33).

This foundation of the religion and state, or cult and monarchy at Bethel is connected with land. At Bethel, Amaziah says, 'the land cannot bear' Amos' words (7:10) and Amos responds with the announcement of exile from the land (7:17). Koch argues that the faith of Israel has at its heart a bond with its אדמה, its native land. It has been the goal of their history under the guidance of YHWH since the days of their forefathers (Gen 15:18) and its bond is the matter of a covenant between YHWH and his

---

231. Polley, *Davidic Empire*, 85; Linville, *Cosmic*, 143.
232. See Francis Landy, 'Vision and Poetic Speech in Amos,' *HAR* 11 (1987): 236; Linville, *Cosmic*, 143; Pierre Berthoud, 'The Covenant and the Social Message of Amos,' *EJT* 14, no. 02 (2005): 106; Tucker, 'Historical Framework,' 93.
233. Paul, *Amos*, 243.
234. Polley, *Davidic Empire*, 17.
235. Coote, *Amos Among the Prophets*, 108.
236. See Coote, *Amos Among the Prophets*, 108; Patrick D. Miller, Jr., *Sin and Judgment in the Prophets: A Stylistic and Theological Analysis*, (Chico, California: Scholars Press, 1982), 24.
237. Koch, *Prophets*, 1: 37.

people.[238] Especially Bethel is regarded as the place where the land is promised to Jacob for a possession, and as a place of the worship of YHWH, where the people of Israel celebrated (Gen 28:10-22; 1 Kgs 12:28-29), and offered sacrifices and feasts (cf. 4:4-5; 5:5-6).[239] As argued by Koch,[240] the cultic place at Bethel is connected with YHWH's gift of the land to Israel and it was celebrated in remembrance of the promise of YHWH to the patriarchs in the ancient days.

At Bethel, a conflict takes place between two men: a prophet and a priest who bear responsibility to YHWH and the king respectively. Therefore, the narrative offers two different understandings of Bethel. The first is Amaziah's understanding, according to which Bethel is the 'royal sanctuary' for Jeroboam's kingdom. Amaziah is claiming the historic status of Bethel as support for the kingdom and priesthood that operate there, instituted by Jeroboam I. It seems, therefore, that for Amaziah, the priest at Bethel who is a representative of the royal sanctuary and monarchy (7:10), the defence of the king is to protect the land, which is for him, in practice, the northern kingdom.

On the other side, for Amos, Bethel is a 'house of God' associated with Jacob (Gen 28:19) and the patriarchal promises (Gen 12:8; 13:3; 28:10-22). Bethel is thus unmistakeably connected to the ancient promise of the land. Jacob repeats publicly the naming of Bethel on his return home when YHWH again appeared to him and confirmed the change of his name to 'Israel', along with the patriarchal promise of land (Gen 35:1-15). It apparently functioned at one point as the worship centre for all historic Israel (Judg 20:18, 26-27). For Amos, the prophet who is commissioned by YHWH to prophesy to the whole covenant people, 'my people Israel' (7:15), the obligation to prophesy against Israel is to defend the people of YHWH and the land. Therefore, two different understandings of Bethel could be drawn from the narrative. For Amaziah, the Bethel tradition means that Amos has no right to prophesy there; for Amos, it means the opposite, because it belongs to all Israel.

---

238. Ibid.
239. See Koch, *Prophets*, 1: 37; Marlow, *Ethics*, 151.
240. Koch, *Prophets*, 1: 55.

3.2.4.2 The Terms חֹזֶה and נָבִיא and the Concept of Land

The narrative uses two different words for 'prophet', namely חֹזֶה and נָבִיא in relation to land. In the context of the narrative, Amaziah addresses Amos perhaps derisively with the word חֹזֶה, 'seer' (7:12), not נָבִיא, 'prophet'. The title itself is legitimate however,[241] and the context suggests that Amaziah recognizes that Amos was one of the professional seers.[242] The terms 'prophet' (נָבִיא) and 'seer' (חֹזֶה) are sometimes synonymous and used interchangeably (2 Sam 24:11; 2 Kgs 17:13; Isa 29:10).[243] In addition, the verb חָזָה 'he saw'[244] is used in Amos 1:1 to refer to the whole prophecy: 'the words of Amos . . . which he saw.'[245] Apparently it was a custom to give money when enquiring of a seer (1 Sam 9:7-8). In this sense, Amaziah treats Amos as one of the professional diviners who earn money (cf. Mic 3:5, 11). Again, the individual members of the guild are called בני־הנביאים 'sons of prophets' (1 Kgs 20:35; 2 Kgs 2:3, 5, 15; 4:1). Amaziah then treats him as such, and thus orders him to leave the country and make money in Judah (7:12).[246]

As suggested by a number of scholars above, although the terms נָבִיא (prophet) and חֹזֶה (seer) can be used interchangeably, David L. Petersen argued that the term חֹזֶה tends to identify the prophet in the south, whereas the term נָבִיא does so in the north.[247] Petersen believed that there is no distinction in meaning between these two titles, and that the work of the

---

241. Paul, *Amos*, 240-241.
242. For example, see Polley, *Davidic Empire*, 10-11; Simundson, *Hosea, Joel, Amos, Obadiah, Jonah, Micah*, 218; Hammershaimb, *Book of Amos*, 116; Gary Smith, *Amos: A Commentary*, 238.
243. See Hayes, *Amos*, 233-234; Hammershaimb, *Book of Amos*, 116; Simundson, *Hosea, Joel, Amos, Obadiah, Jonah, Micah*, 219; Mays, *Amos*, 136; Paul, *Amos*, 240-241; Sweeney, *The Twelve Prophets*, 1:258; Jimmy J. Roberts, 'A Note on Amos 7:14 and Its Context,' *RQ* 8, no. 03 (1965): 175-176.
244. The title חֹזֶה (seer) is used in the verb form חָזָה, 'he saw' in 1:1. The root meaning of חזה (to see) is used of visions and dreams (cf. Num 24:2, 4, 16) and the word for 'vision' (חָזוֹן) is from the same root. See Smith and Page, *Amos, Obadiah, Jonah*, 137. The visions consistently use the other verb for seeing (ראה), a synonym of חזה. See Hayes, *Amos*, 234; Hubbard, *Joel and Amos*, 213.
245. Hayes, *Amos*, 233-234.
246. Hammershaimb, *Book of Amos*, 116.
247. David L. Petersen, *The Roles of Israel's Prophets* (JSOTSS 17; Sheffield: JSOT, 1981), 51-69.

חֹזֶה could equally well be depicted by the term נָבִיא. On this basis, for both Amaziah and Amos, the title חֹזֶה would be an appropriate title for Amos.[248] Similarly, following Petersen, Hubbard suggests that the term חֹזֶה connotes the morality prophets in Judah (cf. Gad, 2 Sam 24:11), for instance, Micah (3:5-8) and Isaiah (28:15; 29:10; 30:10), and the term נָבִיא connotes the morality prophets (נביאים) in Israel (Amos 2:11-12).[249]

Therefore, when Amaziah calls Amos a חֹזֶה, an appropriate title indicating a prophet in Judah, Amos neither rejects it nor accepts it.[250] Right after addressing Amos with this title חֹזֶה, Amaziah goes on to order him to prophesy in Judah not in Israel, using the verb נבא (7:12).[251] Amaziah's use of the words חזה and נבא even shows that Amos' prophecy cannot be restricted only to Judah.[252] Amos replies to Amaziah using נבא, unexpectedly perhaps. However, Amos is not claiming to be a נביא rather than a חזה – the terms do not seem to function in that way for him.

Rather, Amos rejects the charge that he is a professional prophet who earns money by prophesying. Thus he says: I am neither a prophet (לֹא־נָבִיא), nor a son of a prophet (וְלֹא בֶן־נָבִיא) (7:14).[253] At the same time he may be rejecting Amaziah's implication of some distinction between חזה and נבא, and thus between prophetic competences in north and south. Curiously, both Amaziah and Amos use the verb נבא for the activity of prophesying (7:12-13, 15). This is the real issue. Amaziah tells Amos to 'prophesy' (נבא) in Judah only, but YHWH has told Amos to 'prophesy' (נבא) to 'my people Israel'.

---

248. Ibid., 57.
249. Hubbard, *Joel and Amos*, 213.
250. See Hubbard, *Joel and Amos*, 214; Yair Hoffmann, 'Did Amos Regard Himself as a NĀBÎ?,' *VT* 27, no. 02 (1977): 209-212.
251. Hubbard, *Joel and Amos*, 214.
252. Ibid.
253. For a helpful study of בֶן־נָבִיא ('a son of prophet') in Amos 7:14, see Jack P. Lewis, '"A Prophet's Son" (Amos 7:14) Reconsidered,' *RQ* 49, no. 04 (2007): 229-240, who attempts to call attention to the terms בני־נביאים and בן־נביא in the Old Testament and tries to define the term.

Amos is a shepherd, בּוֹקֵר, and a dresser of sycamore trees, בּוֹלֵס שִׁקְמִים.[254] According to Driver cited in Paul,[255] Amos' statement about his profession contains a rhetorical question: 'Do you suppose that I am not a true prophet because I am a seasonal labourer? Why the Lord called me…' Perhaps Amos is economically independent and he does not actually need to live by means of prophecy (7:12b) because he can make his living by his occupation on the land (7:14). However, YHWH calls him to prophesy to the covenant people.

Amos asserts his divine commission to prophesy. In opposing Amaziah, he does not intend to deny the prophetic order,[256] but he rather refuses to be like professional prophets as Amaziah assumes. Amos believes that prophets are called by YHWH to warn his people (cf. 2:11; 3:7).[257] Amaziah also acknowledges Amos' communal activity as 'prophesying.'[258] In Amos' commission to prophesy to 'my people Israel' (7:15),[259] Amos speaks to the covenant people of YHWH who belong neither to Jeroboam nor to Amaziah, nor even to Amos.[260] The commission of Amos depends completely upon the covenant language 'my people Israel' (7:15), which is associated with the story of David (2 Sam 5:2).[261]

In addition, the commission of Amos 'YHWH took me from following the flock' (וַיִּקָּחֵנִי יְהוָה מֵאַחֲרֵי הַצֹּאן, 7:15) also applied to the call of David (לְקַחְתִּיךָ מִן־הַנָּוֶה מֵאַחַר הַצֹּאן, 2 Sam 7:8; cf. Ps 78:70), who was anointed

---

254. Giles, 'A Note on the Vocative of Amos in 7:14,' 690-692. For some significant study of Amos' vocation (7:14), also see Wright, 'Amos and the "Sycamore Fig,"' 362-368; Zalcman, 'Piercing the Darkness at Bôqēr (Amos 7:14),' 252-255.
255. Godfrey Rolles Driver, 'Amos 7:14,' *ExpTim* 67, no. 03 (December 1955): 91-92 quoted in Paul, *Amos*, 244.
256. See Anderson, *The Living World of the Old Testament*, 271; Linville, *Cosmic*, 145; Wolff, *Prophets*, 313; Achtemeier, *Minor Prophets I*, 1: 223; Coogan, *The Old Testament: A Historical and Literary Introduction to the Hebrew Scriptures*, 313.
257. Anderson, *Living World*, 270-271.
258. Thomas W. Overholt, 'Prophecy in History: The Social Reality of Intermediation,' in *The Prophets: A Sheffield Reader*, ed. Philip R. Davies (BSem 42; Sheffield: Sheffield Academic Press, 1996), 67.
259. Von Rad, *Message*, 102, considers that the prophetic call of Amos in 7:15 is linked with the reception of the visions (Amos 7:1-3; 4-6; 7-9; 8:1-3; 9:1-4).
260. Smith and Page, *Amos, Obadiah, Jonah*, 141.
261. Stuart, *Hosea-Jonah*, 377.

to be king over the entire people of Israel.²⁶² The verb לקח (took) is also used for the divine appointment of Levites to their cultic function (Num 18:6),²⁶³ and YHWH's election of the people of Israel or king (e.g. Deut 4:20; 1 Kgs 11:37).²⁶⁴ Here, Amos was once a shepherd like David, and now he becomes a prophet of YHWH by his appointment to serve in a special way.²⁶⁵ The offices of king and prophet are made legitmate only by YHWH (Deut 17:15; 18:15). Moses is another example. While he was tending the sheep he was called by YHWH to deliver the covenant people out of the bondage of Egypt and bring them into the Promised Land (Exod 3:1-22). In this sense, it is possible to assume that Amos intended that Amaziah should perceive the similarity,²⁶⁶ in which he received the commission only from YHWH to prophesy to the entire covenant people, and thus the entire land.

In this way, the land is treated in relation to the terms חֹזֶה and נָבִיא. Amaziah's implication of some distinction between חזה and נביא, or between prophetic competences in north and south, even functions to indicate the whole land. Amaziah calls Amos a 'seer' (חֹזֶה), and orders him to prophesy (נבא) in the *land* of Judah (7:12), because the *land* of the northern Israel (in Amaziah's view) cannot bear all his words (7:10). Therefore, it seems that the implication of the terms חֹזֶה and נָבִיא is a debate about land.

3.2.4.3 Exile and the Concept of Land

The confrontation between Amos and Amaziah ends with the oracle concerning the judgment of Amaziah, the land, and the people into exile (7:16-17). This oracle is expressed in the messenger formula and an announcement of prophetic judgment: 'hear the word of YHWH' (7:16) and 'thus said YHWH' (7:17). The accusation repeats the sin of Israel indicated in Amos 2:12b: 'and you commanded the prophets, saying, "you shall not prophesy".'²⁶⁷ Two things can be drawn from this attack of Amos

---

262. See, for instance, Mays, *Amos*, 139; Stuart, *Hosea-Jonah*, 377; Paul, *Amos*, 249.
263. Mays, *Amos*, 139.
264. Hubbard, *Joel and Amos*, 216.
265. Mays, *Amos*, 139.
266. Stuart, *Hosea-Jonah*, 377.
267. Tucker, 'Prophetic Authenticity,' 434.

on Amaziah: the impending specific judgment for opposing YHWH's authority and the repetition of the announcement against Israel.[268] Finally the attempt of Amaziah to drive out Amos from Israel is now turned round so that Amaziah himself will be driven by YHWH from the land of Israel (7:17).[269]

The punishment of Amaziah includes his family in which his wife will become a prostitute and his children will fall by the sword (7:17). This fate in which Amaziah's wife is the only one who survives among the family, and becomes a prostitute has overtones of the reference to father and son going together to the same girl in 2:7.[270] The prophecy connotes both the bringing of judgment upon the family of the priest and the destiny of Israel (7:17).[271] The prophecy against the whole people of Israel (7:8) is shifted to a threat against the dynasty of Israel (7:10). When Amaziah cites Amos' threat against the house of Jeroboam (7:9, 11), Amos reacts to his false perception of it, with the announcement of YHWH's punishment (7:9) upon his family (7:17).[272] However, as Amos pronounces the ruin of Israel, his prophecy advances to Judah as well. When Amos is commanded by YHWH to prophesy to 'my people Israel' (7:15), his climactic vision has as its same target 'my people Israel' (8:2), which includes both Judah and Israel.[273] In the narrative, then, the prediction of the end of 'my people Israel' shows Amos' confirmation of the end of the whole people:[274] 'Israel must go into exile away from its land' (7:11, 17).

In the closing verse of the narrative (7:17), the 'land' (אדמה) is mentioned three times. What do the three occurrences of 'land' mean specifically? The references to 'land' here recall the 'land' in verse 10, where it was used by Amaziah to mean the kingdom of Jeroboam. Therefore, there is irony in Amos now turning a word about land against Amaziah. First, Amos states that Amaziah's land (אדמה) will be divided up by a measuring

---

268. Ibid.
269. Gary Smith, *Amos: A Commentary*, 241.
270. Linville, *Cosmic*, 147.
271. Ibid., 147-148.
272. Wood, *Song*, 74.
273. Ibid., 75.
274. Ibid.

line (7:17). Does this refer to Amaziah's family property? Or does it refer to the land of Israel? Or indeed, is there any relationship between Amaziah's own land and that of Israel? It is not clear whether Amaziah would have possessed land of his own. If priests in the north were like Levites in Judah, they would have lands granted to them by their neighbors (Num 35:1-8; see also 1 Kgs 2:26-27; 1 Chr 6:54-72; Jer 32:6-15).

Wolff thinks that although the 'land' (אדמה) generally connotes the whole of the 'cultivable land' (3:2; cf. 5:2; 7:11b, 17b; 9:8), it cannot mean this in the case of Amaziah's 'land'.[275] The land of Israel (cf. 5:2), YHWH's gift (2:9), will be taken by foreigners, and Amaziah will die where no worship of YHWH is available.[276] Wolff concluded that possibly Amaziah had his own land, and supposed that there is a relationship between his property and the land of Israel.[277] Amaziah's land may also indicate his share in the whole territory of Israel. More importantly, it could be Amos' ironic reversal to Amaziah, who identifies the land to the northern kingdom Israel. Amos particularly specifies the fate of Amaziah in relation to the punishment of Israel by exile away from its land.

Further, there is a parallel between Amaziah's land and the 'unclean land' in which he will die. Israel's own land (cf. 5:2) which once YHWH gave them as a gift (2:9; cf. 9:15) will be destroyed, and the people will go into exile, so that the priest must die in an unclean land.[278] The phrase the 'unclean land' may also picture the land in a more universal sense, the foreign land where YHWH is absent (Hos 9:3; Ezek 4:13; cf. Deut 4:28; 1 Sam 26:19; Jer 16:13; Ps 137:4).[279] Any foreign land may be considered unclean due to the control of the foreign deities in place of YHWH (1 Sam 26:19; Hos 9:3-4; Ezek 4:13).[280] Or it could be ironically, the 'polluted

---

275. Wolff, *Prophets*, 315.
276. Ibid., 315-316.
277. Ibid., 316.
278. Ibid.
279. See Gerhard Pfeifer, *Die Theologie des Propheten Amos* (Frakfurt: Peter Lang, 1995), 115; Wolff, *Prophets*, 316; Jeremias, *Book of Amos*, 141; Sweeney, *The Twelve Prophets*, 1:261; Paul, *Amos*, 251; Gary Smith, *Amos: A Commentary*, 242.
280. Mays, *Amos*, 140; Von Rad, 'Promised Land,' 87.

soil of Israel',[281] because it has lost the essential meaning of Bethel 'house of God'.

What land, in contrast, is 'clean'? The land that YHWH had given to Israel was clean, since on it alone was access to God in worship possible.[282] The primary function of Amaziah as a priest was to defend the cult, sanctuary, and people from being unholy (Lev 10:10).[283] Therefore, Amaziah is expected to protect the holiness of the sanctuary at the 'house of God'. Because of the concept of the sanctuary as a holy place, the land also is regarded as 'holy'.[284] Koch's point about Amos' criticism in connection with a 'religious attitude to the land' is significant in dealing with the land as a cultic place. He refers to it as a 'sacral' or 'cultic' one, that is, the land is 'holy' because God makes his dwelling in it.[285] The terms 'clean' or 'holy' thus denote the place where YHWH is present (e.g. Exod 3:5; 25:8). Bethel was the 'house of God' where YHWH made his dwelling. However, Bethel in 7:13 is no longer the 'house of God', or a 'holy' place where YHWH dwells, but rather it has become the king's sanctuary and the temple of the kingdom, and also a place of covenant disloyalty.

Finally, in the statement, 'And Israel must go into exile away from its land' (וְיִשְׂרָאֵל גָּלֹה יִגְלֶה מֵעַל אַדְמָתוֹ) in the closing verse of the narrative (7:17), the 'land' (אדמה) is used in reference to the fortunes of the king, the people, and the place itself. At the end of the narrative (7:17), Amos reaffirms the threat of the exile of the whole people, which has already been reported by Amaziah to the king (7:11).[286] The land and Israel here could have a double meaning. First, in response to the accusation of Amaziah, Amos possibly in turn predicts that Israel (Jeroboam's kingdom) will go into exile at the hands of Assyria (Hos 9:3). Amos' oracle creates a rhetorical emphasis on the punishment of the northern kingdom, an ironic reversal of what Amaziah has reported. Second, as Paul argues that the 'unclean land' applies to any foreign land, including Assyria (Hos 9:3) and

---

281. Gary Smith, *Amos: A Commentary*, 242.
282. Pfeifer, *Theologie*, 115.
283. Mays, *Amos*, 140.
284. Sweeney, *The Twelve Prophets*, 1:261.
285. Koch, *Prophets*, 1: 50.
286. Hammershaimb, *Book of Amos*, 119.

Babylonia (Ezek 4:13),[287] it is part of Amos' argument that his prophecy is to all Israel (7:15), and hence, the historic land. Therefore 'Israel' (historic Israel) will go into exile in the 'unclean land' at the hands of Assyria (Hos 9:3), and the prophecy would find later fulfilment for Judah in the Babylonian exile (Ezek 4:13). In this narrative, Amos announces judgment against the priest and his family, and finally the people of Israel as a whole (7:17).

The book of Amos thus makes exile an important part of the picture of the fate of Israel in the future. In the narrative (7:10-17), according to Donald E. Gowan, the punishment of Israel in exile (7:11, 17) is assumed to be YHWH's death sentence on Israel. The reason for this punishment lies in the election of Israel in relation to the exodus tradition (3:1-2).[288] Gowan argues that the election tradition functioned significantly in the theology of the northern kingdom. Therefore, Amos reinforces the belief of the people of Israel that they are elected for a special relationship with YHWH but also especially responsible in consequence,[289] which is mainly represented by exile.

The passage thus concludes with a strong statement about the announcement of the exile of Israel. 'And Israel must go into exile' (7:11, 17) has several parallels throughout the book of Amos (4:2-3; 5:5, 26-27; 6:7; 9:4). These references show that the descriptions of the land and Israel in this narrative are best understood as the fate of the whole land and historic Israel. Moreover, as already noted, the specific expression 'high places of Isaac' in 7:9 is used as 'the house of Isaac' in 7:16 which connotes all 'Israel'. The parallel of 'Israel' with 'Isaac' in 7:9, 16 points to the inclusion of both kingdoms. Further, Amos uses the 'house of Israel' (5:1, 3, 4, 25; 6:1, 14; 9:9) to refer to historic Israel and thus the whole land. In this way, Amos' announcement of exile is appropriately used in the narrative account (7:11, 17) to refer to the fate of both kingdoms.

---

287. Paul, *Amos*, 251.
288. Donald E. Gowan, *Theology of the Prophetic Books: The Death and Resurrection of Israel* (London: Westminster John Knox Press, 1998), 29-30.
289. Ibid., 30.

3.2.5 Conclusion

In the narrative, by announcing the destruction of the cultic and royal institutions, Amos aims to persuade his audience to learn from their sin and failure to comply with the covenant and to respond properly to his message. In his rhetoric, Amos confirms his commission to prophesy to 'my people Israel' (7:15). In retrospect, it traces back the announcement of the punishment by setting a plumb-line in the midst of 'my people Israel' (7:8), and looking forward to the end of the same entity 'my people Israel' (8:2), which alludes to the ancient covenant with YHWH.

The conflict of Amos with Amaziah has taken place at Bethel. Bethel is a significant place for historic Israel in relation to the gift of the land by YHWH. It has a connection with Israel's patriarch, Jacob who named it (Gen 28:19) and it served as an important place for worship after the conquest (Judg 20:18). YHWH promised to give Bethel to Jacob as a possession for him as well as all his descendants (Gen. 28:10-22). Therefore, Bethel is connected with YHWH's gift of the land to all Israel. Even after the division of the kingdom it became an important place for cultic celebration (1 Kgs 12:28-29). In the time of Amos, the people of Israel offered sacrifices and feasts at the sanctuaries of Bethel (Amos 4:4-5; 5:5-6). However, in Amos' view it came to symbolize covenant disloyalty and empty ritual. Therefore, Amos ironically calls Israel to come to Bethel and sin (4:4); he then says that YHWH rejects their worship, feasts, and songs (5:21-24). Amos mentions that YHWH will punish the altars of Bethel (3:14) and rebukes the people for seeking Bethel (5:5). In this way, Amos' rhetoric intends to oppose the concept of Amaziah, priest at Bethel (7:10), who strongly identifies Bethel as the temple of the kingdom, the royal sanctuary (7:13) but does not understand the true significance of worship or land.

Having known Bethel in connection with the gift of YHWH to the covenant people, Amos was commissioned by YHWH to prophesy among them. In the narrative, the message of Amos ends with the prophecy of the exile of the covenant people into an unclean land (7:17). The narrative (7:10-17) shows that the gift of land and the covenant people of YHWH will be destroyed. The narrative (7:10-17) is essentially about the question of Israel and land. Land is not simply a territory. It cannot be equated with the territories of either kingdom in Amos' time. The legitimate possession of land, for Amos, depends on a true understanding of what is meant by the covenant and the people of Israel.

CHAPTER 4

The Land in Amos 8

4.1 The Land in Amos 8:1-3

4.1.1 Introduction

The fourth vision-report in Amos 8:1-3 employs the prophet's experience as a farmer (7:14). Knowing YHWH's intentions for Israel, now Amos pictures the 'summer fruit' (קָיִץ) in connection with the end (קֵץ) of the covenant people, 'my people Israel' (עַמִּי יִשְׂרָאֵל), and utters YHWH's statement of judgment, 'I will never again pass them by' (לֹא־אוֹסִיף עוֹד עֲבוֹר לוֹ). The image of destruction is vivid: all happiness will disappear and be transformed into lament, and even in the temple (הֵיכָל), festival songs will be replaced by wailing and many dead bodies will be cast out everywhere.

4.1.2 The Summer Fruit

The fourth vision follows the same model as the third; that is, the vision itself, a question, an answer, and a word of judgment. Only the object of the vision changes from the plumb-line (אֲנָךְ) to a basket of summer fruit (קָיִץ).[1] The name of the object קָיִץ is used in other contexts both to refer to the summer season (Gen 8:22; Isa 28:4; Jer 8:20; Ps 32:4; Amos 3:15) and to the ripe fruit in the summer, hence 'summer fruit' (2 Sam 16:1-2).[2] Mays suggests that this basket of summer fruit could be the offering

---

1. For example, see Mays, *Amos*, 140; Smith and Page, *Amos, Obadiah, Jonah*, 142.
2. See, for instance, Hammershaimb, *Book of Amos,* 120; Hayes, *Amos,* 207; Hubbard, *Joel and Amos*, 218; Smith and Page, *Amos, Obadiah, Jonah,* 143.

brought to the sanctuary of Bethel in which the people celebrated with thanksgiving for the coming new year in order to retain prosperity and blessing.[3]

Jeremias also claims that originally, the 'basket of summer fruit' (כְּלוּב קָיִץ) is a sign of joy in which the people of Israel celebrated. It is a festival of wine, oil, sycamore, and pomegranates and more importantly it is a thanksgiving festival for the good gift of the land,[4] a connection that is found in the confession of faith in Deuteronomy 26.[5] Amos' vision of the basket of summer fruit brought to the sanctuary or temple is thus connected with the Deuteronomic understanding of the gift of the land by YHWH.

However, as the people of Israel are ripe for 'harvest', this has become a symbol of judgment in the prophecy of Amos and the message is the 'end'.[6] The ripe fruit designates the fate of Israel that they are ripe for the punishment of exile, carrying them off perhaps as in a 'basket' (cf. 4:2-3).[7] In wordplay, Amos identifies a basket of summer fruit (קָיִץ)[8] with YHWH's announcement of the end (קֵץ) of Israel. In the connection between the two words קָיִץ and קֵץ,[9] the wordplay could arise from similar sounds in different dialects.[10]

---

3. Mays, *Amos*, 141.
4. Jeremias, *Book of Amos*, 134.
5. Landy, 'Vision,' 232.
6. Jeremias, *Book of Amos*, 134.
7. Hubbard, *Joel and Amos*, 218.
8. The 'summer fruit' (קָיִץ) is harvested at the end of the summer (August, September), see Paul, *Amos*, 253; or around the time of Sukkoth (July, August), see Sweeney, *The Twelve Prophets*, 1: 261.
9. The term קָיִץ derives from the root קיץ (to be hot, to awaken) while קֵץ is connected to קצץ (to cut off, or hew off). See Wolff, *Prophets*, 319; Hammershaimb, *Book of Amos*, 120; Paul, *Amos*, 253-254.
10. For the suggestion of the terms קָיִץ and קֵץ referring to the difference between the southern (Judah) and northern (Israel) dialects, see Al Wolters, 'Wordplay and Dialect in Amos 8:1-2,' *JETS* 31, no. 04 (December 1988): 407-410. Walters thinks Amos may have sold ripe sycamore-figs (קָיִץ) in the markets of the north, which sounded to the ears of Judah like a prophet announcing, קֵץ 'the end.' Also see the discussion in Eduard Yechezkel Kutscher, *A History of the Hebrew Language* (Jerusalem: Magnes Press, 1982), 66, 70, 78; Paul, *Amos*, 254.

There is a connection between the third and fourth visions, in content and use of wordplay.[11] The announcement of the end of Israel by YHWH (8:2) echoes the miserable sounds of grieving predicted with the setting of the אֲנָךְ in the midst of Israel (7:8), and these cries of misery are intimated as the turning of the songs of the temple into wailing (8:3). The prediction of the destruction of the house of Jeroboam with the sword in 7:9 also indicates the picture of the many dead bodies which shall be cast out in every place in 8:3.[12]

The same situation of grief and misery is previously found in the pronouncement of the אֲנָךְ which also features a wordplay on the ח of [13]אָנַח and the ק of אָנַק.[14] Both of these denote moaning and groaning,[15] and therefore בְּיָדוֹ אֲנָךְ evokes the sounds of someone crying in grief and misery, אָנַח or אָנַק,[16] respectively 'to sigh in grief' and 'to cry in distress'.[17] In this sense, the wailing in the third vision has a connection with the fourth vision. Stuart believes that the central focus in this fourth vision moves from 'what is seen to what sounds like' as in the third vision, where the visual אֲנָךְ (plumb-line) gives way to the sounds of moaning or groaning (אָנַח or אָנַק).[18] Yvonne Sherwood considers the relationship between what is heard (wailing) and seen (corpses) and the exploration of Amos 8:1-3 as audio-vision.[19] The end (קֵץ) of Israel in 8:2 is in harmony with the symbol of dead bodies and wailing in 8:3,[20] and both these elements recur in 8:10.[21]

---

11. See Andersen and Freedman, *Amos*, 757, 759; Linville, 'Visions and Voices', 30; Jeremias, *Book of Amos*, 132-133.

12. Linville, 'Visions and Voices', 34.

13. The term אָנַח indicates moaning or sighing (Isa 24:7; Joel 1:18; cf. Isa 35:10). See Stuart, *Hosea-Jonah*, 373; Linville, *Cosmic*, 139; Linville, 'Visions and Voices', 30; Auld, *Amos*, 20.

14. The term אָנַק indicates moaning or crying out (see Jer 51:52; Ezek 26:15). See Stuart, *Hosea-Jonah*, 373; Linville, *Cosmic*, 139; Linville, 'Visions and Voices', 30; Auld, *Amos*, 20.

15. Auld, *Amos*, 20.

16. Linville, *Cosmic*, 139.

17. Linville, 'Visions and Voices', 30.

18. Stuart, *Hosea-Jonah*, 379.

19. Yvonne Sherwood, 'Of Fruit and Corpses and Wordplay Visions: Picturing Amos 8:1-3,' *JSOT* 92 (March 2001): 5-27.

20. Ibid., 12.

21. Gary Smith, *Amos: A Commentary*, 248.

This vision pronounces the end of the forgiveness of YHWH upon Israel. The same picture is anticipated in the third vision (7:7-9).[22] The קֵץ 'end' implies the final punishment that will bring the nation to an end[23] or the destruction of people and the land which is the result of the end of YHWH's covenant relationship with Israel, 'my people Israel'. This concept of the end of the people and land is incorporated with the earlier oracles of the remnant (5:14-15), the survival of people in exile (4:2-3; 5:27; 7:11, 17), and the promise of the restoration of the people and land (9:11-15). However, in reality the 'end' has come for Israel, 'my people Israel'.[24] Therefore, the summer fruit (קָיִץ) is not simply indicating the end of the summer but more importantly it is a sign of the disastrous end of the people of YHWH, [25] 'my people Israel'. YHWH himself will bring the end of Israel by discontinuing his covenant contact with his people (3:2).[26]

The language Amos chooses in this vision is drawn from the realm of agriculture and land. It is therefore not only wordplay on קֵץ, nor a 'mere' metaphor, but expresses the subject matter in a powerful way. The good land, with its promised gifts, is coming to an end. Offering the fruit at the sanctuary is associated with thanksgiving for the gift of the land (Deut 26:1-4). Therefore, the ripe fruit indicating the 'end' may also affect the gift of the land.

4.1.3 I Will Never Again Pass Them By

As we saw, the theme of the first two visions reflects the theme of destruction of agriculture (4:6-11; 5:16-17) in the land of the covenant people Israel. Amos cries out on behalf of Jacob and YHWH relents. In the first two visions, through the intercession of Amos, the punishment is postponed (cf. 7:7-9; 8:1-3). However, there would finally be no forgiveness. Therefore, this pattern of YHWH's longsuffering is about to draw to a conclusion, which is confirmed by the expression 'I will never again pass them

---

22. Ibid.
23. Andersen and Freedman, *Amos*, 797.
24. Gary Smith, *Amos: A Commentary*, 251.
25. Watts, *Vision*, 72.
26. Craig A. Satterlee, 'Amos 8:1-12,' *Int* 61, no. 02 (April 2007): 203.

by' (לֹא־אוֹסִיף עוֹד עֲבוֹר לוֹ).[27] Again, the present vision (8:2) locates the bringing of judgment among the people of Israel and the land as a whole.

As already argued, the term עָבַר ('pass over')[28] is used to indicate the thought of passing through a land in connection with entering into it, as the gift of YHWH (Num 20:17; 21:22; Deut 9:1; 27:3; 30:18; Josh 1:2). However, this instance of עָבַר has become a judgment on the land and people.[29] As mentioned previously, the connection of the two terms קָיִץ and קֵץ makes the meaning of the vision clear in relation to the destruction of the covenant people and the land by bringing the 'end' of Israel. This prophecy, then, is without hope of change, for YHWH 'will never again pass them by' or pardon; instead he will bring the judgment of destruction on the land and the people.[30] The end (קֵץ) of Israel sounds the grieving situation in the midst of all Israel (7:7, 8) as the songs of the temple are turned into wailing in the fourth vision (8:3). Again, the destruction of the house of Jeroboam by the sword (7:9, 11) also envisages the many corpses YHWH will cast out in the fourth vision (8:3). The third vision, then, is reinforced in the fourth vision in which the punishment is increased.[31] Therefore, the announcement of YHWH's judgment 'I will never again pass them by' (7:8; 8:2) foreshadows the terrible fate of the covenant people in the future. Elsewhere too, Amos predicts the end of 'my people Israel' in exile (4:2-3; 5:5, 27; 6:7; 7:11, 17; 9:4) away from their native land (7:11, 17).

4.1.4 The Temple and Land

The announcement of judgment also includes turning the songs of the temple (הֵיכָל) into wailing (8:3). Which temple is referred to here? Besides Bethel, could it also suggest Jerusalem? Neither place is named here. In 7:13, the reference was to Bethel, a royal sanctuary (מִקְדַּשׁ־מֶלֶךְ), or temple of the kingdom (בֵּית מַמְלָכָה). It was closely connected with Jeroboam I,

---

27. Cf. Noble, 'Amos and Amaziah', 427.
28. Though not identical, the similar expression עָבַר עַל (to pass over) occurs in Proverbs 19:11; Micah 7:18.
29. Cf. Robert H. O'Connell, 'Telescoping N+1 Patterns in the Book of Amos,' *VT* 46, no. 01 (January 1996): 69; Brueggemann, *Genesis*, 76.
30. Gary Smith, *Amos: A Commentary*, 251.
31. Linville, 'Visions and Voices', 34.

who established a sanctuary there (1 Kgs 12) to replace Israel's national sanctuary at Jerusalem.[32] Amaziah's accusation (7:13) is connected with Bethel, the royal house and temple, in connection with the concept of land. However, in the wider context of the book, the unnamed temple in 8:3 could also suggest Jerusalem. YHWH utters his word from Jerusalem (1:2). As I have discussed already, the narrative (7:10-17) offers two different understandings of temple, people and land. The first is Amaziah's understanding, according to which Israel, land, temple, and prophecy are closely related to the north; for Amos, it means the opposite, because his rhetoric intends to suggest that his prophecy toward a temple audience in 8:3 includes all Israel, 'my people Israel' (8:2), and thus the whole land. It is possible that the absence of a name leaves room for an allusion to Jerusalem.

As previously stated, YHWH confirms that the prophecy of punishment on the sanctuary or temple (מִקְדָּשׁ) in 7:9 will surely occur in the destruction of the temple (הֵיכָל) in 8:3. Even the portrayal of the destruction of the temple (הֵיכָל) in 8:3 could be a response to Amaziah's allusion to the temple (מִקְדָּשׁ or בַּיִת) in 7:13.[33] In Israel, the temple (מִקְדָּשׁ) is portrayed in cosmic extent and the world is a macro-Temple (Ps 78:69).[34] The temple is a link between the heaven and earth,[35] that is, the symbolism of temple denotes the entire cosmos. For this reason, it is the 'centre' of the land, and the place of pilgrimage and agricultural festival (Amos 4:4-5; 5:21-22).

Then, what are the songs (שִׁירוֹת) of the Temple? For some, it refers to the singers, connected with the royal palace or court (2 Sam 19:35; 2 Chr 35:25; Eccl 2:8).[36] According to Andersen and Freedman, the הֵיכָל could be either the 'temple' or 'palace' because both priest and king are thought of

---

32. See Stuart, *Hosea-Jonah*, 375-376; Hammershaimb, *Book of Amos*, 114; Mays, *Amos*, 135; Gary Smith, *Amos: A Commentary*, 246, 252.
33. Stuart, *Hosea-Jonah*, 370.
34. Jon Douglas Levenson, *Creation and the Persistence of Evil: The Jewish Drama of Divine Omnipotence* (Princeton, New Jersey: Princeton University Press, 1988), 86-87.
35. See Othmar Keel, *The Symbolism of the Biblical World: Ancient Near Eastern Iconography and the Book of Psalms*, trans. Timothy J. Hallett (London: SPCK, 1978), 171; Carol Meyers, 'Jerusalem Temple,' in *ABD (Si-Z)*, ed. David Noel Freedman (London: Double Day, 1992), 359; John M. Lundquist, 'Temple,' in *EDB*, ed. David Noel Freedman (Grand Rapids, Michigan: William B. Eerdmans, 2000), 1282.
36. See Wolff, *Prophets*, 319-320; Paul, *Amos*, 254-255; Jeremias, *Book of Amos*, 143, 145; Hubbard, *Joel and Amos*, 219.

as the objects of punishment (7:10-17). And thus, the songs are either for the cult (5:23; 6:5; 8:10) or secular festivals, as evidenced by the contrast of celebrative songs with wailing in 8:10.[37] Although kings in ancient Israel controlled religious matters,[38] the northern kings did not make Bethel their royal court or palace. Smith takes הֵיכָל to refer to the 'temple', not the 'palace',[39] and thinks the songs (שִׁירוֹת) sung at the temple (Amos 5:23; 6:5; 8:10) fit a cultic context. For Mays, the songs of the temple are songs of 'joy and hope in YHWH'.[40] However, the wrath of YHWH turns these joyful songs at 'harvest time'[41] or at the 'Autumn Festival'[42] to disastrous wailing (8:3; cf. 8:10). Therefore, the 'songs of the temple' probably connote ironically the joyful celebration of the gift of the land, and the change to wailing implies its loss.

The fourth vision presents the contrast between divine and human, and between utterance and silence.[43] Amos 8:3 reads:[44] רַב הַפֶּגֶר בְּכָל־מָקוֹם הִשְׁלִיךְ הָס 'Many are dead bodies, they shall be cast in every place. Silence!' 'Dead bodies in every place' is a negation of life-giving land. The changing of 'songs of the temple' into lament also continues in the symbol of the destruction of the cultic centres or shrines which is identified by מָקוֹם 'place'. The term מָקוֹם could refer to a sanctuary.[45] Yet it can also suggest ordinary places or towns throughout the land, and even the whole land (Deut 26:9). There are dead bodies in the מָקוֹם, every place, that is, the whole land. And to this image is added a demand for silence. As Linville suggests, the use of the term הָס in 8:3, as an interjection, has

---

37. Andersen and Freedman, *Amos*, 798.
38. See Hammershaimb, *Book of Amos,* 114; Mays, *Amos*, 135; Stuart, *Hosea-Jonah*, 375-376; Polley, *Davidic Empire*, 17; Achtemeier, *Minor Prophets I*, 222.
39. Gary Smith, *Amos: A Commentary*, 252.
40. Mays, *Amos*, 141.
41. Gary Smith, *Amos: A Commentary*, 252.
42. Hammershaimb, *Book of Amos,* 120.
43. Linville, 'Visions and Voices', 35.
44. The BHS suggests that הִשְׁלִיךְ could be corrupt, and suggests reading אַשְׁלִיכֵם ('I shall cast them out') or הִשְׁלִיכָם ('he cast them out').
45. Mays, *Amos*, 142.

a connection with Amos 6:10, which also mentions both dead bodies and silence.[46]

Francis Landy points out that the speaker in this vision in the command of silence (הַס) is none other than YHWH, and this command corresponds to the attempt of Amaziah to silence the word of YHWH, which came through Amos.[47] The 'songs of the temple' turn to wailing and silence in 8:3 and to lamentation in 8:10. This turning song to silence is accomplished in 8:11-13 in which there is a silence of the word of YHWH. Therefore, it will be a fruitless search for YHWH's word.[48] YHWH is probably demanding silence from the survivors before the casting out of the dead, an order which seems to go against the order of silence commanded by Amaziah.[49] Furthermore, the 'silence' in 8:3 makes a catchword link to the opening phrase 'hear this' in 8:4. This shows the corrupted nature of the rich merchants, who desire to start their exploitation upon the needy and poor of the land (8:4-6).[50] Therefore, the turning of the 'songs of the temple' to wailing is the consequence of the sins of the corrupt (8:10), and the famine of the word of YHWH also reflects 'silence'.[51]

The fourth vision of wailing in the temple and many dead bodies (8:1-3) gives a foundation for the particular punishment of the wealthy merchants (8:4-6).[52] In this way, Paul Noble considers 8:4-6 as further thematic development of the fourth vision.[53] As will be shown in detail later, the wailing in the temple results the punishment of the greedy merchants with their empty ritual in 8:4-6. While the merchants are obliged to keep the New Moon and Sabbath holy, they consider that this religious matter merely interferes with their business, and they are impatient for it to end (8:5).

The concept of the temple may well relate to the notion of land. The basket of summer fruit in the fourth vision designates the fruitful, life-giving

---

46. Linville, *Cosmic*, 152; Linville, 'Visions and Voices', 35.
47. Landy, 'Vision', 231-232, 238.
48. See Landy, 'Vision,' 238; Linville, 'Visions and Voices', 36.
49. Linville, 'Visions and Voices', 35; Linville, *Cosmic*, 134.
50. Linville, 'Visions and Voices', 36.
51. Ibid.
52. Noble, 'Literary Structure', 223-224.
53. Ibid., 223; also in his article 'Amos and Amaziah', 433.

land. People offered sacrifices and songs of praise (4:4-5; 5:21-23; 6:5) in order to celebrate the gift of land. However, the 'songs of the temple' turn to wailing and there are 'dead bodies in every place'. These images negate the land as life-giving, but announce its loss and the end of the people of Israel.

Koch too argues that the descriptions of the visions (7:7-9; 8:1-3; 9:1-4) connote the idea of the fruitful earth, which is rooted in the temple at Bethel, and/or Jerusalem as well.[54] The violation of the holy cultic places and festivals because of sin brings lament (2:6-16). YHWH's prophecy against the rich women of the court (4:1-3) is followed by the description of the pilgrimage to the cultic places (4:4-5). People sang a lament at their cultic ceremony (6:1-7). The sacred festivals are affected by YHWH's indignation due to the social and economic injustice of the merchants towards the poor (8:4-6).[55] Koch thinks that for Amos sin is 'never so grave as when it touches the sphere of the holy'.[56] Koch's argument about Amos' criticism in relation to a 'religious attitude to the land'[57] suggests land as a cultic place. That is, the land is 'holy' because it is the place where YHWH dwells, symbolized by temple and cult.

4.1.5 Conclusion

The fourth vision designates the fruitful land, identified by the summer fruit, a symbol of the year's greatest time of joy in which the people of Israel celebrated. Offering the fruit at the sanctuary is connected with the land, and by it people expressed thanksgiving for the gift of it (Deut 26:1-4). However, this has become a sign of judgment, and the announcement of punishment is the 'end' of the covenant people, 'my people Israel' (4:2-3; 5:27; 6:7; 7:11, 17; 9:4). The good and fruitful land, with its promised gifts, is coming to an end.

This prophecy of summer fruit with its message of 'end', then, is the judgment of destruction on the land and the people, for YHWH 'will

---

54. Koch, *Prophets,* 1: 50.
55. Ibid.
56. Ibid.
57. Ibid.

never again pass them by'. Consequently, the 'songs of the temple' turn to wailing. The imagery of temple signifies the centre of the land. This is the cultic place where people celebrated their agricultural festival and offered sacrifices along with songs (Amos 4:4-5; 5:21-22; 6:5; 8:5). Conversely, the change to wailing implies loss of land and its life-giving properties.

Further, that the end (קֵץ) has come to 'my people Israel' (8:2) is portrayed in the 'dead bodies' throughout the land. This too implies a cancellation of the life-giving and fruitful land. Consequently, this judgment gives a foundation for the punishment of the rich merchants (8:4-6), who abused the benefit of the gift of land, and thus their cultic festivals became empty ritual. This will be now explored in depth.

4.2 The Land in Amos 8:4-6

4.2.1 Introduction

The aim of this section is to explore how the Sabbath[58] in Amos 8:4-6 relates to the theme of land in the book. We will first attempt to show what was known and practiced in the Ancient Near East and suggest whether it has any relevant connection with the Sabbath in Israel. The investigation of Sabbath (Amos 8:4-6) will then explore the relationship of Amos to other Old Testament theological traditions, especially in Exodus, Leviticus, and Deuteronomy. These show different strands of theological interpretation of the Sabbath in Israel possibly at different times. On the basis of Amos 8:4-6, the study will show what Amos knows and thinks about the Sabbath and what he and his audience might understand by it. Finally, it will demonstrate the relation of Sabbath in Amos 8:4-6 to the land and to justice.

---

58. Laws about the Sabbath occur in Exodus (20:8-11; 31:12-17), Leviticus (23:3; 25:1-7), and Deuteronomy (5:12-15). Other important biblical references to the Sabbath are: Gen 2:2-3; Exod 34:21; 35:3; Num 15:32-36; 28:9-10; Neh 13:15-22; Isa 58:13-14; 66:23; Ezek 20:12.

4.2.2 Sabbath in the Ancient Near East

The origin of Sabbath remains uncertain both in the Ancient Near East and in the Old Testament.[59] The noun form for Sabbath in Hebrew, שַׁבָּת, means 'cessation from work'. The relation of the Hebrew term for Sabbath to the Akkadian term, šabattu/šapattu is uncertain.[60] The number seven has a symbolic significance in both Ancient Near East and Old Testament.[61] The šabattu/šapattu in Akkadian or Babylonian is an observance of the seventh day, perhaps at the full moon or on the fifteenth of the month.[62] In the Babylonian cycle of ominous days (ūmê lemnūti), there were four phases which occurred at approximately seven-day intervals.[63] The Sabbath in the Ancient Near East was observed in connection with the lunar cycle.[64] In Babylonia and Assyria, the four phases of the moon, the seventh, fourteenth, twenty-first, and twenty-eighth days, were considered to be 'evil days' (ūmê lemnūti)[65] or a 'day of quieting of the heart'.[66] These cultic evil days affected the king, soothsayer, and sorcerer.[67] Even the king was forbidden to ride on his chariot, and among other prohibitions, the physician should not treat the sick.[68] The restriction of work is not because these days were intended for rest;[69] rather it is probably due to the belief that they were 'evil days', and therefore inauspicious.

According to Mays, the Ancient Near East observance of Sabbath seems to have been adopted by Israel.[70] However, others argue that there is no

---

59. John E. Hartley, *Leviticus*, vol. 4 (WBC; Dallas, Texas: Word Books, 1992), 376; Lester L. Grabbe, *Leviticus* (OTG; Sheffield: Sheffield Academic Press, 1993), 88.
60. See Brevard S. Childs, *Exodus* (OTL; London: SCM Press, 1974), 413; Hartley, *Leviticus*, 376; Grabbe, *Leviticus*, 88.
61. Grabbe, *Leviticus*, 88.
62. A. Noordtzij, *Leviticus*, trans. Raymond Togtman (BSC; Grand Rapids, Michigan: Zondervan Publishing House, 1982), 229.
63. Grabbe, *Leviticus*, 89.
64. Hartley, Leviticus, 376.
65. See Benno Jacob, *The Second Book of the Bible: Exodus*, inter. Benno Jacob; trans. with an introduction by Walter Jacob in association with Yaakov Elman (Hoboken, New Jersey: Ktav Publishing House, 1992), 561; Noordtzij, *Leviticus*, 229.
66. Noordtzij, *Leviticus*, 229.
67. Ibid.
68. Weinfeld, *Deuteronomy 1-11*, 301.
69. Ibid., 302.
70. Mays, *Amos*, 144.

reference in the Old Testament which connects with the Ancient Near East concept of Sabbath in terms of the lunar cycle or phases of the moon.[71] William Hallo agrees with this view, and thinks that rather the biblical calendar was gradually regulated to the concept of Sabbath.[72] Therefore, although the name Sabbath is etymologically related with the Ancient Near East term šabattu/šapattu, the concept of Sabbath is unique to Israel. Sabbath in the Ancient Near East is not necessarily a day of rest whereas the Sabbath in Israel is characterized in this way.[73] Wenham agrees that there is no other ancient culture which had a weekly day of rest apart from the Sabbath of Israel.[74] And Peter C. Craigie argues that 'there is no clear evidence of a *sabbath day* apart from the Israelite tradition'.[75] Even the inner relationship within the week makes the Sabbath of Israel unique and significant. The Babylonian week had no inner relationship between the seventh day and the other six days. However, the Sabbath is a day of rest after six days of work.[76] We conclude therefore, that the concept of Sabbath in Israel has no connection with the Ancient Near Eastern traditions. It is unique to Israel.

4.2.3 Sabbath in the Pentateuch

4.2.3.1 Theology of Sabbath in Exodus

In Exodus, Moses clarifies how the Sabbath is observed by the people of Israel in relation to the manna (Exod 16).[77] Brevard S. Childs has pointed out that the word שַׁבָּת 'Sabbath' first appears in Exodus 16:23, regarded as an early text, before Israel comes to Sinai. Therefore, the text assumes that

---

71. See William W. Hallo, 'New Moons and Sabbaths' *HUCA* 48 (1977): 1-18; Benno Jacob, *Second Book*, 561; Weinfeld, *Deuteronomy 1-11*, 301; Grabbe, *Leviticus*, 89; Noordtzij, *Leviticus*, 229.
72. Hallo, 'New Moons and Sabbaths' 1-18.
73. See Noordtzij, *Leviticus*, 229; Hartley, *Leviticus*, 376.
74. Gordon J. Wenham, *Exploring the Old Testament Volume 1, The Pentateuch* (London: SPCK, 2003), 70.
75. Peter C. Craigie, *The Book of Deuteronomy* (NICOT; Grand Rapids, Michigan: William B. Eerdmans Publishing Company, 1976), 157.
76. Benno Jacob, *Second Book*, 561.
77. W. Gunther Plaut, *The Torah: A Modern Commentary*, ed. W. Gunther Plaut (New York: Union of American Hebrew Congregations, 1981), 500, 547.

the Sabbath law was not given for the first time at Sinai to the Israelites (Exod 16:22-31); rather they are urged to remember their responsibility to YHWH since their beginning.[78] Similarly, Houtman considers that Israel had observed the commandment of Sabbath as a pattern for their social life prior to YHWH's revelation at Sinai (Exod 16:4, 5, 22-30).[79] However, a detailed command about Sabbath is given for the first time at Sinai (Exod 20:8-11).[80]

The Sabbath rest is a prominent and recurring theme in the book of Exodus (20:8-11; 31:12-17; cf. 23:12; 34:21; 35:2-3).[81] The instruction of Sabbath in Exodus affirms that the world did not come into existence by chance but by the only creative act of YHWH, and thus 20:11 affirms the design of a creator, grounded in YHWH's creation.[82] YHWH himself kept the Sabbath day after the completion of his work of creation; thus, the people of Israel have that responsibility.[83] Exodus (20:8) uses זָכַר 'remember', meaning the Sabbath day is 'not to be overlooked and not to remain unnoticed', while Deuteronomy (5:12) uses שָׁמַר 'observe', meaning 'keep'. In both cases, the descriptive definition means that the Sabbath is to be 'kept holy'.[84]

'Remembering', as Fretheim argues, is an active observance, and therefore observing the Sabbath is patterned after YHWH's creation.[85] Again, Fretheim asserts that in the creation what YHWH intended is to have a rhythm in the created order. Therefore, the Sabbath functions as a means for all creatures to live in harmony with the created order. In this sense, keeping the Sabbath is primarily fulfilling the intention of YHWH's

---

78. Childs, *Exodus*, 416.
79. Cornelis Houtman, *Exodus* (Leuven: Peeters, 2000), 42.
80. See Allen P. Ross, *Holiness to the Lord: A Guide to the Exposition of the Book of Leviticus* (Grand Rapids, Michigan: Baker Academic, 2002), 398; Ronald E. Clements, *Exodus* (Cambridge: Cambridge University Press, 1972), 100.
81. Terence E. Fretheim, *Exodus* (IBCTP; Louisville: John Knox Press, 1991), 185; also see Plaut, *Torah*, 547.
82. See Preuss, *Old Testament Theology*, 2: 235; Fretheim, *Exodus*, 185; Plaut, *Torah*, 547.
83. John I. Durham, *Exodus* (WBC; Waco, Texas: Word Books, 1987), 290.
84. Martin Noth, *Exodus: A Commentary* (OTL; London: SCM Press, 1962), 164.
85. Fretheim, *Exodus*, 229.

rhythmic creation.[86] The theology of Sabbath in Exodus clearly asserts that it is a religious institution connected with the recognition of YHWH's creation of the world.[87] Houtman believes it has 'a stamp' of YHWH as creator of the world.[88] Therefore, ignoring the Sabbath is a kind of violation of the created order, and this explains its result in the penalty of death (Exod 31:12-17; 35:2).

Not only does Sabbath have a creation context, it also has social implications. YHWH blessed (ברך) the Sabbath day and made it holy (Exod 20:11). Its social and humanitarian character is represented by the word ברך 'bless' or 'blessing' which grows out of the primary purpose of the seventh day, Sabbath.[89] This blessing is shared by the whole family in celebration, making the Sabbath a symbol of the humanitarian treatment of fellow human beings regardless of status.[90] Therefore, Sabbath is primarily liberating, because not only are the land-owners given rest but also all the household members, along with the servants and aliens; and even the animals are to take rest (Exod 20:10; cf. Deut. 5:14).[91] Furthermore, the Sabbath signifies a consecration of time to YHWH.[92] This idea of Sabbath in terms of consecration to YHWH is further developed in Exodus 31:12-17 as a sign between YHWH and Israel.[93]

Many scholars think that Exodus 31:12-17 emphasizes strict observation of Sabbath during the construction of the sanctuary.[94] The reference

---

86. Fretheim, *Exodus*, 230.
87. See Plaut, *Torah*, 1360; Preuss, *Old Testament Theology*, 2: 235; Fretheim, *Exodus*, 185; U. Cassuto, *A Commentary on the Book of Exodus*, trans. from the Hebrew by Israel Abrahams (Jerusalem: The Magnes Press, 1983), 244; Christopher D. Ringwald, *A Day Apart: How Jews, Christians, and Muslims Find Faith, Freedom, and Joy on the Sabbath* (Oxford: Oxford University Press, 2007), 16; Noth, *Exodus*, 164; J. Gerald Janzen, *Exodus* (Louisville, Kentucky: Westminster John Knox Press, 1997), 222.
88. Houtman, *Exodus*, 42.
89. Ibid., 43.
90. Houtman, *Exodus*, 43.
91. Hartley, *Leviticus*, 376.
92. Clements, *Exodus*, 125.
93. See Clements, *Exodus*, 200-201; Cassuto, *Exodus*, 403-405; Noth, *Exodus*, 241; Benno Jacob, *Second Book*, 844-849; Durham, *Exodus*, 413; Hartley, *Leviticus*, 376; Ross, *Holiness*, 399.
94. See Benno Jacob, *Second Book*, 844; Janzen, *Exodus*, 222; Houtman, *Exodus*, 3: 588-589.

to Sabbath in Exodus 31:12-17 indicates a similarity between the creation of the world by YHWH and the building of the sanctuary by Israel.[95] YHWH's creation of the world is obviously observed as holy. In this sense, the work of building the sanctuary is holy because it is sanctified by the sign of the covenant between YHWH and Israel.[96] It is a reminder that Israel is particularly chosen for YHWH (Exod 31:13) and that they are to keep it in memory of YHWH's work of creation (Exod 31:17).[97]

4.2.3.2 Theology of Sabbath in Leviticus

Since the Sabbath is a sign of covenant, YHWH requires an occasion for the people of Israel to come to assembly (Lev 23:3). The expression מִקְרָא־קֹדֶשׁ, translated as a 'sacred assembly',[98] 'holy convocation',[99] or 'sacred day of celebration',[100] shows that the Israelites gathered together before YHWH to observe the Sabbath. The phrase שַׁבַּת שַׁבָּתוֹן, literally 'the most restful cessation',[101] or 'Sabbath of complete rest'[102] (see also Exod 31:14; 35:2), presupposes the ownership of YHWH: שַׁבָּת הִוא לַיהוָה, 'it is a Sabbath to YHWH'.[103] The designation of the Sabbath year (Lev 25:4) as a שַׁבַּת שַׁבָּתוֹן, is also related to the expression, שַׁבָּת לַיהוָה, 'a Sabbath to YHWH' in which work is forbidden. The expression, שַׁבָּת הִוא לַיהוָה, 'it is a Sabbath to YHWH', signifies that it is to be observed in honor of YHWH especially in worship (cf. Isa 58:13-14).[104] Although there is no specific instruction about sacrificial rite here, the Sabbath is to be observed in giving worship to YHWH.[105]

---

95. John H. Sailhamer, *The Pentateuch as Narrative: A Biblical-Theological Commentary* (Grand Rapids, Michigan: Zondervan Publishing House, 1992), 309.
96. Sailhamer, *Pentateuch*, 286.
97. Houtman, *Exodus*, 589.
98. NIV, NEB.
99. See Sailhamer, *Pentateuch*, 286; Gordon J. Wenham, *The Book of Leviticus* (NICOT; London: Hodder and Stoughton, 1979), 301; also see ASV, ESV, KJV, NAS, RSV.
100. Noordtzij, *Leviticus*, 227.
101. Baruch A. Levine, *Leviticus: The Traditional Hebrew Text with the New JPS Translation* (JPSTC; Philadelphia: The Jewish Publication Society, 1989), 155.
102. See Noordtzij, *Leviticus*, 230; Levine, *Leviticus*, 155.
103. Levine, *Leviticus*, 155.
104. Hartley, *Leviticus*, 376.
105. Levine, *Leviticus*, 155.

Again, the law of Sabbath in Leviticus 23:3 is intended to preserve the weekly remembrance of YHWH's creation.[106] The observance of Sabbath supposes the people's imitation of their Creator who rested on the seventh day after six days of creation (Gen 2:1-3; Exod 20:11).[107] Another evidence of Sabbath is found in Leviticus 25:1-7. In Leviticus 23:15-16, the seven weeks are called שַׁבָּתוֹת, 'Sabbaths', weeks of days. In Leviticus 25:1-7, these are weeks of years.[108] In Leviticus 25:1-7, the Sabbath year also shares the fundamental principles of the weekly Sabbath and the Sabbaths of all other festivals.[109] The concept in Leviticus 25 is based on the Sabbath rest for the land, recognizing that the land belonged to YHWH.[110] Therefore, the Sabbath observance makes clear that people are acknowledging YHWH's ownership of the land (cf. 25:23).[111] YHWH, the owner of the land (Lev 25:23), grants it to Israel and the land itself must observe a Sabbath to the Lord (Lev 25:2).

In Leviticus 25:1-7, the land is to be left untilled and to have rest after having produced food,[112] and it is thus protected from exploitation.[113] As in Exodus (23:10-11), Leviticus chiefly focuses on the land's right to have a 'Sabbath of rest' in the seventh year (25:4).[114] A Sabbath rest for the land recognizes YHWH's faithful provision, the right of his people to enjoy the abundance of his provision, and also their responsibility to share YHWH's bounty with one another (Lev 25:6-7).[115] YHWH wants his people to enjoy the gift of the Promised Land by taking a rest from continuous work.[116]

---

106. Ross, *Holiness*, 397.
107. Wenham, *The Book of Leviticus*, 301-302.
108. Levine, *Leviticus*, 169-170.
109. Ross, *Holiness*, 450.
110. Ibid., 451.
111. See Martin Noth, *Leviticus: A Commentary* (OTL; London: SCM Press, 1965), 186; Ross, *Holiness*, 451-453; Hartley, *Leviticus*, 433; Noordtzij, *Leviticus*, 250.
112. See Plaut, *Torah*, 940; Wenham, *The Book of Leviticus*, 318; Bernhard J. Bamberger, *Leviticus: A Modern Commentary* (New York: Union of American Hebrew Congregations, 1979), 271.
113. Thomas W. Mann, *The Book of the Torah: The Narrative Integrity of the Pentateuch* (Atlanta: John Knox Press, 1988), 122.
114. Noordtzij, *Leviticus*, 250.
115. Ross, *Holiness*, 452-454; Sailhamer, 361.
116. Hartley, *Leviticus*, 433.

Further, a Sabbath rest for the land includes a social and humanitarian concern for the poor (Lev 25:6-7) as in Exodus (23:10-11).[117] Exodus (23:10-11) especially gives its focus on the poor and animals. However, Leviticus is more inclusive than Exodus, embracing a larger community including land-owners and poor alike, and animals too (Lev 25:6-7),[118] who are to enjoy whatever the land produces.

4.2.3.3 Theology of Sabbath in Deuteronomy

While the Sabbath in Exodus emphasizes YHWH as creator, the Sabbath in Deuteronomy bears the stamp of YHWH as redeemer;[119] each therefore emphasizes people's dependence upon YHWH in a different way.[120] In Exodus, YHWH ceased from his work of creation (20:11). In Deuteronomy, the Israelites remember their slavery in Egypt (5:15).[121] In these ways the traditions explore the meanings of Sabbath, as both 'to cease' and 'to rest'.[122]

Childs observes that in addition to the replacement of the reminder of YHWH's creation in Exodus with YHWH's redemption in Deuteronomy, the structure of Sabbath itself has also changed in its focus.[123] To the introduction: 'Observe the Sabbath to keep it holy' is added a clause, כַּאֲשֶׁר צִוְּךָ יְהוָה אֱלֹהֶיךָ, 'as YHWH your God has commanded you' (Deut 5:12). And a similar phrase is repeated,

---

117. Noordtzij, *Leviticus*, 250.
118. Philip J. Budd, *Leviticus* (NCBC; Grand Rapids, Michigan: William B. Eerdmans Publishing Company, 1996), 341; Elmer A. Martens, *God's Design: A Focus on Old Testament Theology*, 2nd ed. (Grand Rapids, Michigan: Baker Books, 1994), 117.
119. See Houtman, *Exodus*, 42-43; Sailhamer, *Pentateuch*, 437; Plaut, *Torah*, 1360; Calum M. Carmichael, *Women, Law and the Genesis Traditions* (Edinburgh: Edinburgh University Press, 1979), 36; Christensen, *Deuteronomy*, 120; Patrick D. Miller, *Deuteronomy* (IBCTP; Louisville: John Knox Press, 1990), 79-82; Ross, *Holiness*, 399; Weinfeld, *Deuteronomy 1-11*, 302; Hallo, 'New Moons and Sabbaths,' 11.
120. See Craigie, *Deuteronomy*, 157; Ross, *Holiness*, 399.
121. Merrill, *Deuteronomy*, 150.
122. See Christensen, *Deuteronomy*, 119; Craigie, *Deuteronomy*, 157; Merrill, *Deuteronomy*, 150-151.
123. Childs, *Exodus*, 416. For more discussion on the different structure of Deuteronomy see J. A. Thompson, *Deuteronomy: An Introduction and Commentary* (Leicester: Inter-Varsity Press, 1974), 116; J. Ridderbos, *Deuteronomy* (BSC; Grand Rapids, Michigan: Zondervan Publishing House, 1984), 108.

עַל־כֵּן צִוְּךָ יְהוָה אֱלֹהֶיךָ לַעֲשׂוֹת אֶת־יוֹם הַשַּׁבָּת, 'therefore YHWH your God has commanded you to observe the Sabbath day' (Deut 5:15).[124]

The replacement of the focus on 'remember' with 'observe'[125] shows the distinctiveness of Deuteronomy from Exodus. The word זָכַר 'remember'[126] does not necessarily mean 'recall to mind' but it is 'to remember to do', or 'to keep it'.[127] However, Deuteronomy's usage adds rhetorical force. The form שָׁמוֹר (like זָכוֹר) is an infinitive form, but it functions as an imperative, to form an exhortation, together with the following infinitive לְקַדְּשׁוֹ (Deut 5:12).[128] The commandment begins with 'observe' (שָׁמוֹר) and adds the word 'remember' (זָכוֹר) at the end (5:15), recalling their historical experience under the bondage of Egypt.[129] This double exhortation, using both verbs (שָׁמוֹר, זָכוֹר) provides a distinctive motivation for Sabbath.[130] Friedman argues that both terms are necessarily complementing each other: 'in the mind, one must remember it. In actions, one must observe it'.[131] The people of Israel are urged to observe the Sabbath by remembering their history with YHWH's act of redemption.

Deuteronomy's additional expression, כַּאֲשֶׁר צִוְּךָ יְהוָה אֱלֹהֶיךָ 'as YHWH your God has commanded you' (5:12b), is another unique characteristic of that book.[132] The other addition of 'your ox, your donkey or any of your animals' (Deut 5:14) once again illustrates a characteristic of Deuteronomy.[133] Weinfeld observes that this enumeration of ox (שׁוֹר) and

---

124. Childs, *Exodus*, 416-417.
125. See Thompson, *Deuteronomy*, 116; Miller, *Deuteronomy*, 80; Ridderbos, *Deuteronomy*, 108; Weinfelf, *Deuteronomy 1-11: A New Translation with Introduction and Commentary*, 302.
126. For the study of זָכַר see John D. W. Watts, 'Infinitive Absolute as Imperative and the Interpretations of Exodus 20:8,' *ZAW* 74, no. 02 (1962): 141-145.
127. Allan M. Harman, 'Decalogue (Ten Commandments),' in *NIDOTTE*, ed. Willem A. VanGemeren et al., vol. 4 (Carlisle: Paternoster Press, 1996), 517.
128. Merrill, *Deuteronomy*, 149-150.
129. Richard Elliott Friedman, *Commentary on the Torah: With a New English Translation and the Hebrew Text* (San Francisco: Harper San Francisco, 2001), 583.
130. Weinfeld, *Deuteronomy 1-11*, 302-303.
131. Friedman, *Commentary on the Torah*, 583.
132. See Merrill, *Deuteronomy*, 150; Thompson, *Deuteronomy*, 116; Childs, *Exodus*, 416-417; Ridderbos, *Deuteronomy*, 108.
133. See Ridderbos, *Deuteronomy*, 108; Thompson, *Deuteronomy*, 116; Richard D. Nelson, *Deuteronomy: A Commentary* (OTL; London: Westminster John Knox Press,

donkey (חֲמוֹר) is absent in Exodus, which rather uses the word בְּהֵמָה to refer to domestic animals generally (cf. Gen 1:24-26; Lev 1:2; 25:7; 27:26) while Deuteronomy uses שׁוֹר and חֲמוֹר in addition to בְּהֵמָה (Deut 5:14).[134] Deuteronomy, therefore, is more inclusive by asserting the ox and the donkey in addition to the general term בְּהֵמָה for 'animal' or 'cattle'.[135]

A further additional expression, לְמַעַן יָנוּחַ עַבְדְּךָ וַאֲמָתְךָ כָּמוֹךָ, 'so that your manservant and maidservant may rest, as you do' (Deut 5:14) also illustrates the unique characteristic of Deuteronomy, with its concern for the humanitarian treatment of servants.[136] Childs concluded that only if the slaves also observed the Sabbath would it be fully realized.[137] Exodus put the animal and human being together on the same level in Sabbath rest (23:12). However, Deuteronomy particularly stresses the equality of human beings by adding 'so that your manservant and maidservant may rest, as you do' (Deut 5:14).[138] As McConville suggests, this clause makes clear that the granting of rest applies to the servants who are weak and unprotected.[139] Deuteronomy's Sabbath command shows that it is specially orientated towards the weak, poor, and marginalized people in the society.

The Sabbath in Deuteronomy draws attention to the participation of slaves in Sabbath rest and the salvation history of Israel, by reminding its hearers that all Israelites had been slaves in Egypt (cf.15:15; 16:12; 24:18, 22),[140] and brought them by the mighty act of YHWH to a new land. Sabbath is an occasion for remembering that freedom for everyone is ensured by YHWH. The rhetorical use of 'you' shows a desire for 'alternative community.'[141] Sabbath is not limited to a particular class but it applies to all social classes (land-owners, slave, alien), gender (son, daughter or man-

---

2002), 83.
134. Weinfeld, *Deuteronomy 1-11*, 308.
135. McConville, *Deuteronomy*, 121.
136. Childs, *Exodus*, 417.
137. Ibid.
138. Weinfeld, *Deuteronomy 1-11*, 308.
139. McConville, *Deuteronomy*, 121. Also see Ridderbos, *Deuteronomy*, 108.
140. See Preuss, *Old Testament Theology*, 2: 235; McConville, *Deuteronomy*, 128; Nelson, *Deuteronomy: A Commentary*, 83; Thomas W. Mann, *Deuteronomy* (Louisville, Kentucky: Westminster John Knox Press, 1995), 75.
141. Walter Brueggemann, *Deuteronomy* (Nashville: Abingdon Press, 2001), 73-74.

servant or maidservant), or even species, all household members at large,[142] and so portrays the whole Israel, brought by YHWH to give the land.

4.2.4 Amos' Theology of Sabbath

4.2.4.1 Sabbath in Amos 8:4-6

The Sabbath (שַׁבָּת) has been understood as one of the most important festivals and days in the life of Israel.[143] This observance of Sabbath is carried out in the prophets as early as the eighth century BC (Amos 8:5; Hos 2:11; Isa 1:13) and later in the exilic and post-exilic time (Isa 56; Neh 13:15-22).[144] The book of Amos shows that Sabbath was already known and practiced in the prophet's time. However, what was its character then? In biblical tradition, since the essential character of Sabbath is undoubtedly designated by 'rest', any work is in principle prohibited (Exod 16:23-24; 20:10; 31:14; 34:21; Lev 23:3; Num 15:32-36; Deut 5:12-14; Amos 8:5; cf. Isa 58:13-14; Jer 17:21-27; Ezek 20:13; 22:8; Neh 13:15-22).[145] Therefore, avoiding 'work' is the key element of Sabbath.[146] Repeatedly Sabbath observance means the cessation of work and trading or business.[147] What is work in Amos 8:4-6? Sabbath law strictly prohibits marketing

---

142. Nelson, *Deuteronomy: A Commentary*, 83.
143. See Abraham E. Milgram, *Sabbath: The Day of Delight*, 14th imp. (Philadelphia: The Jewish Publication Society of America, 1981), 1. For further discussion on the modern or traditional Jewish practice of Sabbath see Rabbi Solomon Goldman, *A Guide to the Sabbath* (London: Jewish Chronicle Publications, 1961); Rabbi Adin Steinsaltz, *The Miracle of the Seventh Day: A Guide to the Spiritual Meaning, Significance, and Weekly Practice of the Jewish Sabbath* (San Francisco: Jossey-Bass, 2003); Dayan Dr. I. Grunfeld, *The Sabbath: A Guide to Its Understanding and Observance*, 4th reset ed. (Jerusalem: Feldheim Publishers, 1981). For Sabbath as peace, see Ron H. Feldman, 'The Sabbath versus New Moon: A Critique of Heschel's Valorization of the Sabbath,' *Jud* 54, no. 1-2 (Winter-Spring 2005): 27-33.
144. Preuss, *Old Testament Theology*, 2: 235; Grabbe, *Leviticus*, 88.
145. See Houtman, *Exodus*, 44; Hartley, *Leviticus*, 375; Weinfeld, *Deuteronomy 1-11*, 307; Andersen and Freedman, *Amos*, 806; Heather A. McKay, *Sabbath and Synagogue: The Question of Sabbath Worship in Ancient Judaism* (Leiden: E. J. Brill, 1994), 30.
146. See Houtman, *Exodus*, 43; J. R. Porter, *Leviticus* (CBC; Cambridge: Cambridge University Press, 1976), 179-180.
147. See McKay, *Sabbath and Synagogue*, 13; Noordtzij, *Leviticus*, 230; Gary Smith, *Amos: A Commentary*, 253.

because it is a part of work (Amos 8:5; cf. Exod 20:8; 23:12; 34:21; Deut 5:12-15; cf. Neh 13:15-22).[148]

It is interesting that work stops at New Moon, as well as Sabbath, in Amos 8:5. Does New Moon function in the same way as Sabbath? Or was New Moon in effect a Sabbath, so that no work was to be done on it? The fact that New Moon and Sabbath,[149] referring to monthly and weekly religious festivals, are dealt with together in Amos 8:4-6, shows that these two days were important in the religious life of Israel in Amos' time. New Moon and Sabbath are connected together on many occasions throughout the Bible.[150] Amos' contemporary prophets also cited the New Moon in association with Sabbath as a religious festival (Isa 1:13-14; Hos 2:11 [Heb 2:13]).[151] Both Isaiah and Hosea take up a more negative perspective,[152] stressing YHWH's condemnation of their meaningless offerings and feasts without any concern for the oppressed and needy.

Noth has observed that the combination of the New Moon and Sabbath in the Old Testament (2 Kgs 4:23; Isa 1:13-14; Hos 2:11 [Heb 2:13]; Amos 8:5) might indicate the Sabbath's connection with the phases of the moon, though incongruously.[153] However, Hans Wildberger has argued that this combination is not due to the Sabbath's relationship with the moon since there is no suggestion in the Old Testament that the Sabbath originated as a moon day.[154] Similarly, Houtman argues that the juxtaposition is due to the fact that both are observed at regular times throughout the year by abstaining from ordinary work (Ezek 46:1, 3; 1 Chr 23:31; 2 Chro 2:4;

---

148. Wolff, *Prophets*, 326; Stuart, *Hosea-Jonah*, 384.

149. Soggin, *The Prophet*, 134, dates the observance of New Moon and Sabbath to be pre-exilic and thinks that Amos pursues the observance in connection with the cultic criticism (Amos 4:4-5; 5: 5-6).

150. New Moon and Sabbath occur in the texts as holy days such as, New Moon, Sabbath, and solemn assemblies (Isa 1:13); feasts, New Moon, Sabbath, appointed feasts (Hos 2:13); New Moon, Sabbath (2 Kgs 4:23; Isa 66:23; Amos 8:5); Sabbath, New Moon (I Chr 23:31; 2 Chr 2:4; 8:13; 31:3; Neh 10:33; Ezek 46:1, 3); appointed feasts, Sabbath (Lam 2:6; Ezek 44:24); New Moon, other feasts (Ezra 3:5; Isa 1:14; Ps 81:3). McKay, *Sabbath and Synagogue*, 26-28.

151. Paul, *Amos*, 257.

152. Andersen and Freedman, *Amos*, 806.

153. Noth, *Exodus*, 165.

154. Hans Wildberger, *Isaiah 1-12: A Commentary*, trans. Thomas H. Trapp (CC; Minneapolis: Fortress Press, 1991), 44.

31:3).¹⁵⁵ New Moon, then, is not necessarily identical with Sabbath, but has its own character.

Regarding New Moon, in Numbers (10:10; 28:11), the word 'new' does not appear separately, just חֹדֶשׁ, alone. The expression, בְּרָאשֵׁי חָדְשֵׁיכֶם (Num 10:10; 28:11) points to the beginning of the month or the first day of the month. However, it may be noted that the word חֹדֶשׁ (month or new moon) is itself related to the adjective form of חָדָשׁ, translated as 'new'.¹⁵⁶ Therefore, it is possible to take it to refer to the New Moon in those texts because New Moon is a monthly religious festival on the first day of the month.

That the New Moon was popularly observed appears from 1 Samuel 20:5, 18, 24-25. A celebration is implied, but it is not known whether all work really stopped. The Mosaic Law does not specify that no work shall be done on New Moon, but only presupposes a celebration. What is noteworthy is that Sabbath is to be observed as holy and so free from work, whereas New Moon is named as a day with celebration and offering (Num 28:11-15; 1 Sam 20:5, 24; 2 Kgs 4:23; 1 Chr 23:31; 2 Chr 2:4).¹⁵⁷ However, the offering and celebration on New Moon may signify that no ordinary work is done on it, but rather that people should pay attention to the worship of YHWH. Niehaus concludes that 'consequently, by custom if not explicitly by law, the people did not buy and sell at this time.'¹⁵⁸ Amos gives an important example of the restriction of selling and buying on the New Moon as well as Sabbath.

However, it is only the Amos text that makes it perfectly clear that business activity was forbidden, and work actually stopped on the New Moon and Sabbath (8:5).¹⁵⁹ The observance of New Moon and Sabbath is attested early by Isaiah and Hosea (Isa 1:13; Hos 2:11 [Heb 2:13]) but only Amos

---

155. Houtman, *Exodus*, 41.
156. See Pieter A. Verhoef, 'חדש,' in *NIDOTTE*, ed. Willem A. VanGemeren et al., vol. 2 (Carlisle: Paternoster Press, 1997), 30, 38.
157. Cf. Hayes, *Amos*, 208; Mays, *Amos*, 144; Grabbe, *Leviticus*, 86; Stuart, *Hosea-Jonah*, 384; A. A. Macintosh, *A Critical and Exegetical Commentary on Hosea* (ICC; Edinburgh: T & T Clark, 1997), 61; Mordechai Cogan and Hayim Tadmor, *II Kings: A New Translation with Introduction and Commentary* (New York: Doubleday, 1998), 57.
158. Niehaus, 'Amos,' 470.
159. Paul, *Amos*, 257-258.

gives evidence of cessation of work. It is clear that they were holidays with rest and worship.[160] It is interesting that this light on the New Moon comes from the prophets and not from the Mosaic Law. It does not mean that the prophetic texts show that the worship practices of Israel were different in their time from the Mosaic Law's requirements. It seems that the practice of offering and celebration was neglected and discredited before YHWH in terms of lacking social justice (Amos 5:21-24).

Given the aspects of the Sabbath noticed above, a minimal conclusion could be drawn. It is possible that the reason for restriction of work on New Moon and Sabbath could be taken from their observance by giving offering and sacrifice and paying attention to YHWH in which normal work stops on that occasion. The Sabbath along with New Moon, with the theme of worship, is connected with the land by means of offering such as grain, wine, oil, honey, and all that the land produced (Num 28:9-14; 2 Chr 8:12-13; 31:3-5; Neh 10:33ff; Amos 8:5).

This celebration of New Moon and Sabbath in Amos' time has become disgraceful in the sight of YHWH because of social injustice and religious idolatry in Israel's nation (Amos 8:4-6; cf. Isa 1:13; Hos 2:11 [Heb 2:13]).[161] Therefore, Sabbath also has its significant connection with social and economic justice (8:4-6). The relation of Sabbath in Amos 8:4-6 to the land and justice will be now explored in depth.

4.2.4.2 Sabbath in Relation to Land as a Gift of YHWH

In Deuteronomy, YHWH is recognized as the owner of the land in which Israel is to follow the Torah (Deut 4:39; 10:14, 17).[162] Israel's possession of the land depends on obedience to YHWH and his law.[163] Israel in its land is under the command of YHWH to keep Torah and to enjoy the gift of land which will help them not to forget whose land it is and how it was given to

---

160. See Graham I. Davies, *Hosea* (NCBC; Grand Rapids, Michigan: William B. Eerdmans Publishing Company, 1992), 76; Wildberger, *Isaiah 1-12*, 44.
161. R. Dennis Cole, *Numbers* (NAC; Nashville: Broadman and Holman Publishers, 2000), 474.
162. Norman C. Habel, *The Land is Mine: Six Biblical Land Ideologies*, forward by Walter Brueggemann (OBT; Minneapolis: Fortress Press, 1995), 37.
163. Miller, 'The Gift of God', 456, 458.

them.[164] The land as a gift of YHWH is connected with the responsibility of Israel to keep Sabbath (Deut 5: 12-15). Amos also shows the connection of the gift of land in terms of Sabbath (Amos 8:4-6).[165] The people of Israel are tempted to initiate a sabbathless society to abandon the criteria of Sabbath including social concern and resting the land.[166] Brueggemann sees this concept of sabbathless existence as coveting without limit among the covenanted people of Israel.[167]

For Brueggemann, the land is the means of YHWH's word becoming real and perfect (Deut 6:10-11; 11:10-12). Israel has thus to receive it with 'listening or hearing' (שמע). The exhortation to 'listen' or 'hear' (שמע) is primary in Deuteronomy (Deut 6:4).[168] This same verb (שמע) is used in Amos 8:4, also in the imperative, to gain the attention of the audience of Amos. Again, Brueggemann argues that land will become meaningless and void of covenant if Sabbaths are abolished.[169] Elmer A. Martens pointed to the Deuteronomic extension of Sabbath in relation to land-use, which is for the benefit of the poor (Deut 15:1-3).[170] In Amos, the rich attempt to abuse the products of the land by selling the grain and wheat with unjust prices and balances (8:5). This deprives the poor and needy of their true interest in the land, and the Sabbath is meant to prevent this mistreatment of its bounty.

4.2.4.3 Sabbath and Justice

Andersen and Freedman point to the merchants' impatience, expressed by the question מָתַי 'when?'[171] For them, Sabbath is merely waiting time, and

---

164. Brueggemann, *The Land*, 56-58.
165. Ibid., 59.
166. Ibid., 60-61.
167. Ibid., 61.
168. Ibid., 45-48.
169. Ibid., 61.
170. Elmer A. Martens, *Plot and Purpose in the Old Testament* (Leicester: Inter-Varsity Press, 1981), 111-112; Martens, *God's Design*, 117.
171. Andersen and Freedman, *Amos*, 805.

in effect this means they are not keeping it.[172] Mays expresses the impatient merchants' attitude as follows:

> 'Ah, we can hardly bear the interruption of holy days, so impatient we are to get on with our business, our wheeling and dealing that brings the property and person of every man into our hands!'[173]

The greedy merchants may have taken part in formal worship and dutifully closed their shops, but their priority was expressed in their intention: 'that we may sell grain and that we may market wheat.'[174] Further, Amos characterizes them rhetorically as enthusiastically waiting for the day when they can sell and buy the indebted poor into slavery.[175] Amos apparently shares with the laws 'the social concern of protecting slaves' (cf. Exod 21:1-11; 23:12; Deut 5:14-15; 15:12-18).[176] It is the only event that defends the needy and poor from social exploitation, that is, from 'being bought and sold'[177] The Sabbath grounds the relationship between YHWH and the people, and the concern is social and economic justice within the entire household (see Exod 20:10; Deut 5:14).[178]

In Amos 8:4, those who oppressed the poor are the main target for Amos' condemnation: 'Hear this, you who trample upon the needy, and bring the poor of the land to an end.' Here, the verb שאף 'to trample' designates to those who abusively treat to the poor and needy which recalls

---

172. See Simundson, *Hosea, Joel, Amos, Obadiah, Jonah, Micah*, 227; Satterlee, 'Amos 8:1-12,' 202.
173. Mays, *Amos*, 144.
174. Smith and Page, *Amos, Obadiah, Jonah*, 145; also see D. N. Premnath, 'Amos and Hosea: Sociohistorical Background and Prophetic Critique,' *WW* 28, no. 02 (Spring 2008): 130; Hammershaimb, *Book of Amos*, 122.
175. Gunther H. Wittenberg, 'The Significance of Land in the Old Testament,' *JTSA* 77 (1991): 59.
176. Wolff, *Prophets*, 327. Also see Brueggemann, *The Land*, 59.
177. Brueggemann, *The Land*, 61.
178. See Richard H. Lowery, *Sabbath and Jubilee* (St. Louis, Missouri: Chalice Press, 2000), 106-109; Norman Wirzba, *Living the Sabbath: Discovering the Rhythms of Rest and Delight* (Grand Rapids, Michigan: Brazos Press, 2006), 38.

Amos' earlier description in 2:7[179] in his first judgment oracle against Israel (2:6-8),[180] referring to the cruel and unjust conduct of undefended members of society.[181] The 'needy, poor, afflicted' connote those who are helpless and are protected by YHWH (cf. Pss 22:24, 26; 34:2; 37:11; 69:32; 72:12-13; 83:3-4).[182] At the same time the legal traditions of Israel (Exod 22:20-23; Deut 16:11, 14; 24:19-21) also demand sharing openly with the poor and needy.[183] It is clear that the conditions of the poor and needy show that they need their share in the land to be protected.

'Landed' Israel, as argued by Brueggemann, is to care for the poor (Exod 23:6; Deut 15:7-11), the stranger (Exod 21:21-24; 23:9), the sojourner (Deut 10:19), the widow and orphan (Deut 24:19-22), and the Levite (Deut 14:27).[184] However, 'land' becomes an occasion to pervert justice (Deut 24:17-18; see Amos 5:10-12)[185] and to trample and oppress the poor (Amos 8:4-6; 5:10-12).[186] In this sense, it is possible to notice that the concept of land seems to diminish its value, integrity, and essence as gift of YHWH due to lack of justice.

The Sabbath brings to mind that the poor are also to enjoy the gift of land. Amos is concerned with the poor's relationship with the land. If the people do not enjoy the benefits of the gift of land there must be a disturbance of the ordinary people's relationship with it. As Niels Peter Lemche argues, this state of affairs relates to monarchic Israel. The king believed that he had the right to control everything including land (1 Sam 8:11-17).[187] In pre-Israelite Canaan the kings and their officials possessed the

---

179. Sweeney, *The Twelve Prophets*, 1: 263; Coggins, *Joel and Amos*, 147.

180. Hubbard, *Joel and Amos*, 220.

181. Smith and Page, *Amos, Obadiah, Jonah*, 145, further note that YHWH requires his people to work with the poor, orphan, widows, aliens (Deut 10:14-26; 24:19-21) and thus to be on YHWH's side is to be on the side of the poor and needy.

182. See Jeremias, *Book of Amos*, 147; Gary Smith, *Amos: A Commentary*, 253.

183. Gary Smith, *Amos: A Commentary*, 253.

184. Brueggemann, *The Land*, 61.

185. Ibid., 62.

186. For the status of the poor and needy in the Old Testament, see T. Raymond Hobbs, 'Reflections on 'the Poor' and the Old Testament,' *ExpTim* 100, no. 08 (May 1989): 291-294.

187. Niels Peter Lemche, *Ancient Israel: A New History of Israelite Society* (Sheffield: JSOT Press, 1988), 152.

land. In Israel, the kinship pattern comprises the tribe, the clan, and the household (Judg 6:15). It was on the household that the land tenure system was based and that the territory was distributed (Josh 15-22).[188]

During the monarchy, however, the families of Israel still possessed their land, including Naboth (1 Kgs 21:3), Jeremiah's cousin Hanamel (Jer 32:6-13), Naomi (Ruth 4).[189] This family land was made inalienable, intending to protect the system of kinship distribution of land, and to maintain it within the extended family. It is explicit in Naboth's refusal to King Ahab (1 Kgs 21).[190] The story of Naboth's vineyard (1 Kgs 21) indicates the king's illegal treatment of the ordinary landowner and the land,[191] according to the traditional view of ownership in families and tribes, as in Deuteronomy (where it is assumed the land is owned by ordinary Israelites, e.g. Deut 15:12-18; 16:1-17, and the king has limited property, Deut 17:15-17), and in Joshua, where the land is distributed among the families and tribal groups (Josh 13:7; 14:4; 15:13; 17:2).

In Amos' time, the ordinary people's relationship with the land was disturbed by the politics of monarchic Israel.[192] The rich received wealth through the unjust business. The poor of the land who were farmers lost their own lands (Amos 8:4-6) because of exploitation and injustice.[193] To describe the corrupt situation regarding social and economic conditions in Amos 8:4-6 (cf. 2:6), Bernhard Lang uses the term 'rent capitalism' and asserts that Amos condemns particularly the upper classes who exploit the peasant population.[194]

Why do the poor have debts and why have they lost their land? Traditionally in the ancient peasant society, every family owned their own

---

188. Wright, *Mission,*, 291.
189. John Rogerson and Philip Davies, *The Old Testament World*, (Cambridge: Cambridge University Press, 1989), 39.
190. Wright, *Mission,* 291-292.
191. Lemche, *Ancient Israel,* 151.
192. See Davis, *Scripture,* 124, 127; J. David Pleins, *The Social Visions of the Hebrew Bible: A Theological Introduction* (Louisville, Kentucky: Westminster John Knox Press, 2001), 373.
193. See Polley, *Davidic Empire,* 131, 133; Pleins, *Social Visions,* 369; Dearman, *Property Rights,* 28-29.
194. Bernhard Lang, 'The Social Organization of Peasant Poverty in Biblical Israel,' *JSOT* 24 (1982): 53.

land and was economically sufficient. Therefore, trading did not play an important role.[195] However, due to the rise of urban culture under the monarchy, commerce took an important role in the royal economy, and it was monopolized by the royal circle.[196] Many farmers were forced through poor harvests and debt to become landless and dependent on the market. Consequently, powerful merchants could monopolize the market.[197]

One can take the historical analysis of the social and economic practices that lie behind Amos 8:4-6 further. The modern scholarly trend in interpreting the history of Israel supposes that Israel was native to Canaan, and that it shared with other Canaanites its essential religious beliefs, that is, polytheism, with each people having its own particular god (in Israel's case, YHWH), in a pantheon in which El may have been the high god (as at Ugarit).[198] Like YHWH, El in Ugarit was acknowledged as creator of heaven and earth and thus the maintainer of the created world.[199] This ensures the god's control of everything including land. Like YHWH, the national gods of Israel's neighbours controlled the political and social life of the states.[200] Therefore, political and social institutions would have been broadly similar too, that is, small royal states, in which the king as divine was the chief executive and controlled everything including land.[201] The national god was thought to guarantee the possession of land in this way. These states could have developed out of pre-monarchical tribal societies. This analysis is, of course, quite different from that which we see in the biblical narrative. There, Israel becomes a people *outside* the land of Canaan, and enters Canaan with its belief in YHWH fully formed and different from Canaanite belief.

---

195. Mays, *Amos*, 143.
196. See Mays, *Amos*, 143; Premnath, 'Amos and Hosea', 128, 130; Lemche, *Ancient Israel*, 149-150.
197. See Mays, *Amos*, 143; Lemche, *Ancient Israel*, 149-150.
198. See Lemche, *Ancient Israel*, 155, 203; Alice A. Keefe, *Women's Body and the Social Body in Hosea* (London: Sheffield Academic Press, 2001), 78-79; Mark S. Smith, *The Early History of God: Yahweh and the Other Deities in Ancient Israel*, 2nd ed. (Grand Rapids, Michigan: William B. Eerdmans Publishing Company, 2002), xx, 1-2.
199. Lemche, *Ancient Israel*, 203.
200. Keefe, *Women's Body*, 83.
201. For discussion see Lemche, *Ancient Israel*, 152, 205; Keefe, *Women's Body*, 84.

Hosea and Amos worked in this world. However, there is a conflict in Israel at the time because of different beliefs about YHWH, Israel and land to those assumed in the modern view. These are the beliefs that we find in the Pentateuch, according to which YHWH gave the land to Israel centuries before; when he also gave them Torah. In relation to land, the main Pentateuchal ideas are found in Leviticus and Deuteronomy. According to the modern view, however, these ideas may have grown up as a special development within Yahwism. Hosea would then be one of the earliest to express them strongly. Hosea is often regarded as paving the way for theology we find in Deuteronomy. It may be, however, that the ideas of Amos and Hosea are not actually new, but that they are really looking back to ancient tribal traditions as they express their opposition to the practices of kings and the wealthy class. It is not possible to know this for sure. Both Amos and Hosea certainly *claim* to be drawing on historical traditions as they make their appeal to their hearers.

This is the context in which Amos' saying on the Sabbath may be understood. Amos was a near contemporary of Hosea, actually a little earlier. If we assume the modern view, outlined above, he may have shared Hosea's basic convictions about Yahwism and land. Köckert's reading of both Amos and Hosea is based on this kind of historical analysis. According to him, up until the eighth century, the relationship between YHWH, Israel and the land was 'natural'. However, the eighth century prophets Amos and Hosea began to loosen this 'natural' bond. He thinks Amos and Hosea are doing something entirely new in Israel.[202]

The origins of the Sabbath in Israel remain unclear. Deuteronomy and Leviticus represent theologies of the Sabbath which may have been developing in Amos' day. Leviticus especially sees in it a relationship between people and land that is completely different from the 'royal' model in which land is controlled by the king. As noted above, it is not possible to know just how ancient and traditional these ideas are. But of course it is possible that the Sabbath in some form has ancient tribal roots.

Amos' saying in Amos 8:4-6 rests on a belief about the just and proper use of land. In his time, the Sabbath is *at the least* an established institution

---

202. Köckert, 'Gottesvolk und Land', 43.

in which people cease from work, presumably one day in seven. And this institution must have had force, because the greedy merchants have to observe it, even though they don't like it! Amos uses the merchants' impatience with the Sabbath to illustrate a point: the wealthy class have no respect for anything except increasing their profit! Their attitude is deeply flawed; it rests on a corrupt view of the whole economic process. They will use their power to acquire for themselves as much of the goods in Israel that they can. This is quite contrary to the theology of both Deuteronomy and Leviticus: in Deuteronomy the land is a gift of YHWH to the whole people, not to a king or a particular class; in Leviticus it remains perpetually in the possession of families, and Sabbath and Jubilee function to keep it that way. Amos may have had concepts of this sort in mind as he spoke. His allusion to the Sabbath may be an ironic reminder that the economic process in Israel is meant to be profoundly different from the prevailing practice. For Amos then, the Sabbath has become an empty ritual to the merchants, just like the feasts and sacrifices (5:21-24).

Sabbath functions in reminding people of the proper use of the land. The land is intended for all people including the poor and needy (Lev 25:1-7), the people will be punished if they defile the land, a gift of YHWH, and the land will vomit out the inhabitants (Lev 18:25, 28). Therefore, they have to follow and keep the laws and decrees of YHWH so that the land that YHWH brought them to live may not vomit them out (Lev 20:22). The immoral social behaviour of the rich merchants (8:4-6) by defiling the land results the collapse of the community of YHWH, bringing the disaster and mourning in the land (Amos 8:8; cf. Hos 4:3). That is, the land is by no means insecure due to the failure to observe the Sabbath, a call to economic justice - just and proper use of the land.

4.2.5 Conclusion

The Sabbath as an institution has several theological emphases, such as YHWH's creation of the world (Exod 20:8-11), the everlasting sign of the covenant between YHWH and Israel (Exod 31:12-17), YHWH's ownership of the land (Lev 25:1-7), and YHWH's redemption from the slavery of Egypt (Deut 5:12-15) by bringing them into a new land (Amos 2:9-10; 3:1). The Sabbath also connects to the themes of social and humanitarian concern within the entire household: land-owners, manservant, maidservant, and alien.

Although the law of Sabbath functions differently in Exodus and Deuteronomy, the primary concern is Israel's dependence upon YHWH, creator and redeemer. Therefore, the law of Sabbath shows the nature of YHWH and character of YHWH's relationship with the world and the people of Israel in terms of creation and redemption, recognizing that the land belonged to YHWH (Lev 25:23) and that it is a gift to Israel (Lev 25:2). The Sabbath in Amos primarily prevents the abuse of enjoying the bounty of the gift of land. The rich want to monopolize the land-produce such as grain and wheat by economic injustice. The Sabbath rather suggests that the poor and the needy are also to enjoy the gift of land. Amos condemns the desire to have a sabbath-less society, which brings about social and economic exploitation of the poor. Sabbath, of course, is not only about land; rather it is broadly about the relationship with Israel and their covenant keeping. However, Amos' word about Sabbath in 8:4-6 rests on a belief about the just and proper use of land.

4.3 The Land in Amos 8:7-14

4.3.1 Introduction

The immoral social behaviour of the rich merchants (Amos 8:4-6) defiles the land and results in the collapse of the community of YHWH, bringing about disaster and mourning in the land (Amos 8:8; cf. Hos 4:3). That is, the land is put at risk by the failure to observe the Sabbath, hence Amos' call to economic justice – just and proper use of the land. Because of the misconduct of the people the land will once again turn against them in a dreadful earthquake and eclipse, which are seen as YHWH's wrath and punishment for the sins of the people.[203] We now turn to Amos' theology of land, as implied in the natural disaster of earthquake (8:8), a Day of YHWH (8:9) for judgment, and consequently, famine of the word of YHWH all over the whole land (8:11-12).

---

203. Snyman, 'Eretz and Adama', 143.

4.3.2 Earthquake

The land is expected to be a place where justice is to be practiced. However, it has become a place where justice is ignored and the poor and needy are trampled. Every Israelite farmer depends upon the land for the life of his family. Amos' preaching suggests that the people maintain their freedom of action in the land only by recognizing that it is a gift of YHWH.[204] Acknowledging YHWH's gift of land also implies a respect for fellow-Israelites who live on the same land, and to whom YHWH also gave a particular share of it. In this sense, the poor should not be dispossessed from their land.[205] Therefore, violating the laws of the land means 'rising against the Almighty and the order he has created through salvation history; and it is this order alone which provides the conditions and possibilities for a successful and harmonious life.'[206]

However, the land is no longer securely held. The farmers have been probably dispossessed of their land (Amos 8:4-6), and accordingly, the land itself will turn against the people (Amos 8:8)[207] in a dreadful earthquake as YHWH's wrath and punishment for their sin.[208] Amos says: 'Because of this shall not the land tremble and all who dwell on it mourn?' (8:8),[209] and as Smith and Page point out, the phrase 'because of this' (הַעַל זֹאת) retraces the oath of YHWH which brings the consequences of trembling and mourning in the land.[210] The 'mourning' in 8:8 and 9:5 is the reaction of the people to the earthquake.[211]

What does the verbal form רגז (tremble) refer to in 8:8? According to Smith and Page, it is not an earthquake (1:1), but rather it is possibly a trembling in fear, a fear that their wrong deeds would not be forgotten by

---

204. Koch, *Prophets*, 1: 62.
205. Ibid.
206. Ibid.
207. Davis, *Scripture*, 128.
208. Snyman, 'Eretz and Adama', 143.
209. This rhetorical question is associated with the judgment. Previously Amos uses the questions to relate to YHWH's accusations (cf. 2:11; 5:18, 20, 25-26; 6:2-3, 12; 9:7); Hubbard, *Joel and Amos*, 221.
210. Smith and Page, *Amos, Obadiah, Jonah*, 147.
211. Wolff, *Prophets*, 329.

YHWH and thus he would bring the punishment of 'mourning'.[212] Hayes also thinks that verse 8 relates to 8:4-7 rather than 8:9-10, where the context is in connection with Jeroboam's oppressive social and economic policies, his officials, and greedy merchants. In this sense, the term רגז 'to tremble' does not simply imply the earthquake; rather it connotes the distress already there in the land due to the economic and political oppression under Jeroboam II.[213] Hayes further argues that it seems that Amos addresses a simple question to his hearers: 'are not the social oppression and economic exploitation under Jeroboam II the main reasons for the agitation already present in the land which, like the Nile inundation, swells, stirs up, and subsides but is certain to repeat itself?'[214] For them, the description of an earthquake could be a metaphor for social disturbance.

However, Amos' description of the wrath of YHWH is closely associated with natural disasters (1:1; 9:1). A number of scholars see the term רגז (tremble) as the description of an actual earthquake,[215] and that this is the judgment threatened in 8:7b. The earthquake was already referred to in the superscription (1:1), and also in 9:1.[216] The word רגז used in 8.8 (cf. Joel 2:10) is in effect a synonym of רעש, which is otherwise found in Amos.[217] The earthquake, as a disclosure of divine power, is probably also in view in 3:14-15; 9:1,[218] because it is one of the central themes of divine judgment in Amos.[219] By noting the trembling of the land, rising and sinking like the Nile, it seems that Amos employs the symbol of an earthquake to depict the judgment of YHWH.[220] Amos started his ministry two years before the earthquake (1:1), and it is possible that the event occurred after two years

---

212. Smith and Page, *Amos, Obadiah, Jonah*, 147.
213. Hayes, *Amos,* 210.
214. Ibid.
215. For instance, see Wolff, *Prophets*, 328-329; Mays, *Amos*, 145; Satterlee, 'Amos 8:1-12,' 203; Sweeney, *The Twelve Prophets*, 1: 265.
216. Wolff, *Prophets*, 328-329.
217. Hubbard, *Joel and Amos*, 222.
218. Mays, *Amos*, 145.
219. Hubbard, *Joel and Amos*, 222.
220. Sweeney, *The Twelve Prophets*, 1: 265.

of his prophecy (8:8).[221] Can the text refer to both the earthquake and the inner experience of the people?

Outside the context of Amos, a number of texts also speak of 'quaking' or 'quivering' in terms of a threat of earthquake (1 Sam 14:15; Pss 18:7; 77:18).[222] Again, this earthquake, referred to by the verbal form רגז (see 1 Sam 14:15; Joel 2:10; Ps 77:18; Prov 30:21), is a common signal of the wrath of YHWH (see Hab 3:6; Zech 14:4-5).[223] This earthly disruption with all its natural disasters will cause the mourning of the whole people.[224]

However, in addition to the term רגז, another possible pointer to the meaning of the image lies in the important use of the term אָבַל 'mourn'. As we mentioned already, 'because of this' (הַעֲל זֹאת) in 8:8 refers to the sin of the people. This sin affects human beings and extends even to the sphere of nature. Jeremias argues that the seventh century prophets saw the sin of the people causing the land to be sterile, and bringing disasters as in Amos (8:8; also see Hab 3:17; Jer 3:3; 12:4; 14:2-6; 23:10; Hos 4:3). The collapse of the community of the people of YHWH brings disaster and mourning on the land, that is, world order becomes subject to disaster (Hos 4:3).[225] Furthermore, Jeremias thinks that while in relation to human beings, the word אָבַל means to 'mourn', with nature (cf. 1:2), it suggests 'dry up',[226] or 'wither'.[227] 'Mourning' is thus the way in which people experience 'the failure of nature's powers of blessing'.[228] Therefore, Amos 8:8 recreates this traditional perception, interpreting the earthquake in 1:1 (cf. 9:1) in a cosmic sense, as the results of the sins in 2:13 and 8:4-6, and 'in anticipation of 9:5a, from which 8:8a is presumably drawing.'[229] Equally importantly, both רגז and אבל in the context of Amos show that the earthquake as cosmic event is his description of the wrath of YHWH which is

---

221. Gary Smith, *Amos: A Commentary*, 255.
222. See Cripps, *Exegetical Commentary*, 246; Paul, *Amos*, 260.
223. Paul, *Amos*, 260-261.
224. Ibid., 260.
225. Jeremias, *Book of Amos*, 149.
226. Ibid.
227. Coggins, *Joel and Amos*, 153.
228. Jeremias, *Book of Amos*, 149.
229. Jeremias, *Book of Amos*, 149.

associated with natural disaster (1:1; 2:13; 9:1). Earthquake and mourning may not just express the potential of language for metaphor. Rather, it is the language of ambiguity, showing both YHWH's punishment through the natural disaster of an earthquake and the inner description in the lives of the people.

It emerges, therefore, that the assumption that the earthquake is YHWH's punishment prevails in the land. According to Cripps, perhaps in these passages (8:8; also in 2:13-16; 9:1), the destruction is local, the land of Israel. Since the following passage, Amos 8:10-14, is concerned about the mourning of Israel, the use of the term ארץ essentially represents the ideal land of Israel.[230] Some translate the term ארץ in Amos 8:8 as the 'whole earth'[231] while others translate it as 'land'.[232] Perhaps it could mean the land of Israel if the subject is used as a parallel with the expression 'and everyone who dwells in it mourns?' (8:8Ab).[233] The ארץ itself will turn against the people in a dreadful earthquake as a result of people's injustices. Again in Amos 8:11, the term ארץ refers to 'land'.[234] Regarding the term ארץ in 8:4, 8, 11, Niehaus argues that as Amos' prophecies are addressed particularly to the people of Israel, it seems convenient to translate ארץ as referring to 'land', the land of Israel, for in his view the judgment is not for the whole earth.[235]

The subject הָאָרֶץ is ambiguous, however. It may have a cosmic dimension as well. In a wider sense referring to the earth, the verb רגז (to tremble or quake) can refer to the anxiety and distress of all nations on earth (Jer 33:9), corresponding to חרד (tremble) (Isa 32:11; cf. Amos 3:6). Again, if

---

230. Cripps, *Exegetical Commentary*, 246.
231. See Andersen and Freedman, *Amos*, 381; Paul, *Amos*, 256.
232. See Wolff, *Prophets*, 322; Mays, *Amos*, 142; Jeremias, *Book of Amos*, 143; Niehaus, 'Amos,' 473; Snyman, 'Eretz and Adama', 143.
233. Andersen and Freedman, *Amos*, 811.
234. See Wolff, *Prophets*, 322; Mays, *Amos*, 147; Stuart, *Hosea-Jonah*, 381; Paul, *Amos*, 256; Jeremias, *Book of Amos*, 144; Snyman, 'Eretz and Adama', 143.
235. Niehaus, 'Amos,' 473.

8:8b[236] is viewed in the light of 9:5,[237] it seems that there is a more cosmic disruption, which affects all its inhabitants.[238] Amos 8:8b compares this disruption to the rising of the Nile. This comparison is ironic, because the Nile gives life to the land, that is, of Egypt, whereas an earthquake brings death. The 'land' here is ambiguous and it could be a territory or the whole earth, or could even simply be land as the physical entity, that which shakes in an earthquake, or dries up in a famine. This context shows the overlapping meanings of the word.

4.3.3 Eclipse

The wrath and judgment of YHWH also brings the natural disaster of eclipse which affects the land. The expressions 'In that day, declares the Lord YHWH' (בַּיּוֹם הַהוּא נְאֻם אֲדֹנָי יְהוִה), and 'I will make the sun go down at noon and darken the earth in broad daylight' (8:9) suggest YHWH's bringing of another disaster on Israel. This oracle starts with [239]בַּיּוֹם הַהוּא 'in that day', introducing the coming events in the indefinite future.[240] What does 'in that day' (cf. 8:11) refer to in the context of Amos? Does it refer to the Day of YHWH? Is it apocalyptic language or ordinary judgment language?

As we shall see, a number of scholars consider that the expression 'in that day' in 8:9-10 can be conceptually related to the 'Day of YHWH' context of Amos 5:18-20,[241] in which YHWH's punishment affects the whole earth. For instance, Paul contends that this expression בַּיּוֹם הַהוּא mainly

---

236. Amos 8:8b reads: 'The whole land will rise like the Nile; it will be stirred up and then sink like the river of Egypt' (NIV).

237. Amos 9:5 reads: 'The Lord GOD of hosts, he who touches the earth and it melts, and all who dwell in it mourn, and all of it rises like the Nile, and sinks again, like the Nile of Egypt' (ESV).

238. Andersen and Freedman, *Amos*, 811.

239. This prophetic formula can be found in other prophetic books (see Isa. 7:18; Jer. 4:9; Ezek. 38:18; Hos. 1:5; Joel 3:18; Mic. 5:10). Smith and Page, *Amos, Obadiah, Jonah*, 148.

240. Stuart, *Hosea-Jonah*, 385.

241. For example, see Mays, *Amos*, 146; Harper, *Amos and Hosea*, 181; Paul, *Amos*, 262; Gary Smith, *Amos: A Commentary*, 255; Hubbard, *Joel and Amos*, 222; James D. Nogalski, 'The Day(s) of YHWH in the Book of the Twelve,' in *Thematic Threads in the Book of the Twelve*, ed. Paul L. Redditt and Aaron Schart (New York: Walter de Gruyter, 2003), 205; Kenneth D. Mulzac, 'Amos 5:18-20 in its Exegetical and Theological Context,' *AJT* 13, no. 02 (2002): 296; Mowvley, *Amos and Hosea*, 84.

connotes the day of punishment (see 2:16; 8:3, 13) which focuses on the celestial world. In the first section in 8:8, the focus is on the 'terrestrial world', in the earthquake; while in 8:9-10, the imagery includes the 'celestial world', in an eclipse. In this sense, YHWH's punishment embraces the entire cosmos.[242] The same event of earthquake and eclipse is mentioned in Joel 2:10:[243] 'The earth quakes before them, the heavens tremble. The sun and the moon are darkened, and the stars withdraw their shining' (RSV).

Commentators note that two solar eclipses had already been visible on February 9, 784 BC,[244] and June 15, 763 BC,[245] and thinks that the eclipse could suggest not only that the end of Israel was coming, but that the whole cosmos was affected as well.[246] The singers of the temple (8:3), all the people of the earth (8:8), and even the heavens would join in the event of mourning (8:9-10).[247] As this eclipse,[248] turning light into darkness, brings mourning, then, this transforms religious feasts into occasions for mourning, and singing into weeping (see 5:16-17; 8:3, 10; cf. Jer 7:34; Lam 5:15).[249]

The essential significance of 'in that day' – an eclipse, darkening the earth – (8:9) is closely associated with the characteristics of the 'Day of YHWH' in which the day will be darkness, not light (5:18, 20; Isa 13:10; Joel 2:10; 3:15).[250] The imagery of darkening over the land echoes 5:18, 20, and the turning of festivals and songs into mourning in 8:10 recalls

---

242. Paul, *Amos*, 262.
243. See Paul, *Amos*, 262.
244. For instance, Wolff, *Prophets*, 329; Hammershaimb, *Book of Amos,* 126; Hayes, *Amos,* 210.
245. See Wolff, *Prophets*, 329; Hammershaimb, *Book of Amos,* 126; Hayes, *Amos,* 210; Samuel Rolles Driver, ed., *The Books of Joel and Amos* (Cambridge: The University Press, 1897), 212-213; Harper, *Amos and Hosea*, 181. Both Driver and Harper noted the eclipse centred at Asia Minor at about 38-39° N; and reasonably visible in the latitude of Jerusalem 31° 46' N.
246. Wolff, *Prophets*, 329.
247. Ibid.
248. References to the eclipse can also be found in other parts of the prophetic books, for example, Isa. 13:10; 50:3; Joel 3:3-4; 4:15. Paul, *Amos*, 262.
249. See Wolff, *Prophets*, 329; Paul, *Amos*, 263; Smith and Page, *Amos, Obadiah, Jonah*, 148; Hubbard, *Joel and Amos*, 222-223; Hayes, *Amos*, 210.
250. Mays, *Amos*, 146-147.

5:21-23.²⁵¹ This imagery (8:9; cf. Isa 5:30; Joel 2:2) is presumably Amos' presentation of the concept and the language of the 'Day of YHWH' (see 5:18, 20)²⁵² and Amos describes it more clearly in the first creation hymn (5:8).²⁵³ Amos consistently uses this term 'in that day' in his oracles (2:16; 8:3, 13; 9:11) in association with YHWH's judgment upon Israel.²⁵⁴ It refers then to the 'eschatological future of the Day of YHWH' (5:18-20).²⁵⁵ Further, in addition to the 'Day of YHWH', the expression 'in that day' is, according to Richard Coggins, apocalyptic language, which speaks of the overthrowing of the natural order, and turning the sun into darkness (cf. Matt 24:29).²⁵⁶ This language is also used in Joel (Joel 2:10, 30-31; 3:15) and Zechariah (14:6, 7) and the darkening of the sun is joined with earthquake also in the New Testament (cf. Matt 27:51; Luke 23:44).²⁵⁷

Another understanding of the term 'in that day' is that it is ordinary judgment language. For instance, Hammershaimb considers that it refers to the day of judgment (cf. 8:3) and leads up to the disaster in 8:11-13.²⁵⁸ Similarly, Hayes believes that Amos uses the metaphor of the eclipse to designate the imminent disasters. These disasters are further announced by the terms 'and it shall come to pass on that day', 'behold the days are coming', and 'in that day' (8:9, 11; also 2:16; 8:3, 13).²⁵⁹

In light of above mentioned different theories in terms of the use of 'in that day', in my view, it refers to the 'Day of YHWH', capable of bringing natural disasters of earthquake and eclipse. It directs the audience's perception towards the turning of the land against the people, and at the same time the effect on the land itself. Originally, the 'Day of YHWH'

---

251. Nogalski, 'The Day(s) of YHWH', 205.
252. See Mulzac, 'Amos 5:18-20,' 296; Mowvley, *Amos and Hosea*, 84; Paul, *Amos*, 262; Mays, *Amos*, 146; Gary Smith, *Amos: A Commentary*, 255; Hubbard, *Joel and Amos*, 222; Nogalski, 'The Day (s) of YHWH', 205.
253. Paul, *Amos*, 262.
254. See Mays, *Amos*, 146; Harper, *Amos and Hosea*, 181.
255. Hubbard, *Joel and Amos*, 222.
256. Coggins, *Joel and Amos*, 149. For discussion of apocalyptic genre, see John J. Collins, *The Apocalyptic Imagination: An Introduction to Jewish Apocalyptic Literature*, 2ⁿᵈ ed. (BRS; Grand Rapids, Michigan: William B. Eerdmans Publishing Company, 1998), 1-43.
257. Cripps, *Exegetical Commentary*, 247-248.
258. Hammershaimb, *Book of Amos*, 126.
259. Hayes, *Amos*, 210.

may have been considered as YHWH's act of salvation for the protection of his people Israel.[260] However, Amos tries to convince his audience, who believed it was a day of salvation, that it is rather depicted in terms of cosmic disaster which affects the land as well.[261] Therefore, the concept of the 'Day of YHWH' is a vital theme of Israel's faith,[262] which occurs only in prophetic texts.[263] Particularly, in the context of Amos, the theme 'in that day' is prominent (8:3, 9, 13). It bears directly on the land question in these passages, but it also has a cosmic dimension. The fate of the land seems to have wider implications.

4.3.4 *Famine*

As suggested above, the term 'in that day', along with 'the days are coming', connotes the 'Day of YHWH' which has a cosmological sense. In Amos 8, the 'Day of YHWH' brings cosmic disasters on the land. YHWH intervened in the created natural order by bringing earthquake (8:8) and eclipse (8:9), and now he brings a famine of his word (8:11). The imminent end symbolised by the imagery of the disasters of the ארץ affects not only Israel but also the whole cosmos.[264] It seems that the famine of the word of YHWH may also have a cosmic dimension.

Amos 8:11 says: 'Behold, the days are coming, says the Lord God, when I will send a famine on the land; not a famine of bread, nor a thirst for water, but of hearing the words[265] of the Lord' (RSV). The expression הִנֵּה יָמִים בָּאִים 'behold, the days are coming', indicates absolutely a judgment of YHWH by famine. This famine will afflict the whole people

---

260. See Gerhard Von Rad, 'The Origin of the Concept of the Day of Yahweh,' *JST* 4, no. 02 (April 1959): 104-105; Yair Hoffmann, 'The Day of the Lord as a Concept and a Term in the Prophetic Literature,' *ZAW* 37, (1968): 43.
261. See Hoffmann, 'The Day of the Lord,' 43; K. A. D. Smelik, 'The Meaning of Amos 5:18-20,' *VT* 36, no. 02 (1986): 247.
262. A. Joseph Everson, 'The Days of Yahweh,' *JBL* 93 no. 03 (1974): 329; Mays, *Amos*, 103.
263. For example, Isa 2:12; 13:6, 9; 22:5; 34:8; Jer 46:10; Ezek 7:19; 13:5; 30:3; Joel 1:15; 2:1, 11; 2:31; 3:14; Obad 15; Zeph 1:7, 14-18; Zech 14:1; Mal 4:5. Mays, *Amos*, 103.
264. See Wolff, *Prophets*, 329; Paul, *Amos*, 265; Cripps, *Exegetical Commentary*, 246.
265. LXX reads λόγον κυρίου the singular form דְּבַר־יְהוָה 'YHWH's word.' Wolff, *Prophets*, 322; Paul, *Amos*, 265.

throughout the whole land.[266] Is it a metaphorical famine here, that is, of the word of YHWH? Or is it a literal one?

This is the day that people will suffer from 'the famine of the word of YHWH'.[267] What does the word of YHWH refer to? Stuart asserts that the word of YHWH includes both the Mosaic Law and the prophetic revelation since the latter is based on the former.[268] Similarly, Andersen and Freedman consider that the words of YHWH (אֶת דִּבְרֵי יְהוָה) in plural form refer to the prophetic message (Jer 36:4, 6, 8, 11; 37:2), and the Book of Covenant or Decalogue (Exod 24:3-4; 34:27-28; Deut 5:5). Therefore, in Amos, a famine of hearing the words of YHWH could connote the people's failure to comply with basic commands such as the Decalogue (Hos 4; cf. Jer 7).[269] It is 'a famine of hearing as obeying' YHWH's word (cf. Isa 6; Ezek 33:30-33).[270] However, Wolff considers it to be the people's longing to hear the words of YHWH, since apart from Amos 8:11, the expression 'to hear [all] the words of YHWH' occurs only in Jeremiah (Jer 36:11; 37:2; 43:1) in close meaning with the Deuteronomic understanding: 'man lives not by bread alone but by the words of YHWH' (Deut 8:3; cf. 30:15-16; 32:47).[271] Furthermore, 'those who refused to hear the prophetic word (2:11-12; cf. 7:16) are punished by that very word being withheld from them,'[272] although they shall wander from sea to sea, and from north to east to seek it (8:12).

YHWH uses famine as one of the disasters to reveal his wrath. In Amos 4:6-11, Amos speaks of the famine and drought on Israel, but they failed to return to YHWH. Here in 8:11, YHWH brought again a different famine, not of food and water, but a famine, that is, the absence of his words.[273]

---

266. Paul, *Amos*, 265.
267. When Jesus responded to the tempter quoting from Deut 8:3: 'Man does not live on bread alone but on every word that comes from the mouth of the LORD' (NIV), it implies that starvation of food is better than that of YHWH's word. Smith and Page, *Amos, Obadiah, Jonah*, 148.
268. Stuart, *Hosea-Jonah*, 386.
269. Andersen and Freedman, *Amos*, 824.
270. Ibid.
271. Wolff, *Prophets*, 330.
272. Ibid.
273. Mays, *Amos*, 148.

Within Amos, it is clear that the people of Israel already had YHWH's word earlier (4:6-11) and they are warned with the invitation to hear his word, but they refused to return to him.[274] Rather, they commanded Amos not to prophesy (2:11-12), and they refused him and his message when he delivered the word of YHWH to them (7:10-17).[275]

Since YHWH's word refers particularly to the word and vision of a prophet, Amos previously reminded the people of Israel to seek YHWH (5:4-6, 14-15). At the final stage, they seek to hear the word of YHWH, but the time of the famine of YHWH's word is coming, and thus their deep desire for it is unfulfilled (8:11-12).[276] Therefore, this failure of the prophetic word may mean that YHWH had forsaken the people (Ps 74:9; Jer 37:17: Ezek 7:26).[277] In this sense, bringing a famine of YHWH's word in the land connotes the absence of YHWH himself for Israel.[278] This is another case of a metaphor, which lies close to a literal reality. There is 'famine' of the word of YHWH. But ironically this may mean a famine of his promises, and thus the people's life in the land. In Deuteronomic theology, one would expect real famine as the outcome of Torah-unfaithfulness (Deut 28:17-18).

Amos 8:12 confirms this famine which has taken place throughout the land: 'They shall wander from sea to sea, and from north to east; they shall run to and fro, seeking the word of the LORD, but they shall not find it' (NRS). The universal sovereignty of YHWH's ownership can be clearly seen through the use of the term ארץ.[279] Undoubtedly, the use of the term ארץ in light of seeking the word of YHWH (8:11) is not limited only to the boundaries of Israel, but alludes to the whole earth in a cosmological sense, as suggested by the expression 'from sea to sea' (מִיָּם עַד־יָם) in 8:12. In the use of מִיָּם עַד־יָם, Wolff argues that this does not necessarily mean the Dead Sea to the Mediterranean; rather it denotes the ends of the earth

---

274. Gary Smith, *Amos: A Commentary*, 256.
275. Ibid.
276. See Gary Smith, *Amos: A Commentary*, 256; Mays, *Amos*, 148-149.
277. Mays, *Amos*, 148-149.
278. See Paul, *Amos*, 265; Mays, *Amos*, 148-149; Snyman, 'Eretz and Adama', 143.
279. Wright, 'אֶרֶץ,' 518-524.

or the whole boundaries of the earth (cf. Ps 72:8; Zech 9:10).[280] Similarly, Stuart refers to it as the whole earth.[281]

Andersen and Freedman further argue that 'from sea to sea' (מִיָּם עַד־יָם) is the boundary of YHWH's rule as king (Zech 9:10; Ps 72:8).[282] Significantly, the expression 'north and east' gives a clear direction. And the expression 'from sea to sea', often alludes to the Mediterranean as the 'west' and the Dead Sea as the 'south'.[283] In this sense, by taking the four corners: north, east, west, south, it is clear that they cover all directions in a simple way; hence, the concept of searching the word of YHWH covers the whole land, that is, the whole earth. Therefore, the expressions from 'sea to sea', and from 'north to east' embrace the people's entire search everywhere,[284] and suggest the absence of any geographical limits (cf. Zech 9:10; Ps 72:8).[285] The 'land,' where a famine of the word of YHWH took place (8:11), is ambiguous and Amos chapter 8 illustrates the overlapping meanings of the word. It seems that the term ארץ, referring to the whole land of Israel (8:11), is possibly expanded to cover the whole earth in light of Israel's searching for the word of YHWH, indicating YHWH's universal ownership of the whole earth, and the validity of his word there. Amos builds up the idea of this land-concept here towards a wider theme of the whole earth or creation. And this is all affected by the failure of Israel to hear YHWH's words.

4.3.5 Conclusion

The land as gift of YHWH reinforces the indebtedness of Israel to YHWH. In the Deuteronomic tradition, the land as the gift of YHWH for Israel is associated with ethical, social, and cultic responsibilities (Deut 12:1; cf. 11:31-32; 4:5, 14; 5:31; 6:1; 8:1). The possession of the land means obedience to YHWH and his law (Deut 4:1, 5-14.; 5:31; 6:1-3; 10:14, 17). The people of Israel have to care for the poor (Deut 15:7-11 cf. Exod 23:6)

---

280. Wolff, *Prophets*, 330-331. Also see Harper, *Amos and Hosea*, 183.
281. Stuart, *Hosea-Jonah*, 386.
282. Andersen and Freedman, *Amos*, 825.
283. Ibid., 825-826.
284. Smith and Page, *Amos, Obadiah, Jonah*, 151.
285. Hubbard, *Joel and Amos*, 224.

but rather they use it as an occasion to pervert justice and to oppress the poor (Amos 5:10-12; 8:4-6; see Deut 24:17-18), which leads to a weakening of the meaning of land – a gift whose benefit everyone is supposed to enjoy. The message of Amos is essentially based on his deep consciousness of YHWH's demand of justice and righteousness (5:24). However, the inhabitants of the land do not share equal opportunities as the people of YHWH (8:4-6).

Consequently, the land itself turns against the people due to their lack of obedience to YHWH. The earthquake as YHWH's punishment comes upon the covenant people, and affects the whole earth. The eschatological nature of the Day of YHWH also promises disaster (8:8-9) and punishment upon the people of Israel, so that they will even experience the lack of YHWH's presence and his word (8:11). They will go beyond their defined territory in searching for YHWH's word throughout the entire earth (8:12). That is, Amos has in his mind a concept of land in relation to YHWH's universal sovereignty of the whole earth.

Amos' use of language in 8:7-14 is significant. In his rhetorical way, Amos uses language like earthquake, eclipse, and famine in relation to land in order to convey his message. It can be a real earthquake. At the same time, it can also be metaphorical for trembling in fear. The metaphor expresses the reality (cf. 'the land mourns' in Hos 4:3; Jer 12:4; 14; 'the land whores' Hos 1:2). The point is that the sin of Israel is so unnatural that it deeply affects the whole created order. In a deep sense, Israel's sin could lead to such things. The famine of the word of YHWH (8:11) is another metaphor which lies close to a literal reality of famine (4:6-11; 5:16-17; 7:1-6), and the people's life in the land is threatened (8:8-9). The land is affected by Israel's perversion of the covenant and Amos' language expresses this. Amos' metaphorical language helps to establish the close connection between Israel's sin and their position in the land itself. In Deuteronomic theology, one would expect real famine as the result of disobedience to the covenant (Deut 28:17-18). Theologically, this is Deuteronomic, but in Amos' metaphors we see how he expresses this theology in his own way.

CHAPTER 5

The Land in Amos 9

5.1 The Land in Amos 9:1-6

5.1.1 Introduction
Amos 9:1-6 presents a vision concerning the destruction of the temple and the inescapability of YHWH's judgment, along with a doxology that recognizes and praises YHWH's sovereign authority over the whole creation. The unnamed temple strikingly anticipates the concept of YHWH's rule in the entire earth and cosmos. We shall consider how Amos pays attention to the universality of YHWH and the certainty of judgment. We shall also examine YHWH's sovereign power in both the natural world and human history, and how the mythological and cosmological picture of the whole creation has the intention of indicating the work of YHWH in the ordinary world of time and space.

5.1.2 Temple (Altar): A Symbol of YHWH's Universal Rule
Amos 9 begins with a picture of YHWH's judgment, which includes both the temple and the people. The temple is shaken from top to bottom, and this also affects 'all the people' in that they will suffer from its collapse. The inclusive language – heaven, earth, sheol, sea, and Mt Carmel – acknowledges YHWH's presence and sovereign power over all creation (9:2-4). YHWH can bring judgment upon Israel and the other nations because he is authoritative over the whole natural world and there is no place to hide from his presence. Where is YHWH when he brings such judgment? Is he in 'heaven'? It does not appear so, according to 9:1-4, since the one fleeing

is apparently trying to escape in heaven (9:2). Is he on earth? It is not said. However, we read that YHWH made his abode in heaven and made its foundation on the earth (9:6), implying that he dwells, and therefore is powerful, in both heaven and earth.

As Aaron Schart suggests, Amos' vision of YHWH standing by the altar or temple (9:1) shows that YHWH is at the centre of the land and the universe.[1] When the fourth vision (8:1-3) describes the end of the covenant people, the site of the judgment is the sanctuary itself. In the final vision (9:1-4), Amos envisages YHWH's judgment on Israel and the specific destruction of the altar. Wolff, for example, suggested that this altar is located in the outer court of the temple.[2] In Amos 9:1, there is, of course, no indication of which altar is referred to. Does it refer to the altar of Jerusalem or Bethel? Or does this destruction of the altar refer to the cosmic dimension of the sanctuary? What does Amos have in mind when he mentions the destruction of the temple? Does he mean the heavenly or earthly temple or both? Why is it unnamed?

In the beginning of the book, YHWH utters his word from Jerusalem (1:2). However, the Jerusalem temple as a theme is not developed in Amos. Some consider that by observing the use of the definite article ה, *the* altar (הַמִּזְבֵּחַ), it could be understood that the nucleus of the final vision is the great altar in the royal sanctuary at Bethel.[3] The commonly accepted interpretation of the location of the altar among several scholars is the identification with Bethel,[4] the place of Amos' ministry, and a sanctuary whose worship he condemned (3:14; 4:4).[5] Because of the motif of fleeing judgment in vain, Amos 9:1-4 has echoes of 2:13-16 which is part of Amos'

---

1. Aaron Schart, 'The Fifth Vision of Amos in Context,' in *Thematic Threads in the Book of the Twelve*, ed. Paul L. Redditt and Aaron Schart (Berlin: Walter de Gruyer, 2003), 46.
2. Wolff, *Prophets*, 339.
3. See Paul, *Amos*, 274; Andersen and Freedman, *Amos*, 835; Schart, 'Fifth Vision', 49.
4. See Hammershaimb, *Book of Amos*, 131; Gary Smith, *Amos: A Commentary*, 266; Wolff, *Prophets*, 338; Paul, *Amos*, 274; Andersen and Freedman, *Amos*, 835, 838; Hayes, *Amos*, 216; Stuart, *Hosea-Jonah*, 391; Wood, *Song*, 83-84; Sweeney, *The Twelve Prophets*, 1: 268-269; Soggin, *The Prophet*, 122; Schart, 'Fifth Vision', 49, 52; Simundson, *Hosea, Joel, Amos, Obadiah, Jonah, Micah*, 231.
5. Sweeney, *The Twelve Prophets*, 1: 269.

oracle against the northern kingdom.[6] The phrase נצב על may allude to YHWH's standing on the stairway to heaven in the narrative of Jacob at Bethel (Gen 28:13) and it may imply his readiness to act.[7] Instead of being seated on a throne as in Jerusalem, it seems that in Bethel YHWH is seen unusually as standing on or over the altar. This belongs to the picture of the frightening scene of destruction.[8]

In the ancient Israelites' sacrificial practice, the sacrifices are burned and animals are killed. The imagery of the sacrifice at the altar, with its destruction of life, may underlie the picture of the destruction of the temple in Amos' vision.[9] This is the consequence of the corruption of the shrines, which have misled the people of Israel into sin (cf. 2:8; 4:4-5; 5:4-5, 21-26; 8:14). Further, its destruction is nothing other than the fulfilment of the prophecies both 'implied (5:6) and expressed (7:9)'.[10] The fifth vision can therefore be taken in connection with the destruction of the Bethel sanctuary (7:7-9; 10-17).[11]

The vision contains the imperatives הַךְ (smite) and וּבְצַעַם (break), signifying the destruction.[12] Henceforth, the usual meeting of the priests and the people with YHWH for the purpose of reconciliation and relationship would no longer be possible. Again, YHWH's presence would then be for evil (9:4) when the people of Israel do not seek good (5:14).[13] What then is the intention of the destruction of this Bethel temple? Does it imply a favourable view of Jerusalem?

Having seen the place of the altar at Bethel, some scholars consider that the destruction of the Bethel temple relates to Amos' attack on the northern kingdom and its cult. Robert Coote, for instance, suggests that Amos announces that YHWH utters his voice from Jerusalem (1:2) against

---

6. Gary Smith, *Amos: A Commentary*, 261.
7. Schart, 'Fifth Vision', 48-49.
8. Ibid., 49.
9. Sweeney, *The Twelve Prophets*, 1:269.
10. Hubbard, *Joel and Amos*, 227.
11. Linville, 'Visions and Voices', 37-38.
12. See Andersen and Freedman, *Amos*, 835, 839; Mays, *Amos*, 153; Schart, 'Fifth Vision', 49; Linville, *Cosmic*, 161; Jeremias, *Book of Amos*, 155-156.
13. Smith and Page, *Amos, Obadiah, Jonah*, 157.

the northern kingdom. YHWH roars his condemnation against the cult of Bethel (4:4; 5:4-5).[14] The northern sanctuaries of Bethel, Gilgal, and Beersheba were associated with false leaders who were outwardly pious. In this sense, true worship cannot be found in these sanctuaries.[15] They are not regarded as the centres of YHWH's revelation and power.[16] The judgment of YHWH is based on measuring of their sin especially the corruption of the political and religious institutions specifically at Bethel (7:10-17; 4:4; 5:5).[17]

Still some think that the destruction of the temple is not only a consequence of Amos' condemnation of the northern monarchy and cult, but also essentially it is the prophet's call to the northern kingdom to return to allegiance to Jerusalem. Harry Mowvley, for instance, noted that since the time of David Jerusalem had been the place where people expected to encounter YHWH and listen to his word.[18] Polley points to Jerusalem as the temple associated with the Davidic monarchy, and with YHWH's justice in the courts. As Amos 1:2 also functions as an introduction to his polemic against northern shrines (Amos 5:4-6), Amos' intention was to call the northern kingdom to seek YHWH in Jerusalem.[19] Amos condemned the nations including Israel for rebelling against Davidic rule, and its own priesthood and monarchy.[20] Therefore, for Polley, true worship will be established only through the north's reunion with the south, and rejection of the northern cult and monarchy. Amos expected the restoration of the two kingdoms under Davidic rule (9:9-12).[21]

Sweeney, in line with Polley, asserts that Amos' announcement of the death of Jeroboam (7:10-17), the destruction of Israel (9:1-10), and the restoration of the fallen house of David (9:11-15) are the facts that led Amos to call for 'the reunification of the entire nation of Israel around YHWH's

---

14. Coote, 'Bethel,' 441.
15. See Marsh, *Amos and Micah: Thus Saith the Lord*, 53; Polley, *Davidic Empire*, 101.
16. Hubbard, *Joel and Amos*, 126.
17. Koch, *Prophets*, 1: 37.
18. Mowvley, *Amos and Hosea*, 13.
19. Polley, *Davidic Empire*, 154.
20. Ibid., 94-107.
21. Ibid., 138.

Jerusalem and the Davidic monarchy.'[22] Amos is therefore considered as a prophet of re-union of the two kingdoms.[23] Sweeney argues that although the sanctuaries in the north would have been places for offerings and worship Amos calls them to return to the Jerusalem Temple.[24] For these scholars, the vital message of Amos in the fifth vision is the announcement of judgment against Bethel and the northern kingdom of Israel.

However, it remains true that the temple is unnamed here and this may be significant. The effect may be that Amos' message is not really about calling the northern kingdom back to unite with Jerusalem or condemning the northern cult in this context. Rather, there may be a general reference to the theology of temples, as the place where the realms of heaven and earth meet.[25] As previously mentioned, Amos argues with Amaziah about the nature of Israel. Amos does not actually condemn the north, Bethel, or favour the south, Jerusalem. This perspective may similarly apply to the concept of the temple. Amos is really concerned with the character of YHWH's people and expresses a universal vision. In this way the vision serves to support Amos' teaching that YHWH rules in the entire earth and cosmos.

The essential point is about what applies to temple imagery generally. The temple in its most basic sense symbolizes the dwelling place of YHWH. Theologically, the belief is that YHWH is present in the temple. Clements suggests that the presence of YHWH can be seen in the Israel's worship in which YHWH's glory will be in their midst (Exod 25:8-9), and that he will dwell among them (Exod 29:43-46).[26] The temple is YHWH's

---

22. Sweeney, *The Twelve Prophets*, 1: 200.
23. G. Henton Davies, 'Amos—the Prophet of Reunion,' 196-199.
24. Sweeney, *The Twelve Prophets*, 1: 234.
25. See Lundquist, 'Temple,' 1282; Meyers, 'Jerusalem Temple,' 359; Keel, *Symbolism*, 171; David Noel Freedman, 'Temple Without Hands,' in *Temples and High Places in Biblical Times: Proceedings of the Colloquium in Honor of the Centennial of Hebrew Union College-Jewish Institute of Religion*, ed. Avraham Biran (Jerusalem: The Nelson Glueck School of Biblical Archaeology of Hebrew Union College-Jewish Institute of Religion, 1981), 23-29.
26. Ronald E. Clements, *God and Temple: The Idea of the Divine Presence in Ancient Israel* (Oxford: Blackwell, 1965), 114-115.

dwelling place because in their worship he reveals his presence among them (1 Kgs 6:12-13).[27]

Jon Levenson recognizes that the temple and the world are the realization of YHWH's command (Exod 39, 40 and Gen 1:1-2:3). The creation and temple are closely connected and verbal parallels relating to them are significant.[28] These parallels highlight the portrayal of the 'sanctuary as a world,' that is an order; and the portrayal of the 'world as a sanctuary,' that is, a place where YHWH reigns. In many cultures, the temple is considered as a 'microcosm' but the temple in Israel, conversely, is clearly portrayed in cosmic extent, and the world as a 'macro-Temple' (Ps 78:69).[29] Levenson concludes that 'the Temple is a visible, tangible token of the act of creation, the point of origin of the world, the "focus" of the universe.'[30] This macro-cosmic conception of the temple designates the creator YHWH's cosmic sovereignty.

In the terms of Psalm 78:69, 'He built his sanctuary (מִקְדָּשׁוֹ) like the high heavens, like the earth, which he has founded forever' (ESV), the earthly temple is comparable to the heavens and earth.[31] For the people of

---

27. See Clements, *God and Temple*, 63-64; J. G. McConville, *God and Earthly Power: An Old Testament Political Theology* (London: T & T Clark, 2006), 58; Stephen F Noll, 'Tabernacle, Temple,' in *EDT*, ed. Walter A. Elwell (Grand Rapids, Michigan: Baker Book House, 1984), 1068; Lundquist, 'Temple,' 1280; Stephen Westerholm, 'Temple,' in *The International Standard Bible Encyclopaedia Volume Four (Q-Z)*, ed. Geoffrey W. Bromiley et al., rev. ed. (Grand Rapids, Michigan: Williams B. Eerdmans Publishing Company, 1988), 764; Menahem Haran, 'Temples and Cultic Open Areas as Reflected in the Bible,' in *Temples and High Places in Biblical Times: Proceedings of the Colloquium in Honor of the Centennial of Hebrew Union College-Jewish Institute of Religion*, ed. Avraham Biran (Jerusalem: The Nelson Glueck School of Biblical Archaeology of Hebrew Union College-Jewish Institute of Religion, 1981), 32-35.

28. Levenson, *Creation*, 82-86, further illustrates the parallels between the creation and temple: Gen 1:31 with Exod 39:43; Gen 2:1 with Exod 39:32; Gen 2:2 with Exod 40:33b-34; Gen 2:3 with Exod 39:43; and Gen 2:3 with Exod 40:9-11. Also, see Jon Douglas Levenson, 'The Temple and the World,' *JR* 64 (1984): 275-298; especially 287-288, for temple in Exodus and creation in Genesis.

29. Levenson, , 86.

30. Levenson, 'Temple,' 283. For the typological relationship between the temple and the creation, particularly the Garden of Eden, see Gregory K. Beale, *The Temple and the Church's Mission: A Biblical Theology of the Dwelling Place of God* (NSBT 17; Downers Grove, Illinois: InterVarsity Press, 2004), 66-80; Jon Douglas Levenson, *Theology of the Program of Restoration of Ezekiel 40-48* (HSMS 10; Cambridge: Scholars Press, 1976), 25-35.

31. Beale, *The Temple and the Church's Mission*, 31-32.

Israel, the temple is one of the essential means of conducting a relationship with YHWH because YHWH manifests his nature and acts in the temple. People came to the temple to experience the power of YHWH (cf. Pss 27:4; 34:8), and their longing for him can be expressed as a longing for the temple (Pss 42; 84), since it represents YHWH through his presence and revelation.[32] The temple is assumed to be located at the centre of the universe in the ancient world.[33] The earthly and heavenly bodies are depicted as complementary, that is, the temple also denotes the entire cosmos. In this sense, as the temple represents all creation, Habakkuk announces, 'But the Lord is in his holy temple; let all the earth keep silence before him' (2:20).[34]

In Amos, the temple, a place of blessing and blissful fellowship with YHWH,[35] is turned into a place of YHWH's judgment.[36] People expected that YHWH would accept their offerings at the altar. Upon the announcement of Amos that he saw the Lord standing by the altar, the worshippers may have expected to hear that YHWH has accepted their offerings.[37] However, Amos declares that the altar is now the place of YHWH's furious and final judgment.

Schart perceptively suggests that Amos is commanded to smite the capital (כפתור) and the thresholds (ספים), that is, essential and prominent parts of the temple. This denotes the complete destruction of the temple, and hence the foundation of the earth or universe.[38] Schart argues that 'the temple is the center that gives refuge, stability, and prosperity to life to the land.'[39] In addition, the thresholds mark the border between the sacred and profane. And the shaking of the thresholds signifies that they can no

---

32. Keel, *Symbolism*, 179.
33. Meyers, 'Jerusalem Temple,' 359-360.
34. See Leland Ryken, James C. Wilhoit, Tremper Longman III, eds., 'Temple,' in *Dictionary of Biblical Imagery: An Encyclopedic Exploration of the Images, Symbols, Motifs, Metaphors, Figures of Speech and Literary Patterns of the Bible* (Leicester: InterVarsity Press, 1998), 849. Keel, *Symbolism*, 174.
35. Hubbard, *Joel and Amos*, 229; Wolff, *Prophets*, 339; Smith and Page, *Amos, Obadiah, Jonah*, 154.
36. Gary Smith, *Amos: A Commentary*, 266.
37. Smith and Page, *Amos, Obadiah, Jonah*, 154.
38. Schart, 'Fifth Vision', 50.
39. Ibid., 51.

longer protect the sacred from the profane world because the temple is no longer functioning, and no longer a place of harmony with YHWH.[40] The people are not usually allowed to approach the boundary of a sacred place without any ritual preparation. The priests had to properly sanctify themselves before approaching YHWH and coming to the sacred place (Exod 19:22), and the people also are not permitted even to touch the sacred object without prior consecration (2 Sam 6:6-8).[41] Amos' message about the striking of the temple is a sign which shows how a profane people has been offensively assaulting the boundaries of the sacred, the temple.[42] Specifically, in the context of Amos 9:1, the primary concern is the centrality of the religious institution, with the temple as the foundation of YHWH's judgment.

Jeremias recognizes that the closest parallel to the language for the destruction of the temple (9:1) is found in Isaiah 6:4, which points to the cosmic dimension. This is because only YHWH, the founder of that sanctuary, can smite and shake such things of the capitals and the thresholds.[43] As Jeremias argues, it is certain that 'God's standing on the altar, along with his stroke against the temple columns, possesses cosmic significance for Israel insofar as it means the end of all contact with God as well as the end of asylum, that is, of all protection with God.'[44] Similarly, Linville recognizes that the altar in 9:1 could be 'anywhere', or in fact it could be 'everywhere', since all of the Israelites' land is included in the territory extending from Dan to Beersheba (8:14; 1 Sam 3:20; 2 Sam 3:10; 17:11; 24:2).[45] It is also possible that the unnamed temple is perceived as a symbol of the fate of all Israel and the full extent of the land.

Regarding the destruction of the people in association with the destruction of the temple, the crucial question arises at this point. Who are the people who will be killed? Amos 9:1 mentions only כֻּלָּם 'all of them'. Schart suggests that the fourth vision mentions the end of 'my people Israel' (8:2).

---

40. Ibid., 50-51.
41. Linville, *Cosmic*, 165.
42. Ibid.
43. Jeremias, *Book of Amos*, 156-157.
44. Ibid., 157.
45. Linville, *Cosmic*, 159-160.

Although the expression 'my people Israel' (8:2) could be identified with 'all of them' here in the final vision (9:1), the expression 'my people Israel' does not appear in it.[46] In 9.1, 'here is the last connection between YHWH and Israel torn apart.'[47] In 8.2, at least Israel was still 'my people' – but now no more. YHWH is against 'them all'.[48] The clear indication of the covenant people, 'my people Israel' is not addressed in YHWH's judgment of the temple and the people. It is replaced with 'all of them'. According to Schart, this language indicates the end of the personal relationship between YHWH and his chosen historic Israel.[49] If 'my people Israel' is the covenant people of YHWH, the expression 'all of them' becomes understandable as the end of covenantal relationship between YHWH and his covenant people.

Significantly, the unnamed temple may correspond to the fact that the people of Israel are not mentioned either, but rather 'all the people'. These points together support the universalizing tendency that YHWH is the centre of the universe and rules the entire earth and cosmos. This concept also applies to the concept that 'Israel' is not limited to the political conditions that prevailed in Amos' day, but rather must be understood in terms of its ancient calling and mission.

5.1.3 The Certainty of YHWH's Judgment

The primary theme of Amos 9 is that YHWH can bring both judgement and salvation to Israel and to other nations of the world. Just as YHWH created the heavens and the earth he can bring a flood to destroy the earth (9:5-6; cf. Gen 6-8), so that no one can escape from him (9:1-4). YHWH also brought salvation not only to Israel but also to other nations of the earth (9:7).[50] Again, the picture of a fertile land in 9:13-15 corresponds to the picture of devastation in 8:1-3. These scenes show that YHWH is able to bring both judgment and restoration to historic Israel and all other

---

46. Schart, 'Fifth Vision', 51-52.
47. Köckert, 'Gottesvolk und Land,' 54.
48. Ibid.
49. Schart, 'Fifth Vision', 51.
50. Cf. Smith and Page, *Amos, Obadiah, Jonah*, 155; Linville, *Cosmic*, 163.

nations in both history and the natural order because YHWH is sovereign in all time and space.

Wolff argued that YHWH's sovereign authority extends from the sphere of the cosmos (9:3) to the realm of human history, as when the people of Israel are to be driven off to distant lands as captives by their enemies (9:4).[51] In the context of Amos, the judgment of exile (9:4) is mentioned elsewhere (3:11-12; 4:2-3; 5:27; 6:7; 7:11, 17; 9:9) to designate the removal of YHWH's giving of the land as a gift and the reversal of the exodus from Egypt (3:1; 9:7).[52]

The punishment of YHWH also includes the remnant (9:1), the people who escape into exile (9:4). The word אַחֲרִית 'remnant'[53] occurs three times in Amos (4:2; 8:10; 9:1) with different pronominal suffixes. In 4:2, Israel's אַחֲרִית is taken away with hooks; in 8:10, her אַחֲרִית is grieved; and finally in 9:1, the אַחֲרִית will be killed with the sword. The context of Amos shows that the primary understanding of this term is 'remnant'.[54] According to Hasel, the remnant concept has two meanings in Amos. In a positive perspective the remnant has a hope of mercy from YHWH with an eschatological idea (5:3, 14-15; 9:11-12). However, a negative aspect of the remnant brings home the force of YHWH's judgment (3:12; 4:1-3; 5:3; 6:9-10; 9:1-4).[55] In Amos 9:1-4, the remnant concept shows the inescapable judgment of YHWH without any hope for the people.

Having seen a clear picture of the certainty of YHWH's judgment, the doxology (9:5-6) reminds the people of Israel that YHWH is creator and destroyer who controls the whole earth and the destiny of all creation.[56] The passage (9:5-6) makes clear that YHWH is creator of the heaven and the sea, which proves the certainty of YHWH's judgment that extends in sheol, heaven (9:2), or even to the bottom of the sea (9:3). YHWH's au-

---

51. Wolff, *Prophets*, 341.
52. Hubbard, *Joel and Amos*, 227.
53. The usual term for 'remnant,' שְׁאֵרִית, is used by Amos in 1:8, for the remnant of the Philistines; in 5:15, for the remnant of Joseph; and in 9:12, for the remnant of Edom.
54. Andersen and Freedman, *Amos*, 836.
55. Hasel, *Understanding of Amos*, 113-114, 116; also see Hasel, 'Alleged "No"' 8-12; Gerhard F. Hasel, *The Remnant: The History and Theology of the Remnant Idea from Genesis to Isaiah*, 2nd ed. (Berrien Springs, Michigan: Andrews University Press, 1974), 173-215.
56. Jeremias, *Book of Amos*, 159.

thority also extends to the earth, and he can make it rise like the Nile (9:5). People will mourn who live on the earth (9:5) because YHWH will bring destruction upon them (9:1).[57] As Paul suggests, in Amos, no geographical land is beyond the control of YHWH.[58] Amos mentions the inescapable judgment of YHWH upon all people (e.g. 1:3-2:16) and thus 9:5-6 is not a new indication about the punishment of death, destruction, and exile.[59] Amos 9:1-4 speaks of the certainty of YHWH's judgment, and Amos 9:5-6 deals with the corresponding idea of YHWH's creation not only of Israel, but also of all other inhabitants of the earth, and his judgment on all.

5.1.4 YHWH's Presence and His Power over the Creation

The idea that YHWH is the creator of the whole universe is in harmony with Amos' theology. This harmony can be seen in the reference to YHWH's sending of the famine and withholding the rain (4:6-7). In the same way, Amos can affirm that YHWH's presence pervades the universe, including the heavens and sheol (9:2).[60] There is no way to pass beyond the limits of YHWH's sovereignty (9:1-4). The essential elements of the ancient worldview – heaven, earth, and sea – show that there is no place for human beings to escape from the power of YHWH. Where could people expect to escape from YHWH? According to Amos 9:2-4, the possibilities would be sheol, heaven, the top of Carmel, the bottom of the sea, and other nations in exile. They contain both mythic places and natural world.

First, the mythological picture of creation functions to illustrate the idea that YHWH has power over all the mythic places: sheol, heaven, and sea.[61] Sheol (שְׁאוֹל)[62] is commonly understood as the place of the dead, the grave, the nether world where everyone went after death, located vari-

---

57. Gary Smith, *Amos: A Commentary*, 264.
58. Paul, *Amos*, 279.
59. Stuart, *Hosea-Jonah*, 394.
60. Thomas Edward McComiskey, 'The Hymnic Elements of the Prophecy of Amos: A Study of Form-Critical Methodology' *JETS* 30, no. 02 (June 1987): 148.
61. In addition to heaven, sheol, and sea as mythic places, Andersen and Freedman include Carmel as a mythic place. Andersen and Freedman, *Amos*, 837.
62. Sheol (שְׁאוֹל), as subject of the sovereignty of YHWH, appears several places in the Old Testament (e.g. 26:6; Pss 9:17; 16:10; 30:3; 49:15 [Heb 16]; 86:13; 139:8; Prov 15:11; Isa 14:15; Ezek 31:16, 17; Hos 13:14; Amos 9:2; Jonah 2:2).

ously under the earth (Gen 37:35; 42:38; Num 16:30, 33; Deut 32:22; Isa 14:15),[63] in the lower part of the cosmic sea (Job 26:5-6), beneath the foundations of the mountain (Jonah 2:6).[64] This concept has parallels in Ancient Near Eastern cultures. In Babylonian myth, the concept of sheol is seen in the myth of Ishtar's Descent into the underworld and in the Gilgamesh Epic.[65] At Ugarit, the abode of dead lay under the earth and the mountains.[66] Significantly, the concept of sheol in the Old Testament may well be rendered to portray the sovereign power of YHWH. Although it is the region outside the earth it is accessible to YHWH (Job 26:6; Ps 139:8; Amos 9:2).[67] According to Psalm 139:8, as in Amos' view, it is evident that both sheol and heaven will not provide a place of escape from YHWH.[68]

Another element of the mythic place, the bottom of the sea, is a dark and subterranean region where the roots of the earth are laid (Jonah 2:3-6). YHWH can send a sea-serpent to bite them even though people hide there (Amos 9:3). This sea-serpent is reminiscent of the creation myth in which YHWH defeated the primeval serpent of chaos.[69] In the mythologi-

---

63. See, for instance, Coggins, *Joel and Amos*, 152; Douglas K. Stuart, 'Sheol,' in *The International Standard Bible Encyclopaedia Volume Four (Q-Z)*, ed. Geoffrey W. Bromiley et al., rev. ed. (Grand Rapids, Michigan: Williams B. Eerdmans Publishing Company, 1988), 472; R. Laird Harris, 'שְׁאוֹל,' in *Theological Word Book of the Old Testament*, eds. R. Laird Harris, Gleanson L. Archer, Jr., and Bruce K. Waltke, vol. 2 (Chicago: Moody Press, 1980), 892-893; Theodor H. Gaster, 'Abode of the Dead,' in *IDB (A-D)*, ed. George Arthur Buttrick et al. (Nashville: Abingdon Press, 1962), 787-788; Jim West, 'Sheol,' in *EDB*, ed. David Noel Freedman (Grand Rapids, Michigan: Williams B. Eerdmans, 2002), 1206-1207; Donald E. Gowan, 'Amos,' in *New Interpreter's Bible: Introduction to Apocalyptic Literature; Daniel; the Twelve Prophets*, eds. Leander E. Keck et al. (Nashville: Abingdon Press, 1996), 421; Walther Eichrodt, *Theology of Old Testament*, vol. 2 (OTL; London: SCM Press, 1967), 210-211.

64. Gaster, 'Abode of the Dead,' 787-788.

65. Eichrodt, *Theology*, 2: 211-212; for discussion of Gilgamesh epic in connection with Old Testament, see Alexander Heidel, *Gilgamesh Epic and Old Testament Parallels* (Chicago: University of Chicago Press, 1949); William L. Moran, *The Most Magic Word: Essays on Babylonian and Biblical Literature* (Washington DC: Catholic Biblical Association of America, 2002); K. Lawson Younger, Jr., 'Gilgamesh Epic,' in *EDB*, ed. David Noel Freedman (Grand Rapids, Michigan: William B. Eerdmans, 2000), 505.

66. Gaster, 'Abode of the Dead,' 787.

67. Ibid.

68. Coggins, *Joel and Amos*, 152.

69. Paul, *Amos*, 278; Hammershaimb, *Book of Amos*, 132, further noted that the serpent (נָחָשׁ) is sometimes called רַהַב (Isa 51:9; Ps 89:10 [Heb 89:11]; Job 9:13; 26:12) and sometimes לִוְיָתָן? (Isa 27:1; Ps 74:14).

cal motif in both sea (יָם) and serpent (נָחָשׁ),[70] the sea is depicted as the deified power of chaos (cf. Pss 74:13; 93:3-4; Job 7:12) and the sea-serpent as a mythological personification of the destructive power of the sea.[71] In Amos, the mythological serpent is regarded as YHWH's servant or representative whom he commands 'to bite' (נשׁך) those who attempt to escape from YHWH (9:3; cf. Job 9:13) and destroy to those who mistakenly consider that they are safe (5:19).[72] Since the sea-serpent is formed by YHWH (Ps 104:26) and recognized as part of his creation the serpent will act to fulfil YHWH's command on his behalf.[73] To this point, it is clear that the ancient cosmology or worldview underlies this all-embracing language. Therefore, Amos affirms YHWH's mobility and universal sovereign might.

Second, in close connection with the mythological language, there is a specific place namely Carmel. The Carmel (כַּרְמֶל, meaning 'vineyard', or 'garden-land') is characterized by its beauty, plentiful forests and fruitful land, and pasture land (1:2; 9:3; cf. Isa 33:9; 35:2; Jer 50:19; Nah 1:4; 2 Kgs 19:23).[74] According to Andersen and Freedman, even Carmel is regarded as 'a legendary, not an ordinary place'.[75] However, they do not give reasons apart from its position here alongside mythical places. Unlike Andersen and Freedman, several scholars observe that Carmel (כַּרְמֶל) is a

---

70. It is commonly understood that both sea and serpent have mythological connotations. See Wolff, *Prophets*, 341; Paul, *Amos*, 278; Hammershaimb, *Book of Amos*, 132; Andersen and Freedman, *Amos*, 838; Wood, *Song*, 84. However, Gary Smith, *Amos: A Commentary*, 268, considers that the sea (יָם) and serpent (נָחָשׁ) are not regarded as mythological deified powers because the serpent obeys YHWH's order (cf. Job 41).

71. Wolff, *Prophets*, 341.

72. See Wolff, *Prophets*, 341; Andersen and Freedman, *Amos*, 838; Wood, *Song*, 84; Paul, *Amos*, 278-279.

73. See Coggins, *Joel and Amos*, 152; Paul, *Amos*, 278-279.

74. See Paul, *Amos*, 40; Wolff, *Prophets*, 125; Jeremias, *Book of Amos*, 14; Hammershaimb, *Book of Amos*, 21; Jill L. Baker, 'Mount Carmel,' in *NIDB (A-C)*, eds. Katharine Doob Sakenfeld et al. (Nashville, Tennessee: Abingdon Press, 2006), 569; R. Laird Harris, 'כַּרְמֶל(Carmel)' in *Theological Word Book of the Old Testament*, eds. R. Laird Harris, Gleanson L. Archer, Jr., and Bruce K. Waltke, vol. 1 (Chicago: Moody Press, 1980), 455; O. Odelain and R. Séguineau, *Dictionary of Proper Names and Places in the Bible*, trans. and adapted by Matthew J. O'Connell (Garden City, New York: Doubleday, 1981), 81; J. Kenneth Kuntz, 'Mount Carmel,' in *DBR*, ed. William H. Gentz (Nashville: Abingdon, 1986), 183; Henry O. Thompson, 'Mount Carmel,' in *ABD (A-C)*, ed. David Noel Freedman (London: Doubleday, 1992), 874; Rick W. Byargeon, 'Carmel' in *EDB*, ed. David Noel Freedman (Grand Rapids, Michigan: Williams B. Eerdmans, 2002), 224.

75. Andersen and Freedman, *Amos*, 837.

specific place in Israel with its fruitful land and forest.[76] Linville suggests that heaven and sheol are undoubtedly recognized as mythic places while the top of Carmel is a place in the real world.[77] In Amos 1:2, Carmel is withered by the utterance of YHWH, so that there too it is associated with judgment on the land. In addition, mountains are described as YHWH's creation in 4:13. Therefore, the Carmel is a place where YHWH meets the physical or real world in 9:3.[78]

Historically, Mount Carmel has been described in the writing of Egypt in the lists of three Egyptian Pharaohs Thutmose III, Ramses II, and Ramses III [79] under the name *Rosh Qishu* ('holy cape' or 'holy head' or 'holy peak'), and its character as an ancient sanctuary is implied.[80] In the Old Testament, Mount Carmel is known especially as the scene of the contest between the prophets of Baal and Elijah (1 Kgs 18) or rather, between YHWH and Baal. Possibly an altar of YHWH stood along with that of Baal since it is portrayed as a place for the contest of faith (1 Kgs 18:30).[81] It may have been a place of worship from an early period.

It is clear then that Amos refers here to both mythological places and a 'real' place as a way of encompassing all of creation. Though Carmel is in one sense an 'ordinary' place in the land, it is also, as we noticed, symbolic of the land's fruitfulness. As a mountain used for worship, it has the

---

76. See Wolff, *Prophets*, 121, 125; Hammershaimb, *Book of Amos*, 21; Mays, *Amos*, 21; Jeremias, *Book of Amos*, 14; Paul, *Amos*, 40.

77. Linville, *Cosmic*, 163.

78. Ibid.

79. Thompson, 'Mount Carmel,' 875, gives the dates of the Egyptians Pharaohs Thutmose III (ca. 1490-1436 BC), Ramses II (ca. 1301-1234 BC), and Ramses III (ca. 1195-1164 BC).

80. See, for instance, Kuntz, 'Mount Carmel,' 182; William Ewing and Roland K. Harrison, 'Mount Carmel,' in *The International Standard Bible Encyclopaedia Volume One (A-D)*, ed. Geoffrey W. Bromiley et al., rev. ed. (Grand Rapids, Michigan: Williams B. Eerdmans Publishing Company, 1979),618; Gus W. Van Beek, 'Mount Carmel,' in *IDB (A-D)*, ed. George Arthur Buttrick et al. (Nashville: Abingdon Press, 1962), 538; Thompson, 'Mount Carmel,' 875.

81. For discussion, see Martin J Mulder, 'Carmel,' in *DDD*, ed. Karel van der Toorn, Bob Becking, and Pieter W. van der Horst (Grand Rapids, Michigan: William B. Eerdmans Publishing Company, 1999), 182; H. Thompson, 'Mount Carmel,' 875; Baker, 'Mount Carmel,' 569; Ewing and Harrison, 'Mount Carmel,' 618; Van Beek, 'Mount Carmel,' 538; Michael. C. Astour, 'Mount Carmel,' in *IDBSup*, ed. Keith Crim (Nashville: Abingdon Press, 1976), 141.

usual symbolic significance of a meeting-place between heaven and earth. Andersen and Freedman may overstate when they say that Carmel here 'is a legendary, not an ordinary place'. Yet it may also symbolize the land as part of YHWH's wider creation. This means that the judgment pronounced upon it (1:2; 9:3) is particularly terrible.

As in Amos 9:1-4, YHWH's sovereignty over humanity and the cosmos is described in Psalm 139. It praises YHWH for his omniscience (vv. 1-6) and omnipresence (vv. 7-11); here too escape is impossible from the presence of YHWH for there is no hiding place in heaven or sheol. However, this positive concept of YHWH's presence is inverted in Amos 9:1-4 into a dreadful image.[82] Linville concludes that the mutually beneficial relationship of heaven, nature, and the human world is obviously overturned in YHWH's act of bringing the devastation of the cosmos.[83] The language of the final vision (9:1-4) and the idea of YHWH's sovereignty and authority over the entire universe is repeated and carried out in the doxology (9:5-6).[84] The doxology (9:5-6) portrays YHWH's presence as pervading the universe: heaven and earth. This idea is in harmony with the affirmation that there is no place in the universe to escape from the presence of YHWH in 9:2-4.[85]

In his rhetoric, Amos uses different techniques, including wordplay, analogy, and explicit imagery in his theology of the sovereignty of YHWH, to persuade Israel to live in a right relationship with YHWH the creator.[86] Finally, to summarize, Amos uses mythological and cosmological language to convey a true picture of YHWH's presence and power throughout the whole universe. The language about the whole universe, including the mythological language, supports the idea that YHWH has power everywhere and over everything. Yet it goes closely together with language about a specific place, namely Carmel. Therefore, the picture of Amos 9:1-4 combines the world of myth and the ordinary world. The mixing of the 'real' and 'mythological' locations is very interesting. It seems that the land in

---

82. Linville, *Cosmic*, 164.
83. Ibid.
84. Wood, *Song*, 85.
85. McComiskey, 'Hymnic Elements', 154.
86. Rich R. Marrs, 'Amos and the Power of Proclamation,' *RQ* 40, no. 01 (1998): 17.

Amos takes on a symbolical significance in itself, that is, as a *symbol* of the whole creation. Therefore, YHWH is completely sovereign in both the natural world, the whole cosmos and in time and human history.

5.1.5 YHWH's Power in Heaven and Earth

5.1.5.1 YHWH's Lordship

In the book of Amos, YHWH as creator is celebrated in three doxologies (4:13; 5:8-9; 9:5-6). These doxologies picture YHWH as creator and controller of the universe including the foreign nations (1:3-2:3)[87] who are linked in their different ways with the description of YHWH in judgment.[88] YHWH is extolled as creator and judge in three doxologies, but the order is reversed in the last doxology, where YHWH is celebrated as judge in 9:5 and as creator in 9:6. This change of order suggests an immediate connection with 9:2–4, and the inescapability of YHWH's judgment.[89] The focus on YHWH as creator in 9:6 evidently envisages his lordship over all nations (Amos 1-2), in addition to Israel (9:7).[90]

The characteristics of doxologies are significant. Interestingly, the first doxology (4:13) begins with the earth: mountains (הָרִים) and wind (רוּחַ); the second (5:8) with the heavenly bodies: Pleiades, a cluster of stars (כִּימָה) and Orion (כְּסִיל); and the third (9:6) combines the two: earth (אֶרֶץ) and heaven (שָׁמַיִם), summarizing the previous two.[91] What is interesting is the description of YHWH as both creator and destroyer in each doxology. Amos 4:13 focuses on the sovereign power of God of creation, whose judgment Israel is about to face in 4:12. Amos 5:8-9 pictures destruction on Israel's strongholds and YHWH's power over the natural order.

YHWH's lordship over all creation is also conveyed by the term צְבָאוֹת. The word צְבָאוֹת occurs nine times in Amos,[92] designating YHWH's title

---

87. See Cullen I. K. Story, 'Amos—Prophet of Praise,' *VT* 30, no. 01 (1980): 67-80; Smith and Page, *Amos, Obadiah, Jonah*, 31.
88. Paas, *Creation and Judgment*, 310, 324.
89. Story, 'Prophet of Praise,' 76.
90. See Story, 'Prophet of Praise,' 76; Marrs, 'Proclamation,' 15-16.
91. Paas, *Creation and Judgment*, 295.
92. Amos 3:13; 4:13; 5:14, 15, 16, 27; 6:8, 14; 9:5.

in different formulations.[93] The divine names and titles are consistently organized in Amos to accentuate that YHWH is the God of Hosts, צְבָאוֹת.[94] Taking the name of God, יְהוִה הַצְּבָאוֹת אֲדֹנָי 'the Lord, YHWH of Hosts',[95] Joyce Wood suggests that Amos 9:5 reaffirms YHWH's lordship over the heavenly bodies.[96] The title יְהוִה הַצְּבָאוֹת אֲדֹנָי 'the Lord, YHWH of Hosts', in 3:13 is applied in the context of the altar of Bethel in 3:14, and is now applied again in the doxology (9:5-6). Other references (4:13; 5:8-9, 14-15, 16-17, 26-27; 6:14; 8:7-8) also confirm YHWH's transcendent omnipotence and made the use of the term comprehensible here (9:5).[97]

The term צְבָאוֹת, means 'hosts'[98] or 'armies'[99] and its use shows YHWH as a mighty warrior.[100] In 1 Samuel 17:45, יְהוִה צְבָאוֹת is further clarified with 'the God of the armies (מַעַרְכוֹת) of Israel'. Therefore, the expression יְהוִה הַצְּבָאוֹת אֲדֹנָי, 'YHWH, God of the armies', could be intended to be 'the army hosts of Israel'.[101] Paas argues that although this could indicate the 'war hypostasis of YHWH', the essential nature of it links with the worship of יְהוִה צְבָאוֹת which had a strong connection with Zion and the Jerusalem temple elsewhere in the Old Testament (cf. Isa 6:3, 5; 8:18; 24:23; 25:6;

---

93. Different formulations are יְהוָה אֱלֹהֵי הַצְּבָאוֹת (4:13; 5:14, 15, 27; 6:8); אֲדֹנָי יְהוִה אֱלֹהֵי הַצְּבָאוֹת (3:13); יְהוִה אֱלֹהֵי הַצְּבָאוֹת אֲדֹנָי (5:16); יְהוִה הַצְּבָאוֹת (6:14); and אֲדֹנָי יְהוִה הַצְּבָאוֹת (9:5). See Wolff, *Prophets,*, 287, 341; Hubbard, *Joel and Amos*, 233; Smith and Page, *Amos, Obadiah, Jonah*, 158; Wood, *Song*, 85; Stephen Dempster, 'The Lord is His Name: A Study of the Distribution of the Names and Titles of God in the Book of Amos,' *RB* 98 (1991): 185.
94. Dempster, 'The Lord is His Name,' 170-189. Dempster has contributed to a greater awareness of the use of the Divine names and titles in Amos. In each of the major sections: Prologue (1-2), Book of Words (3-6) Book of Visions (7:1-9:6), and Epilogue (Amos 9:7-15) the focus is on YHWH as the God of Hosts.
95. BHS suggests that אֲדֹנָי יְהוִה הַצְּבָאוֹת 'the Lord, YHWH of hosts' could be an addition.
96. Wood, *Song*, 84.
97. Ibid., 85.
98. The term צְבָאוֹת 'hosts' is a common interpretation. See Wolff, *Prophets*, 341; Hubbard, *Joel and Amos*, 233; Paul, *Amos*, 280; Smith and Page, *Amos, Obadiah, Jonah*, 158; Mays, *Amos*, 155; Jeremias, *Book of Amos*, 160; Gary Smith, *Amos: A Commentary*, 268.
99. Stuart thinks that the 'armies' are all the heavenly hosts, and thus translates the expression אֲדֹנָי יְהוִה הַצְּבָאוֹת as 'YHWH, God of the Armies.' Stuart, *Hosea-Jonah*, 393.
100. Gary Smith, *Amos: A Commentary*, 268.
101. Stuart, *Hosea-Jonah*, 393.

Zech 14:16-17; Pss 46:8, 12; 48:9; 84:2, 4, 9, 13).[102] Paas strengthens his argument by asserting that 'YHWH of the armies, who is enthroned upon the cherubim' (1 Sam 4:4; 2 Sam 6:2) serves the idea that YHWH, as king, was enthroned invisibly. The cherubim were located in the temple (1 Kgs 6:23-28). Therefore, the יְהוָה צְבָאוֹת has connotations of the worship of YHWH in the temple.[103] Significantly, the two occurrences of אֲצַוֶּה 'I will command' in 9:3-4 may suggest the fact that YHWH has 'army personnel' to execute his command for judgment. YHWH's address here as 'the Lord, YHWH of Hosts' emphasizes his control over nature,[104] universal lordship, and is associated with the temple.

The lordship of YHWH over the whole earth (Ps 47:8; Zech 14:9) and of all peoples (Ps 47:9; 103:19; 145:13; Jer 10:7) is related to the concept of YHWH as creator.[105] Sweeney suggests that the title of 'YHWH of Hosts' designates not only the creative power of YHWH who builds his upper chambers in the heavens and founds his vault upon the earth, but also his destructive power.[106] In 9:5-6, YHWH, as 'hosts' also has destructive power, so that the earth rises and sinks like the Nile (cf. 8:8); he summons the waters and pours them out upon the surface of the earth.[107] What does the ארץ mean in 9:5? Is it the same as in 8:8 where the image of the rising of the Nile also occurs?

As we saw, some translate the ארץ in Amos 8:8 as the 'whole earth'[108] while others translate it as 'land'.[109] Niehaus argues that as Amos' prophesies are addressed particularly to the people of Israel, ארץ in 8:8 refers to 'land', the land of Israel.[110] Perhaps it could mean the land of Israel if the subject is used as a parallel with the expression 'and everyone who dwells

---

102. Paas, *Creation and Judgment*, 233.
103. Ibid., 234, 236.
104. Story, 'Prophet of Praise,' 76.
105. Paas, *Creation and Judgment*, 238.
106. Sweeney, *The Twelve Prophets*, 1: 270.
107. Ibid., 1: 270-271.
108. See Andersen and Freedman, *Amos*, 800, 810; Stuart, *Hosea-Jonah*, 381; Paul, *Amos*, 256.
109. See Wolff, *Prophets*, 322; Mays, *Amos*, 142; Jeremias, *Book of Amos*, 143; Niehaus, 'Amos,' 473; Snyman, '*Leitmotiv*,' 536.
110. Niehaus, 'Amos,' 473.

in it mourns' (8:8aB).[111] We saw, however, that the ארץ in 8:8 is ambiguous, and illustrates the overlapping meanings of the word. The 'land' in 8:8 might be simply 'land' as the tangible reality, that which shakes like the Nile. The echo of Amos' language in the earlier text shows us his rhetorical technique. He could be using it here to extend his thought from 'land' to 'whole earth'.

The context of Amos 9:5-6 shows that YHWH, the supreme Lord, is the only supernatural power controlling the cosmic orders. YHWH manifests his purpose to human beings and demands their obedience to him, and thus the judgment will follow from their refusal of this.[112] The language and imagery of creation in 9:5 stresses the sovereignty of YHWH, his covenant relationship with his people Israel, and his lordship even over the heavenly bodies.[113] The emphasis on the cosmic picture (9:6) is a continuation from 9:1-4,[114] in which YHWH is characterized as the one who controls the whole earth and all nations. Amos praises YHWH by extolling him as God of creation: 'He who builds his upper chambers[115] in the heavens, and founds his vault upon the earth' (הַבּוֹנֶה בַשָּׁמַיִם מַעֲלוֹתוֹ וַאֲגֻדָּתוֹ עַל־אֶרֶץ) (9:6). All this has to do with YHWH's control of the cosmos and human history. What Amos understood by YHWH's lordship is characterized by the name, יְהוָה הַצְּבָאוֹת אֲדֹנָי 'the Lord, YHWH of Hosts'. Therefore, the people who hear the word of YHWH must affirm his name and attributes.[116] The passage begins with the divine name יְהוָה הַצְּבָאוֹת אֲדֹנָי and closes with the divine name יְהוָה שְׁמוֹ 'YHWH is His name' (cf. Exod 15:3). The whole cosmos is subordinate to YHWH's lordship for he is powerful in heaven and earth.

---

111. Andersen and Freedman, *Amos*, 811.
112. Watts, *Vision*, 19.
113. Smith and Page, *Amos, Obadiah, Jonah*, 158.
114. Jeremias, *Book of Amos*, 159.
115. MT reads מַעֲלוֹתוֹ, 'his upper chambers "while LXX reads it a singular ἀνάβασιν αὐτοῦ, his ascent."' Stuart, *Hosea-Jonah*, 389.
116. Linville, *Cosmic*, 167.

5.1.5.2 YHWH and Cosmos/Natural Order

The essential point of the prophetic message in the doxology (9:5-6) is not simply the relationship between YHWH and his covenant people Israel. Attention is paid to the concept that YHWH is creator, ruler, and sustainer of the whole cosmos and its order.[117] It is important to ask how Israel and its land are related to the whole earth and the created order. One important question in this connection is whether Amos accepts or challenges received views about God and the creation in Israel.

A significant study by Gillingham has shown the relationship between God and the created order in Amos. Gillingham notes that YHWH as creator and destroyer are combined in Amos' 'creation theology'.[118] Amos' view of Israel's God comes not only as creator but also as the destroyer of the created order.[119] The threat begins in YHWH's call to worship (4:4-5), and the bringing of famine, drought, and disasters is to warn his own people (4:6-9). YHWH's destructive power is developed in the Day of YHWH (5:18-20; 8:9-10), which will be a day of darkness, not of light. The crisis includes the natural order. As a result, it will have an effect both locally (9:1) and to a cosmic extent (9:2-4).[120]

YHWH also brings natural disasters in the first two visions (7:1-6). This belief in YHWH's power over nature contributes to the belief in his sovereign control over the cosmos. Finally, the doxology in Amos (9:5-6; also in 3:14; 5:8-9) describes YHWH as bringer of both order and destruction.[121] For Gillingham, it is this conception of YHWH and the created order that is employed in Amos as the basis of how YHWH acts against Israel.[122] The correlation of YHWH and the created order is obvious in Amos 9:5-6.[123] Amos 9:5 depicts a destructive theophany of YHWH, and 9:6 illus-

---

117. See Schart, 'Fifth Vision', 57; Story, 'Prophet of Praise,' 76-77.
118. Gillingham, 'Morning Darkness', 165-184.
119. The picture of YHWH as creator and destroyer is less prominent in Hosea. See Paas, *Creation and Judgment*, 327-348; Gillingham, '"Who Makes the Morning Darkness": God and Creation in the Book of Amos,' 173.
120. Gillingham, 'Morning Darkness', 167-169.
121. Ibid., 170-172.
122. Ibid., 173.
123. Farr, 'The Language' 323, further noted that the oracles of Amos echo the Psalms. Amos 9:5, 'He who touches the earth and it quakes' recalls Ps 104:32, 'Who looks on the

trates his cosmic creation, heaven and earth, as his dwelling place,[124] or his dominion.[125] YHWH as the builder (בונה) and founder (יסד) of the heaven and earth denotes the fact that the heaven and earth are his handiwork.[126] Therefore, YHWH is not limited to Israel alone (Amos 2:10; 3:2); other nations are under his judgment (1:3-2:3) and they are part of his concern (9:7). In this way, YHWH's particular dealing with Israel is extended to the whole created order in the bringing of judgment upon the other nations as well.[127] Therefore, Amos' conviction is that YHWH is the absolute Lord of the natural order, and of the whole creation.

As we have seen, the earthquake is a key symbol in Amos, indicating the natural order. The earthquake is a sign that the created order has turned to disorder (cf. Jer 4:23-26), which is associated with the final judgment (e.g. Ezek 38:19-20; Hag 2:6, 7, 21; Joel 2:10; 3:16).[128] Following the destructive natural order of the earthquake in 9:1, the doxology (9:5) refers to the mourning of all people who live on the earth. The people of Israel had to acknowledge that YHWH controls the cosmos and all natural order.[129]

The description of the earthquake is differently used in Amos (1:1, 8:8; 9:1, 5). In 9:5, the term מוג pictures the quaking or shaking of the earth. It is paralleled by רעש 'quake' or 'shake' in 9:1, 1:1.[130] Amos 8:8 describes רגז to refer to the earthquake as YHWH's sovereign authority over the creation and the human history. All these terms provide a picture of an earthquake as YHWH's punishment (2:13; 3:14, 15; 9:1).[131] The earthquake thus comes at the beginning and end of the book, strengthening the impression

---

earth and it trembles, who touches the mountains and they smoke!' And 9:6 'He builds His chambers in the heavens and found His vault upon the earth' is like Ps 104:3, 'Who lays the beams of His chambers on the water.'

124. Andersen and Freedman, *Amos*, 844-845.
125. Smith and Page, *Amos, Obadiah, Jonah*, 158.
126. Stuart, *Hosea-Jonah*, 393.
127. Gillingham, 'Morning Darkness', 174.
128. Hubbard, *Joel and Amos*, 227.
129. Wolff, *Prophets*, 342.
130. See Mays, *Amos*, 145; Paas, *Creation and Judgment*, 268.
131. Mays, *Amos*, 145.

of danger to the land. It is a reaction of the ארץ itself to the failures of some of the people (8.4-6).[132]

As Linville suggests, Amos is closely associated with earthquakes as his ministry is dated to 'two years before the earthquake' (1:1). Amos 9:5 primarily evokes 8:8:[133] 'Shall not the land "tremble"[134] on this account, and everyone mourn who dwells in it, and all of it rise like the Nile and be tossed about and sink again like the Nile of Egypt?' Since the natural order is absolutely under YHWH's control, the land reacts to an earthquake like that of the Nile that rises and sinks by the touch of YHWH on the earth.[135]

As we saw, the expression in Amos 9:5 recalls Amos 8:8, and therefore the rhetorical questions of Amos 8 are significantly answered in Amos 9 in the form of the liturgical hymn[136] which praises YHWH who controls the earth and all the inhabitants in it. Amos 9:5 reads: 'The Lord, YHWH of Hosts, he who touches the earth (אֶרֶץ) and it quakes (מוּג),[137] and all who dwell in it mourn; and all of it rises like the Nile, and sinks like the Nile of Egypt.' The doxology (9:5-6) thus also echoes the hymn in 5:8 (9:6) and the eschatological orientation in 8:8 (9:5).[138] In the expression הַקֹּרֵא לְמֵי־הַיָּם וַיִּשְׁפְּכֵם עַל־פְּנֵי הָאָרֶץ, the doxology closes with the message of flood. The breaking of the mass of waters in heaven is assumed to connect with YHWH's power in heaven. It is evident that the earthquake, which is followed by the flood, shows YHWH's creative power in heaven and earth.[139] Therefore, YHWH's punishment on all creation and the people with the threat of earthquake and flood shows that YHWH is in complete

---

132. Keita, *Gottes Land*, 265.
133. Linville, *Cosmic*, 167.
134. The different terms רגז in 8:8, מוג in 9:5, and רעש in 1:1; 9:1 are used in Amos to refer to the image of earthquake. See Linville, *Cosmic*, 167.
135. Smith and Page, *Amos, Obadiah, Jonah*, 158.
136. Linville, *Cosmic*, 167.
137. Most scholars read 'quake' or 'totter' here. For instance, see Paul, *Amos*, 273; Wolff, *Prophets*, 336; Mays, *Amos*, 151; Gary Smith, *Amos; A Commentary*, 263; Coggins, *Joel and Amos*, 152. However, Andersen and Freedman, *Amos*, 844; Smith and Page, *Amos, Obadiah, Jonah*, 157, read 'melt.'
138. Noble, 'Literary Structure', 225.
139. Paas, *Creation and Judgment*, 295.

control of the natural order and human history, and thus nature and history are connected.

5.1.6 Conclusion

The confession in Psalm 24:1 celebrates YHWH as creator: 'To Yahweh belong the earth and all it contains, the world and all who live in it.' YHWH takes his place as creator of the whole cosmos and thus has sovereign authority over creation. Similarly in Amos, the theological emphasis on the universal rule of YHWH authenticates the notion that it is impossible for the people to escape from his presence (9:1-4). In his own characteristic way, Amos uses this creation concept to refute the false notions of his audience who are confident that they are secure, who say, 'God is with us' (5:14); 'disaster shall not overtake or meet us' (9:10) by describing YHWH's creation in terms of a threat of destruction: the temple is destroyed by the earthquake; the natural order becomes chaos and affects all people who dwell on the earth (9:1, 5-6). Amos sets out an absolute theological claim for the universality of the power of YHWH. The vision of YHWH standing by the altar shows that he rules in the entire earth and cosmos represented by the unnamed temple, the place where the heaven and earth meet. YHWH's dwelling in both heaven and earth shows his sovereign power and thus the whole earth responds to him.

Therefore, YHWH can bring both judgment and salvation to Israel and to other nations, and destruction on the earth. YHWH is completely sovereign in both the natural world (the cosmos) and in time/history. The language about the whole universe, including the mythological language, supports the idea that YHWH has power everywhere and over everything. Yet it goes closely together with language about specific places, like Carmel and the Nile. The mythological and cosmological picture of the whole creation serves the purpose of demonstrating YHWH's work in the ordinary world of time and space. That is, the land is a symbol of the cosmos. Ordinary places become symbols of YHWH's work in the entire cosmos. Therefore, YHWH can bring judgment in human history; this judgement might be by means of natural events, and at the same time, the people's sin might have an effect on the natural world.

5.2 The Land in Amos 9:7-10

5.2.1 Introduction

Having seen YHWH's complete control over all creation, created order, and human history, the concept of the election of Israel is further established in a wider context in Amos 9:7-10, presenting the idea of YHWH's concern for and interest in the whole world. Whereas Amos 3:2 addresses the special status of Israel as the elected people among the nations of the earth, 9:7 refers to YHWH's dealings with other nations and their lands by revealing him as God of the universe who brought them from far places to lands of their own. Does this annul the theology of election? Or does it aim to make Israel think about itself in a new perspective? In this section we shall consider each text in its context, its rhetorical purpose and their relationship to each other. As will be shown, the different rhetorical purposes of each text may well render the possibility of theological development; that is, election has become inclusive, applying to the possession of land as well. Both texts relate to the theology of exodus-election and the occupation of land.

5.2.2 Election in Relation to Land in 3:2

In an earlier section on covenant-election in Amos 3:2, we showed in detail that election requires responsibility for justice, and is closely connected with the concept of land as gift. Amos 3:2 addresses Israel as the 'chosen people' among the nations of the world. Their historical opportunity is to be maintained through obedience to the covenant demands of justice and righteousness (5:24).[140] And to practise them is the demand of YHWH who brought Israel into its land (2:9-10; 3:1).[141] Amos sees that failure to comply with the covenant demand of justice has significant effects on their land (3:9-11), in effect leading to the loss of it.[142] Amos wants the people of Israel to acknowledge that the land was given by YHWH (2:9-10; 3:1),

---

140. See Wright, *People of God*, 36; Childs, *Old Testament*, 95, 233; also see Boadt, *Reading*, 316; Dumbrell, *Covenant and Creation*, 168; Mays, *Amos*, 56-57; Gary Smith, *Amos: A Commentary*, 104.

141. Zimmerli, 'Land', 248.

142. Wright, *People of God*, 36.

and that this was part of a close covenant relationship (3:2), through which the gift of land was to be maintained.[143]

5.2.3 Election in Relation to Land in 9:7

Amos 9:7 says that YHWH has acted for other nations in just the way that he has done for Israel. YHWH's deliverance of Israel from Egypt into the land is viewed no differently from his actions in giving land to other nations. It suggests that neither the people of Israel nor its land have a special status in comparison with other peoples and their lands, and therefore it seems to stand in opposition to the idea of Israel's election. Does this revoke the theology of election?

In 9:7, YHWH who brought the other nations to their lands also determines their destiny and history as he did to Israel. In this sense, it seems that the unique status of Israel as an elected or covenant people is radically called into question.[144] Amos 9:7 lists the nations: Cushites, Israelites, Philistines and Arameans. The Masoretic text reads Cushites,[145] referring to the land south of Egypt near the Nile River,[146] known as Nubia (modern Sudan) and referred to in LXX as Ethiopia.[147] The migrations of the Philistines from Caphtor (Crete) and of the Arameans (Syrians) from Kir, a Mesopotamian location (cf. 1:5) had occurred not long after Israel settled in Palestine.[148] Although the Philistines and Arameans are Israel's archenemies

---

143. Zimmerli, 'Land', 247.
144. See Regina Smith, 'New Perspective', 47; Paul, *Amos*, 101, 283; Wood, *Song*, 90; Gary V. Smith, 'Continuity and Discontinuity in Amos' Use of Tradition,' *JETS* 34, no. 01 (March 1991): 40; Buber, *Faith*, 45; Howard Moltz, 'A Literary Interpretation of the Book of Amos,' *Hor* 25, no. 01 (1998): 64-65.
145. Cushites are described as enemies during the reigns of Asa (2 Chr 14:9-15) and Jeroboam (2 Chr 21:16), and a Cushite served in David's army (2 Sam 18:21-23, 31-32). Hayes, *Amos*, 219.
146. See Regina Smith, 'New Perspective', 40-41; Wolff, *Prophets*, 347; Gary Smith, *Amos: A Commentary*, 270; Cripps, *Exegetical Commentary*, 262-263; Paul, *Amos*, 282; Stuart, *Hosea-Jonah*, 393.
147. See Hayes, *Amos*, 219; Andersen and Freedman, *Amos*, 869; Mays, *Amos*, 157; Gary Smith, *Amos: A Commentary*, 270; Stuart, *Hosea-Jonah*, 393; McKeating, *Amos, Hosea, and Micah*, 67.
148. Beebe, *The Old Testament*, 228; also see Mays, *Amos*, 157-158; Cripps, *Exegetical Commentary*, 263.

from the very beginning (cf. 1:6-8; 1:3-5),[149] Amos here uses them to show that the God of creation has sovereign power over all nations.[150] Amos 9:7 does not actually mention an exodus for the other nations as he did for Israel, but just YHWH's action in taking them from a far place to the land they have come to possess.

5.2.4 The Relation of 3:2 with 9:7: A Rhetorical Purpose

Amos 3:2 and 9:7 appear to give quite different views of the election of Israel. Amos 3:2 affirms Israel's election, and declares that Israel will be punished *because of* it. Amos 9:7 puts Israel's exodus and occupation of land on the same level as the histories of other nations. Both texts relate to the election of Israel and their occupation of land. Amos 3:2 follows immediately on 2:9-16, in which Amos recalls the exodus from Egypt and the occupation of land, and shows the same logic as 3:2, that is, YHWH gave special treatment to his people, but they were not faithful and thus he punished them. These texts together show the connection between Israel's election and their occupation of land. Amos 9:7 also presupposes the concept of the election of Israel, and its exodus from Egypt and occupation of land. This text, however, rather than emphasizing the distinctness of Israel from other nations, puts the other nations on the same footing as Israel. YHWH has also brought them from various locations to occupy lands that he has given them.

Do these texts contradict or complement each other? Some scholars have seen them as contradictory. John Barton believes that Amos 3:2 affirms Israel's election, and shows that their unique status led them to think

---

149. See Jeremias, *Book of Amos*, 25; Mays, *Amos*, 158; Stuart, *Hosea-Jonah*, 393; Walter Brueggemann, *Old Testament Theology: Essays on Structure, Theme, and Text*, ed. Patrick D. Miller (Minneapolis: Fortress Press, 1992), 50.

150. See Wright, *Mission*, 96-97; Ettien Koffi, 'Theologizing about Race in Study Bible Notes: The Case of Amos 9:7,' *JRT* 57-58, 2-1/2 (2001-2005): 160-161; Marrs, 'Proclamation,' 16; Yehezkel Kaufmann, *The Religion of Israel: From Its Beginnings to the Babylonian Exile*, translated and abridged by Moshe Greenberg (Chicago: The University of Chicago Press, 1960), 364; Arvid S. Kapelrud, 'God as Destroyer in the Preaching of Amos and in the Ancient Near East,' *JBL* 71, no. 01 (March 1952): 37; Regina Smith, 'New Perspective', 47; Bramer, 'Structure', 273; Preuss, *Old Testament Theology*, 2: 284-285; Walter C. Kaiser Jr., *Toward Old Testament Ethics* (Grand Rapids, Michigan: Zondervan, 1983), 35, 291.

that punishment would not fall upon them (9:10). They disregarded the surrounding nations (Amos 1-2) and believed that YHWH would forgive their iniquity for they were the only people whom he knew.[151] Amos 9:7, in contrast, denies that Israel had any special status – the tradition of election is in effect rejected. Amos then overturns Israel's popular notion of election.[152] Barton argued, regarding election, that 'in Amos 3:2, Amos seems to accept the premise but deny the conclusion; in 9:7, to deny both.'[153] Another interpretation is given by Koch,[154] who argued that the idea of the exodus of the peoples in 9:7 is offered as evidence against a connection between YHWH and Israel's redemptive history.

Also slightly differently from Barton, J. Alberto Soggin asserted that the notion of election in 3:2 is described with the root ידע while the description in 9:7 is different. In 9:7, the concept of election is reduced in its *dimension*, emphasizing that the people of Israel are not greater than other nations.[155] The literal point of 9:7, however, seems here to be that YHWH's action in taking them from far places to their lands is a special event in their histories. It does not mean that the exodus is an ordinary event in the history of Israel. Israel's unique status remains to the same degree, but simply does not exceed other peoples; rather than Israel's status being reduced, in 9:7, other nations are made *like* them.

Others take a similar view in an attempt to reconcile the two texts. Andersen and Freedman, for instance, consider that 9:7 affirms the election of Israel as in 3:2, but it puts other nations on the same footing as Israel. That is, other nations are now included in the pattern of exodus and land-settlement; election has become inclusive. This assumes and develops the idea of election that underlies 3:2.[156] They argue that 'every nation is elect; every nation has a special history created for it by the same God, Yahweh.

---

151. John Barton, *Amos's Oracles against the Nations: A Study of Amos 1:3-2:5* (Cambridge: Cambridge University Press, 1980), 36.
152. Ibid., 49-50.
153. Barton, *Amos's Oracles*, 47. Other scholars also take Barton's view. For instance, see McKeating, *Amos, Hosea, and Micah*, 67; Wood, *Song*, 88; Pfeifer, *Theologie*, 112.
154. Koch, *Prophets*, 1: 75.
155. Soggin, *The Prophet*, 55.
156. Andersen and Freedman, *Amos*, 93.

It is an extraordinary feature of Amos' theology: election is universal.'[157] In line with Andersen and Freedman, Joyce suggests that Amos 9:7 is a radical text which describes the election of Israel in a wider context, namely, YHWH's ultimate purposes for the whole world. Amos builds up Israel's unique status and brings it into a universal scope, so that the entire world becomes the domain of YHWH's historical activity.[158]

Considering both texts as complementary, Mays puts them within a relational context. Mays asserted that since the term יָדַע refers to intimate relationship between YHWH and Israel, it has a relational meaning. YHWH knew that to choose Israel alone would limit his nature since YHWH also deals with the other nations (Amos 1-2). Therefore, this relational meaning in 3:2 also applies to YHWH's active involvement in the history of other peoples in 9:7.[159] Similarly, Bernard A. Asen argues that Israel's special relationship with YHWH is Amos' 'yes' to YHWH's action toward Israel in 3:2 and Amos also says 'yes' to YHWH's similar action toward the other peoples in 9:7.[160]

Israel's exodus does not prevent YHWH from punishing them (2:4-16). Similarly, the exodus for the Philistines (1:6-8) or Arameans (1:3-5) does not prevent YHWH from punishing them. The essential factor that unites 3:2 and 9:7 is each nation's relationship to YHWH. Again, the people of Israel will be punished for their iniquities (3:2) and the sinful kingdom will also be destroyed (9:8). For Amos, therefore, 'the key that determines a nation's relationship to God is sin.'[161]

In its rhetorical purpose, Amos 9:7 is a development of 3:2, and has a wider context. That is, the election of Israel becomes the election of all nations; hence, exodus and occupation of land applies to all. Both texts refer to other nations: the families of the earth (3:2) and the nations such as Cushites, Philistines, and Arameans (9:7); and both compare Israel with other nations. YHWH brought both Israel and other peoples to

---

157. Ibid.
158. Joyce, 'Amos,' 231.
159. Mays, *Amos*, 56.
160. Bernhard A. Asen, 'No, Yes and Perhaps in Amos and the Yahwist,' *VT* 43, no. 04 (October 1993): 434.
161. Gary Smith, 'Continuity and Discontinuity', 39-40.

occupy lands and at the same time punished all of them. Amos 9:7 extends YHWH's action from local to universal scope. In this sense, Amos then puts other nations on the same basis as Israel, and they all share the same opportunity of specific settlement in land. The theme of election is affected by Amos' theology of creation and universality. And he shows a deep connection between human beings and land.

5.2.5 Election: YHWH's Ultimate Purpose for the Whole World

Amos 9:7 can be understood in the context of 9:7-10 which puts Israel's election in the wider context of YHWH's ultimate purpose for the whole world and also in the light of tendencies in Amos 9:1-6 which speaks of YHWH's power throughout the entire cosmos. YHWH maintains a special relationship with Israel (3:2). Thus the election of Israel becomes decisive for all peoples. Verse 8 brings the thought back to Israel's election – YHWH will not after all utterly destroy Jacob. While the 'sinful kingdom' will be destroyed, the 'house of Jacob' will not be utterly destroyed. What does the sinful kingdom refer to? Is it simply the northern kingdom? That seems unlikely, since Amos has just made his audiences think about the election of historic Israel as a whole.

The 'sinful kingdom'[162] (הממלכה החטאה) which is not identified here, seems to be an important clue to the meaning of Amos 9:7-10. At first glance, the article הַ, '*the* sinful kingdom', might suggest a reference to the northern kingdom of Israel. However, this is not the whole meaning.[163] The article most likely connotes class, that is, 'every sinful kingdom,' designating a 'general policy of YHWH's government'.[164] This unidentified kingdom, therefore, indicates that it can be any sinful kingdom of the

---

162. Some commentators think that the 'sinful kingdom' refers to the Northern Kingdom. For example, Andersen and Freedman, *Amos*, 881-882, think that this refers especially to the leaders, the priest, kings and royal house, in analogy and connection with 9:1-4 and 7:10-17. Also see Hammershaimb, *Book of Amos*, 135, 138; Paul, *Amos*, 284; Wood, *Song*, 90; Smith and Page, *Amos, Obadiah, Jonah*, 161; Soggin, *The Prophet*, 144; Niehaus, 'Amos,' 486; A. Cohen, *The Twelve Prophets: Hebrew Text and English Translation with Introductions and Commentary*, rev. A. J. Rosenberg, rev. 2nd ed. (London: The Soncino Press, 1994), 122.
163. See Stuart, *Hosea-Jonah*, 394; Mays, *Amos*, 159.
164. Mays, *Amos*, 159.

world.¹⁶⁵ Having understood 'the sinful kingdom' in 9:8b as *any* kingdom of the world, the logic of 9:7-8a is then that YHWH says, in effect, 'I have brought all these nations from one place *A* to another *B* and settled them in their lands; *therefore* I will punish them for their sins.' This is like the logic of 3:2, except that it now applies to all nations. Therefore, once again, this supports the idea that all nations are included in the theology of exodus-election.

This sinful kingdom may include the people who do not believe Amos' message while those who believe his message may belong to the 'house of Jacob'.¹⁶⁶ The antithetical parallelism with 'house of Jacob' connotes Israel as a whole¹⁶⁷ who are brought by YHWH from bondage.¹⁶⁸ In the study of 'Jacob' in Amos 7, I have already argued that it connotes the historic Israel and implies the unity of both people and land. Therefore, the context can be interpreted to focus on all historic Israel who participated in the event of exodus (2:10; 3:1; 9:7).

The previous oracle against Israel has shown that Israel could be included in this concept of sinful kingdom. YHWH has acted for other nations just as he has done for Israel. The oracles against the nations (1:3-2:16) indicate that Israel is not the only 'sinful kingdom'; rather it is one among the sinful nations that YHWH is about to destroy. However, Israel will not be completely destroyed.¹⁶⁹ Therefore, Israel is 'both like and unlike the other nations of earth'.¹⁷⁰ The announcement of the destruction of the 'sinful kingdom' is intended to refer to the fate of those upon whom YHWH set his eyes in 9:4.¹⁷¹ The ambiguity of the reference to the 'sinful kingdom' is answered in 9:10 which suggests כֹּל חַטָּאֵי עַמִּי, the people of Israel as a whole.¹⁷² The חַטָּאֵי עַמִּי are those who consider that YHWH will protect

---

165. See Garrett, *Hebrew Text*, 273; Mays, *Amos*, 159; Stuart, *Hosea-Jonah*, 394; Gary Smith, *Amos: A Commentary*, 271.
166. Schart, 'Fifth Vision', 55.
167. See McConville, 'Jacob', 132-133, 150; Stuart, *Hosea-Jonah*, 395; Regina Smith, 'New Perspective', 274.
168. Stuart, *Hosea-Jonah*, 395.
169. See Garrett, *Hebrew Text*, 273-274; Stuart, *Hosea-Jonah*, 394; Paul, *Amos*, 286.
170. Garrett, *Hebrew Text*, 273.
171. Paul R. Noble, 'Amos' Absolute "No",' *VT* 47, no. 03 (July 1997): 333-334, 337.
172. Noble, 'Amos' Absolute "No",' 334-336.

the nation saying, 'the evil shall not overtake or meet us'.[173] The election of Israel is reaffirmed here with the theme of remnant, bound up with the covenant (Lev 26:44; Deut 4:31), as in other prophetic texts (e.g. Hos 1:10-11 [Heb 2:1-2]; Joel 2:18-19; Isa 11:11).[174] Judgment will be selective; only the sinners will be taken for punishment and a remnant in the house of Jacob will be left. The thought continues in 9:9 in the image of the sieve, presumably saving those who are not 'sinners'. Again, the expression 'among all the nations' (בְּכָל־הַגּוֹיִם) in 9:9 is a reminder of YHWH's universal sovereignty, as in 1:3-2:5 and 9:7.

The historical information of the exodus event of the people and the concept of the sinful kingdom in 9:7-10 puts the election of Israel in a wider context, namely, YHWH's ultimate purpose for the whole world. The election of Jacob remains valid and has a continuing purpose, but the *kingdoms* are not necessarily permanent. Similarly, the land has no permanent or absolute status – since YHWH has also brought other people to other lands. Rather, it is subject to YHWH's purpose in electing Israel, which is not bound conclusively only to Israel.

5.2.6 Conclusion

YHWH entered a special relationship (Amos 3:2) with Israel whom he brought out of the land of Egypt (3:1). YHWH also has brought other peoples from distant lands to a new land (9:7). The relationship of YHWH with Israel also applies to the other nations, and so the concept of exodus-election has become inclusive. All the people of the whole world are part of YHWH's concern, but YHWH has given a special responsibility to those who claim a unique relationship with him. YHWH alone is the Lord of history, creator of the universe, ruler of all nations, and judge of the world. Amos' theology of election is in the context of YHWH's universal sovereign control over the entire created order or nature (9:2-6), and other nations (9:7-10). Election does not mean that YHWH is limited finally to Israel alone.

---

173. See Sweeney, *The Twelve Prophets*, 1: 273; Noble, 'Amos' Absolute "No",' 338.
174. Stuart, *Hosea-Jonah*, 394.

The fundamental theme of Amos 9:7-10 is most likely to correspond to the oracles against the nations in chapters 1-2 and 3:1-2, respectively implying YHWH's rule over the other peoples on one hand and Israel on the other, and that each nation is responsible to YHWH. YHWH's equal dealing with other peoples confirms and develops his special interest in Israel, so as to express his lordship over the universe. In other words, Amos develops the new idea that other nations are also included in the pattern and theology of exodus-election and land-settlement. Amos 9:7 extends to the nations the responsibility implied in the gift of land.

5.3 The Land in Amos 9:11-15

5.3.1 Introduction

The following section aims to show how the topic of the land of Israel relates to Amos' eschatology. This requires a consideration of the place of Amos 9:11-15 in the book. We will first consider the authenticity of the passage, and will suggest that because of the intertextual relations between Amos 9:11-15 and the rest of the book, and the continuity of ideas, Amos 9:11-15 is in fact theologically consistent with the rest of the book. Finally, it is also suggested that the various aspects of Amos' land-theology come to an impressive theological climax in 9:11-15, exploring the land as fruitful, as a gift to people in covenant, and as a universal theme, which confirms YHWH as God of creation and of all nations who are called by his name.

5.3.2 Authenticity

Doubts about the authenticity of Amos 9:11-15 go back to Wellhausen's observation of the change of tone in Amos from judgment to restoration.[175] In 1892, Wellhausen declared this section inconsistent with the rest of the book of Amos, finding in it: 'roses and lavender instead of blood and iron'.[176] Based upon the change of tone and language many scholars have rejected

---

175. See Wolff, *Prophets*, 352; Hasel, *Understanding of Amos*, 116; Hayes, *Amos*, 223; Paul, *Amos*, 288.
176. Julius Wellhausen, *Die Kleinen Propheten*, 4th ed. (Berlin: W. de Gruyter, 1963), 96 quoted in Wolff, *Prophets*, 352; Paul, *Amos*, 288; Hasel, *Understanding of Amos*, 116.

its authenticity and ascribed it to a late, presumably Deuteronomic, addition.[177] However, in contrast, many scholars have regarded this last section as an integral part of the prophecy of Amos.[178]

The first argument concerning authenticity is based on the belief that the eschatological message of restoration is inconsistent with Amos' repeated message of judgment in the rest of the book.[179] Hasel argues, however, that the true understanding of the message of Amos requires recognition of it as eschatological in nature.[180] Robert Martin-Achard argues that YHWH's plan for Israel could not end with judgment; rather 'judgment was not Yahweh's last word upon his own people. Between God and his people a new page had to be written in a totally different manner, and based solely upon divine grace'.[181] In this restoration, Amos carries the traditional concept of covenant blessings (e.g. 5:14-15) and curses (e.g. 4:6-11; 8:1-3).[182] Further, Amos is in line with his contemporary prophets in the sense that they foresaw a restoration beyond judgment, based on the hope that

---

177. Before 1930, see Driver, *The Books of Joel and Amos*, 119-124; Harper, *Amos and Hosea*, 195-196; Cripps, *Exegetical Commentary*, 67-77; before 1980 see, Otto Eissfeldt, *The Old Testament: An Introduction* (Oxford: Blackwell, 1965), 400-401; Wolff, *Prophets*, 113, 352-353; Mays, *Amos*, 164-165; Georg Fohrer, *Introduction to the Old Testament*, trans. David Green (London: SPCK, 1970), 436-437; Childs, *Introduction to the Old Testament as Scripture*, 405-406; and for recent scholarship see Coote, *Amos Among the Prophets*, 120-127; Blenkinsopp, *History of Prophecy*, 92; James D. Nogalski, 'The Problematic Suffixes of Amos 9:11,' *VT* 43, no. 03 (July 1993): 416-417; Kenneth E. Pomykala, *The Davidic Dynasty Tradition in Early Judaism: Its History and Significance for Messianism* (EJL 07; Atlanta, Georgia: Scholars Press, 1995), 61-63.

178. Before the 1970s, Watts, *Vision*, 58-60; Kaufmann, *Religion of Israel*, 368; Ronald E. Clements, *Prophecy and Covenant* (London: SCM Press, 1965), 111; Gerhard von Rad, *Old Testament Theology*, trans. D. M. G. Stalker, vol. 2 (Edinburgh: Oliver and Boyd, 1965), 138; Hammershaimb, *Book of Amos*, 135-138. For recent scholarship, see Koch, *Prophets*, 1: 69-70; Stuart, *Hosea-Jonah*, 397; Hayes, *Amos*, 223-228; Gary Smith, *Amos: A Commentary*, 277-290; Hubbard, *Joel and Amos*, 236-239; Andersen and Freedman, *Amos*, 893-894; Paul, *Amos*, 288-290; Hasel, *Understanding of Amos*, 116-120; Bramer, 'Structure', 275-277.

179. For instance, Driver, *The Books of Joel and Amos*, 119-122; Harper, *Amos and Hosea*, 195; Cripps, *Exegetical Commentary*, 67-71, 75-77; Wolff, *Prophets*, 353; Mays, *Amos*, 164-165; Nogalski, 'Problematic Suffixes', 416-417; Eissfeldt, *The Old Testament*, 400-401; Fohrer, *Introduction to the Old Testament*, 437.

180. Hasel, *Understanding of Amos*, 118-120.

181. Robert Martin-Achard, 'A Commentary on the Book of Amos,' in *God's People in Crisis* (Edinburgh: The Handsel Press, 1984), 67.

182. Gary Smith, *Amos: A Commentary*, 280.

was placed in the Davidic line (Hos 2:14-23 [Heb 2:16-25]; 3; 11:8-11; 14:2-9; Isa 9:2-7 [Heb 9:1-6]; 11; Mic 2:12-13; 4:1-8; 5:2-9 [Heb 5:1-8]; 7:7-20).[183] In Amos, the misfortune[184] is described as the destruction and judgment of people and land. Although Amos announces this destruction he does not announce the total end of the people and land (cf. 4:6-11; 5:4-6, 14-15; 9:8, 10). The restoration promises in 9:11-15 affirm Amos' underlying message of hope for the people of Israel.

The second objection lies in the fact that the reference to the Davidic dynasty in 9:11 does not fit Amos' audience, the northern kingdom.[185] Only one other time does Amos directly refer to David, in 6:5. However, 2 Samuel (1:11-27; 3:20-39; 4:1-12) shows the close relationship of David with Israel, the northern people.[186] In addition, in 1 Kings 12, where the kingdom is divided, and Israel chooses Jeroboam I as king, the prophet Ahijah promises that YHWH would establish an everlasting kingdom in Israel like the Davidic dynasty if Jeroboam would keep YHWH's law (1 Kgs 11:30-38).[187] YHWH holds up the Davidic dynasty as an example to Jeroboam I (1 Kgs 11:38).[188] The eschatological hope for YHWH's people has a connection with the Davidic kingdom, connoting the unity of people and land (2 Sam 7:13, 16; Hos 1:11 [Heb 2:2]; 3:5).[189] In line with this hope, the text in Amos concentrates upon the restoration of the Davidic dynasty together with the giving of the fruitful land and security, which were features of the time of the united Israelite kingdom.[190]

---

183. See Hammershaimb, *Book of Amos*, 137-138; Gary Smith, *Amos: A Commentary*, 278; Chisholm, *Handbook*, 402.
184. Outside Amos and the Old Testament, the change from misfortune to good fortune is found in Egyptian oracles from about 2000 BC. Hammershaimb, *Book of Amos*, 137-138.
185. For this objection, see Cripps, *Exegetical Commentary*, 67, 71-72; Harper, *Amos and Hosea*, 195.
186. Gary Smith, *Amos: A Commentary*, 279-280.
187. Ibid., 280.
188. Bramer, 'Structure', 276.
189. Ibid.
190. Paul, *Amos*, 289-290.

Thirdly, the reference to 'the fallen booth of David' with its breaches and its ruins is taken as evidence of an exilic or postexilic setting.[191] However, in the reference to 'the fallen booth of David' (אֶת סֻכַּת דָּוִיד הַנֹּפֶלֶת), Stephen J. Bramer translates נֹפֶלֶת, a *qal* participle, as 'falling', to refer to the declining condition of the kingdom in the time of Amos.[192] Similarly, Paul asserts that the word 'fallen' or 'falling' refers to the state of the Davidic kingdom, not the destruction of Jerusalem in 586 BC.[193] 'The booth of David' (סֻכַּת דָּוִיד), like the more usual 'house of David', refers to his kingdom (2 Sam 7:5, 11, 13, 16).[194] The status of the Davidic kingdom can be recognized by the expression 'as in the days of old' (כִּימֵי עוֹלָם) (cf. Mic 7:14), in which Amos perhaps refers to the glorious period of Davidic rule over all Israel.[195] The expression כִּימֵי עוֹלָם foreshadows the time of YHWH's establishment of the Davidic dynasty (cf. 2 Sam 7).[196] In this sense, the view of 'the fallen booth of David' is contemporaneous with Amos.

The fourth objection is that the reference to 'Edom' does not fit Amos' time, but seems to imply the fate of the Edomites when they were occupied by the Babylonians (cf. Isa 63:1-6; Obad 10-14; Lam 4:21-22; Ps 137:7).[197] However, there are traditions in the Old Testament that assume a long previous history between Israel and Edom. Edom was descended from Esau, the older brother of Jacob (Gen 25:30; 36:1).[198] The conflict had started in the womb (Gen 25:23) and carried on in the time of Jacob and Esau (27:41), and finally they became enemies after coming as the nations

---

191. Those who rejected the authenticity are, for example, Driver, *The Books of Joel and Amos*, 122-123; Harper *Amos and Hosea*, 195; Fohrer, *Introduction to the Old Testament*, 437; Soggin, *The Prophet*, 149; Nogalski, 'Problematic Suffixes', 416-417.
192. Bramer, 'Structure', 276.
193. Paul, *Amos*, 290.
194. See Gordis, 'Structure of Amos,' 245; Cripps, *Exegetical Commentary*, 270-271; Hammershaimb, *Book of Amos*, 140; Kaiser, 'The Davidic Promise and the Inclusion of the Gentiles (Amos 9:9-15 and Acts 15:13-18): A Test Passage for Theological Systems,' 101; Gary Smith, *Amos: A Commentary*, 280-281.
195. For example, Hammershaimb, *Book of Amos,* 140; Hayes, *Amos*, 223-225; Niehaus, 'Amos,' 490-491; Paul, *Amos*, 290-291; David G. Firth, 'Promise as Polemic: Levels of Meaning in Amos 9:11-15,' *OTE* 9, no. 03 (1996): 379.
196. Jeremias, *Book of Amos*, 167.
197. See Wolff, *Prophets*, 353; Mays, *Amos*, 164; Eissfeldt, *The Old Testament*, 400; Harper, *Amos and Hosea*, 198.
198. Hubbard, *Joel and Amos*, 241.

(Num 20:14-21; 1 Sam 14:47; 2 Sam 8:13-14; 2 Kgs 8:20-22).[199] Amos refers to both Esau (Edom; 1:6, 9, 11; 2:1) and Jacob (7:2, 5), and so seems to know these traditions. They show that Edom was ruled by the Davidic dynasty and that there was enmity between them even before Amos' time.[200] Edom was subject to David, and Amos 1:11-12 shows that they have been put under YHWH's authority.[201]

While Israel sometimes dominated Edom (1 Sam 14:47; 2 Sam 8:11-14), Edom had at times successfully opposed the rule of Israel and Judah (1 Kgs 11:14-22; 2 Kgs 8:20-22).[202] Although Uzziah rebuilt Elath and restored it to Judah (2 Kgs 14:21-22) he could not subdue all of Edom. Since Uzziah was king over Judah in his time, Amos might have expected Uzziah to restore the remnant of Edom and other nations.[203] Stuart argues that Amos had already referred to 'Edomite war atrocities prior to his own time (1:11-12) and had good reason to address the subject of the restoration of Israel in terms of power over Edom.'[204] The restoration of the fallen booth of David includes the possession of the remnant of Edom (שְׁאֵרִית אֱדוֹם).[205] In the oracle of Balaam in Numbers 24:18, Edom was regarded as the possession of Israel (וְהָיָה אֱדוֹם יְרֵשָׁה). This tradition of an ancient relationship between Israel and Edom is the background to Amos 9.

The fifth reason for rejection of the oracle is that the vision of material prosperity in the passage contains no ethical elements which are characteristic of Amos.[206] However, it may be argued that this material prosperity could be obtained only by observing the ethical requirement of YHWH's covenant. The bringing back of the people into their own land which is fruitful, inheriting permanently, and enjoying life with peace and security in it (9:13-15), is the result of observing the covenant of YHWH (Lev

---

199. Bramer, 'Structure', 277.
200. Gary Smith, *Amos: A Commentary*, 281.
201. Martin-Achard, 'Commentary,' 68.
202. See Stuart, *Hosea-Jonah*, 397; Sweeney, *The Twelve Prophets*, 1: 273.
203. Sweeney, *The Twelve Prophets*, 1: 273.
204. Stuart, *Hosea-Jonah*, 397. Also see Paul, *Amos*, 291.
205. See the similar expressions about 'remnant' in Amos, such as 'the remnant of the Philistines' (שְׁאֵרִית פְּלִשְׁתִּים) (Amos 1:8), and 'the remnant of Joseph' (שְׁאֵרִית יוֹסֵף) (Amos 5:15). Paul, *Amos*, 291.
206. See Harper, *Amos and Hosea*, 195; Cripps, *Exegetical Commentary*, 67, 72-73.

26:1-6).²⁰⁷ It is Amos' rhetoric that for the sake of encouraging the people, he addresses this eschatological hope of material prosperity, which indicates YHWH's purpose to keep his previous promises. The passage refers back to YHWH's covenantal promises, which involve ethical demands.²⁰⁸

The sixth factor is centred on the closing formulas, 'declares YHWH who does this' (נְאֻם־יְהוָה עֹשֶׂה זֹּאת) (9:12b) and 'says YHWH your God' (אָמַר יְהוָה אֱלֹהֶיךָ) (9:15) which do not occur in other parts of Amos.²⁰⁹ However, it may be argued that the new concluding formulas in 9:12 and 9:15 signal Amos' significant change of message. The first formula נְאֻם־יְהוָה is an affirmation that YHWH will surely do what he has said in the previous oracles.²¹⁰ YHWH does what has been said in the former oracles in a continuous and consistent way. Further, regarding the concluding messenger formula, 'says YHWH your God', Hubbard reasonably argues that it is a fitting conclusion to the book. The closing formula 'says YHWH or Lord God' occurs several times in the rest of the book (cf. 1:5, 8, 15; 2:1; 5:17, 27; 7:6) to assert Amos' prophetic role as the messenger to the people (1:1; 2:11-12; 3:7-8; 7:14-15).²¹¹ However, the present expression is not just a repetition of the previous formula, but a unique form: 'Says YHWH *your God*.'²¹² This second person suffix 'your' uniquely introduces a new thing with great hope,²¹³ reaffirming particularly YHWH as 'your God' which is the language of trust,²¹⁴ confirming the promise of YHWH who made covenant with Israel,²¹⁵ and assuring them of protection (4:2).²¹⁶ Amos uses the covenantal language 'YHWH, your God' (יְהוָה אֱלֹהֶיךָ) 'to redouble the reassurance' that this same God entered into covenant with Abraham and his descendants²¹⁷ and that Israel's earlier relationship to YHWH is

---

207. Gary Smith, *Amos: A Commentary*, 278.
208. Bramer, 'Structure', 277.
209. For example, Harper, *Amos and Hosea*, 195; Wolff, *Prophets*, 353; Mays, *Amos*, 165.
210. Hammershaimb, *Book of Amos*, 141.
211. Hubbard, *Joel and Amos*, 245.
212. Ibid.
213. Bramer, 'Structure', 279.
214. Jeremias, *Book of Amos*, 169.
215. Smith and Page, *Amos, Obadiah, Jonah*, 170.
216. Hammershaimb, *Book of Amos*, 143.
217. Niehaus, 'Amos,' 494.

continued.²¹⁸ It was in covenantal language that אֱלֹהֶיךָ portrayed YHWH's punishment upon the disobedient people (4:12), and now it turns to the future condition of his people (9:15).²¹⁹ YHWH is no longer their enemy (cf. 9:4, 8) for he has made them his own again, confirming him as their God; thus, says YHWH *your* God (9:15).

Finally, some scholars argued that the linguistic terms, ideas, and expressions like 'falling' (נֹפֶלֶת), 'ruins' (הֲרִיסוֹת), 'the days of old' (כִּימֵי עוֹלָם), 'restore the fortunes' (שׁוּב שְׁבוּת) belong principally to the post-exilic prophetic literature (Isa 49:19; 58:12; 63:9; 65:21; Mal 3:4; Jer. 24:6, 29:14; 42:10).²²⁰ However, this is not certain. As we have seen, these linguistic terms link back to earlier material in Amos.²²¹ In addition, the terms 'falling' (נֹפֶלֶת) refers to the weak condition of the Davidic dynasty, and 'as in the days of old' (כִּימֵי עוֹלָם) connotes the status of the Davidic kingdom in Amos' time. Furthermore, the expression 'ruins' (הֲרִיסוֹת) is already found in earlier Hebrew,²²² and שׁוּב שְׁבוּת has been documented in the Aramaic inscription from Sefire in the eight century.²²³ The metaphors of ruins, rebuilding, and planting in the land (9:11-15) show what will happen after the exile. In his previous oracles, Amos frequently envisaged the exile and destruction of the people (3:11-15; 4:2-3; 5:1-3, 9-13, 27; 6:7-11, 14; 7:9-17; 8:1-3; 9:1-4).²²⁴ Seen as prediction not yet fulfilled, Smith further argues that 'this does not require that the exile is now history'.²²⁵ Based upon Amos' repeated references to exile, Stuart concludes that the linguistic

---

218. Garrett, *Hebrew Text*, 291.

219. M. D. Terblanche, '"Rosen und Lavendel nach Blut und Eisen": Intertextuality in the Book of Amos,' *OTE* 10, no. 02 (1997): 318.

220. See Harper, *Amos and Hosea*, 195; Cripps, *Exegetical Commentary*, 67, 73-74; Mays, *Amos*, 164-165.

221. Cf. Warning, 'Patterns', 133.

222. Paul, *Amos*, 289.

223. Ibid., 294, a quotation from Fitzmyer, further mentions the Aramaic inscription from Sefire (III 24-25): וכעת השבו אלהן שיבת ב [ית אבי] ('But now, the gods have brought about the return of the hou[se of my father . . .]') as evidence of the origin of the expression in pre-exilic times.

224. Gary Smith, *Amos: A Commentary*, 279.

225. Ibid.

terms do not reflect a later addition.²²⁶ The predictions of exile in the rest of the book of Amos finally receive an answer.

5.3.3 Intertextual Relationship between Amos 9:11-15 and Other Parts of the Book

In the light of the intertextual relationship between Amos 9:11-15 and the preceding oracles, I shall suggest that the message of restoration in Amos 9:11-15 is in fact theologically consistent with Amos' prophecy elsewhere in the book. The literary links show the possibility of such a theological development in Amos' message.

5.3.3.1 Amos 9:11-15 in Relation to 9:7-10

Regarding the literary link of Amos 9:11-15 and the immediately preceding section, Bramer sees Amos 9:7-15 as consisting of two related units: 9:7-10 and 9:11-15. Amos 9:7-10 has maintained the message of judgment. These verses serve as a transition between the previous judgment oracles (7:1-9:6) and the succeeding oracle of restoration in 9:11-15.²²⁷ Amos 9:11-15 is intended as a continuation of the preceding section of 9:7-10.²²⁸ Sweeney also looks at the literary connection between Amos 9:11-15 and the previous section. He suggests that the phrase 'in that day' in 9:11 relates to the time of punishment referred to in 9:9-10.²²⁹

Considering the link of 9:11-15 with 9:7-10, Amos 9:7 addresses how the Israelites are like the Cushites. Amos 9:7 describes Amos' concept of universalism and links with the first unit of the restoration (9:11-12). The Cushites represent the rest of the other peoples in addition to the eight nations under YHWH's punishment in 1:3-2:3. This concept of the nations is illustrated in part in 9:9 and entirely in 9:11-12.²³⁰ Similarly, Smith asserts that there is a structural connection and contrast between the two units of 9:7-10 and 9:11-15. The destruction of the land אדמה (9:8) is transformed into restoration of fruitful land (9:13-15), and the destruction of the sinful

---
226. Stuart, *Hosea-Jonah*, 397.
227. Bramer, 'Structure', 272-275.
228. Jeremias, *Book of Amos*, 166.
229. Sweeney, *The Twelve Prophets*, 1: 273.
230. Andersen and Freedman, *Amos*, 912-913.

kingdom (9:8) into the restoration of the fortunes of Israel (9:14). Israel will be shaken among all the nations (9:9) but will possess all the nations (9:12). All the sinners will die (9:10) but the nations who bear YHWH's name will be blessed (9:12). Whatever disaster will overtake them (9:10) is replaced with YHWH's blessing (9:13). False belief in YHWH's protection (9:10) will turn into peace and security (9:15).[231] From the arguments above, the literary connection of 9:7-10 and 9:11-15 shows the consistency of Amos' message. It is Amos' rhetoric that this literary link or intertextual relations also support his theological continuity.

Table 1: Intertextual relations between Amos 9:11-15 and 9:7-10

Amos 9:7-10	Amos 9:11-15
Cushites stand for all the nations besides eight nations under divine judgment (9:7).	All the nations are restored by YHWH; no divine judgment (9:11-12).
The land is destroyed (9:8).	The land is restored (9:13-15).
The sinful nation is destroyed (9:8).	The people are restored (9:14).
Israel will be shaken among all the nations (9:9).	Israel will possess all the nations (9:12).
The sinners will be destroyed (9:10).	The nations who are called by YHWH's name will be blessed (9:12).
Disaster will overtake them (9:10).	God's blessing will overtake them (9:13).
False hope in the protection of YHWH (9:10).	Israel will have peace, security, and protection of YHWH (9:15).

5.3.3.2 Amos 9:11-15 in Relation to the Rest of the Book

Amos 9:11-15 includes several vocabulary and verbal links to earlier oracles of Amos.[232] Hubbard argues that their relationship can be seen in the pattern of 'continuity and contrast'.[233] First, Amos uses certain language and

---

231. Gary Smith, *Amos: A Commentary*, 277.
232. Bramer, 'Structure', 277.
233. Hubbard, *Joel and Amos*, 237.

theological themes throughout his book. Arguably, one of the most influential themes in Amos is covenant, which is related to the giving of the land (3:1-2). The covenant tradition is widely dealt with and serves as a prominent theme in Amos (3:1-4:13),[234] and this concept is carried to a conclusion with the covenant blessing of the land in 9:11-15.[235] Several times Amos has used covenantal concepts in his oracles before referring to the restoration of the covenant of David in the last part of the book. Bramer thinks that YHWH's proclamation about the covenant in 3:2, the covenant lawsuits in 3:1-15 and 4:1-13, and the covenant curses in 4:6-11 show that the concept of covenant is an integral part of the book of Amos, culminating in covenant blessing in 9:11-15.[236] Again, von Rad considered Amos 9:11-15 as authentic and understood this passage of Amos' prophecy as a 'prophetic religion' in which covenant is continued and restored. The essential element of covenant includes the restoration of the fallen booth of David.[237]

Another prominent theme in the book of Amos is the concept of eschatology. Amos uses this language and theme throughout the book. I have already argued that the eschatological message of restoration is consistent with the rest of Amos' message of punishment in the sense that it serves as a complement, continuation, and development of his prophecy. Within the context of Amos 9:11-15, the eschatological theme is present in the use of 'in that day' (בַּיּוֹם הַהוּא) and 'the days are coming' (יָמִים בָּאִים) (9:11, 13). The book of Amos is dominated by oracles of punishment or doom. Hubbard shows that this dominant message of punishment could end with such a great hope of restoration. These two eschatological formulas answer the oracles of doom and of restoration. They must mean respectively "'in that day when judgment has run its course" and "the days are coming after the divine judgment has done its righteous work'".[238] Significantly, the

---

234. For a detail discussion see Brueggemann, 'Covenant Worship,' 1-15; Boyle, 'Covenant Lawsuit,' 338-362; Bramer, 'Structure', 280; Bramer, 'Literary Genre' 45-49.
235. Bramer, 'Structure', 280.
236. Ibid. Bramer observes that all these references (3:1-15; 4:1-13; 9:11-15) confirm that the book of Amos is a covenant enforcement document. Also see Stephen J. Bramer, 'Literary Genre,' *BS* 156, no. 621 (January-March 1999): 45-49.
237. Von Rad, *Old Testament Theology*, 2: 138.
238. Hubbard, *Joel and Amos*, 236.

eschatological term 'in that day' (9:11) is already used in 2:16; 8:3, 9, 13 and 'the days are coming' (9:13) in 4:2, 8:11. Therefore, these two eschatological formulas introduce the oracle of restoration instead of the oracle of judgment in the last section. In other words, Amos' use of eschatology is a process of continuity and development, not a static thing.

Second, the fact that the tone of the message is contrasted and changed from negative to positive is due to Amos' rhetorical purpose of showing the link between 9:11-15 and the rest of the book in a particular way. The fallen nation 'never to rise again' (5:2; 8:14) is contrasted as being restored (9:11). These verses use the same root קוּם.[239] The same verb קוּם, 'Who will raise (מִי יָקִים) Jacob, for he is so small?' (7:2, 5) is answered in the expression 'I will raise up (אָקִים) the fallen booth of David and its ruins' (9:11).[240] The 'fallen' (נפל) Israel (5:2) as YHWH's punishment is changed into YHWH's restoration of the 'fallen' (נפל) booth of David (9:11).[241] The breaches in the city walls (4:3) will be repaired (9:11). Both verses use פֶּרֶץ in plural form to refer to the broken places.[242] Edom, once portrayed as the object of YHWH's judgment (1:11-12), is embraced under YHWH's name (9:12).[243] The reference to 'the remnant of Edom' (9:12) is an allusion to its former punishment (1:11-12).[244]

The expression עֹשֶׂה זֹאת (who does this) (9:12) recalls the expressions כֹּה אֶעֱשֶׂה־לְךָ (thus I will do to you) and זֹאת אֶעֱשֶׂה־לָּךְ (I will do this to you) in Amos 4:12.[245] Covenant curses (4:6-11) will be changed to covenant blessings (9:13).[246] The building of houses, which they could not live in (5:11), is contrasted to living in them again (9:14).[247] The planting of vineyards from which they could not drink (5:11) will be changed into

---

239. See Terblanche, 'Rosen', 315; Bramer, 'Structure', 277; Hubbard, *Joel and Amos*, 237.
240. Warning, 'Patterns', 128.
241. Wood, *Song*, 88.
242. See Hubbard, *Joel and Amos*, 237; Bramer, 'Structure', 277.
243. Hubbard, *Joel and Amos*, 237.
244. See Wood, *Song*, 92; Terblanche, 'Rosen', 316.
245. Terblanche 'Rosen', 316.
246. Bramer, 'Structure', 278, 280.
247. See Park, *Antiquity*, 107; Hubbard, *Joel and Amos*, 238; Wood, *Song*, 90; Bramer, 'Structure', 278; Terblanche, 'Rosen', 317.

the planting of vineyards and drinking their wine (9:14).[248] The drinking of wine as an abuse of the Nazirites (2:12) is turned to wine-drinking as a sign of the people's restored fortunes (9:13-15).[249] The gardens struck with blight and mildew (4:9) will again be fruitful gardens (9:14).[250]

The phrase 'I will not turn' (לֹא אֲשִׁיבֶנּוּ) (2:4, 6) is contrasted to 'I will return' (שַׁבְתִּי) to Israel (9:14), that is, the wrath of YHWH is changed to his blessing.[251] The people are called עַמִּי יִשְׂרָאֵל (9:14) which recalls Israel's covenant relationship with YHWH (3:2).[252] The announcement of exile (3:11; 4:2-3; 5:5, 17; 6:14; 7:11, 17; 9:4, 8) is turned into the planting of Israel on their own land (9:15).[253] YHWH's announcement to overthrow his people like Sodom and Gomorrah (4:11) becomes a promise to plant Israel in their own land (9:15).[254] The expression עוֹד 'never again' in 7:8 and 8:2 (לֹא־אוֹסִיף עוֹד עֲבוֹר לוֹ 'I will never again pass them by') is contrasted with עוֹד 'never again' in 9:15, about taking back the gift of the land (וְלֹא יִנָּתְשׁוּ עוֹד מֵעַל אַדְמָתָם 'And they shall never again be uprooted from their land').[255] The divine name 'YHWH God of Hosts' (יְהוָה אֱלֹהֵי צְבָאוֹת; 5:14-16; 6:14) is altered to 'YHWH your God' (יְהוָה אֱלֹהֶיךָ; 9:15).[256] אֱלֹהֶיךָ is used to portray YHWH's punishment upon the disobedient people (4:12) while the same טורם דס now used in the context of YHWH's restoration of the people (9:15).[257] The destiny of Israel, 'never again to rise' (לֹא־תוֹסִיף קוּם) (5:2) is pictured as 'never again to be uprooted' (וְלֹא יִנָּתְשׁוּ עוֹד) (9:15).

Finally, in relation to the fruitful land in Amos 9:13-15, Amos 1:2 is an important text in the book with a reference to the land. The roar of

---

248. See Hubbard, *Joel and Amos*, 238; Park, *Antiquity*, 107; Niehaus, 'Amos,' 493-494; Bramer, 'Structure', 278; Wood, *Song*, 90.
249. Wood, *Song*, 92.
250. See Niehaus, 'Amos,' 494; Bramer, 'Structure', 278; Hubbard, *Joel and Amos*, 238; Wood, *Song*, 91; Terblanche, 'Rosen', 317.
251. Smith and Page, *Amos, Obadiah, Jonah*, 169; Wood, *Song*, 92; Terblanche, 'Rosen', 317.
252. Terblanche, 'Rosen', 317.
253. See Hubbard, *Joel and Amos*, 238; Terblanche, 'Rosen', 318.
254. Terblanche, 'Rosen', 317-318.
255. Jeremias, *Book of Amos*, 169.
256. Bramer, 'Structure', 279.
257. Terblanche, 'Rosen', 318.

YHWH from Zion (1:2a), as we have seen, shows its effect especially upon the land, and thus the land is at risk in 1:2b: 'the pastures of the shepherds shall dry up, and the top of Carmel wither.'[258] The drying and withering of the land (1:2) will be changed into a fruitful land (9:13-15). By observing the given literary context of Amos, it is clear that there exists a literary connection or intertextual relations between 9:11-15 and the preceding sections. These show the possibility of Amos' theological development, which is firmly built into the land-theme.

Table 2: Intertextual relations between Amos 9:11-15 and the rest of the book

Other parts of Amos	Amos 9:11-15
The eschatological term בַּיּוֹם הַהוּא 'in that day' is used (2:16; 8:3, 9, 13).	The eschatological term בַּיּוֹם הַהוּא 'in that day' is used (9:11).
The fallen nation never to rise again (5:2; 8:14); the root קוּם is used.	The fallen nation will be raised up or restored (9:11); the root קוּם is used.
The 'fallen' (נפל) Israel is described as YHWH's punishment (5:2).	The 'fallen' (נפל) booth of David is restored as YHWH's promise (9:11).
Who will raise Jacob? (7:2, 5); קוּם is used.	I will raise up the fallen booth of David and raise up its ruins (9:11); קוּם is used.
The breaches in the city will be left (4:3). The word פֶּרֶץ is used in plural form.	The breaches will be repaired (9:11). The word פֶּרֶץ is used in plural form.
Edom under divine judgment (1:11-12).	Edom bears YHWH's name (9:12).
The destruction of Edom is announced (1:11-12).	The destruction of Edom is confirmed (9:12).
The זֹאת אֶעֱשֶׂה־לָּךְ is used (4:12).	The expression עָשָׂה זֹאת is used (9:12).
The eschatological term יָמִים בָּאִים 'the days are coming' is used (4:2, 8:11).	The eschatological term יָמִים בָּאִים 'the days are coming' is used (9:13).

---

258. Snyman, 'Leitmotiv,' 533.

People are addressed בְּנֵי יִשְׂרָאֵל in covenant-election tradition (3:1-2).	People are addressed עַמִּי יִשְׂרָאֵל to recall the covenant-election of Israel (9:14).
People will not live in their houses (5:11).	People will live in them (9:14).
People will plant vineyards but will not drink their wine (5:11).	People will plant vineyards and drink their wine (9:14).
The drinking of wine symbolizes people's rejection (2:12).	The drinking of wine symbolizes people's prosperity and fortune (9:13-15).
The gardens are fruitless (4:9).	The gardens are fruitful (9:14).
The prophecy of exile is in force (3:11; 4:2-3; 5:5, 17; 6:14; 7:11, 17; 9:4, 8).	The prophecy of exile is ended (9:15).
Covenant curses are illustrated (4:6-11).	Covenant blessings are addressed (9:13).
The land will be dry and wither (1:2).	The land will be fruitful and prosperous (9:13-15).
The phrase 'I will not turn' (לֹא אֲשִׁיבֶנּוּ) is used (2:4, 6).	The phrase 'I will return' (שַׁבְתִּי) is used (9:14).
YHWH will overthrow Israel like Sodom and Gomorrah (4:11).	YHWH will plant Israel in their own land (9:15).
The emphatic עוֹד 'never again' is used with YHWH's punishment of Israel (7:8; 8:2).	The emphatic עוֹד 'never again' is used with YHWH's reassurance of giving the land to Israel (9:15).
The destiny of Israel is pictured as 'never again to rise' (לֹא־תוֹסִיף קוּם) (5:2).	The destiny of Israel is pictured as 'never again to be uprooted' (וְלֹא יִנָּתְשׁוּ עוֹד) (9:15).
אֱלֹהֶיךָ is used to depict that YHWH punishes the disobedient people (4:12).	אֱלֹהֶיךָ is used to depict that YHWH blesses the restored people (9:15).
The name, 'YHWH God of Hosts' (יְהוָה אֱלֹהֵי צְבָאוֹת) is used in judgment context (5:14-16; 6:14).	The name, 'YHWH your God' (יְהוָה אֱלֹהֶיךָ) is used in a unique way to affirm hope (9:15).

5.3.4 Eschatology: Various Aspects of Amos' Land-Theology

Amos 9:11-15 has shown how the topic of the land of Israel relates to Amos' eschatology. In this vision of the future, several aspects of Amos' land-theology are apparently in view, namely, the eschatological theme as unity of both people and land, land as a universal theme, as fruitful, and as a gift to the covenant people.

5.3.4.1 Land as a Universal Theme

The oracle of restoration starts with the future promise: 'I will raise up the fallen booth of David' (אָקִים אֶת־סֻכַּת דָּוִיד הַנֹּפֶלֶת) (9:11).[259] This restoration includes the possession of Edom and all nations. That is, land in a universal sense is in view here. How does 'the fallen booth of David' function in relation to land as a universal theme? As will be shown, this restoration brings about the unity of the whole people of Israel and their land and assures their possession of the whole land. With regard to סֻכָּה,[260] many scholars take it to be a metaphor for the Davidic dynasty or kingdom.[261] Mays claimed that since booths are used for shelter and protection (Lev 23:42; 2 Sam 11:11), in Amos it is a metaphor for the Davidic kingdom which gives security to the people under Davidic rule.[262] The term 'booth of David' (סֻכַּת דָּוִיד)[263] appears only in Amos 9:11, and apparently takes

---

259. For a proper understanding of סֻכּוֹת in the Old Testament see Richardson, 'SKT (Amos 9:11): "Booth" or "Succoth"?,' 375-381; Michael M. Homan, 'Booths or Succoth? A Response to Yigael Yadin,' *JBL* 118, no. 04 (Winter 1999): 691-697; Polley, *Davidic Empire*, 72-74.

260. Regarding the use of סֻכָּה in Amos 9:11, translations are varied: booth (NAS, RSV), tabernacle (ASV, KJV), hut (NAB, NJB), tent (NIB, NIV), house (NEB), and kingdom (NLT). Homan, 'Booths or Succoth?', 693, notes that probably 'booth' סֻכָּה, 'tent' אֹהֶל (Josh 18:1, 1 Sam 2:22), 'house' בַּיִת (Judg 18:31, 1 Sam 1:7, 24), 'temple' הֵיכָל (1 Sam 1:9, 33), and 'tabernacle' מִשְׁכָּן (Ps 78:60; Josh 18:1) are used interchangeably.

261. For example, Cripps, *Exegetical Commentary*, 270; Wolff, *Prophets*, 353; Hammershaimb, *Book of Amos*, 140; Mays, *Amos*, 163-164; Childs, *Introduction*, 407; Kaiser, 'Davidic Promise', 101; Blenkinsopp, *History of Prophecy*, 92; Koch, *Prophets*, 1: 69-70; Hayes, *Amos*, 224; Andersen and Freedman, *Amos*, 889; Smith and Page, *Amos, Obadiah, Jonah*, 165. Against this, Pomykala, *Davidic Dynasty*, 62-63, considers 'booth of David' סֻכַּת דָּוִיד as referring to Jerusalem (Isa 1:8; 16:5), not Davidic dynasty or kingdom.

262. Mays, *Amos*, 164.

263. For the comparison of *byt dwd* and *swkt dwyd* see Philip R. Davies, '*BYTDWD* and *SWKT DWYD*: A Comparison,' *JSOT* 64 (1994): 23-24, who considers that the former has a literal rather than metaphorical sense.

the place of the 'house of David' (2 Sam 7:11, 13, 16).[264] Support for this view lies in the expression 'and I will build it as in the days of old' (וּבְנִיתִיהָ כִּימֵי עוֹלָם) (9:11), probably referring to the promise of Nathan to build David a house in 2 Samuel 7:11-16.[265] The fallen booth of David is thus a prophetic symbol of the condition of the Davidic kingdom.[266]

The plural form סֻכֹּת (Sukkoth) is used for the 'Feast of Booths or Tabernacles', recalling the shelters made during Israel's wilderness wanderings (Lev 23:42-43).[267] For Sweeney, the picture of the 'booth' also hints at the festival of Sukkoth (סֻכֹּת) in Amos.[268] Therefore, the memory of the booths (סֻכֹּת) in the wilderness wandering combines with the metaphor for the house of David, that is, the Davidic kingdom. In Amos' rhetoric, the metaphor סֻכַּת דָּוִיד has the power to evoke Israel in its seasonal agricultural life, a 'fruitful land,' as well as carrying a historical memory of a strong and prosperous Israel.

Before the time of Amos, both kingdoms had struggled against the surrounding nations to maintain their own independence. The restoration of 'the fallen booth of David' would bring about the reunion of the two kingdoms and thus greater security (see Isa 9:1-7; 11:10-14; Hos 1:11; 3:5), and all the nations including Edom would become subject to Davidic rule (2 Sam 8:1-14; 10:1-19; 1 Kgs 11:15).[269] This hope could imply the actual reunification of the two kingdoms of Israel and Judah under the Davidic dynasty again,[270] since David had first united both peoples (Hos 3:5; Isa 9:7).[271] However, it may rather portray the restored simplicity of the Davidic days, that is, security and well-being of the whole people and

---

264. See Hayes, *Amos*, 223; Cripps, *Exegetical Commentary*, 270-271; Kaiser, 'Davidic Promise', 101; Kaiser, *Theology*, 196; Gary Smith, *Amos: A Commentary*, 280-281; Gordis, 'Structure of Amos,' 245.
265. Pomykala, *Davidic Dynasty*, 211.
266. Gary Smith, *Amos: A Commentary*, 281.
267. Smith and Page, *Amos, Obadiah, Jonah*, 165.
268. Sweeney, *The Twelve Prophets*, 1: 273.
269. Chisholm, *Handbook*, 402.
270. See Richardson, 'SKT (Amos 9:11): "Booth" or "Succoth"?,' 381; Polley, *Davidic Empire*, 138; Sweeney, *The Twelve Prophets*, 1: 200; G. Henton Davies, 'Amos—the Prophet of Reunion,' 196-199; Stuart, *Hosea-Jonah*, 398.
271. Stuart, *Hosea-Jonah*, 398.

land before its slide into injustice. As Hasel suggests, Amos is not simply looking for the people and land to be united, as a prophet of eschatological doom and hope, he looks forward to a successful future of the people and land.[272]

Throughout the study, I have argued that Amos directs his prophecy to all Israel (7:15), and hence, to the historic land. Restoration of the Davidic kingdom suggests a reference to historic Israel whom YHWH brought from Egypt. However, the restoration of 'the fallen booth of David' could be understood in a wider context, namely, YHWH's ultimate purpose for the whole world. As Sweeney suggests, the restored Davidic kingdom extends its rule over the remnant of Edom and all the nations (cf. 2 Sam 8:1-14). Amos expected Israel to regain the remnant of Edom, and all other nations to be put under Davidic rule as in the days of old.[273] The MT text of Amos 9:12 reads, לְמַעַן יִירְשׁוּ אֶת־שְׁאֵרִית אֱדוֹם וְכָל־הַגּוֹיִם אֲשֶׁר־נִקְרָא שְׁמִי עֲלֵיהֶם, 'so that they may possess the remnant of Edom and all the nations who are called by my name.' However, the LXX reads, 'that the remnant of humanity (ἀνθρώπων, אָדָם, not אֱדוֹם), and all the nations who are called by my name, may search (ἐκζητήσωσιν, יִדְרְשׁוּ, not יִירְשׁוּ 'possess') for me, says the Lord God who does all these things.'

For Barry Alan Jones, the reading of LXX Amos 9:12 was not a mistaken translation, rather it reflects the translator's Hebrew *Vorlage*.[274] Jones considers that the LXX reading is appropriate to this context. YHWH worship, that is, 'seeking YHWH', is inclusive, and thus LXX Amos 9:12 universalizes it to embrace the remnant of humanity and all nations. For Jones, that 'the remnant of humanity' אָדָם (ἄνθρωπος) will 'seek' (יִדְרְשׁוּ) (the term דָּרַשׁ 'seek' appears four times in Amos, at 5:4, 5, 6, and 14) YHWH, fits with Amos' description of the remnant (שְׁאֵרִית, 'remnant' appears two times in 1:8; 5:15) who survive in the metaphor of the sieving process (9:8-10).[275]

---

272. Hasel, 'Alleged "No",' 18.
273. Sweeney, *The Twelve Prophets*, 1: 273.
274. Barry Alan Jones, *The Formation of the Book of the Twelve: A Study in Text and Canon* (SBLDS 149; Atlanta, Georgia: Scholars Press, 1995), 183.
275. Jones, *Formation*, 187-188.

Like Jones, Michael Braun prefers reading Amos 9:12 in the LXX, 'the remnant of men will seek God' as opposed to the reading of the MT, 'they will possess the remnant of Edom'.[276] Wright agrees, and thinks this fits better with the expression 'all the nations'.[277] James' use of Amos 9:11-12 in Acts 15:17 seems to look forward to the 'fallen booth of David', which refers to the eschatological temple (cf. Hos 3:5; Jer 12:15; Isa 45:21), on one hand, and the inclusion of Gentiles who are called by YHWH's name on the other.[278]

However, a number of scholars consider that the LXX misread or changed 'possess' (יָרַשׁ) as 'seek' (דָּרַשׁ) and 'Edom' (אֱדוֹם) as 'Adam' (אָדָם, 'mankind').[279] Unlike Jones and others, some such as Hammershaimb, Stuart, and Niehaus have argued that MT is certainly the original reading.[280] Although LXX, like MT, implies the inclusion of other nations, the LXX's 'the remnant of humanity'[281] seems contradictory and impossible with the parallel use of כָּל־הַגּוֹיִם 'all the nations'.[282] In the LXX, the original words of Amos are thus expanded from remnant of Edom to all humankind.[283]

Both MT and LXX can be taken to imply the universal concept. Although Jones and others prefer the LXX reading, in my view, MT is entirely appropriate in Amos, since Israel's possession of אֱדוֹם is paralleled by the inclusion of כָּל־הַגּוֹיִם. And, as we saw, the references to Edom (1:6, 9, 11; 2:1; cf. Gen 25:30; 36:1) correspond to Jacob (7:2, 5). Since Edom has been under Davidic rule and regarded as the constant enemy of Israel

---

276. Michael A. Braun, 'James' Use of Amos at the Jerusalem Council: Steps toward a Possible Solution of the Textual and Theological Problems,' *JETS* 20, no. 02 (June 1977): 113-121.

277. Wright, *Mission*, 495.

278. Wright, *Mission*, 518.

279. See Wolff, *Prophets*, 350; Hammershaimb, *Book of Amos*, 141; Chisholm, *Handbook*, 402; Gary Smith, *Amos: A Commentary*, 276; Stuart, *Hosea-Jonah*, 396; Smith and Page, *Amos, Obadiah, Jonah*, 167; Schart, 'Fifth Vision', 63; Niehaus, 'Amos,' 491.

280. See Stuart, *Hosea-Jonah*, 396; Niehaus, 'Amos,' 491. Hammershaimb, *Book of Amos*, 141.

281. In Acts 15:16-17, James quoted Amos 9:11-12 from the Septuagint (LXX) rather than the Hebrew text (MT). See Smith and Page, *Amos, Obadiah, Jonah*, 167; Chisholm, *Handbook*, 402; Niehaus, 'Amos,' 491.

282. Stuart, *Hosea-Jonah*, 396; Niehaus, 'Amos,' 491.

283. Niehaus, 'Amos,' 491.

(Exod 15:15; Num 20; 1 Sam 14:47; 2 Sam 8:11-14; 1 Kgs 11:14-22; Amos 1:11-12), it makes sense that the restored booth of David may again possess, not the remnant of humanity, but the remnant of Edom. Numbers 24:18a reads: וְהָיָה אֱדוֹם יְרֵשָׁה 'Edom will become a possession.' This intertext supports the MT reading and harmoniously leads to MT's inclusion of other nations.

YHWH's concern is not limited to the people of Israel alone (cf. Amos 1:3-2:3). The Philistines, Moab, Ammon, Aram of Zobah, Damascus, Amalek, and Edom (2 Sam 8) had been conquered by David, and are regarded as the possession of YHWH, and so under his rule. If Amos takes this view, the expression אֲשֶׁר־נִקְרָא שְׁמִי עֲלֵיהֶם denotes the concept of YHWH's 'ownership' and his 'act of possession,'[284] and thus it implies his possession of all the nations, among which only Edom is mentioned by name (9:12).[285] In other words, it can be said that all the nations are subject to YHWH, or will be subordinated under his rule (Amos 1-2), and will be called by his name.

Furthermore, the reference to 'all the nations' (וְכָל־הַגּוֹיִם) here, corresponds to the concept of universalism in 9:7.[286] Although only Edom is mentioned by name, other nations are also included under the umbrella of YHWH's name. In dealing with the theology of land as a universal theme, Amos links the Cushites, the Philistines, and the Arameans. Further, the nations (כָל־הַגּוֹיִם) alluded to are found in the oracles against the nations in which Amos includes the eight nations, namely, Damascus or Philistines (1:3-5), Gaza (1:6-8), Tyre (1:9-10), Edom (1:11-12), Ammon (1:13-15), Moab (2:1-3), and the southern (2:4-5) and northern kingdoms (2:6-16). Therefore, it is probable that all nations can be regarded in the wider sense of a universal theme, namely that YHWH, God of creation and the universe, controls the destiny of all nations and their lands. In this sense, Amos suggests that the theology of land functions to carry a universal theme. Amos presupposes the concept of the occupation of land by Israel (2:9-10; 3:1-2, 9; 9:7; 14-15) and by other nations (9:7). This possession of land is

---

284. See Paul, *Amos*, 292; Jeremias, *Book of Amos*, 167; Kaiser, *Theology*, 196; Niehaus, 'Amos,' 491-492.
285. Jeremias, *Book of Amos*, 167.
286. Wood, *Song*, 89.

the result of YHWH's activity in human history. YHWH controls all the nations (Amos 1-2) and can also grant them their land (9:7).

5.3.4.2 Land as Fruitful

The land as fruitful can be seen as a recurring topic in Hosea, Joel, and Amos. YHWH's punishment affects the land's fertility with natural disaster (Hos 2; Joel 1; Amos 4:6-11). In Amos 4:6-11, YHWH used natural disasters to try to change Israel. Nevertheless, the people of Israel have not returned to YHWH. In this sense, the land suffers.[287] However, the restoration of the fruitful land along with the restoration of the people (9:13-14) serves as a signal that YHWH's relation to the people of Israel has been restored. YHWH's call to repentance (4:6-11) is connected with the pattern of the fruitful land and the restoration of the land (9:13-14).[288] In Amos (4:6-11), YHWH's judgment corresponds to the covenant curses of Leviticus 26 and Deuteronomy 28. And the prophecy of blessings of the fruitful land (9:11-15) may well be intended to balance the curses of natural disasters (4:6-11), just as the covenant curse and blessing in Leviticus and Deuteronomy correspond to each other in relation to covenant.[289]

The fruitfulness of both people and land depends upon the people's obedience to the covenant of YHWH (Lev 26:3-5, 9), and failure to obey the covenant results in the unfruitful land (Lev 26:20). Therefore, land as fruitful is the 'natural' result of covenant faithfulness.[290] Similarly in Deuteronomy, through obedience to covenant, people enjoyed abundant prosperity and the fruits of the land (Deut 28:4; 11-12). However, disobedience to covenant will hinder people from enjoying the fruitfulness of the land (28:18, 38-40, 42). Köckert points to the theology of the gift of land in Deuteronomy, where it is the pre-condition for the command to keep the Torah. Deuteronomy 26:5-10 contains an ancient ritual of thanksgiving for harvest, which focuses on land as fruitful (cf. Deut 6:10-11;

---

287. James D. Nogalski, 'Recurring Themes in the Book of the Twelve: Creating Points of Contact for a Theological Reading,' *Int* 61, no. 02 (April 2007): 128.
288. Ibid., 129-130.
289. Bramer, 'Literary Genre,' 50, 55.
290. Davis, *Scripture*, 60-61.

7:12-13; 8:7-9; etc).²⁹¹ As Snyman observes, the people of Israel are in a position to lose the land in exile (3:11; 5:2, 5, 27; 6:7; 7:11, 17; 9:4, 8-9) and the land itself will turn against them (1:2; 4:6-13; 7:2-4; 8:8-11) because they do not live in accordance with the covenant laws (Lev 26; Deut 28). However, finally they will reoccupy the land and enjoy its prosperity again (9:13-15).²⁹²

Amos 9:11-15 introduces the restoration of the land, which includes agricultural prosperity, and the people's peace and security in the land. Israel will be planted in the land (אדמה) never to be taken away again from it. Why are the images in 9:11-15 agricultural? The term אדמה needs to be considered more carefully to enhance the agricultural concept. Is it correct to translate אדמה as 'soil', which connotes agricultural bounty? Davis considers that Amos and Hosea are the world's first agrarian writers whose characteristics are the 'soil-centred tradition of prophecy' and translates אדמה always as 'soil', because Amos' prophecy is persistently oriented to the fertile soil, that is, the fruitful land.²⁹³ As Linville suggests, the term אדמה in Amos stresses the actual 'life-giving soil'. ²⁹⁴ And for Wolff, אדמה is used elsewhere to refer to the native 'soil' of Israel (5:2; 7:11b, 17b; 9:8).²⁹⁵

As previously mentioned, the terms ארץ and אדמה for land function almost as synonyms and are used interchangeably in Amos. In addition to אדמה, ארץ can also denote the fruitful land. The promise of the land (ארץ) flowing with milk and honey (Deut 6:3; 11:9; 26:9) also indicates the land's capacity to give enough pastures for the animals and a plenty of produce from the fertile land.²⁹⁶ The land (ארץ) is pictured as a land with brooks of waters, of fountains and springs; a land with wheat and barley, vines and fig trees, pomegranates; and a land of olive trees and honey (Deut 8:7-8).²⁹⁷ The land (ארץ) gives increase (Deut 32:22) and fruit (פְּרִי) (Deut

---

291. Köckert, 'Gottesvolk und Land', 46.
292. Snyman, '*Leitmotiv*,' 540.
293. Davis, *Scripture*, 120-138. Also see Preuss, *Old Testament Theology*, 1: 118; Garrett, *Hebrew Text*, 290.
294. Linville, *Cosmic*, 148.
295. Wolff, *Prophets*, 315.
296. Snyman, 'Eretz and Adama', 139.
297. See Snyman, 'Eretz and Adama', 139; Gordon Wenham, 'The Old Testament and the Environment: A Response to Chris Wright,' in *A Christian Approach to the*

1:25).²⁹⁸ This פְּרִי is also used with אדמה to designate the fertility of the land. YHWH promised to give the פְּרִי of the אדמה to the people of Israel (Deut 7:13; 26:2; 28:11).

Amos reasserts the relationship between the ordinary people of Israel and the fruitful land (9:15), which was disturbed due to the politics of monarchic Israel (8:4-6).²⁹⁹ As Davis argues, the soil-centred prophecy in Amos concludes not only in images of fruitfulness, but also in a restoration of the relationship between the people and the land (9:13-15).³⁰⁰ The ordinary people are also to 'inherit' the land.³⁰¹ This aspect of 'inheritance' is illustrated by the story of Ahab, Jezebel, and Naboth in 1 Kings 21.³⁰² It implies that the people of Israel should all have access to the good things of the land. And this is what the kings of Israel and Judah put under threat by creating a centralized administration and a rich upper class. This is not explicit in Amos 9:11-15. The term ירש ('possess') occurs only in relation to possessing Edom, and נחלה ('inheritance') does not occur here at all. However, the imagery implies a traditional kind of possession of land. In fact 'restoring the fortunes of my people Israel' (שַׁבְתִּי אֶת־שְׁבוּת עַמִּי יִשְׂרָאֵל) (9:14) could mean a restoration after the ravages of the kings themselves.

Further, Davis considers that there is a profound connection between ordinary people as 'heirs' to the land and an order in the universe since Amos' constant reference to the soil-centred prophecy is in fact regulated in the creation of the universe. In this way the idea of fruitful land connects with the cosmos.³⁰³ In Amos, the term צְדָקָה (5:7, 10-15; 5:21-6:14) also occurs in a creation context.³⁰⁴ When people do not practice justice and righteousness (Amos 5:7; 6:12), the earth is disordered, and the land

---

Environment, Sam Berry et al. (n.p.: The John Ray Initiative, 2005), 52.
298. Magnus Ottosson, 'אֶרֶץ,' in *TDOT*, ed. G. Johannes Botterweck and Helmer Ringgren, trans. John T. Willis, vol. 1 (Grand Rapids, Michigan: William B. Eerdmans Publishing Company, 1974), 397-398.
299. Davis, *Scripture*, 127.
300. Ibid., 129.
301. Ibid., 127, 130.
302. See Wright, *Mission*, 291-292; Lemche, *Ancient Israel*, 151.
303. Davis, *Scripture*, 127, 130.
304. Fretheim, *God and World*, 170.

is unfruitful (Amos 8:4-10; cf. Hos 10:4; Isa.24: 1-13).[305] Schmid considered the connection between 'creation' and 'justice' (צְדָקָה). The concept of צְדָקָה implies the well-balanced created order of the world.[306] That is, YHWH's 'justice' is imprinted on the creation. Therefore, Amos' view of צְדָקָה might come in part from his understanding of creation, the cosmos. In this sense the notion of fruitful land relates to a more cosmic view. This is perhaps what is most interesting about Amos' view of land – that these two perspectives are closely related to each other.

The land becomes a fruitful land in which the former curse of planting vineyards that produce no wine (5:11) is turned into planting vineyards that do so (9:14),[307] and so the curse turns to blessing (9:13-14). The gardens and vineyards struck with blight and mildew (4:9) will again be fruitful gardens and vineyards (9:14).[308] In this context, the סֻכֹּת also is an agricultural image. Sweeney sees that Amos' image of the 'booth' hints at the festival of Sukkoth (סֻכֹּת). In the harvest time, people used to go to the vineyard and dwelt there in Sukkoth or temporary booths.[309] The metaphor סֻכָּה has the power to evoke Israel in its seasonal agricultural life, carrying a historical memory, pointing to an agricultural feast, and 'fruitful land'. Sweeney further asserts that the metaphor of planting conforms well to the setting of Sukkoth. The description that 'the plowman shall overtake the reaper and the treader of grapes him who sows the seed' shows that there will be agricultural bounty (9:13).[310] Therefore, the oracle points to a complete change in the destiny of Israel.[311]

This vision of fruitful land given by YHWH to Israel resembles the descriptions of the fertility of the land in the Ras Shamra texts in connection with the good fortune brought about by Baal.[312] In the context

---

305. See Schmid, 'Creation', 105; Koch, *Prophets*, 1: 59; Marlow, *Ethics*, 268.
306. Schmid, 'Creation', 107-108.
307. Hubbard, *Joel and Amos*, 238; Niehaus, 'Amos,' 493-494; Bramer, 'Structure', 278; Wood, *Song*, 90.
308. See Niehaus, 'Amos,' 494; Bramer, 'Structure', 278; Hubbard, *Joel and Amos*, 238; Wood, *Song*, 91.
309. Sweeney, *The Twelve Prophets*, 1: 273.
310. Ibid., 1: 274.
311. Martin-Achard, 'Commentary,' 68.
312. Hammershaimb, *Book of Amos*, 142.

of Amos, both the building and agricultural pictures seem to evoke the theme of creation.[313] The message of restoration, that is, the fruitful land, is in harmony with the creation theology found in the doxologies (4:13; 5:8-9; 9:5-6). The mountains, hills, vineyards, and gardens may be taken as creation imagery (9:13-15).[314] This creation imagery of fruitful land has clear connections with a 'recreated cosmos'.[315] As we previously mentioned, Deuteronomy's description of the fruitful land (Deut 8:7-8) may even be 'Eden overtones' in it.[316] It reflects the picture of Eden in Genesis. 'It is as if the Garden of Eden were reborn when Yahweh causes the land to produce his blessings for his remnant who are called by his name (cf. Joel 3:18 [Heb 4:18]).'[317]

Several aspects of 'land' in Amos relate to creation. The soil-centred character of Amos' prophecy is in fact rooted in the creation of the universe.[318] Davis makes the important point that in this creation theme, there is a close relationship between human beings and the earth, that is, the fertile soil. YHWH made אָדָם, the human being, from the fertile soil אֲדָמָה (Gen 2:7).[319] אדמה is connected to the root אדם which reflects 'a reddish brown' soil.[320] The indication of the relationship between the people and 'soil', characterized by the wordplay אָדָם – אֲדָמָה clearly implies the image of agricultural life (Gen 2:5).[321] Therefore, creation of אָדָם from אֲדָמָה pictures the 'land' or 'earth' as essentially agricultural.[322]

As such, this aspect of 'land' relates to the creation: אֲדָמָה as fruitful land recalls Adam's (אָדָם) vocation, who was to 'work the land' (אֲדָמָה) (Gen 2:5). As Davis suggests, Noah, who continues the story of אָדָם, was

---

313. Gerald A. Klingbeil and Martin G. Klingbeil, 'The Prophetic Voice of Amos as a Paradigm for Christians in the Public Square,' *TB* 58, no. 02 (2007): 180.
314. Gillingham, 'Morning Darkness', 180-181.
315. Linville, *Cosmic*, 173.
316. See Wenham, 'Response,' 53.
317. Gary Smith, *Amos: A Commentary*, 282.
318. Davis, *Scripture*, 127, 130.
319. Davis, *Scripture*, 29. Also see Wenham, *Genesis 1-15*, 59.
320. Preuss, *Old Testament Theology*, 1: 118.
321. Westermann, *Genesis 1-11*, 199.
322. Wenham, *Genesis 1-15*, 58.

a man of the fertile 'soil' (אֲדָמָה) (Gen 9:20).[323] The 'fertile soil' or more simply, the 'cultivated land' is to be cultivated by אָדָם (Gen 2:5; 3:23; 4:2, 12; 9:20; 47:23).[324] More than a political territory, this fruitful cultivated land is the dwelling place of 'all man' (כֹּל הָאָדָם) (Gen 6:1; Num 12:3), 'all peoples' (כֹּל הָעַמִּים) (Deut 7:6; 14:2), and 'all families' (כֹּל מִשְׁפְּחֹת) (Gen 12:3; 28:14; Amos 3:2).[325] With that in mind, it is possible to see that Amos reflects the creation theme in Genesis with the intention of bringing out the close connection between humankind and fertile land, and thus the images in 9:11-15 are very agricultural.

The final eschatological restoration oracle (9:11-15) reviews the title of Amos 1:2 and confirms the prospect of future restoration of the land. The drying and withering of the land (1:2) becomes a fruitful and bountiful land (9:13-15).[326] That is, YHWH turns the land again into a productive and fruitful land. In the context of Amos, the picture of the land as fruitful implies that YHWH works freely throughout the whole world-order, not only to bring destruction and disaster (as in the doxologies) but also to cultivate, recreate, and restore the land.[327] The political system, which brought about a disturbance of the relationship between the ordinary people and land, is overturned in the soil-centred character of Amos' prophecy, which is finally underlined in the restoration of the land and people (9:14-15).[328]

YHWH's punishment by famine and the destruction of land is now completely annulled (cf. 3:11, 15; 4:6-11; 5:11; 6:8, 11).[329] The oracle rather recalls the idea of Israel's land as YHWH's gift, 'a land flowing with milk and honey' (Exod 3:8, 17; 13:5; Lev 20:24; Deut 6:3; 11:9; 26:9). This concept is widely regarded as 'Deuteronomic'. In Deuteronomy 8:7-8, the land is pictured as a land with streams and springs, wheat and barleys, vines and fig-trees, olive and honey, etc.[330] Furthermore, the verb נתן,

---

323. Davis, *Scripture*, 32.
324. Plöger, 'אֲדָמָה,' 90.
325. Ibid., 93.
326. Bramer, 'Structure', 280-281.
327. Gillingham, 'Morning Darkness', 182.
328. Davis, *Scripture*, 127, 129.
329. Wolff, *Prophets*, 354.
330. Snyman, '*Leitmotiv*,' 531-532.

indicating the gift of this fruitful land to Israel as possession (Deut 1:25; 4:21; 4:40; 6:10; 7:13; 8:10; 9:6; 11:9; 26:9; 27:3; 28:8; 11; 31:20) could also imply land as a defined territory. The picture of a fertile land in 9:13-15 corresponds to and contrasts with the picture of devastation at the beginning of chapter 8. The vision of the summer fruit (8:1-3) alludes to YHWH's gift of blessing on the land for the people's life. The logic of this scene depends on the perspective that YHWH is in all time and space; he is able to bring both judgment and restoration to historic Israel and all other nations, in both time/history and natural order.

The perspective of all nations on the earth (הָאָרֶץ) is also introduced in Genesis (Gen 1:28 – 'fill the earth' (הָאָרֶץ), developed in Gen 10). This perspective of all nations on the earth is inherent in Amos (cf. 1:3-2:16; 9:7; 9:12). Further, there is the cosmic dimension, 'the heavens and the earth' (הַשָּׁמַיִם וְאֵת הָאָרֶץ) (Gen 1:1; cf. Amos 9:6), where הָאָרֶץ corresponds to the heavens and together they designate the whole cosmos.[331] As Gillingham asserts, the mountains, hills, vineyards, and gardens in Amos are cosmic creation imagery (9:13-15).[332] All these things therefore come together in Amos: the land is a fruitful land, giving life to people; it is also a defined territory, but, in addition, it is cosmic, symbolizing the whole earth, the whole world-order. As previously mentioned, the term צְדָקָה (5:7, 10-15; 5:21-6:14), which occurs in creation context, plays an important part in this concept of a well-ordered cosmos.

5.3.4.3 Land as a Gift to People in Covenant

The last five verses in the book of Amos include YHWH's restoration of his people and land. The reaffirmation of land as a gift to people in covenant is in view in the closing of the book. Most scholars suggest that the last section of 9:11-15 consists of two oracles introduced by the phrases 'in that day' (בַּיּוֹם הַהוּא) (9:11) and 'the days are coming' (יָמִים בָּאִים) (9:13).[333] Both expressions are connected with 'time', treating the theme of restora-

---

331. Wenham, *Genesis 1-15*, 15.
332. Gillingham, 'Morning Darkness', 180-181.
333. See Bramer, 'Structure', 277; Wolff, *Prophets*, 351; Gary Smith, *Amos: A Commentary*, 276-277; Jeremias, *Book of Amos*, 166; Smith and Page, *Amos, Obadiah, Jonah*, 164; Andersen and Freedman, *Amos*, 886.

tion. The former depicts a time of restoration of the Davidic dynasty with possession of the nations, and the latter communicates a time of restoration of the people with inheritance of its land.[334] The oracles of destruction and of restoration are clearly answered by these two eschatological formulas[335] with aspects of the unity of both people and land. The key terms 'building or restoring' of the 'ruins' and 'planting' the 'land' in 9:11-15 are used as a positive contrast to Amos' previous oracles of judgment and destruction.[336]

The theme of land serves a significant and important role in Amos as in other parts in the Old Testament. The land is promised and granted (2:9-10; 3:1-2, 9) to Israel.[337] In dealing with the land as a gift to people in covenant, it is important to consider the expression וְשַׁבְתִּי אֶת־שְׁבוּת in relation to Israel, both people and land. There is disagreement about how שׁוּב is to be understood in this verse (9:14). Why do scholars read שׁוּב שְׁבוּת in different ways? Is שְׁבוּת related to שׁבה (take into exile) or שׁוב (return)? The views of some scholars and the English versions reflect disagreement on this point. Some read it as 'turn the captivity' or 'I will bring back the captivity'.[338] Driver maintained that 'turn the fortune' (lit. 'turn the turning') could be the true meaning of the expression. However, taking the references to 'exile' in several parts in Amos (4:2-3; 5:5, 27; 7:11, 17; cf. Hos 11:11), Driver preferred to read 'turn the captivity' as one of the changes of the people's fortunes.[339] For Cripps, the phrase שׁוּב שְׁבוּת can mean a general sense of 'restore the fortunes' only in itself. It rather refers exclusively to a return from captivity, which fits the context.[340] שְׁבוּת could be from שׁוּב or probably the roots became confused. However, Cripps preferred to take שְׁבוּת from שָׁבָה to emphasize the return from exile. At any rate, 'there is no

---

334. See Chisholm, *Handbook*, 402; James D. Nogalski, *Literary Precursors to the Book of the Twelve* (BZAW 217; Berlin: Walter de Gruyter, 1993), 105.
335. Hubbard, *Joel and Amos*, 236.
336. Gary Smith, *Amos: A Commentary*, 277. Also see Paul R. House, 'Amos and Literary Criticism,' *RE* 92, no. 02 (Spring 1995): 182.
337. Snyman, 'Leitmotiv,' 529.
338. For example, see Driver, *The Books of Joel and Amos*, 225; Cripps, *Exegetical Commentary*, 275-276.
339. Driver, *The Books of Joel and Amos*, 225.
340. Cripps, *Exegetical Commentary*, 276.

essential difficulty in supposing that a prophet who announces punishment of exile could foretell also a return from exile.'³⁴¹

However, others observe that the term rather points to the restoration of peoples' fortunes. Sweeney, for example, notes that the phrase לְהָשִׁיב שְׁבוּת, with both words deriving from שׁוּב, refers to 'restoring the returning'.³⁴² That is, the restoration of the general welfare of the people, such as the return of the people, the rebuilding of the ruined cities, and planting of the agricultural crops.³⁴³ Wolff and others translated as 'restore the fortunes'.³⁴⁴ In Amos 1-2, as 'I will not return them' (לֹא אֲשִׁיבֶנּוּ) has been overturned, YHWH will then 'reverse the reversal' (שַׁבְתִּי אֶת־שְׁבוּת) for the people of Israel.³⁴⁵ The evidence of the reversal of fortunes (שַׁבְתִּי אֶת־שְׁבוּת) will be the rebuilding of the ruined cities in order that they will dwell again there (9:14).³⁴⁶

Another suggestion is that the שַׁבְתִּי אֶת־שְׁבוּת includes planting vineyards and gardens, and enjoying the land's blessing.³⁴⁷ John M. Bracke argues that שׁוּב שְׁבוּת in Amos, deriving from the root שׁוּב, embraces the rebuilding of cities, yielding vineyards and gardens, as well as returning from exile, indicating the restoration to the earlier time of well being. They reverse YHWH's judgment described in the earlier oracles in Amos (4:6, 9; 5:11, 16-17; 6:8).³⁴⁸ Taking שׁוּב שְׁבוּת from the root שָׁבָה seems too restrictive, rather the term שׁוּב שְׁבוּת contributes to the broader context of restoration of the fortunes of the people characterized by YHWH's reversal of the judgment.³⁴⁹ Niehaus asserts that the expression וְשַׁבְתִּי אֶת־שְׁבוּת is rooted in the covenant tradition (Deut 30:3) and used in that tradition

---

341. Ibid.
342. Sweeney, *The Twelve Prophets*, 1: 274.
343. See Sweeney, *The Twelve Prophets*, 1: 274; Nogalski, *Literary Precursors*, 107; Smith and Page, *Amos, Obadiah, Jonah*, 169.
344. Wolff, *Prophets*, 76, 351; Andersen and Freedman, *Amos*, 886; Paul, *Amos*, 288; Hubbard, *Joel and Amos*, 243; Gary Smith, *Amos: A Commentary*, 276.
345. Linville, *Cosmic*, 171-172.
346. See Sweeney, *The Twelve Prophets*, 1: 274; Linville, *Cosmic*, 172; Smith and Page, *Amos, Obadiah, Jonah*, 169.
347. Smith and Page, *Amos, Obadiah, Jonah*, 169.
348. John M. Bracke, 'šûb šebût: A Reappraisal,' *ZAW* 97, no. 02 (1985): 241, 244.
349. Ibid., 243-244.

(e.g. Jer 29:14; 30:3, 18; 31:23; 32:44; 33:7, 11; 33:26; Ezek 16:53; Hos 6:11; Joel 3:1; Zeph 3:20).[350] That is, it means to restore the fortunes or bring about a great change for the people of Israel.

From the literal translation, 'I shall turn a turning' (וְשַׁבְתִּי אֶת־שְׁבוּת), Paul argues that in all the Old Testament literature in which this phrase occurs, it never refers to a return from captivity; rather it means the restoration of Israel into its previous state of well being.[351] This restoring of fortunes to the former state of well-being is 'a concept suitable to many settings even in or before the time of Amos.'[352] This wider meaning of the phrase is evident elsewhere (Job 42:10). Planting Israel in their land (9:15) shows that 'return from exile' is merely one of the elements of the restored fortunes.[353]

The positive view of Israel and the land in Amos 9:13-15 has several similarities to Hosea's visions of the future (e.g. Hos 14.8). Most striking is the idea of YHWH as 'gardener' or 'farmer,' planting Israel in its land (9.15; Hos 2.23 [Heb 2:25]). Both these texts (Amos 9:13-15; Hos 2:23 [Heb 2:25]) combine return from exile *and* planting in the land.[354] The expression שְׁבִתִּי שְׁבוּת does not only embrace people who return from exile, but also suggests a total change of their destiny.[355] For Amos, Israel's political system could have had the effect of disturbing the close relationship between ordinary people and their land. In this way not only enemies but also rulers in Israel can in effect remove people from their land.[356] This also relates to a proper understanding of שׁוּב שְׁבוּת, a restoration of the fortunes of the people. It fits well with the idea that Amos wants a return to an older, traditional form of relationship between ordinary people and their land.

Following the restoring of the fortunes, the metaphor of planting in the last verse relates to YHWH's promise of peace and security to Israel in

---

350. Niehaus, 'Amos,' 493.
351. Paul, *Amos*, 294. Also see Smith and Page, *Amos, Obadiah, Jonah*, 169.
352. Smith and Page, *Amos, Obadiah, Jonah*, 169.
353. Andersen and Freedman, *Amos*, 892, 923-924.
354. Keita, *Gottes Land*, 275.
355. See Martin-Achard, 'Commentary,' 68; Firth, 'Promise as Polemic' 380; Sweeney, *The Twelve Prophets*, 1: 274; Nogalski, *Literary*, 107.
356. Davis, *Scripture*, 127.

their land. That is, YHWH changes the condition of the people. YHWH's blessing, mercy, and forgiveness and possession of land will be permanent. YHWH restored the covenant of Israel and this covenant blessing is an 'unconditional promise' because reference to repentance on Israel's part is absent.[357] The phrase 'And I will plant them upon their land, and they shall never again be uprooted from their land' recalls the promise of YHWH in 2 Samuel 7:10.[358] As previously mentioned, the terms נתן and ירש are Deuteronomic language concerning YHWH's giving of the land (ארץ, אדמה).[359] The Book of Amos concludes the theology of the land with the idea of *gift* in the phrase אֲשֶׁר נָתַתִּי לָהֶם 'which I have given to them' (9:15). This phrase clearly recalls the covenantal vocabulary of 'the land that I have given them' (e.g. Deut 1:8; 6:3; 7:13; 11:9; 26:9; 30:5).[360]

As Snyman argues, the concluding verse solemnly brings the concept of land in Amos together with a clear insight about both the past and the future. The people of Israel are reminded that it was YHWH who brought them into the land and at the same time it was YHWH who will plant them in their land.[361] Regarding the restoration, there are two possibilities here. First, what YHWH expects from Israel about true return (4:6-11) finally happens. Second, more probably, the restoration comes from YHWH alone as a result of his absolute mercy and love since there is no indication of Israel's repentance. It is the sovereign act of YHWH physically restoring Israel to its former state of well-being and bringing them back into the land.

What makes the theme of land in Amos extremely significant is the fact that the theological tradition is in some way associated with the covenant promise and giving of the land to the covenant people of Israel (2:9-10; 3:1-2; 9:7). This specific covenantal tradition is specifically Deuteronomic (Deut 6:3; 8:1; 11:8-12; 12:1). The book of Amos, then, solemnly

---

357. See Smith and Page, *Amos, Obadiah, Jonah*, 169-170; Mays, *Amos*, 167-168; Paul, *Amos*, 295.
358. Niehaus, 'Amos,' 494.
359. See McConville, *Law and Theology*, 11-13; Miller, 'The Gift of God', 451-465; Eryl Davies, 'Land: Its Rights and Privileges,' 350-351.
360. Niehaus, 'Amos,' 494.
361. Snyman, '*Leitmotiv*,' 538.

concludes with the reassurance of the gift of the Promised Land which YHWH once promised Israel, to inherit it forever: 'I will plant them upon their own land, and they shall never again to be uprooted from their land which I have given them' (9:15).

Finally, several aspects of 'land' in Amos 9:11-15 relate to each other. First, the land is a defined territory, which can be equated with the 'historic Israel'. That is, Israel is a nation among the other nations of the earth. As such, it is also 'given', in covenant with Israel. Second, it is a fruitful land, giving life to people (אדמה/אדם). Finally, it is cosmic. The land of Israel is not only a defined territory, and fruitful, but also symbolizes the whole earth as part of the cosmos, heavens and earth (9:6; cf. Gen 1:1). And further, it exemplifies YHWH's dealings with all nations (cf. 9:7); hence, all the land of the whole world. YHWH's restoration of Israel after judgment (9:11-15) is part of his renewal of the whole creation.

5.3.5 Conclusion

Amos 9:11-15 serves as a concise conclusion to all the previous sections. I have already argued that Amos 9:11-15 has its literary connection with the immediately preceding passage of 9:7-10 and with the rest of the book of Amos. This connection is communicated by continuity and contrast. In other words, the themes and theological ideas of covenant and eschatology, with attention to the theology of the land, run up to the climax of the book, which ends with the restoration. Linguistic terms, vocabulary, and verbal connections also play a part in this. There is, then, a continuity of thought in the prophecy of Amos, which is related throughout to the land-theme.

Amos' understanding of the relationship between YHWH and Israel is built essentially on the concept of the covenantal blessings of land and people. YHWH would plant them again in their own land forever. In this regard, the ultimate covenant curse, misfortune, or judgment, which is mainly represented by the prediction of 'exile' in the rest of the book of Amos, finally receives an answer. The newly bestowed land will bind the historic people to the historic land that had already once been given by YHWH to the covenant people. It is in this sense that the book of Amos, filled with Wellhausen's 'Blut und Eisen' (judgment), now ends with 'Rosen und Lavendel' (restoration).

Through this restoration, YHWH is known as the God of the universe and of creation. All nations will worship him, and be called by his name. The later prophets confirmed this concept that YHWH, the God of creation, and king, is to be worshipped and served by all nations and peoples of every language (Isa 66:23; Zech 14:9; Dan 7:14). Amos 9:11-15 has shown how the topic of the unity of land and Israel relates to Amos' eschatology. Various aspects of Amos' land-theology are brought together, namely, land as a universal theme, land as fruitful, and land as a gift to people in covenant. When the land suffers the people who live in it also suffer; when the land is restored the people are restored as well. The book comes to an end with a significant statement on the issue of the land. In this way, the restoration in Amos 9:11-15 finally recaps the theology of land in Amos.

Conclusion

The aim of this publication has been to give an account of Amos' specific contribution to the Old Testament's theology of land. It has explored the theme of land as a key aspect of the background to Amos' prophecy, and also of the book's overall theology of the relationship between YHWH, Israel, and the world.

The study was set in a wide context in the Old Testament, and raised questions about the relation of Amos to other important traditions about land. In support of the theological analysis, the study employed textual and literary, and some historical criticism. The text of Amos 7-9 has been analysed carefully for its literary coherence and inner relationships. Insights from rhetorical criticism were applied, because it asks the question how theological traditions are used in order to make an impact on and draw a response from an audience. This work has attempted to focus on what theological assumptions are made about the land in one section of the book, chapters 7-9, in order to explore the topic in close detail. But I have attempted to set the findings in the context of the book as a whole.

The language for land itself is essential to the study, and was found to have geographical, political, social and agricultural aspects. I began by considering the leading terms אֶרֶץ and אֲדָמָה for 'land', and the range of their meaning, namely 'earth,' 'land,' 'ground,' or sometimes 'soil,' as well as an understanding of land as territory, land as cosmic, and land as fruitful.[1] It was often difficult to decide between these meanings, and this already suggested, for instance, that there might be important theological links between the land of Israel and the whole earth.

---

1. Cf. Snyman, 'Eretz and Adama', 137-146.

In researching the way in which the land functions in Amos' theology, through an analysis of Amos 7-9, I have considered important scholarly treatments of land in the Old Testament to help build a theology of the land in Amos. For instance, Köckert distinguishes several possibilities for the understanding of land in Amos' time: land promised to the patriarchs, land given by YHWH, land taken by YHWH in war, and land as YHWH's property.[2] According to him, land as promised to the patriarchs is not the same as mere occupation of land.[3] However, it might be argued that the Jacob and Bethel traditions serve as hints of the theme of promise, since Bethel is associated with the promise to give the land to Israel (Gen 28:13). Differently from Köckert's view, I have highlighted some of the significant theological ideas about land in Amos, and also asked a question about the theological traditions underlying Amos concerning land, namely, land as gift of YHWH, land as inheritance, and land as a place to practice justice.[4] Amos refers to the land in different ways, using a range of language, and with different theological implications, including YHWH's 'gift' and 'ownership,' 'conquest' and Israel's 'inheritance' and 'possession' of the land, a kind of land-possession defined by a connection with justice. This is understood in relation to the theology of election, and also to an eschatological vision for the creation.

Amos is like Deuteronomy in certain ways, and there is some evidence of Deuteronomic influence on the book, for example in 9:11-15. But it is also distinctive. First, 'land as gift' is only directly present in 9:15 (e.g. נתן appears once in relation to the gift of land). The idea of 'land as gift' may be implied in texts with עלה and ירש, about Israel's possession of the land (2:9-10; 3:1-2, 9), but it is not explicitly present. Second, 'land as promised' is not present at all. However, arguably the Jacob, Bethel, and exodus and conquest traditions serve as hints of this theme.

There is a relationship between the covenant-election tradition and Israel's responsibility to YHWH. Israel was the only nation among all the families of the earth whom YHWH 'knows' (Amos 3:2). The allusion is

---

2. Köckert, 'Gottesvolk und Land', 43-73.
3. Ibid., 44.
4. Cf. Brueggemann, *The Land*, 3, 133; Wright, *People of God*, 49, 58; Zimmerli, 'Land', 247.

specifically to the election of Abraham. Other aspects of the election and covenant tradition have to be inferred. But the text shows the uniqueness of Israel's historical origin as a nation.[5] Their historical opportunity is to be accompanied by obedience to the covenant demands.[6] Amos perceives that failure to practice the covenantal demand of justice puts Israel on the same level as other nations (9:7), and consequently it threatens the gift of the land as well. This threat to the possession of land is also a threat to Israel's status as a covenant people.

One of the key questions is that of the relationship between the land in Amos 7-9 and the concept of Israel, along with חֹזֶה and נָבִיא, temple and altar, Bethel and the exile. Concerning Israel, it raises the important question of the extent of the land and people Amos has in mind. The study has suggested that the ambiguity of the term 'Israel' in Amos could be best understood to refer to the historic Israel and the whole land. The meaning of 'Israel' is an important factor in the book, and serves to ind_____]os' prophecy to the covenant people, 'my people Israel'.

What Israel truly means is not just the territ___ territory of the north and south. Neither th_____ northern kingdom is in a deep sense tru_____ terminology 'Israel' is addressed _____ people (7:15). Therefore, w_____ related to the ancient cov_____ shown that Israel has failed to _____ explains the judgment of exile. _____ under-stands its true mission, and this m_____ ael's mission is based on its election in relation _____ of justice towards YHWH and all the nations. Therefor_____ ple practicing justice in God's land expresses what Israel truly is_____ e interpretation of Israel and that of land are connected.

In Amos, Zion (1:2) has a specific purpose in relation to the land and people. In the Old Testament, generally, the concept of 'Zion' can develop and become symbolic (e.g. in Isaiah, where it seems to stand symbolically

---

5. Wright, *People of God*, 35, 63.
6. See Wright, *People of God*, 36; Zimmerli, 'Land', 248.

for the place where YHWH dwells, e.g. Isa 62). In Amos too, it is not connected with a specific political programme, but recalls Israel to its true nature. Rather than paying attention to the temple, and the relationship between the northern and southern kingdoms, Amos is more interested in the reality of people's keeping of the covenant of YHWH, which enables them to fulfil the ancient land-promise. Zion in Amos thus points to the true meaning of YHWH's elected people and the gift of land.

The land as a gift of YHWH is closely associated with Israel's responsibility to keep Sabbath (Deut 5: 12-15).[7] In Amos, the saying about the Sabbath (8:4-6) shows concern for the poor, and so has connections with certain Old Testament theological traditions, especially both Deuteronomy and Leviticus, in relation to the proper and right use of the land. Sabbath is assumed to function to defend the poor from exploitation, and implies that the ordinary people are also to enjoy the benefit of the land, since this enjoyment is closely linked with justice.

The right use of the land has its connection with the theme of justice, and failure to do it threatens the gift of the land.[8] The heart of the land in Amos' theology is its social and ethical dimension, its prophetic criticism of injustice in Israel. The prophetic criticism of injustice in Israel is a central part of the land-theme. Justice in Amos appears in social, cultic, and creation contexts, which all relate to the theme of land. Justice and righteousness also have a creation or universal implication, since these concepts are now widely held to belong inextricably with the world order.

The relationship between the land and the earth, or creation is another key topic of Amos. In this the ambiguity of the main terms for land (אֶרֶץ and אֲדָמָה) plays a part, since they can each bear the meanings 'land' and 'whole earth.'[9] In a number of places the language of land has the broader connotations of the whole creation. The theme of YHWH's control over the creation is connected with his rule over all nations, which is raised at the beginning and end of the book (1:3-2:3; 9:7, 12). The study explored

---

7. See Brueggemann, *The Land*, 56-61; Wright, *People of God*, 58.
8. See Davis, *Scripture*, 120-130; Wright, *People of God*, 36; Zimmerli, 'Land', 248.
9. Cf. Paas, *Creation and Judgment*, 183-326; Snyman, 'Eretz and Adama', 137-146; Linville, *Cosmic*, 133-175.

how the topic of Israel and its land relates to that of the nations and the whole earth.

The close connection between land and creation can also be seen in Amos' eschatology. In this vision of the future, various aspects of Amos' land-theology are brought together: land as fruitful, as gift to a people in covenant, as united, and as showing YHWH's control over the whole cosmos. The whole land of Israel is restored to its previous condition of well being, reversing the message of destruction and exile. In particular, the restored fallen booth of David brings about the reunion of the two kingdoms. But this is not just a political programme as such – rather a picture of Israel enjoying its land according to YHWH's purpose. In the closing verse of the book (9:15), Amos, as a prophet of eschatological doom and hope, looks forward to a successful future of the covenant people and covenanted land, which assures Israel's possession of the whole land, so Amos could extend the concept from 'land' to 'whole earth'.

In some ways, Amos' theology of land is like that of other prophets. Isaiah, for example, also has strong links between land and righteousness (Isa 5:1-7; 32). The book of Isaiah also includes the nations in its vision, and makes links between Jerusalem and eschatological Zion. Compared with Isaiah, Amos is more limited in its scope. But it made a key contribution to the message of Israel's prophets, for the following reasons.

Amos was the first to think about the relationship between the two kingdoms, north and south. I have shown that when Amos from the south preached in the north, he challenged the idea that the northern kingdom had an absolute right to hold its land. This was the point of his confrontation with Amaziah. But the same point also applied to Judah. The author of 2:4-5 saw this implication of Amos' message.

Amos' view of the two kingdoms also comes out in his use of David and Zion. These two themes are developed in other parts of the Old Testament into a kind of 'Zion-tradition', which stresses YHWH's relationship with David, and his dwelling on Zion (e.g. Ps 2). This is not strongly developed in Amos. Zion plays a part, as we have seen (1:2). But it is not portrayed as 'inviolable' – a problem that apparently Isaiah had to address (Isa 29:1-8; 31:1-5). In Amos, Zion does not seem to mean that YHWH has a preference for Judah over the north. And David is only a symbol of the unity of historic Israel, not a 'messianic' figure.

So how does Amos think about the land of Israel? As we saw, Köckert reviewed the traditions of land in the Old Testament. Of the various possibilities, it seemed that land as gift was most relevant in Amos, even though it does not use the typical deuteronomic vocabulary for this (except in 9:11-15). Amos thinks about this in relation to the theology of election, and his point is that this is not absolute (3:2). Israel cannot hold its land just because of old promises; instead, it must be truly Israel by doing 'justice and righteousness'. This is why both kingdoms can be accused of failing.

Amos also believes that other nations as well as Israel are within God's interest. This is implied in the Oracles against the Nations (1:3-2:3). And it is clear in 9:7, where YHWH is said to be involved in other nations' history. The theme of the other nations is also close to that of creation. The vocabulary used by the prophet shows that 'land' is close to 'earth'. Land (of Israel) and 'lands' (of other nations) and the whole earth are all related here, and so we can speak of a kind of universalism in Amos. In his view, justice and righteousness should be found throughout the whole created order.

The final vision in the book apparently portrays the salvation of Israel alone. This is odd if Amos believes that YHWH is actually interested in all the nations. It is best to take it, therefore, as an example of what a righteous nation could become. There is no narrow political programme in Amos. This and the features mentioned above make Amos' message suitable to apply to different historical situations.

As we saw in the Introduction, it is important to think about the audiences of the book. We made a working assumption that the events of Amos' own time were relevant to the book's theology. Some further observations may now be made on this. References to the reigns of Jeroboam II and Uzziah, and to the earthquake, and the absence of the explicit threat of Assyria could be taken as evidence that the book has a real connection with the time of Amos. However, the book of Amos makes exile an important part of the vision of the fortunes of Israel in the future (4:2-3; 5:5, 26-27; 6:7; 7:11, 17; 9:4). Amos' use of the 'unclean land' (7:17), in response to the accusation of Amaziah, applies to any foreign land, including Assyria

(Hos 9:3) and Babylonia (Ezek 4:13). Therefore, the audience in this regard could be different from that of the prophet's time.

We can consider what difference it makes to the theology of land if the book was composed in the eighth-century with its audience, or later in the seventh or sixth/fifth-centuries with their own audiences. In the first case, the main point would be that both kingdoms can avoid exile if they do justice, and reform themselves politically and socially. They have misunderstood the basis on which they possess the historic land. Possession of the land means obedience to YHWH's standard of justice and righteousness. However, they misunderstood their own theological traditions. The destruction of the kingdoms apparently depends on the character of the people. If they do not change, the kingdoms will surely fall.

If we think of a seventh-century Josianic audience, the message would be similar to the centralizing message of that programme. Worship should be only at Jerusalem. Judah should learn from the judgment on the north, and so keep its right to its land. From the perspective of an exilic or post-exilic hypothesis in relation to the theology of land, the message of Amos would be remembered in a new situation. By the time of the exile, the northern kingdom had long disappeared. Now that Judah was also in exile, the possibility of losing land became very real. This did not completely change even after the exile, when many Jews had returned to their homeland, since their situation still seemed insecure. So the question becomes urgent: How does 'Israel' now understand the basis on which it is entitled to hold its land again? The historical examples of the kingdoms are made to answer these questions. In all the above examples, the story of Amos' confrontation with Amaziah is at the heart of the book's message.

The confrontation of Amos and Amaziah showed that the life of 'Israel' did not depend on the political and religious institutions of the time. For this reason, I think the Josianic theory is the least convincing. True Israel was rooted in a right understanding of its theological traditions and vocation. YHWH's people practicing justice in YHWH's land expresses what Israel truly is. The message for the exilic and post-exilic times is a hopeful one. If the returned exiles can form their new society according to justice and righteousness, they will again be able to possess their land fully, and they will know what it means to be YHWH's 'elect' according to his purpose.

There is no obvious political programme. For instance, Amos is apparently not 'messianic'. The mention of the 'booth of David' in Amos 9:11-12 probably does not imply that concept. There is no message about an overthrow of empire either. Amos' vision could accommodate to different political situations. It thus lacks the royal-messianic vision of the book of Isaiah. However, in its own way, it shows what it means for a nation to hold its land truly and legitimately. In this sense, it is a message not only for Israel, but also for all nations.

In future research, one could study further the relationship of Amos and Deuteronomy. Especially the nature of Amos' political vision would be interesting here. Amos is like Deuteronomy in that it does not have a strong vision for the role of a king in its model society. It is more like Deuteronomy in this respect (and also Hosea) than, for example, Isaiah or many Psalms. A study of the *people* of Israel in Amos would complement the study of land in the book of Amos as well. One could also study the implications of this thesis for modern situations. For instance, Daniel Carroll did this with Amos with a reference to Latin America.[10] It could no doubt also be done for other parts of the world.

---

10. Carroll R., *Contexts for Amos: Prophetic Poetics in Latin American Perspective* (JSOTSS 132; Sheffield: JSOT Press, 1992).

Bibliography

Achtemeier, Elizabeth. *Minor Prophets I*. NIBC. OTS 17. Peabody, Massachusetts: Hendrickson Publishers, 1996.

_____. 'Righteousness in the Old Testament.' In *IDB (R-Z)*, edited by George Arthur Buttrick et al., 80-85. Nashville: Abingdon Press, 1962.

Ackerman, Susan. 'Amos 5:18-24.' *Int* 57, no. 02 (April 2003): 190-193.

Ackroyd, Peter R. 'A Judgment Narrative between Kings and Chronicles? An Approach to Amos 7:9-17.' In *Canon and Authority: Essays in Old Testament Religion and Theology*, edited by George W. Coats and Burke O. Long, 71-87. Philadelphia: Fortress Press, 1977.

Allen, Leslie C. *The Books of Joel, Obadiah, Jonah, and Micah*. NICOT. Grand Rapids, Michigan: William B. Eerdmans Publishing Company, 1976.

Andersen, Francis I. and David Noel Freedman. *Amos: A New Translation with Introduction and Commentary*. AB. New York: Doubleday, 1989.

Anderson, Bernhard W. *From Creation to New Creation: Old Testament Perspectives*. Minneapolis: Fortress Press, 1994.

_____. *The Living World of the Old Testament*. 3rd ed. London: Longman, 1978.

Anderson, Robert T. 'Bethel.' In *EDB*, edited by David Noel Freedman, 170. Grand Rapids, Michigan: William B. Eerdmans, 2000.

Asen, Bernhard A. 'No, Yes and Perhaps in Amos and the Yahwist.' *VT* 43, no. 04 (October 1993): 433-441.

Astour, Michael. C. 'Mount Carmel.' In *IDBSup*, edited by Keith Crim, 141. Nashville: Abingdon Press, 1976.

Auld, A. G. *Amos*. Sheffield: Sheffield Academic Press, 1995.

Baker, Jill L. 'Mount Carmel.' In *IDB (A-C)*, edited by Katharine Doob Sakenfeld et al., 569. Nashville, Tennessee: Abingdon Press, 2006.

Bamberger, Bernhard J. *Leviticus: A Modern Commentary*. New York: Union of American Hebrew Congregations, 1979.

Barstad, Hans. *The Religious Polemics of Amos: Studies in the Preaching of Amos 2:7b-8; 4:1-13; 5:1-27; 6:4-7; 8:14.* VTSup 34. Leiden: E. J. Brill, 1984.

Barton, John. *Amos's Oracles against the Nations: A Study of Amos 1:3-2:5.* Cambridge: Cambridge University Press, 1980.

Beale, Gregory K. *The Temple and the Church's Mission: A Biblical Theology of the Dwelling Place of God.* NSBT 17. Downers Grove, Illinois: InterVarsity Press, 2004.

Beebe, H. Keith. *The Old Testament: An Introduction to Its Literary, Historical, and Religious Traditions.* Belmont, California: Dickenson Publishing Company, 1970.

Beek, Gus W. Van. 'Mount Carmel.' In *IDB (A-D)*, edited by George Arthur Buttrick et al., 538. Nashville: Abingdon Press, 1962.

———. 'Samaria.' In *IDB (R-Z)*, edited by George Arthur Buttrick et al., 182-188. Nashville: Abingdon Press, 1962.

———. 'Dan.' In *IDB (A-D)*, edited by George Arthur Buttrick et al., 758-760. Nashville: Abingdon Press, 1962.

Berthoud, Pierre. 'The Covenant and the Social Message of Amos.' *EJT* 14, no. 02 (2005): 99-109.

Blenkinsopp, Joseph. *A History of Prophecy in Israel: From the Settlement in the Land to the Hellenistic* Period. London: SPCK, 1984.

Boadt, Lawrence. *Reading the Old Testament: An Introduction.* New York: Paulist Press, 1984.

Boyle, Marjorie O'Rourke. 'The Covenant Lawsuit of the Prophet Amos: 3:1-4:13.' *VT* 21, no. 03 (July 1971): 338-362.

Bracke, John M. 'šûb šebût: A Reappraisal.' *ZAW* 97, no. 02 (1985): 233-244.

Bramer, Stephen J. 'Analysis of the Structure of Amos.' *BS* 156, no. 622 (April-June 1999): 160-174.

———. 'The Structure of Amos 9:7-15.' *BS* 156, no. 623 (July-September 1999): 272-281.

———. 'The Literary Genre of the Book of Amos.' *BS* 156, no. 621 (Jan-March 1999): 42-60.

Braun, Michael A. 'James' Use of Amos at the Jerusalem Council: Steps toward a Possible Solution of the Textual and Theological Problems.' *JETS* 20, no. 02 (June 1977): 113-121.

Bright, John. *A History of Israel.* 4th ed. Louisville: The Westminster John Knox Press, 2000.

Brownlee, William H. 'Gilgal.' In *The International Standard Bible Encyclopaedia Volume Two (E-J),* edited by Geoffrey W. Bromiley et al., 470-472.

Rev. ed. Grand Rapids, Michigan: Williams B. Eerdmans Publishing Company, 1982.

Brueggemann, Walter. *The Land: Place as Gift, Promise, and Challenge in Biblical Faith*. 2nd ed. OBT. Minneapolis: Fortress Press, 2002.

_____. *Deuteronomy*. Nashville: Abingdon Press, 2001.

_____. *Old Testament Theology: Essays on Structure, Theme, and Text*. Edited by Patrick D. Miller. Minneapolis: Fortress Press, 1992.

_____. *Genesis*. IBCTP. Atlanta: John Knox Press, 1982.

_____. 'Amos' Intercessory Formula.' *VT* 19, no. 04 (October 1969): 385-399.

_____. 'Amos 4:4-13 and Israel's Covenant Worship.' *VT* 15, no. 01 (January 1965): 1-15.

Buber, Martin. *The Prophetic Faith*. New York: Harper & Row Publishers, 1960.

Budd, Philip J. *Leviticus*. NCBC. Grand Rapids, Michigan: William B. Eerdmans Publishing Company, 1996.

Byargeon, Rick W. 'Carmel.' In *EDB*, edited by David Noel Freedman, 224. Grand Rapids, Michigan: Williams B. Eerdmans, 2002.

Carmichael, Calum M. *Women, Law and the Genesis Traditions*. Edinburgh: Edinburgh University Press, 1979.

Carroll R, M. Daniel. *Contexts for Amos: Prophetic Poetics in Latin American Perspective*. JSOTSS 132. Sheffield: JSOT Press, 1992.

_____. 'Seeking the Virtues Among the Prophets: The Book of Amos as a Test Case.' *ExA* 17 (2001): 77-96.

Cassuto, U. *A Commentary on the Book of Exodus*. Translated from the Hebrew by Israel Abrahams. Jerusalem: The Magnes Press, 1983.

Childs, Brevard S. *Old Testament Theology in A Canonical Context*. London: SCM Press, 1985.

_____. *Introduction to the Old Testament as Scripture*. London: SCM Press, 1979.

_____. *Exodus*. OTL. London: SCM Press, 1974.

Chisholm, Robert B. Jr. *Handbook on the Prophets: Isaiah, Jeremiah, Lamentations, Ezekiel, Daniel, Minor Prophets*. Grand Rapids, Michigan: Baker Academic, 2002.

Christensen, Duane L. *Deuteronomy 1:1-21:9*. 2nd ed. WBC. Nashville, Tennessee: Thomas Nelson Publishers, 2001.

Clements, Ronald E. 'Amos and the Politics of Israel.' In *Storia e Tradizioni di Israele: Scritti in onore di J.Alberto Soggin*, edited Daniele Garrone and Felice Israel, 49-64. Brescia: Paideia Editrice, 1991.

_____. *Old Testament Theology: A Fresh Approach*. MTL. London: Marshall, Morgan and Scott, 1978.

_____. *Exodus*. Cambridge: Cambridge University Press, 1972.

_____. *God and Temple: The Idea of the Divine Presence in Ancient* Israel. Oxford: Blackwell, 1965.

_____. *Prophecy and Covenant*. London: SCM Press, 1965.

Cogan, Mordechai and Hayim Tadmor. *II Kings: A New Translation with Introduction and Commentary*. New York: Doubleday, 1998.

Coggins, Richard James. *Joel and Amos*. NCBC. Sheffield: Sheffield Academic Press, 2000.

Cohen, A. *The Twelve Prophets: Hebrew Text and English Translation with Introductions and Commentary*. Revised by A. J. Rosenberg. Rev. 2nd ed. London: The Soncino Press, 1994.

Cohen, Simon. 'Beersheba.' In *IDB (A-D)*, edited by George Arthur Buttrick et al., 375-376. Nashville: Abingdon Press, 1962.

Cole, R. Dennis. *Numbers*. NAC. Nashville: Broadman and Holman Publishers, 2000.

_____. 'The Visions of Amos 7-9.' *TE* no. 52 (Fall 1995): 57-68.

Collins, John J. *The Apocalyptic Imagination: An Introduction to Jewish Apocalyptic Literature*. 2nd ed. BRS. Grand Rapids, Michigan: William B. Eerdmans Publishing Company, 1998.

Conrad, Edgar W. *Reading the Latter Prophets: Towards a New Canonical Criticism*. JSOTSS 376. London: T & T Clark International, 2003.

Coogan, Michael D. *The Old Testament: A Historical and Literary Introduction to the Hebrew Scriptures*. Oxford: Oxford University Press, 2006.

Coote, Robert. 'Bethel.' In *NIDB*, edited by Katherine Doob Sakenfeld et al., 438-441. Vol. 1. Nashville, Tennessee: Abingdon Press, 2006.

_____. *Amos Among the Prophets: Composition and Theology*. Philadelphia: Fortress Press, 1981.

Coppes, Leonard J. 'דָּרַשׁ.' In *Theological Wordbook of the Old Testament*, edited by R. Laird Harris, 198-199. Vol. 1. Chicago: Moody Press, 1981.

Craigie, Peter C. *The Book of Deuteronomy*. NICOT. Grand Rapids, Michigan: William B. Eerdmans Publishing Company, 1976.

Cresson, Bruce C. 'Beersheba.' In *EDB*, edited by David Noel Freedman, 161. Grand Rapids, Michigan: William B. Eerdmans, 2000.

Cripps, Richard S. *A Critical and Exegetical Commentary on the Book of Amos*. London: SPCK, 1929.

Davidson, Robert. *Genesis 1-11*. Cambridge: Cambridge University Press, 1973.

Davies, Eryl W. 'Land: Its Rights and Privileges.' In *The World of Ancient Israel: Sociological, Anthropological, and Political Perspectives*, edited by Ronald E. Clements, 349-369. Cambridge: Cambridge University Press, 1989.

Davies, G. Henton 'Amos—the Prophet of Reunion.' *ExpTim* 92, no. 07 (1981): 196-199.

Davies, Graham I. *Hosea*. NCBC. Grand Rapids, Michigan: William B. Eerdmans Publishing Company, 1992.

Davies, Philip R. 'Amos, Man and Book.' In *Israel's Prophets and Israel's Past: Essays on the Relationship of Prophetic Texts and Israelite History in Honor of John H. Hayes*, edited by Brad E. Kelle and Megan Bishop Moore, 113-131. London: T & T Clark, 2006.

———. "*Bytdwd* and *Swkt Dwyd*: A Comparison". *JSOT* 64 (1994): 23-24.

Davies, William David. *The Gospel and the Land: Early Christianity and Jewish Territorial Doctrine*. Berkeley: University of California Press, 1974.

Davis, Ellen F. *Scripture, Culture, and Agriculture: An Agrarian Reading of the Bible*. Cambridge: Cambridge University Press, 2009.

Dearman, John Andrew. *Property Rights in the Eighth-Century Prophets: The Conflict and Its Background*. Atlanta, Georgia: Scholars Press, 1988.

Dempsey, Carol J. *The Prophets: A Liberation-Critical Reading*. Minneapolis: Fortress Press, 2002.

Dempster, Stephen. 'The Lord is His Name: A Study of the Distribution of the Names and Titles of God in the Book of Amos.' *RB* 98 (1991): 170-189.

Denninger, David. 'דרש.' In *NIDOTTE*, edited by Willem A. VanGemeren et al., 993-999. Vol. 1. Carlisle: Paternoster Press, 1996.

Dijkstra, Meindert. '"I am neither a prophet nor a prophet's pupil": Amos 7:9-17 as the Presentation of a Prophet like Moses.' In *The Elusive Prophet: The Prophet as a Historical Person, Literary Character and Anonymous Artist*, edited by Johannes C. de Moor, 103-128. Leiden: Boston, 2001.

Doan, William and Terry Giles. *Prophets, Performance, and Power: Performance Criticism of the Hebrew Bible*. London: T & T Clark, 2005.

Driver, Godfrey Rolles. 'Amos 7:14.' *ExpTim* 67, no. 03 (December 1955): 91-92.

Driver, Samuel Rolles, ed. *The Books of Joel and Amos*. Cambridge: The University Press, 1897.

Dumbrell, William J. *Covenant and Creation: An Old Testament Covenantal Theology*. Exeter: The Paternoster Press, 1984.

Durham, John I. *Exodus*. WBC. Waco, Texas: Word Books, 1987.

Eichrodt, Walther. *Theology of Old Testament*. Vol. 2. OTL. London: SCM Press, 1967.

Eissfeldt, Otto. *The Old Testament: An Introduction.* Oxford: Blackwell, 1965.

Escobar, Donoso S. 'Social Justice in the Book of Amos.' *RE* 92 (Spring 1995): 169-174.

Everson, A. Joseph. 'The Days of Yahweh.' *JBL* 93 no. 03 (1974): 329-337.

Ewing, William and Roland K. Harrison. 'Mount Carmel.' In *The International Standard Bible Encyclopaedia Volume One (A-D)*, edited by Geoffrey W. Bromiley et al., 618. Rev. ed. Grand Rapids, Michigan: Williams B. Eerdmans Publishing Company, 1979.

Farr, Georges. 'The Language of Amos, Popular or Cultic?.' *VT* 16 (1966): 312-324.

Feldman, Ron H. 'The Sabbath versus New Moon: A Critique of Heschel's Valorization of the Sabbath.' *Jud* 54, no. 1-2 (Winter-Spring 2005): 27-33.

Finley, Thomas J. *Joel, Amos, Obadiah: An Exegetical Commentary.* Chicago: Moody Press, 1990.

Firth, David G. 'Promise as Polemic: Levels of Meaning in Amos 9:11-15.' *OTE* 9, no. 03 (1996): 372-382.

Fohrer, Georg. *Introduction to the Old Testament.* Translated by David Green. London: SPCK, 1970.

Freedman, David Noel. 'Confrontations in the Book of Amos.' *PSB* 11, no. 03 (1990): 240-252.

_____. 'Temple Without Hands.' In *Temples and High Places in Biblical Times: Proceedings of the Colloquium in Honor of the Centennial of Hebrew Union College-Jewish Institute of Religion*, edited by Avraham Biran, 21-30. Jerusalem: The Nelson Glueck School of Biblical Archaeology of Hebrew Union College-Jewish Institute of Religion, 1981.

Fretheim, Terence E. *God and World in the Old Testament: A Relational Theology of Creation.* Nashville: Abingdon Press, 2005.

_____. *Jeremiah.* SHBC. Macon: Smith & Helwys, 2002.

_____. 'יָדַע'. In *NIDOTTE*, edited by Willem A. VanGemeren et.al., 409-414. Vol. 2. Carlisle: Paternoster Press, 1997.

_____. *Exodus.* IBCTP. Louisville: John Knox Press, 1991.

Friedman, Richard Elliott. *Commentary on the Torah: With a New English Translation and the Hebrew Text.* San Francisco: HarperSanFrancisco, 2001.

Fyall, Bob. *Teaching Amos: Unlocking the Prophecy of Amos for the Bible Teacher.* TBS. London: Proclamation Trust Media, 2006.

Garrett, Duane A. *Amos: A Handbook on the Hebrew Text.* Waco, Texas: Baylor University Press, 2008.

Gaster, Theodor H. 'Abode of the Dead.' In *IDB (A-D)*, edited by George Arthur Buttrick et al., 787-788. Nashville: Abingdon Press, 1962.

Gilchrist, Paul R. 'יָדַע'. In *Theological Wordbook of the Old Testament*, edited by R. Laird Harris, 366-368. Vol. 1. Chicago: Moody Press, 1981.

Giles, Terry. 'A Note on the Vocative of Amos in 7:14.' *JBL* 111, no. 04 (1992): 690-692.

Gillingham, Susan. '"Who Makes the Morning Darkness": God and Creation in the Book of Amos.' *SJT* 45, no. 02 (1992): 165-184.

Gitay, Yehoshua. 'A Study of Amos's Art of Speech: A Rhetorical Analysis of Amos 3:1-15.' *CBQ* 42, no. 03 (July 1980): 293-309.

Goldingay, John. *Old Testament Theology: Israel's Faith*. Vol. 2. Downers Grove, Illinois: InterVarsity Press, 2006.

Goldman, Rabbi Solomon. *A Guide to the Sabbath*. London: Jewish Chronicle Publications, 1961.

Good, Roger. 'Gilgal.' In *EDB*, edited by David Noel Freedman, 504-505. Grand Rapids, Michigan: William B. Eerdmans, 2000.

Gordis, Robert. 'The Composition and Structure of Amos.' *HTR* 33, no. 04 (October 1940): 239-252.

Gowan, Donald E. *Theology of the Prophetic Books: The Death and Resurrection of Israel*. London: Westminster John Knox Press, 1998.

_____. 'Amos.' In *New Interpreter's Bible: Introduction to Apocalyptic Literature; Daniel; the Twelve Prophets*, edited by Leander E. Keck et al., 339-431. Nashville: Abingdon Press, 1996.

Grabbe, Lester L. *Leviticus*. OTG. Sheffield: Sheffield Academic Press, 1993.

Grisanti, Michael A. 'אֲדָמָה.' in *NIDOTTE*, edited by Willem A. VanGemeren et al., 269-274. Vol. 1. Carlisle: Paternoster Press, 1996.

Grunfeld, Dayan Dr. I. *The Sabbath: A Guide to Its Understanding and Observance*, 4th reset ed. Jerusalem: Feldheim Publishers, 1981.

Habel, Norman C. *The Land is Mine: Six Biblical Land Ideologies*. Forward by Walter Brueggemann. OBT. Minneapolis: Fortress Press, 1995.

Hadley, Judith M. 'Dan.' In *NIDOTTE*, edited by Willem A. VanGemeren et al., 497-498. Vol. 4. Carlisle: Paternoster Press, 1996.

Hallo, William W. 'New Moons and Sabbaths: A Case-Study in A Contrastive Approach.' *HUCA* 48 (1977): 1-18.

Hamilton, Victor P. *The Book of Genesis: Chapters 1-17*. Grand Rapids, Michigan: William B. Eerdmans Publishing Company, 1990.

Hammershaimb, Erling. *The Book of Amos: A Commentary*. Translated by John Sturdy. Oxford: Basil Blackwell, 1970.

Haran, Menahem. 'Temples and Cultic Open Areas as Reflected in the Bible.' In *Temples and High Places in Biblical Times: Proceedings of the Colloquium in Honor of the Centennial of Hebrew Union College-Jewish Institute of Religion*, edited by Avraham Biran, 31-37. Jerusalem: The Nelson Glueck School of Biblical Archaeology of Hebrew Union College-Jewish Institute of Religion, 1981.

Harman, Allan M. 'Decalogue (Ten Commandments).' In *NIDOTTE*, edited by Willem A. VanGemeren et al., 513-519. Vol. 4. Carlisle: Paternoster Press, 1996.

Harper, William Rainey. *A Critical and Exegetical Commentary on Amos and Hosea*. ICC. Edinburgh: T & T Clark, 1905.

Harris, R. Laird. 'כַּרְמֶל Carmel' in *Theological Word Book of the Old Testament*, edited by R. Laird Harris, Gleanson L. Archer, Jr., and Bruce K. Waltke, 455-456. Vol. 1. Chicago: Moody Press, 1980.

_____. 'שְׁאוֹל,' In *Theological Word Book of the Old Testament*, edited by R. Laird Harris, Gleanson L. Archer, Jr., and Bruce K. Waltke, 892-893. Vol. 2. Chicago: Moody Press, 1980.

Hartley, John E. *Leviticus*. Vol. 4. WBC. Dallas, Texas: Word Books, 1992.

Hasel, Gerhard F. *Understanding of Amos: Basic Issues in Current Interpretations* Grand Rapids, Michigan: Baker Book House, 1991.

_____. 'The Alleged "No" of Amos's Eschatology.' *AUSS* 29, no. 01 (Spring 1991): 3-18.

_____. *The Remnant: The History and Theology of the Remnant Idea from Genesis to Isaiah*. 2nd ed. Berrien Springs, Michigan: Andrews University Press, 1974.

Hayes, John H. *Amos, the Eighth Century Prophet: His Times and His Preaching*. Nashville: Abingdon Press, 1988.

Heidel, Alexander. *Gilgamesh Epic and Old Testament Parallels*. Chicago: University of Chicago Press, 1949.

Hobbs, T. Raymond 'Reflections on "the Poor" and the Old Testament.' *ET* 100, no. 08 (May 1989): 291-294.

Hoffmann, Yair. 'Did Amos Regard Himself as a *NĀBÎ* ?.' *VT* 27, no. 02 (1977): 209-212.

_____. 'The Day of the Lord as a Concept and a Term in the Prophetic Literature.' *ZAW* 37, (1968): 37-50.

Homan, Michael M. 'Booths or Succoth? A Response to Yigael Yadin.' *JBL* 118, no. 04 (Winter 1999): 691-697.

House, Paul R. 'The Character of God in the Book of the Twelve.' In *Reading and Hearing the Book of the Twelve*, edited by James D. Nogalski and Marvin A. Sweeney, 125-145. SB 15. Atlanta: Society of Biblical Literature, 2000.

_____. 'Amos and Literary Criticism.' *RE* 92, no. 02 (Spring 1995): 175-187.

Houtman, Cornelis. *Exodus*. Leuven: Peeters, 2000.

Hubbard, David Allan. *Joel and Amos: An Introduction and Commentary*. TOTC. Leicester: Inter-Varsity Press, 1989.

Huffmon, Herbert B. 'The Social Role of Amos's Message.' In *The Quest for the Kingdom of God: Studies in Honor of G. E. Mendenhall*, edited by H. H. Huffmon, F. A. Spina, and A. R. W. Green, 109-116. Winona Lake, Indiana: Eisenbrauns, 1983.

_____. 'The Treaty Background of Hebrew YĀDA'.' *BASOR* 181 (Fall 1966): 31-37.

Jacob, Benno. *The Second Book of the Bible: Exodus*. Interpreted by Benno Jacob. Translated with an introduction by Walter Jacob in association with Yaakov Elman. Hoboken, New Jersey: Ktav Publishing House, 1992.

Jacob, Edmond. *Theology of the Old Testament*. Translated by Arthur W. Heathcote and Philip J. Allcock. London: Hodder and Stoughton, 1958.

Jacobs, Mignon R. *The Conceptual Coherence of the Book of Micah*. Sheffield: Sheffield Academic Press, 2001.

Janzen, J. Gerald. *Exodus*. Louisville, Kentucky: Westminster John Knox Press, 1997.

Janzen, Waldemar. 'Land.' In *ABD (K-N)*, edited by David Noel Freedman et al., 143-154. London: Doubleday, 1992.

Jeremias, Jörg. 'The Interrelationship between Amos and Hosea.' In *Forming Prophetic Literature: Essays on Isaiah and the Twelve in Honor of John D. W. Watts*, edited by James W. Watts and Paul R. House, 171-194. JSOTSS 235. Sheffield: Sheffield Academic Press, 1996.

_____. *The Book of Amos: A Commentary*. OTL. Louisville, Kentucky: Westminster John Knox Press, 1995.

Johnstone, William. *1 & 2 Chronicles - 2 Chronicles 10-36: Guilt and Atonement*. Vol. 2. JSOTSS 254. Sheffield: Sheffield Academic Press, 1997.

Jones, Barry Alan. *The Formation of the Book of the Twelve: A Study in Text and Canon*. SBLDS 149. Atlanta, Georgia: Scholars Press, 1995.

Joyce, Paul. 'Amos.' In *Prophets and Poets: A Companion to the Prophetic Books of the Old Testament*, edited by Grace Emmerson, 218-233. Oxford: The Bible Reading Fellowship, 1994.

Kaiser, Walter C. Jr. *Toward Old Testament Ethics*. Grand Rapids, Michigan: Zondervan, 1983.

———. *Toward an Old Testament Theology*. Grand Rapids, Michigan: Zondervan Publishing House, 1978.

———. 'The Davidic Promise and the Inclusion of the Gentiles (Amos 9:9-15 and Acts 15:13-18): A Test Passage for Theological Systems.' *JETS* 20, no. 02 (June 1977): 97-111.

Kapelrud, Arvid S. 'God as Destroyer in the Preaching of Amos and in the Ancient Near East.' *JBL* 71, no. 01 (March 1952): 33-38.

Kaufmann, Yehezkel. *The Religion of Israel: From Its Beginnings to the Babylonian Exile*. Translated and abridged by Moshe Greenberg. Chicago: The University of Chicago Press, 1960.

Keefe, Alice A. *Women's Body and the Social Body in Hosea*. London: Sheffield Academic Press, 2001.

Keel, Othmar. *The Symbolism of the Biblical World: Ancient Near Eastern Iconography and the Book of Psalms*. Translated by Timothy J. Hallett. London: SPCK, 1978.

Keita, Katrin. *Gottes Land: Exegetische Studien zur Land-Thematik im Hoseabuch in kanonischer Perspektive*. TTS 13. Hildeshheim: Georg Olms Verlag, 2007.

Kidner, Derek. *Genesis: An Introduction and Commentary*. TOTC. London: The Tyndale Press, 1968.

King, Philip J. *Amos, Hosea, Micah: An Archaeological Commentary*. Philadelphia: Westminster Press, 1988.

Kleven, Terence. 'The Cows of Bashan: A Single Metaphor at Amos 4:1-3.' *CBQ* 58, no. 02 (April 1996): 215-227.

Klingbeil, Gerald A. and Martin G. Klingbeil. 'The Prophetic Voice of Amos as a Paradigm for Christians in the Public Square.' *TB* 58, no. 02 (2007): 161-182.

Knierim, Rolf P. *The Task of Old Testament Theology: Substance, Method, and Cases*. Grand Rapids, Michigan: William B. Eerdmans Publishing Company, 1995.

Koch, Klaus. *The Prophets: The Assyrian Period*. Vol. 1. London: SCM Press, 1982.

Köckert, Matthias. 'Gottesvolk und Land: Jahwe, Israel und das Land bei den Propheten Amos und Hosea.' In *Gottesvolk: Beiträge zu einem Thema biblischer Theologie. Festschrift S Wagner*, edited by Arndt Meinhold and Rüdiger Lux, 43-73. Berlin: Evangelische Verlagsanstalt, 1991.

Koffi, Ettien. 'Theologizing about Race in Study Bible Notes: The Case of Amos 9:7.' *JRT* 57-58, 2-1/2 (2001-2005): 157-167.

Kuntz, J. Kenneth. 'Mount Carmel.' In *DBR*, edited by William H. Gentz, 182-183. Nashville: Abingdon, 1986.

Kutscher, Eduard Yechezkel. *A History of the Hebrew Language*. Jerusalem: Magnes Press, 1982.

Landsberger, Benno. 'Tin and Lead: The Adventures of Two Vocables.' *JNES* 24, no. 03 (July 1965): 285-296.

Landy, Francis. 'Vision and Poetic Speech in Amos.' *HAR* 11 (1987): 223-246.

Lang, Bernhard. 'The Social Organization of Peasant Poverty in Biblical Israel.' *JSOT* 24 (October 1982): 47-63.

Lemche, Niels Peter. *Ancient Israel: A New History of Israelite Society*. Sheffield: JSOT Press, 1988.

Levenson, Jon Douglas. *Creation and the Persistence of Evil: The Jewish Drama of Divine Omnipotence*. Princeton, New Jersey: Princeton University Press, 1988.

_____. *Sinai and Zion: An Entry into the Jewish Bible*. Minneapolis: Winston Press, 1985.

_____. 'The Temple and the World.' *JR* 64 (1984): 275-298.

_____. *Theology of the Program of Restoration of Ezekiel 40-48*. HSMS 10. Cambridge: Scholars Press, 1976.

Levine, Baruch A. *Leviticus: The Traditional Hebrew Text with the New JPS Translation*. JPSTC. Philadelphia: The Jewish Publication Society, 1989.

Lewis, Jack P. '"A Prophet's Son" (Amos 7:14) Reconsidered.' *RQ* 49, no. 04 (2007): 229-240.

Limburg, James. 'Sevenfold Structures in the Book of Amos.' *JBL* 106, no. 02 (1987): 217-222.

_____. 'Amos 7:4: A Judgment with Fire?.' *CBQ* 35, no. 03 (July 1973): 346-349.

Lindblom, Johannes. *Prophecy in Ancient Israel*. Oxford: Blackwell, 1962.

Linville, James R. *Amos and the Cosmic Imagination*. Hampshire: Ashgate, 2008.

_____. 'Visions and Voices: Amos 7-9.' *Bib* 80, no. 01 (1999): 22-42.

Loscalzo, Craig. 'Preaching Themes from Amos.' *RE* 92 (Spring 1995): 195-206.

Lowery, Richard H. *Sabbath and Jubilee*. St. Louis, Missouri: Chalice Press, 2000.

Lundquist, John M. 'Temple.' In *EDB*, edited by David Noel Freedman, 1280-1284. Grand Rapids, Michigan: William B. Eerdmans, 2000.

Macintosh, A. A. *A Critical and Exegetical Commentary on Hosea*. ICC. Edinburgh: T & T Clark, 1997.

Mann, Thomas W. *Deuteronomy*. Louisville, Kentucky: Westminster John Knox Press, 1995.

Mann, Thomas W. *The Book of the Torah: The Narrative Integrity of the Pentateuch*. Atlanta: John Knox Press, 1988.

Marlow, Hilary. *Biblical Prophets and Contemporary Environmental Ethics*. Oxford: Oxford University Press, 2009.

Marrs, Rick R. 'Amos and the Power of Proclamation.' *RQ* 40, no. 01 (1998): 13-24.

Martens, Elmer A. *God's Design: A Focus on Old Testament Theology*. 2nd ed. Grand Rapids, Michigan: Baker Books, 1994.

———. *Plot and Purpose in the Old Testament*. Leicester: Inter-Varsity Press, 1981.

Martin-Achard, Robert. 'A Commentary on the Book of Amos.' In *God's People in Crisis*, 1-69. Edinburgh: The Handsel Press, 1984.

Matthews, Victor H. *The Social World of the Hebrew Prophets*. Peabody, Massachusetts: Hendrickson Publishers, 2001.

Mays, James Luther. *Amos: A Commentary*. OTL. London: SCM Press, 1969.

McComiskey, Thomas Edward. 'The Hymnic Elements of the Prophecy of Amos: A Study of Form-Critical Methodology.' *JETS* 30, no. 02 (June 1987): 139-157.

McConville, J. Gordon. *God and Earthly Power: An Old Testament Political Theology*. London: T & T Clark, 2006.

———. '"How Can Jacob Stand? He is So Small!" (Amos 7:2): The Prophetic Word and the Re-Imagining of Israel.' In *Israel's Prophets and Israel's Past: Essays on the Relationship of Prophetic Texts and Israelite History in Honor of John H. Hayes*, edited by Brad E. Kelle and Megan Bishop Moore, 132-151. London: T & T Clark, 2006.

———. *Deuteronomy*. AOTC. Downers Grove, Illinois: Inter-Varsity Press, 2002.

———. *Law and Theology in Deuteronomy*. JSOTSS 33. Sheffield: JSOT Press, 1984.

McKane, William. *A Critical and Exegetical Commentary on Jeremiah: Introduction and Commentary on Jeremiah 1-25*. Vol. 1. Edinburgh: T & T Clark, 1986.

McKay, Heather A. *Sabbath and Synagogue: The Question of Sabbath Worship in Ancient Judaism*. Leiden: E. J. Brill, 1994.

McKeating, Henry. *The Books of Amos, Hosea, and Micah*. CBC. Cambridge: Cambridge University Press, 1971.

McKenzie, Steven L. *1 - 2* Chronicles. AOTC. Nashville: Abingdon Press, 2004.

Merrill, Eugene H. *Deuteronomy*. NAC. Nashville, Tennessee: Boradman & Holman Publishers, 1994.

Meyers, Carol. 'Jerusalem Temple.' In *ABD (Si-Z)*, edited by David Noel Freedman et al., 350-369. London: Double Day, 1992.

Milgram, Abraham E. *Sabbath: The Day of Delight*. 14th imp. Philadelphia: The Jewish Publication Society of America, 1981.

Millar, J. Gary. 'Land.' In *NDBT*, edited by T. Desmond Alexander et al., 623-627. Leicester: InterVarsity Press, 2000.

Miller, Patrick D. *Deuteronomy*. IBCTP. Louisville: John Knox Press, 1990.

⎯⎯⎯⎯. *Sin and Judgment in the Prophets: A Stylistic and Theological Analysis*. Chico, California: Scholars Press, 1982.

⎯⎯⎯⎯. 'The Gift of God: The Deuteronomic Theology of the Land.' *Int* 23, no. 04 (October 1969): 451-465.

Mobley, Gregory. 'Dan.' In *EDB*, edited by David Noel Freedman, 310-311. Grand Rapids, Michigan: William B. Eerdmans, 2000.

Möller, Karl. *A Prophet in Debate: The Rhetoric of Persuasion in the Book of Amos*. JSOTSS 372. London: Sheffield Academic Press, 2003.

⎯⎯⎯⎯. '"Hear This Word Against You:" A Fresh Look at the Arrangement and the Rhetorical Strategy of the Book of Amos.' *VT* 50, no. 04 (2000): 499-518.

Moltz, Howard. 'A Literary Interpretation of the Book of Amos.' *Hor* 25, no. 01 (1998): 58-71.

Moran, William L. *The Most Magic Word: Essays on Babylonian and Biblical Literature*. Washington DC: Catholic Biblical Association of America, 2002.

Motyer, Alec. *Old Testament Covenant Theology: Four Lectures*. Leicester: Theological Students Fellowship, 1973.

Mowvley, Harry. *The Books of Amos and Hosea*. EC. London: Epworth Press, 1991.

Muilenburg, J. 'Gilgal.' In *IDB (E-J)*, edited by George Arthur Buttrick et al., 398-399. Nashville: Abingdon Press, 1962.

Mulder, Martin J. 'Carmel.' In *DDD*, edited by Karel van der Toorn, Bob Becking, and Pieter W. van der Horst, 182-185. 2nd rev. ed. Grand Rapids, Michigan: William B. Eerdmans Publishing Company, 1999.

Mulzac, Kenneth D. 'Amos 5:18-20 in its Exegetical and Theological Context.' *AJT* 13, no. 02 (2002): 286-300.

Nelson, Richard D. *Deuteronomy: A Commentary*. OTL. London: Westminster John Knox Press, 2002.

Nicholson, Ernest W. *God and His People: Covenant and Theology in the Old Testament*. Oxford: Clarendon Press, 1986.

Niehaus, Jeffrey. 'Amos.' In *The Minor Prophets: An Exegetical and Expository Commentary*, edited by Thomas Edward McComiskey, 315-494. Vol. 1. Grand Rapids, Michigan: Baker Book House, 1992.

Noble, Paul R. 'Amos and Amaziah in Context: Synchronic and Diachronic Approaches to Amos 7-8.' *CBQ* 60, no. 03 (July 1998): 423-439.

_____. 'Amos' Absolute "No".' *VT* 47, no. 03 (July 1997): 329-340.

_____. 'The Literary Structure of Amos: A Thematic Analysis.' *JBL* 114, no. 02 (Summer 1995): 209-226.

Nogalski, James D. 'Recurring Themes in the Book of the Twelve: Creating Points of Contact for a Theological Reading.' *Int* 61, no. 02 (April 2007): 125-136.

_____. 'The Day(s) of YHWH in the Book of the Twelve.' In *Thematic Threads in the Book of the Twelve*, edited by Paul L. Redditt and Aaron Schart, 192-213. New York: Walter de Gruyter, 2003.

_____. 'Intertextuality and the Twelve.' In *Forming Prophetic Literature: Essays on Isaiah and the Twelve in Honor of John D. W. Watts*, edited by James W. Watts and Paul R. House, 102-124. JSOTSS 235. Sheffield: Sheffield Academic Press, 1996.

_____. *Literary Precursors to the Book of the Twelve*. BZAW 217. Berlin: Walter de Gruyter, 1993.

_____. 'The Problematic Suffixes of Amos 9:11.' *VT* 43, no. 03 (July 1993): 411-418.

Noll, Stephen F. 'Tabernacle, Temple.' In *EDT*, edited by Walter A. Elwell, 1067-1069. Grand Rapids, Michigan: Baker Book House, 1984.

Noordtzij, A. *Leviticus*. Translated by Raymond Togtman. BSC. Grand Rapids, Michigan: Zondervan Publishing House, 1982.

Noth, Martin. *The History of Israel*. London: SCM Press, 1990.

_____. *A History of Pentateuchal Traditions*. Translated with an Introduction by Bernhard W. Anderson. Englewood Cliffs: Prentice-Hall, 1972.

_____. *Leviticus: A Commentary*. OTL. London: SCM Press, 1965.

_____. *Exodus: A Commentary*. OTL. London: SCM Press, 1962.

O'Connell, Robert H. 'Telescoping N+1 Patterns in the Book of Amos.' *VT* 46, no. 01 (January 1996): 56-73.

Odelain, O. and R. Séguineau. *Dictionary of Proper Names and Places in the Bible*. Translated and adapted by Matthew J. O'Connell. Garden City, New York: Doubleday, 1981.

Ollenburger, Ben C. *Zion, the City of the Great King: A Theological Symbol of the Jerusalem Cult*. JSOTSS 41. Sheffield: JSOT Press, 1987.

Ottosson, Magnus. 'אֶרֶץ.' In *TDOT*, edited by G. Johannes Botterweck and Helmer Ringgren, translated by John T. Willis, 388-405. Vol. 1. Grand Rapids, Michigan: William B. Eerdmans Publishing Company, 1974.

Overholt, Thomas W. 'Prophecy in History: The Social Reality of Intermediation.' In *The Prophets: A Sheffield Reader*, edited by Philip R. Davies, 61-86. BSem 42. Sheffield: Sheffield Academic Press, 1996.

Paas, Stefan. *Creation and Judgment: Creation Texts in Some Eighth Century Prophets*. Leiden: Brill, 2003.

Pace, Sharon. 'Beersheba.' In *NIDB*, edited by Katherine Doob Sakenfeld et al., 419. Vol. 1. Nashville, Tennessee: Abingdon Press, 2006.

Park, Aaron W. *The Book of Amos as Composed and Read in Antiquity*. SBL 37. New York: Peter Lang, 2001.

Paul, Shalom M. *A Commentary on the Book of Amos*. Edited by Frank Moore Cross. Minneapolis: Fortress Press, 1991.

Petersen, David L. *The Roles of Israel's Prophets*. JSOTSS 17. Sheffield: JSOT, 1981.

Pfeifer, Gerhard. *Die Theologie des Propheten Amos*. Frakfurt: Peter Lang, 1995.

Pienaar, Daniel N. 'Samaria.' In *NIDOTTE*, edited by Willem A. VanGemeren et al., 1163-1165. Vol. 4. Carlisle: Paternoster Press, 1996.

Plaut, W. Gunther. *The Torah: A Modern Commentary*. Edited by W. Gunther Plaut. New York: Union of American Hebrew Congregations, 1981.

Pleins, J. David. *The Social Visions of the Hebrew Bible: A Theological Introduction*. Louisville, Kentucky: Westminster John Knox Press, 2001.

Plöger, Josef G. 'אֲדָמָה.' In *TDOT*, edited by G. Johannes Botterweck and Helmer Ringgren, and translated by John T. Willis, 88-98. Vol. 1. Grand Rapids, Michigan: William B. Eerdmans Publishing Company, 1974.

Polley, Max. E. *Amos and the Davidic Empire: A Socio-Historical Approach*. Oxford: Oxford University Press, 1989.

Pomykala, Kenneth E. *The Davidic Dynasty Tradition in Early Judaism: Its History and Significance for Messianism*. EJL 07. Atlanta, Georgia: Scholars Press, 1995.

Porter, J. R. *Leviticus*. CBC. Cambridge: Cambridge University Press, 1976.

Preez, Jannie du. '"Let Justice Roll On Like….": Some Explanatory Notes on Amos 5:24.' *JTSA* 109 (March 2001): 95-98.

Premnath, D. N. 'Amos and Hosea: Sociohistorical Background and Prophetic Critique.' *WW* 28, no. 02 (Spring 2008): 125-132.

Preuss, Horst Dietrich. *Old Testament Theology*. Vol. 2. Edinburgh: T & T Clark, 1996.

_____. *Old Testament Theology*. Vol. 1. Edinburgh: T & T Clark, 1995.

Rad, Gerhard von. *From Genesis to Chronicles: Explorations in Old Testament Theology*. Edited by K. C. Hanson. Minneapolis: Fortress Press, 2005.

_____. *Genesis: A Commentary*. 3rd rev. ed. OTL. London: SCM Press, 1972.

_____. *The Message of the Prophets*. London: SCM Press, 1968.

_____. *Old Testament Theology*. Vol. 2. Translated by D. M. G. Stalker. Edinburgh: Oliver and Boyd, 1965.

_____. 'The Promised Land and Yahweh's Land in the Hexateuch.' In *The Problem of the Hexateuch and Other Essays*, translated by E. W. Trueman Dicken, introduction by Norman W. Porteous, 79-93. London: Oliver & Boyd, 1966.

_____. 'The Theological Problem of the Old Testament Doctrine of Creation.' In *The Problem of the Hexateuch and Other Essays*, translated by E. W. Trueman Dicken; introduction by Norman W. Porteous, 131-143. London: Oliver & Boyd, 1966.

_____. *Old Testament Theology*. Translated by D. M. G. Stalker. Vol. 1. Edinburgh: Oliver and Boyd, 1962.

_____. 'The Origin of the Concept of the Day of Yahweh.' *JST* 4, no. 02 (April 1959): 97-108.

Rainey, Anson F. 'Negeb.' In *The International Standard Bible Encyclopedia Volume Three (K-P)*, edited by Geoffrey W. Bromiley et al., 511-513. Rev. ed. Grand Rapids, Michigan: Williams B. Eerdmans Publishing Company, 1986.

Reventlow, Henning Graf. 'Creation as a Topic in Biblical Theology.' In *Creation in Jewish and Christian Tradition*, edited by Henning Graf Reventlow and Yair Hoffman, 153-171. JSOTSS 319. London: Sheffield Academic Press, 2002.

Richardson, Alan. *Genesis 1-11: Introduction and Commentary*. London: SCM Press, 1959.

Richardson, H. Neil. '*SKT* (Amos 9:11): "Booth" or "Succoth"?.' *JBL* 92, no. 03 (1973): 375-381.

Ridderbos, J. *Deuteronomy*. BSC. Grand Rapids, Michigan: Zondervan Publishing House, 1984.

Ringwald, Christopher D. *A Day Apart: How Jews, Christians, and Muslims Find Faith, Freedom, and Joy on the Sabbath*. Oxford: Oxford University Press, 2007.

Roberts, Jimmy J. 'A Note on Amos 7:14 and Its Context.' *RQ* 8, no. 03 (1965): 175-178.

Rogerson, John. *Theory and Practice in Old Testament Ethics*. Edited and with an introduction by M. Daniel Carroll R. London: T & T Clark International, 2004.

Rogerson, John and Philip Davies. *The Old Testament World*. Cambridge: Cambridge University Press, 1989.

Rooker, Mark F. 'Gilgal.' In *NIDOTTE*, edited by Willem A. VanGemeren et al., 683-685. Vol. 4. Carlisle: Paternoster Press, 1996.

Rosenbaum, Stanley N. *Amos of Israel: A New Interpretation*. Macon, Georgia: Mercer University Press, 1990.

Ross, Allen P. *Holiness to the Lord: A Guide to the Exposition of the Book of Leviticus*. Grand Rapids, Michigan: Baker Academic, 2002.

Ryken, Leland, James C. Wilhoit, Tremper Longman III, eds. *Dictionary of Biblical Imagery: An Encyclopedic Exploration of the Images, Symbols, Motifs, Metaphors, Figures of Speech and Literary Patterns of the Bible*. Leicester: InterVarsity Press, 1998.

Sailhamer, John H. *The Pentateuch as Narrative: A Biblical-Theological Commentary*. Grand Rapids, Michigan: Zondervan Publishing House, 1992.

Sanneh, Lamin O. 'A "New Moon" Sensitivity.' *CC* 106, no. 26 (1989): 118.

Satterlee, Craig A. 'Amos 8:1-12.' *Int* 61, no. 02 (April 2007): 202-204.

Schart, Aaron. 'The First Section of the Book of the Twelve Prophets: Hosea-Joel-Amos.' *Int* 61, no. 02 (April 2007): 138-152.

———. 'The Fifth Vision of Amos in Context.' In *Thematic Threads in the Book of the Twelve*, edited by Paul L. Redditt and Aaron Schart, 46-71. Berlin: Walter de Gruyer, 2003.

Schmid, H. H. 'Creation, Righteousness, and Salvation: "Creation Theology" as the Broad Horizon of Biblical Theology.' In *Creation in the Old Testament*, edited by Bernhard W. Anderson, 102-117. IRT 6. London: SPCK, 1984.

Selms, Andrianus Van. 'Samaria.' In *The International Standard Bible Encyclopedia Volume Four (Q-Z)*, edited by Geoffrey W. Bromiley et al., 295-298. Rev. ed. Grand Rapids, Michigan: Williams B. Eerdmans Publishing Company, 1988.

Sherwood, Yvonne. 'Of Fruit and Corpses and Wordplay Visions: Picturing Amos 8:1-3.' *JSOT* 92 (March 2001): 5-27.

Simundson, Daniel J. 'Reading Amos: Is It an Advantage to Be God's Special People?.' *WW* 28, no. 02 (Spring 2008): 133-140.

_____. *Hosea, Joel, Amos, Obadiah, Jonah, Micah*. AOTC. Nashville: Abingdon Press, 2005.

Smelik, K. A. D. 'The Meaning of Amos 5:18-20.' *VT* 36, no. 02 (1986): 246-248.

Smith, Billy K. and Frank S. Page. *Amos, Obadiah, Jonah*. NAC. Broadman & Holman Publishers, 1995.

Smith, Gary V. 'Continuity and Discontinuity in Amos' Use of Tradition.' *JETS* 34, no. 01 (March 1991): 33-42.

_____. *Amos: A Commentary*. LBI. Grand Rapids: Michigan, Zondervan Publishing House, 1989.

_____. 'Amos 5:13: The Deadly Silence of the Prosperous.' *JBL* 107, no. 02 (June 1988): 289-291.

Smith, Mark S. *The Early History of God: Yahweh and the Other Deities in Ancient Israel*. 2nd ed. Grand Rapids, Michigan: William B. Eerdmans Publishing Company, 2002.

Smith, Regina. 'A New Perspective on Amos 9:7a: "To Me, O Israel, You are just like the Kushites."' *JITC* 22, no. 01 (Fall 1994): 36-47.

Snyder, George. 'The Law and Covenant in Amos.' *RQ* 25, no. 03 (1982): 158-166.

Snyman, S. D. Fanie. 'Eretz and Adama in Amos,' in *Stimulation from Leiden: Collected Communications to the XVIIIth Congress of the International Organization for the Study of the Old Testament, Leiden 2004*, edited by Hermann Michael Niemann and Matthias Augustin, 137-146. BEATAJ 54. Frankfurt am Main: Peter Lang, 2006.

_____. 'The Land as a *Leitmotiv* in the Book of Amos.' *VetEcc* 26, no. 02 (2005): 527-542.

Soggin, J. Alberto. *The Prophet Amos: A Translation and Commentary*. Translated by John Bowden. London: SCM Press, 1987.

Sohn, Seock-Tae. *The Divine Election of Israel*. Grand Rapids, Michigan: William B. Eerdmans Publishing Company, 1991.

Southwell, Peter J. M. 'Bethel.' In *NIDOTTE*, edited by Willem A. VanGemeren et al., 440-441. Vol. 4. Carlisle: Paternoster Press, 1996.

Stacey, W. David. 'The Function of Prophetic Drama.' In *The Place Is Too Small for Us: The Israelite Prophets in Recent Scholarship*, edited by Robert P. Gordon, 112-132. Winona Lake, Indiana: Eisenbrauns, 1995.

_____. *Prophetic Drama in the Old Testament*. London: Epworth, 1990.

Steinsaltz, Rabbi Adin. *The Miracle of the Seventh Day: A Guide to the Spiritual Meaning, Significance, and Weekly Practice of the Jewish Sabbath.* San Francisco: Jossey-Bass, 2003.

Story, Cullen I. K. 'Amos—Prophet of Praise.' *VT* 30, no. 01 (1980): 67-80.

Stuart, Douglas K. 'Sheol.' In *The International Standard Bible Encyclopaedia Volume Four (Q-Z),* edited by Geoffrey W. Bromiley et al., 472. Rev. ed. Grand Rapids, Michigan: Williams B. Eerdmans Publishing Company, 1988.

———. *Hosea-Jonah.* WBC. Waco, Texas: Word Books, 1987.

Sweeney, Marvin A. *Form and Intertextuality in Prophetic and Apocalyptic Literature.* FAT 45; Tübingen: Mohr Siebeck, 2005.

———. *The Twelve Prophets.* Edited by David W. Cotter. Vol. 1. BO. Collegeville, Minnesota: Liturgical Press, 2000.

Tappy, Ron E. 'Samaria.' In *EDB*, edited by David Noel Freedman, 1155-1159. Grand Rapids, Michigan: William B. Eerdmans, 2000.

Tatum, Lynn. 'Negeb.' In *EDB*, edited by David Noel Freedman, 955. Grand Rapids, Michigan: William B. Eerdmans, 2000.

Terblanche, M. D. "Rosen und Lavendel nach Blut und Eisen': Intertextuality in the Book of Amos.' *OTE* 10, no. 02 (1997): 312-321.

Thompson, Henry O. 'Mount Carmel.' In *ABD (A-C)*, edited by David Noel Freedman, 874-875. London: Doubleday, 1992.

Thompson, J. A. *1, 2 Chronicles.* Vol. 9. NAC. Nashville, Tennessee: Broadman & Holman Publishers, 1994.

———. *The Book of Jeremiah.* Grand Rapids, Michigan: William B. Eerdmans Publishing Company, 1980.

———. *Deuteronomy: An Introduction and Commentary.* Leicester: Inter-Varsity Press, 1974.

Towner, W. Sibley. *Genesis.* London: Westminster John Knox Press, 2001.

Tucker, Gene M. 'Amos the Prophet and Amos the Book: Historical Framework.' In *Israel's Prophets and Israel's Past: Essays on the Relationship of Prophetic Texts and Israelite History in Honor of John H. Hayes,* edited by Brad E. Kelle and Megan Bishop Moore, 85-102. London: T & T Clark, 2006.

———. 'Prophetic Authenticity.' *Int* 27, no. 04 (October 1973): 423-434.

Tuell, Steven S. *First and Second Chronicles.* IBCTP. Louisville, Kentucky: John Knox Press, 2001.

Verhoef, Pieter A. 'חדש.' In *NIDOTTE*, edited by Willem A. VanGemeren et al., 30-37. Vol. 2. Carlisle: Paternoster Press, 1997.

Viberg, Åke. 'Amos 7:14: A Case of Subtle Irony.' *TB* 47, no. 01 (1996): 91-114.

Wagner, S. 'דָּרַשׁ.' In *TDOT*, edited by G. Johannes Botterweck and Helmer Ringgren, translated by John T. Wills, Geoffrey W. Bromiley, and David E. Green, 293-307. Vol. 3. Grand Rapids, Michigan: William B. Eerdmans Publishing Company, 1978.

Wal, Adri van der. 'The Structure of Amos.' *JSOT* 26, no. 01 (June 1983): 107-113.

Waldow, Hans Eberhard von. 'Israel and Her Land: Some Theological Considerations.' In *A Light unto My Path: Old Testament Studies in Honor of Jacob M. Myers*, edited by Howard N. Bream, Ralph D. Heim, and Carey A. Moore, 493-508. Philadelphia: Temple University Press, 1974.

Walzer, Michael. 'Prophecy and Social Criticism.' *DG* 55 (1984): 13-27.

Warning, Wilfried. 'Terminological Patterns and Amos 9:11-15.' *DL* 5, no. 02 (2006): 117-134.

Watts, John D. W. *Vision and Prophecy in Amos*. Expanded anniversary ed. Macon, Georgia: Mercer University Press, 1997.

_____. 'Infinitive Absolute as Imperative and the Interpretations of Exodus 20:8.' *ZAW* 74, no. 02 (1962): 141-145.

Weinfeld, Moshe. *Deuteronomy 1-11: A New Translation with Introduction and Commentary*. AB. London: Doubleday, 1991.

Wellhausen, Julius. *Die Kleinen Propheten*. 4th ed. Berlin: W. de Gruyter, 1963.

Wenham, Gordon J. 'The Old Testament and the Environment: A Response to Chris Wright.' In *A Christian Approach to the Environment*, Sam Berry et al., 49-71. N.p.: The John Ray Initiative, 2005.

_____. *Exploring the Old Testament Volume 1, The Pentateuch*. London: SPCK, 2003.

_____. *Genesis 16-50*. WBC. Dallas, Texas: Word Books, 1994.

_____. *Genesis 1-15*. WBC. Nashville, Tennessee: Thomas Nelson Publishers, 1987.

_____. *The Book of Leviticus*. NICOT. London: Hodder and Stoughton, 1979.

West, Jim 'Sheol.' In *EDB*, edited by David Noel Freedman, 1206-1207. Grand Rapids, Michigan: Williams B. Eerdmans, 2002.

Westerholm, Stephen 'Temple.' In *The International Standard Bible Encyclopaedia Volume Four (Q-Z)*, edited by Geoffrey W. Bromiley et al., 759-776. Rev. ed. Grand Rapids, Michigan: Williams B. Eerdmans Publishing Company, 1988.

Westermann, Claus. *Genesis 1-11: A Commentary*. Translated by John J. Scullion S. J. London: SPCK, 1984.

Whybray, R. Norman. *The Good Life in the Old Testament*. London: T & T Clark, 2002.

Wildberger, Hans. *Isaiah 1-12: A Commentary*. Translated by Thomas H. Trapp. CC. Minneapolis: fortress Press, 1991.

Williamson, H. G. M. 'The Prophet and the Plumb-Line: A Redaction-Critical Study of Amos 7.' In *The Place is Too Small for Us: The Israelite Prophets in Recent Scholarship*, edited by Robert P. Gordon, 453-477. New York: Snow Lion Publication, 2002.

_____. *1 and 2 Chronicles*. NCBC. Grand Rapids, Michigan: William B. Eerdmans Publishing Company, 1982.

Wirzba, Norman. *Living the Sabbath: Discovering the Rhythms of Rest and Delight*. Grand Rapids, Michigan: Brazos Press, 2006.

Wittenberg, Gunther H. 'The Significance of Land in the Old Testament.' *JTSA* 77 (1991): 58-60.

_____. 'Amos 6:1-7: "They Dismiss the Day of Disaster but You Bring Near the Rule of Violence."' *JTSA* 58, no. 01 (March 1987): 57-69.

Wolff, Hans Walter. *A Commentary on the Books of the Prophets Joel and Amos*. Translated by Waldemar Janzen, S. Dean McBride, Jr., and Charles A. Muenchow. Edited by S. Dean McBride, Jr. Philadelphia: Fortress Press, 1969.

Wolters, Al. 'Wordplay and Dialect in Amos 8:1-2.' *JETS* 31, no. 04 (December 1988): 407-410.

Wood, Joyce Rilett. *Amos in Song and Book Culture*. JSOTSS 337. London: Sheffield Academic Press, 2002.

Wright, Christopher J. H. *The Mission of God: Unlocking the Bible's Grand Narrative*. Nottingham: Inter-Varsity Press, 2006.

_____. 'Theology and Ethics of the Land.' In *A Christian Approach to the Environment*, Sam Berry et al., 29-47. N.p.: The John Ray Initiative, 2005.

_____. *Old Testament Ethics for the People of God*. Leicester: Inter-Varsity Press, 2004.

_____. 'אֶרֶץ.' In *NIDOTTE*, edited by Willem A. VanGemeren et al., 518-524. Vol. 1. Carlisle: Paternoster Press, 1997.

_____. *Living as the People of God: The Relevance of Old Testament Ethics*. Leicester: Inter-Varsity Press, 1983.

Wright, T. J. 'Amos and the "Sycomore Fig."' *VT* 26, no. 03 (July 1976): 362-368.

Younger, K. Lawson Jr. 'Gilgamesh Epic.' In *EDB*, edited by David Noel Freedman, 505. Grand Rapids, Michigan: William B. Eerdmans, 2000.

Zalcman, Lawrence. 'Piercing the Darkness at Bôqēr (Amos 7:14).' *VT* 30, no. 02 (April 1980): 252-255.

Zimmerli, Walther. 'The "Land" in the Pre-Exilic and Early Post-Exilic Prophets.' In *Understanding the Word: Essays in Honor of Bernhard W. Anderson*, edited by James T. Butler, Edgar W. Conrad, and Ben C. Ollenburger, 247-262. JSOTSS 37. Sheffield: JSOT Press, 1985.

———. *Old Testament Theology in Outline*. Translated by David E. Green. Edinburgh: T & T Clark, 1978.

———. *The Old Testament and the World*. Translated by John J. Scullion, S.J. London: SPCK, 1976.

Zvi, Ehud Ben. *Hosea*. Grand Rapids, Michigan: William B. Eerdmans Publishing Company, 2005.

Langham PARTNERSHIP

Langham Literature and its imprints are a ministry of Langham Partnership.

Langham Partnership is a global fellowship working in pursuit of the vision God entrusted to its founder John Stott –

> *to facilitate the growth of the church in maturity and Christ-likeness through raising the standards of biblical preaching and teaching.*

Our vision is to see churches in the majority world equipped for mission and growing to maturity in Christ through the ministry of pastors and leaders who believe, teach and live by the Word of God.

Our mission is to strengthen the ministry of the Word of God through:
- nurturing national movements for biblical preaching
- fostering the creation and distribution of evangelical literature
- enhancing evangelical theological education

especially in countries where churches are under-resourced.

Our ministry

Langham Preaching partners with national leaders to nurture indigenous biblical preaching movements for pastors and lay preachers all around the world. With the support of a team of trainers from many countries, a multi-level programme of seminars provides practical training, and is followed by a programme for training local facilitators. Local preachers' groups and national and regional networks ensure continuity and ongoing development, seeking to build vigorous movements committed to Bible exposition.

Langham Literature provides majority world pastors, scholars and seminary libraries with evangelical books and electronic resources through grants, discounts and distribution. The programme also fosters the creation of indigenous evangelical books for pastors in many languages, through training workshops for writers and editors, sponsored writing, translation, strengthening local evangelical publishing houses, and investment in major regional literature projects, such as one volume Bible commentaries like *The Africa Bible Commentary*.

Langham Scholars provides financial support for evangelical doctoral students from the majority world so that, when they return home, they may train pastors and other Christian leaders with sound, biblical and theological teaching. This programme equips those who equip others. Langham Scholars also works in partnership with majority world seminaries in strengthening evangelical theological education. A growing number of Langham Scholars study in high quality doctoral programmes in the majority world itself. As well as teaching the next generation of pastors, graduated Langham Scholars exercise significant influence through their writing and leadership.

To learn more about Langham Partnership and the work we do visit **langham.org**